2014

THE FENRIS WOLF

Issue no. 7

Edited by Carl Abrahamsson

TRAPART*books*

The Fenris Wolf, issue no 7

Trapart Books, 2020

ISBN 978-91-986242-2-9

Trapart Books
P.O. Box 8105
SE-104 20 Stockholm
Sweden

info@trapart.net
www.trapart.net

THE FENRIS WOLF, ISSUE NO 7
CONTENTS

Editor's Introduction

Esoteric (**adj**): *Very particularly abstruse and consummately occult. The ancient philosophies were of two kinds, – exoteric, those that the philosophers themselves could partly understand, and* esoteric, *those that nobody could understand. It is the latter that have most profoundly affected modern thought and found greatest acceptance in our time.*

– Ambrose Bierce, The Devil's Dictionary, *1881-1906*

In the summer of 1993 I was criss-crossing the United States on a magical mystery tour that eventually brought me to northern California. Among a lot of interesting people, I was introduced to Adam Rostoker a.k.a. Adam Walks Between Worlds, a neo-pagan Thelemite who immediately struck me as a really bright guy. He could write well too. When I was back in Europe, Adam sent me an essay he'd written, expressing hope it could be included in *The Fenris Wolf 4*. Number 3 had just been published in the spring of '93 and I had high hopes to have number 4 out by 1994... However, it took another 17 years before number 4 actually appeared, but that's an entirely different story.

The piece Adam sent me was called *Whence Came the Stranger?* and it completely blew my mind. As I hadn't read Heinlein's classic *Stranger In A Strange Land* then, I immediately got into it, and saw how perfectly Adam had made sense of Heinlein's intricate and highly esoteric web. In all, a brilliant piece which eventually ended up in *The Green Egg* and in *Rapid Eye*, and I was at least happy it had found a readership.

In 1997 Adam was murdered and that brought back to mind his Heinlein analysis. When I heard of his brutal demise, I regretted not having published it when offered. But there was simply no *Fenris Wolf* around at that time. However, I have decided to include it in this issue, not only to make peace with myself but also to honor Adam's amazing achievement. Heinlein's magical book is a must read, and *Whence Came The Stranger?* really is the perfect introduction to the book.

On that very same journey I met Donald Michael Kraig, author of *Modern Magick*, one of the best-selling books on Western magic ever. Just before I wrote this introduction, I received news of his passing. For many people, his book has been a very user-friendly primer in Golden Dawn-style magic. Easier to read than Regardie's massive *Golden Dawn* tome, and definitely on par with David Griffin's slightly later *The Ritual Magic Manual*. It's sad when people die, but at least Donald left something behind to be remembered by. That in itself is a magical achievement.

As usual, this issue of *The Fenris Wolf* contains an eclectic mix of material new and old: Crowley *en masse*, sacred prostitution, Symbolism, Cannabis, Reich, BDSM, art, humanoid dolls, Steiner, science fiction, psychedelic book covers, Dada and many other things... Perhaps it's wise not to read the entire issue in one stretch. Madness could possibly ensue. But if you pick one piece at a time and savor it, and then another, preferably at random, you'll be just fine. *The Fenris Wolf* is not meant to be strictly an anthology of information. It should work just as well on levels of inspiration and further intuitive associations.

Thanks and praise to the following: *All* the contributors, without whom...

Thanks also to Fredrik Söderberg & Christine Ödlund, Andreas Kalliaridis, Andrew McKenzie, Wera von Essen, Vera Nikolich, William Breeze, Henrik Bogdan, Anthony Stansfeld Jones, everyone at Galleri Riis, Anna Nyman, Henrik Møll, Peder Byberg, Martin Palmer, Genesis Breyer P-Orridge, Peter Gilmore & Peggy Nadramia, Bali & Geraldine Beskin, JD Holmes, Catland Books, Pam Grossman, OTO Sweden, OTO Poland, Camion Noir, Dariusz Misiuna & Joanna John of Okultura, Krzysztof Azarewicz & Ania Orzech of Lashtal Press, Peter Grey & Alkistis Dimech of Scarlet Imprint, Rönnells Antikvariat, Didrik & Aleksandra Søderlind, Pil Cappelen-Smith of Cappelens Forslag in Oslo, Bjarne Salling Pedersen & Isabel Berg of Nekropolis in Copenhagen, TDL & Mr. Greg, and to all our supportive Edda-friends and booksellers.

An editorial note: As the texts in this issue stem from various minds from various cultures, there are obviously some stylistic inconsistencies. I have chosen to keep these, including possible "magical" language quirks and experiments, in the name of heterogeneous and creative integrity. However, for any spelling or typographical errors, pure and simple, I assume full responsibility.

Finally, I would like to say that the views and values expressed in the various texts in this eclectic anthology are those of the respective authors, and do not necessarily represent my own views, those of Edda or any kind of general "Fenris Wolfean" perspective.

Vade Ultra!

Carl Abrahamsson
Stockholm-Monstropolis, March 20th, 2014

AN INTRODUCTION TO
FERNAND KHNOPFF, SYMBOLIST

Sara George & Carl Abrahamsson

"On a que soi" [1]

The 1880s and 90s were the golden days of Symbolist art. It was the period when the Belgian artist Fernand Khnopff (1858-1921) created his literally fantastic images.

Khnopff was born into a wealthy family and spent his childhood in Brugge, a town which made a strong impression on him and which permeated a lot of his art. To meet his parents' expectations he began studying law, but these studies were soon abandoned because of his active disinterest. The young Fernand had already been caught up in literature and read writers like Baudelaire and Flaubert. When he started visiting the painter Xavier Mellery's studio he developed a passionate interest in painting. In 1876 Khnopff began his art studies at the Académie Royale des Beaux-Arts in Brussels. While studying there he discovered the British Pre-Rapahelite artists John Everett Millais and Edward Burne-Jones, both of whom he admired greatly. The Pre-Raphaelite influences are strong in Khnopff's art. Not least in his frequent inclusion of women with dreaming gazes and flowing hair. They also share the general atmosphere of poetic intangibility and a contact with the eternal. With the Pre-Raphaelites and Khnopff alike there's a strong longing to get away from the everyday aspects of life and the temporal. There is, however, a difference between his works and those of a majority of the Pre-Raphaelites. Burne-Jones' art is very much about a romantic yearning for fairy-tales and distant times, and as such sublime. But for Khnopff it is to a higher degree the experiences of the inner world that are in focus. Khnopff was a true Symbolist and as such he was, to borrow a description from the French author and occultist Sar Peladan, a king, priest and magician.

> *Artist... You know art descends from heaven. If you create a perfect work, a soul will come to inhabit it.* [2]   — *Sar Peladan*

Sar Peladan became very influential for Khnopff and many other Symbolist artists. In the 1880s Khnopff and Peladan initiated a close collaboration. Khnopff designed the covers for many of Peladan's novels, including *Istar* and *Femmes Honnettes!* The cover for *Istar* showed a woman who passionately throws her head back while a

---

1 "One has only oneself", quoted in Robert Goldwater, *Symbolism*, Harper & Row, 1979, p. 204
2 www.peladan.org

plant-like phallic shape embraces the lower part of her torso. The Symbolists were seldom afraid of things that could cause a scandal or a sensation. On the contrary, they actively tried to challenge society's norms and limits. They rebelled against the ideals of the day: rationalism, materialism, a focus on economics, and also against regularity in general and a ritualized family life. Opposing these stifling aspects of bourgeois life were fantasy, dreams, sexuality, death, ecstasy, irrationalism, exoticism and spontaneous love.

Sar Peladan was undoubtedly the great missionary of Symbolism and he arranged the first big exhibition of Symbolist art, the *Salon Rose + Croix*, in Paris in the 1890s. Fernand Khnopff exhibited at several of the Salons and his view of art was strongly influenced by Sar Peladan. During a period of six years there were in total six of these Salons in Paris and Brussels. They presented avant-garde art, writing, architecture and music. As an introduction at the first Salon, there was music for the occasion especially written by Erik Satie and there was also a Mass which contained readings from Wagner's *Parsifal*. The poster for the first Salon was designed by the artist Carlos Schwabe and displays the soul's path towards the divine.

Sar Peladan had a very romantic view of artists and he fought for it with great devotion. "Artist, you are the King, you are the Priest, you are the Magician"[3] It was like a crusade against his contemporary times and he assigned an active fighting position to the artist: "The artist should be a knight in armour, engaged in the symbolistic search for the Holy Graal, a crusader in constant battle with the bourgeoisie!"[4] He described art as a mediator between the physical and the metaphysical: "[art] is more an operation of the soul than of the hand; man puts into his creations the best that is in him, i.e. the immaterial; in the creation of a masterpiece – more than any study or effort – there enters mystery".[5]

According to Sar Peladan we live in a spiritual universe that the artist can describe indirectly; he or she can perceive what's invisible to the eye and give the rest of us an apprehension of it. This point of view is central to Symbolism. It is actually the very core of late 19th century Symbolism. This attracted artists who rebelled against realism and naturalism, where the humble and everyday motifs took center stage rather than the dream-like, spiritual and eternal. Symbolism was also a reaction of sorts against impressionism, which was about catching the fleeting moment, here and now in the physical world.

Thus my soul, alone, and which nothing influences: it is as if enclosed in glass and in silence given over entire to its own inner spectacle.[6]
– Georges Rodenbach

Occultism was important to many Symbolist artists. One should probably describe it as general occult ideals and atmospheres, rather than as elaborate systems, even though some artists would maintain specific, systematized occult worldviews. In the

3 Cornell Peter, *Den hemliga källan*, Gidlunds bokförlag, 1988 (1981), p. 146
4 Cornell, ibid, p. 146
5 Goldwater, ibid, p. 186
6 Goldwater, ibid, p. 210

world of Fernand Khnopff, the most important issue was the silence and isolation of meditation, and the related revelations and experiences it brought.

In Khnopff's home in Brussels there was the motto "One has only oneself", written and presented in a prominent place. In several studies and overviews of Symbolism this has been interpreted in a negative sense. Khnopff has even been described as pessimistic nihilist. When delving deeper into his art and into the context in which it bloomed – Belgian 19th century Symbolism – it becomes apparent that the motto was neither connected to pessimism nor to nihilism. Khnopff rather hinted at man's inherent need of the silence and isolation. The solitude contained in the motto could also be interpreted as a notion that every human being is complete in him/herself. This is close to the Thelemic philosophy of life that Aleister Crowley presented in *The Book of the Law* in 1904.

In this ideal of silence was a search for a life that is genuine. If the soul was silent, a communication with the hidden and unknown could manifest itself, according to Khnopff and other Belgian Symbolists. It was an ideal for the artist to strive for: to lead life as a recluse. This idea of the solitary artist is a clear expression of the idealized and romantic view of the artist that was so predominant within Symbolist art. On some levels though, Khnopff and the other Belgian artists were very active within social life. As much as Symbolism carried an ideal of silence, it also put forth a protest against the society of the times. Khnopff had many assignments, not least as a writer for the important English magazine *The Studio*, a forum for the Arts & Crafts movement, in which William Morris was a central figure. Khnopff also maintained good relations with several artist in Europe, not least with Edward Burne-Jones, a key artist in the second wave of Pre-Raphaelities. There is one preserved drawing by Khnopff, a portrait of a woman, dedicated to Burne-Jones. It was also Khnopff who wrote Burne-Jones' death rune in *The Studio*.

Typical of Belgian Symbolism were the artists' strong ties to authors. The Belgian author Georges Rodenbach's works were instrumental in Khnopff's formulations about the need for silence and isolation. In 1888, Rodenbach published *Du Silence* and in 1891 *La Règne du Silence*. Another important influence for Khnopff was the Belgian Symbolist author Maurice Maeterlinck, who also touched upon the need for silence. Both Rodenbach and Maeterlinck advocated an active silence. Rodenbach described it as "a force that makes it possible to communicate with the unknown".[7]

One of Khnopff's paitnings is called exactly that: *Silence*. In it, we can see a solitary, almost priestess-like woman who makes a sign of silence. She exists in a closed world, beyond time and space. In the space there are no objects at all. With her abstract gaze she seems to look somewhere distant or perhaps into herself. There is no real contact between the viewer and the woman in the painting. Khnopff has chosen to portray her slightly from below which further enhances the apparent intangibility. All activity seems to have ceased and she is inside her own dream-like, meditative sphere.

In many of the images of the town Brugge that Khnoppf made it is very much a silent town. The crowds are gone. Khnopff has instead turned Brugge into a calm

---

7 Goldwater, ibid, p. 210

Symbolist dream-sphere wrapped in a magical visionary haze. The only figures that occasionally appear are priestess-like solitaires. This sort of work with ethereal light is typical of Khnopff's art and contributes to a dissolution of the expected. One of the works displaying Brugge is called *The Abandoned Town*. No people remain and even the town square's statue has been removed from its base. There is a desolate atmosphere and the sea seems to be moving into the town, possibly flooding it.

Meditation is a widely used term and can mean many different techniques and attitudes. The "silence of meditation" usually associated with Khnopff's creativity is not quite the same as the one which creates a passive state of mind. It is here rather a question of looking inside, at the space from which images, ideas and atmospheres in deeper psychic spheres surface. Khnopff was like a traveler in the subconscious, and visibly so in a painting like *Etude de Femme*. We can see the upper body of an androgynous woman. She is naked but carries a strange headpiece with a small blue stone on the forehead. The room is dark and vibrates of dynamic black nuances. In the distance we can see a glimpse of something that appears to be a door. In the doorway is something or someone clothed in grey-white nuances. We're not even sure it is an actual door. Khnopff only hints that there is something there. Who the woman is or what she does is equally mysterious. Her piercing gaze is directed, but towards what? In terms of composition this was a radical painting for its time. The woman is at the far left of the image and her long arms stretch out over the entire image. Khnopff moved far away from the conventions of portraiture here. An image like this also builds a bridge between the traditional, figurative art and the abstract art of the 20th century. The woman is figurative but her surroundings abstract. This so-called "naturalistic permutation" was one of the key elements of the Symbolist art of the late 19th century. One reason for doing this was to create scenes in a way so that they could never be able to exist or appear in the "real" reality that we can apprehend with our physical senses.

There were other Symbolist artists who focused on silence. Khnopff's Belgian colleague Alphonse Osbert painted a solitary woman in a meditative pose in his *The Vision*. Her eyes are radiant and she exists in a natural landscape imbued with a visionary blue light. This shows a dream-like state of absolute stillness and silence. Osbert claimed he heard the "occult voices of heaven"[8] and meant that art should be like a prayer in silence. The French Symbolists also worked with silence as a theme. Odilon Redon and Lucien Levi-Dhurmer both painted paintings titled *Silence*, in which androgynes show the sign of silence.

Khnopff's home in Brussels is supposed to have been extraordinary. "Artists' homes" were very popular around the turn of the century and there were many magazines showing images from various artists' houses and studios. Khnopff's house unfortunately no longer exists but both interior and exterior photographs from *The Studio* let us take part of the very strict aura of his home. It was like a temple for contemplation and a life in stillness. The very first impressions that greeted the visitor were the white walls, almost clinically sparse. His home was decorated with an absence of disturbing items. In the entrance hall there was also a brass fence or gate

---

8 Goldwater, ibid, p. 211

which kept visitors out from the holy of holies – Khnopff's studio space. According to Khnopff himself the fence was meant as an incentive for visitors to meditate before they got access to the studio. His home was decorated in the *Secession*-style. It is the *Jugend*-style that was predominantly popular in Vienna and which is more stern, geometric and less elaborate than the usual variants of *Jugend*. This further enhances the feeling of being inside a temple. Khnopff's home definitely had the character of an esoteric temple of some sort. One floor was decorated with a big circle in a golden color, and he often stood inside that circle. Inside his studio was a small pool of water, to remind himself and his visitors of the necessity to ritually integrate the element water in life and work.

There was also an altar dedicated to the god Hypnos centrally placed in his home. Khnopff worshiped Hypnos, who was the god of dreams and sleep during antiquity. A fitting god for a Symbolist! On Khnopff's altar Hypnos had wings. It is a scuplture that can be seen in many of his paintings, for instance in *I Lock the Door Upon Myself* (a title taken from a poem by Christina Rossetti, sister of Pre-Raphaelite painter Gabriel Rossetti). *I Lock the Door Upon Myself* was exhibited at Sar Peladan's first Symbolist Salon and it was one of the paintings that was most talked about. To have altars at home was popular among many other Symbolist artists of the day too. Franz Stück, one of the key people of German Symbolism, had an altar dedicated to sin in his artist home's studio in Munich.

> *Art lives only by harmonies… It must be the evocator of mystery, a solitary repose in life, akin to prayers… In silence.*[9]
> — Alphonse Osbert

The Belgian Symbolist Jean Delville was also tied to Sar Peladan and, like Khnopff, was inspired by the atomspheres at his Salons. A painting like *Satan's Treasure* from 1895 seems, in title and aesthetics, to forebode both the psychedelia of the 1960s and the heavy metal of the 1970s. In a world of strong colors an ecstatic Lucifer seems to be surrounded by dragon-like creatures and dancing amidst a stream of naked bodies. Delville could perceive a spiritual universe beyond the visible. He felt he could look into a world of reincarnation, a world in which each human being is filled with an astral light that surrounds him/her. Based on this, he created his own mystic cosmology. In one significant painting we can see Orpheus' severed head, bathing in an astral glow. The borders between the individual and the universe seem dissolved. The head was painted after Delville's wife, and there's a strong androgyne atmosphere present.

The androgyne is someone who crosses over habitual limits and as such was an ideal being for many Symbolists. They tried to portray what was situated in the very outskirts of the average citizen's experience of normality and reality. Khnopff's images are to a great extent peopled with beings who visually seem to be moving in a border zone of the masculine and feminine. Significant in this regard is that Khnopff in 1884 made an image for Sar Peladan's novel *Le Vice Suprème*, which is

---

9 Goldwater, ibid. p. 193 f

about an artist who creates an androgyne angel. Sar Peladan was, like many other occultists, strongly fascinated by the androgyne. Khnopff was also fascinated by creating unions between humans and animals in the same *Gestalt*. And in Franz Stück's images we can frequently meet fauns and centaurs.

Khnopff took this one step further when he left the fantastic creatures of traditional mythology and created amalgams of humans and animals. In *Avec Veraeren* a human being has merged with an animal body with tiger-like stripes. On the cover of Sar Peladan's *Le Vice Suprême* we can see a cranium-creature adorned with female breasts and a lioness' body. Both these images are worth commenting on further. They both exist in their own right regardless of any Sar Peladan association. In *Avec Verhaeren* the central figure is an androgyne being whose eyes are closed and whose entire being seems on its way to melt into *La Nuit*, the night, with its dark sky and bright stars. There is stillness and the being seems to be in deep contemplation. The upper part of the body, especially the area around the head, is surrounded by a diffuse light. It could be its aura but could also be seen to be indicative of that the borders between the human and the cosmic are about to be dissolved. The human *Gestalt* with its tiger-looking lower body is by the side of the central character, who has a hand against the head of the "man-beast". This beast has a facial expression of pleasure. The mouth is smiling and the eyes closed. This image is very peculiar and some questions that pop up are: Who is this man-beast? What kind of relatonship do these two have?

In *Le Vice Suprème* we can see a naked androgyne character standing on a base, one side of which is adorned by an angel whose head is in the shape of a cranium. The character is in a nocturnal world in what might be a mountainous region. On top of a mountain we can see the being with its skull-head, animal torso and female breasts.

Jean Delville was a militant anti-materialist who in his art portrayed many beings not quite of this world. In his classic painting *Mrs Stuart Merrill* we can see a woman holding a book with a mysterious triangle on the cover. Her eyes are hardly seeing in the traditional sense of the word but are rather turned upward, as if in some kind of ecstatic vision. Despite the fact that the painting has a very distinct human name it's hardly an individual we're watching. This is crucial to Symbolism too: very rarely are human individuals portrayed. They are more like archetypes and representatives of different states of mind and emotion. This is very true of Fernand Khnopff's work too. Even though his sister Marguerite, someone Khnopff worshiped, was his muse and model in a majority of paintings and drawing, these are never meant to be portraits of her. His world is full of immortal, eternal beings existing beyond time and space.

> *The Artist is a creative genius; that is, he is of the nature of Godhead which devised the Soul as a medium for self-realization. Also, as History assures us, the Artist is of the caste of the initiated rulers of Mankind; he understands the theory of the Universe, he is an Epopt of the Mysteries of Nature, and an Hierophant of the Inviolable Sanctuary.* [10]
>
> – *Aleister Crowley*

---

10 *The Nightmare Paintings: Aleister Crowley: Works from the Palermo Collection*, Buratti Fine Art, 2012. Crowley had a Symbolistic view of art and placed the artist higher than even the ritual magician.

Fernand Khnopff, Symbolist

In the painting *De L'Animalité* by Fernand Khnopff we can see a dark, temple-like space. The very subdued sources of light in the image sets the atmosphere. Light and color are used in non-realistic ways and this was primarily meant to stir the emotions, create a vagueness and a sense of uncertainty and confusion in the viewer. The image is dominated by an opening flanked by two pillars. These pillars are decorated with skulls, and behind each skull shines a yellow circle. On the other side of the opening there is a naked woman on the floor. Again, we can't really tell where she's looking as her gaze is veiled and dreaming. That's all Knopff shares, and this is significant of both his own and the general Symbolist art of the late 19th century. Khnopff never wanted to give any answers. The answer lies within the viewer. In this sense, Khnopff was a precursor of much of 20th century art, in which the perspective of the viewer becomes a co-creating force.

In this essay, we have wanted to share some reflections, points of entry and attitudes to the rich artistic world of Fernand Khnopff and the late 19th century Symbolism. We have not, as is common within academic, scholastic art criticism, tried to explain every detail of each artwork in question. We think that would decimate both the work and the individual apprehension of it. Symbolist art is vague in itself and that has always been one of its main traits. You could even go so far as to say that here, even symbols become redundant. In the 1880s Jean Moreau wrote a Symbolist manifesto in which he put forth that the Symbolist art is about hinting. Khnopff's art should not be precised, limited or defined. It should live on in an ambiguous twilight. It should suggest rather than define. His art is to a great extent about getting away from rational thought and preconceived notions. That one consciously central element in his paintings is *silence* is totally in line with this attitude. The silence never explains. It merely suggests and hints.

REFERENCES:

—⁓— www.peladan.org (2014-02-18)
—⁓— Cornell, Peter (1981), *Den hemliga källan. Om initiationsmönster i konst, litteratur och politik*, Gidlunds bokförlag, 1988 (1981)
—⁓— Ehrhardt Ingrid & Reynolds, Simon (ed), *Kingdom of the Soul: Symbolist Art in Germany 1870-1920*, Prestel, 2000
—⁓— *Fernand Khnopff*, Lebeer Hossmann, 1987
—⁓— Gibson, Michael & Nerret, Gilles, *Symbolism*, Taschen 2006 (1996)
—⁓— Goldwater, Robert, *Symbolism*, Harper & Row, 1979
—⁓— Lucie-Smith, *Symbolist Art*, Thames and Hudson Ltd, 1972
—⁓— Rapetti, Rodolphe, *Symbolism*, Flammarion, 2006
—⁓— Wilton, Andrew & Upstone, Robert (ed), *The Age of Rossetti, Burne-Jones & Watts, Symbolism in Britain 1860-1910*, Tate Gallery Publishing, 1997

Making the Invisible Visible

Péladan's Artistic Revolution Meets the 21ˢᵗ Century

Sasha Chaitow

Where Religion becomes artificial, it is reserved for Art to save the spirit of religion by recognising the figurative value of the mythic symbols which the former would have us believe in their literal sense, and revealing their deep and hidden truth through an ideal presentation.
                                                    – Richard Wagner, *Religion and Art.*[1]

Introduction:
Of synchronicity, inspiration, and magic in the mundane

I write these lines in deep midwinter, from a medieval village by a river, on the cultural crossroads that is Corfu, a historically distinctive island in Northwestern Greece known for its long artistic tradition. In this small corner of Europe a sequence of events is unfolding that seems nothing short of miraculous, which reminds us that the impact of history should not be sought in the short term, and which demonstrates the wonder of modern communications technology. It is a tale worth sharing, and a prime example of how culture can be driven, and what it means to apply scholarship to the mundane world. Though Péladan's life and work are the topic of my doctoral research, I maintain that scholarship should serve culture and not remain enclosed in the hallowed halls of academia. A series of serendipitous events led to what is rapidly turning into quite a cultural happening, and it seems fitting that before explaining the background and sharing the source of the inspiration, the story should be recorded first.

It all began when I received an invitation to write an article for the catalogue of a bold new art exhibition that was being organised in Madrid, Spain. The cultural collective behind *Semana Gotica de Madrid*, together with Mentenebre Cultural Association and supported by the Autonomous University of Madrid, were planning a month long sequence of cultural happenings and events. This year's programme included a month-long Neo-Symbolist Salon based on the Rosicrucian Salons of Sâr Péladan. In their call for art submissions, they noted that this exhibition had been inspired by the original Symbolist movement, and spoke of the recontextualisation of key Symbolist motifs within contemporary art, which incorporates "Neo-

---

1 Richard Wagner, "Religion und Kunst," *Sämtliche Schriften und Dichtungen : Volume X. 211-252*, 1880.

Symbolism, new artists of the soul". The brief ended as follows:

> *We look to Decadent Paris, where the Salons were the main way of presenting new artistic developments to the public. But we do not try to emulate the grand salons of the Louvre, or even the Salon des refusés where the Impressionists made their mark; rather we look to the adventure of a visionary, the self-proclaimed Sâr Péladan who founded the Salon de la Rose + Croix which involved mainly the current Symbolist artists. While somewhat removed from Péladan's eccentricity, but following some of the principles that inspired its aesthetic taste, over a century later we present this Neo-Symbolist Salon. Artistic proposals for exhibition should be based on Symbolist iconography but reinterpreted within the parameters of counter-culture, anti-art, in opposition to the market and the establishment. For the true essence of the art of our time is quite far away and must be found in the underground.²*

After an exciting brainstorming session with the organisers, I wrote the catalogue article on Péladan's aesthetics and sent three of my recent illustrations of his work for inclusion in the exhibition. Synchronicity being what it is, within the same week I received a call from a Greek publisher asking me if I'd consider writing a book on Péladan for the general reader, while my editor at the Greek newspaper gave me a weekly art column in which I promptly began to develop a series of articles on the value of the arts in the context of the economic and social crisis currently plaguing Greece.

The weeks and months rolled by, the exhibition in Madrid was mounted to international acclaim, the book had been published, and a few weeks ago I began planning one of several book launches from my medieval hideaway in Corfu. Some of my Greek colleagues began to think it would be a nice idea to pair the book launch with a weekend break in Corfu... And thus the idea for a one-day symposium was born. Being a native, the task of organising the event fell to me, and since my associates and I all have very different areas of interest within the broad sphere of arts, letters, esoteric research and philosophy, I had to find a way of stream-lining the event to give it a central focus. The one, striking common thread was our determination and passion for driving culture forward in spite of the crisis that has stunted the arts and letters across Europe, but particularly in Greece.

So I asked the speakers to focus on the practical value and applications of the arts and letters within this sociocultural context: one in which the world around us is experiencing rapid, vertiginous change to which circumstance calls us to either adapt, or be caught up in a vortex of confusion, and often despair. Further creative brainstorming resulted in a three-day event, which has now taken on the character of a miniature Salon after Péladan's example, incorporating a group art exhibition featuring local Corfiot artists, poetry readings and string quartets, Platonic dialogues unravelling Péladan's vision, and a series of talks on the practical, applicable value

---

2 The original call to artists (in Spanish) may be found at http://www.herejiaybelleza.com/convocatoria-a-artistas-i-salon-neo-simbolista/hayqueponerindex.php/convocatoria-a-artistas-i-salon-neo-simbolista/

of studying and communicating through and about the arts, philosophy, history, culture, and indeed, occulture at times of sweeping cultural change. The lecture topics range from poetry inspired by archival discoveries to Nietzschean thoughts on the re-enchantment of the world, with all the arts – and several of the humanities being well represented.

As I write, the event is less than a month away, yet it seems to have captured the hearts and minds of the inhabitants of Corfu and beyond. Announcements have already begun circulating in the local and national media – without a single press release having been sent out– art submissions are pouring in, and I am already being asked whether it will become an annual fixture. All of which would suggest that Péladan's vision for igniting a social renaissance through the arts is just what the doctor ordered for this embattled corner of Southern Europe. Though Péladan remains a complete unknown outside specialist circles, his idea is being revived and embraced by the very people for whom he conceived it: by artists, poets, philosophers and art-lovers. There is tragic irony in the fact that Péladan was ridiculed and vilified during his life-time, yet over a century later, it may yet be that his grand vision becomes a vehicle for the very dialogue that he so desperately sought to incite.

It is the historian's curse to be constantly mindful of the antecedents and influences weighing on our time, and the similarities between the *fin-de-siècle* and our own time – at least as it is experienced in Southern Europe – are quite stunning. The lived experience of the Greek crisis is quite different to the way in which it is portrayed in the international news alongside info-graphics of wanton spending and accusations of tax evasion, but there is no need for an in-depth account of the harrowing reality faced by the population. Suffice it to note that this is a society being forced to ask itself some hard questions, a nation at the crossroads between east and west still struggling with its own identity and cultural narratives while being subjected to overpowering geopolitical and economic forces. In essence, it is experiencing what anthropologist Victor Turner has aptly termed "moments when common traditional meanings of life and history have become indeterminate", and in such moments, it is to myth and its many modes of expression that societies turn in order to "remake cultural sense".[3] This is the common point of reference between the French *fin-de-siècle* and Greece today, and this is what underpins the rationale behind the decision to introduce and attempt to implement Péladan's idea of a creative crossroads where the arts become a locus for dialogue: for remaking cultural sense.

Our history has yet to be written, and the success or failure of this creative experiment will be judged by others in years to come. When viewed in the here and now, the role of the arts and letters is, among other things, to bear witness. This act of recording this endeavour as it unfolds is just that: to bear witness to an attempt at using scholarship to produce something of real, practical – perhaps delightfully subversive – use to culture as it is created: on street corners, in dusty bookshops, and in the minds and hearts of fellow citizens.

---

3 Victor Turner, 'Social Dramas and Stories about them,' in *On Narrative*, ed. by W.J.T. Mitchell (Chicago: University of Chicago Press, 1981), p. 164.

Making the Invisible Visible

The *fin-de-siècle* was a time when French society was coming to terms with the multiple endings and beginnings witnessed in the wake of the French Revolution. As industry, technology, and science propelled the Western world into the modern era, the multiple rifts within the uneasy French Republic began to heal, new freedoms began to be explored and social boundaries torn down. This was a brave new world where anything might have seemed possible, but apart from these new beginnings, it also marked the end of an era for which Romantic poets and painters had already grieved in the wake of the Enlightenment. Traditionalists mourned the order and security of a world apparently lost to materialism and rampant decadence, and yearned for the romantic notion of a re-imagined glorious past where God was in his heaven, the Pope ruled the Holy Roman Empire, social order was maintained by divine mandate and Catholicism provided both the ritual and the rulebook for aristocrat and pauper alike.

Today this sequence of events may echo as some distant narrative of little relevance, but the inhabitants of the *fin-de-siècle* represented a generation poised on a threshold, many of whom were perhaps prepared to shed their forefathers' dreams of restoring the *ancien régime*, prepared to embrace the idea of creating a new society, but not all of them were prepared to do so at the expense of powerful aspects of their cultural identity; the wounds were perhaps still too fresh, the changes still too radical. To borrow a remark from historian Michael Burleigh, 'eighteen centuries did not disappear from men's characters just by declaring it to be' so, 'the psychological legacy of the *ancien regime* did not simply vanish,' and people were not 'empty glass vessels' to be 'filled with the content of [the revolutionaries'] choice.'[4] This sentiment held true for those circles of intellectuals and visionaries in the following generations, for whom letting go of their past was one sacrifice too many – even though, ironically, it was the Revolution itself that gave them the opportunity to re-imagine it in the ever-more fantastical forms that they did.

It was a mercurial world where established order turned to quicksand; where one had to adapt or be damned. Yet we cannot underestimate the impact on the sensibilities of devout traditionalists faced with the rejection of royal authority by the National Assembly that was to bring a century of political strife, nor that of the abrupt weakening of the Catholic church through the imposition of *laïcité* in what has been read as an echo of the Protestant reformation,[5] whereby the emblematic motto "sola scriptura, sola fide, sola gracia" was replaced by the enduring battle cry of *Liberté, Egalité, Fraternité.* [6]

Within this context, Joséphin Péladan (1858-1918) represented a generation standing on the cusp of modernity, fighting it in name, yet inexorably ushering it in. By his time the internal religious and political turmoil had begun to subside,

---

4 Burleigh, *Earthly Powers*, pp. 92-93; David A. Bell, *The Cult of the Nation in France: Inventing Nationalism 1680-1800* (Cambridge MA: Harvard University Press, 2001).
5 Piers Paul Read, *The Dreyfus Affair: The Story of the Most Infamous Miscarriage of Justice in French History* (London: Bloomsbury 2012), pp. 8-9.
6 Ibid. p. 9.

and the decadent period – literary and literal – coexisted alongside a period of unbridled creativity in many spheres. Where the previous generation – typified by Péladan's father – had reached out to the primordial past to re-enforce the values of the *ancien régime*, Péladan transmuted them into a new *legendarium* for his generation. He revived the archetypal concept of the androgyne, lauded as the ideal to which men and women should strive for harmonious relationships, by extension, harmonious societies, and above all, the way back to reintegration with the divine source. Through his novels and dramas, his tales of fallen angels and lonesome mages, forbidden love and tortuous redemption, he sought to redeem the Great Adversary himself – for Péladan's theology had no place for eternal damnation, only for Promethean self-sacrifice and self-redemption.[7] His invitation, expressed through his Salons, called Paris to rise out of the swamp of decadence and to reach for the light through beauty. It didn't matter if they understood, he thought, if his artist-priests inundated them with ensouled art, they had only to look, and keep on looking until the symbols worked their magic. He took into account that not everyone had the intellectual, educational, or other capacity to explore occult thought in the same way, and selected as democratic a medium as he could: the language of myth and the medium of art – all the while railing against high-minded academic art that he considered overrated and soulless. His grand vision was no less than a spiritual revolution with beauty as his supreme weapon and art as the *coup de grâce* against the 'disenchantment of the world' so prevalent as first the scientific world-view and then the industrial revolution completed their conquest of the Western mind, in an age he regarded as characterized by rampant materialism and futile decadence.

It went disastrously wrong in the end, and the reasons for that are quite another story. Nonetheless, Péladan and his opus represent both the end of an era, and the start of one, where he took the old and turned it into something in tune with his time, where he embraced the democracy of his era even as he strived to raise his compatriots to a new spiritual level. Where his father had tried to use myth to revive the past, Péladan used it to remake the present, and even though he failed in his own objectives, his influence – reaching as far afield as South America, Russia, and Greece, suggests otherwise.

THE SALONS DE LA ROSE-CROIX

In the spring of 1892, the Paris *gendarmerie* were perplexed at the sight of a flood of crowds and carriages on their way to the Galeries Durand-Ruel, where they were met by a curious bearded man wearing purple velvet robes and answering to the name of a Babylonian mage. The exhibition catalogue welcomed them with the lines:

Artist, you are a priest: Art is the great mystery and, if your effort results in a

---

7 See Sasha Chaitow, "Legends of the Fall Retold", *The Fenris Wolf 6* (Stockholm: Edda, 2013), pp. 228-269 for a detailed article on Péladan's Promethean Luciferianism.

masterpiece, a ray of divinity will descend as on an altar. Artist, you are a king: Art is the true empire, if your hand draws a perfect line, the cherubim themselves will descend to revel in their reflection... They may one day close the Church, but [what about] the Museum? If Notre-Dame is profaned, the Louvre will officiate... Humanity, oh citizens, will always go to mass, when the priest will be Bach, Beethoven, Palestrina: one cannot make the sublime organ into an atheist! Brothers in all the arts, I am sounding a battle cry: let us form a holy militia for the salvation of idealism....we will build the Temple of Beauty ...for the artist is a priest, a king, a mage, for art is a mystery, the only true empire, the great miracle...[8]

Péladan proceeded to organise a further five Salons between 1893 and 1897, under the auspices of his organisation, *The Order of the Rose + Croix of the Temple and the Grail*. His purpose was to expose the general public to a form of symbolic art that would "rip Love out of the Western soul and replace it with the love of Beauty, the love of the Ideal, the love of Mystery."

For the organisation of this first, spectacular Salon, he had issued a call to artists some months earlier, with the aim of contravening the academically accepted art of his time, which he despised and frequently railed against in his articles in the French press. The invitation to artists to send their work for consideration for the first *Salon de la Rose + Croix* had the tone of a manifesto:

The Order forbids any contemporary representations, rustic, military, flowers, animals, genres such as history, and portraits or landscapes. But it welcomes all allegories, legends, mysticism and myth, as well as expressive faces if they are noble, or nude studies if they are beautiful. Because you must make BEAUTY to enter the Rose + Croix Salon.[9]

The result was an immense impact on the Parisian art world, and eventually, on the whole Symbolist movement. The first Salon welcomed over fifty thousand visitors, intrigued by the curious poster depicting three women at various stages of initiatory revelation that had covered the walls of Paris a few weeks earlier, as well as by regular articles, announcements, and controversies printed in *Le Figaro* over the preceding year. The Salons included musical and theatrical performances alongside the exhibitions, giving an unparalleled impetus and unity to the Symbolist movement. Yet, the Salons and their instigator were as notorious as they were intriguing, and following numerous public controversies, within a few short years, both Salons and Mage were forgotten, to be recalled only as a utopian fantasy of an eccentric buffoon.

This curious man who in the 1890s went by the name Sâr Merodack and claimed an ancestry of Babylonian royalty, left a spectacular legacy of over one hundred books, several thousand articles, and was responsible for inspiring a generation of

---

8 Josephin Péladan, *Catalogue du Salon de la Rose + Croix* (Paris: Galerie Durand-Ruel, 1892), pp. 7-11.
9 Péladan, "Le Salon de la Rose + Croix", Le Figaro, 2 September 1891, p. 1.

artists and authors as far afield as Russia and South America. Today his works are all but forgotten, encountered only within treatises on the Decadent movement or in brief references in academic studies of *fin-de-siècle* French Occultism, and the majority of these references tend to perpetuate the sense of his eccentricity and peculiarity.

I first encountered Péladan's name in an academic study of Rosicrucianism; one of the few to acknowledge, albeit briefly, that there was more to the man than the tarnished reputation that had survived in most references to his name.[10] Initially, I was sceptical, especially since apart from some rare works by his loyal followers, the vast majority of the existing biographies of Péladan are deeply disparaging, dismissing him as an eccentric fool. His *oeuvre* is vast, and can be disheartening on account of the florid lyricism of his novels, and the turgidity of his theoretical prose. Yet, if one makes the effort to read Péladan on his own terms, what emerges is a man with a clear and coherent vision, whose life's work was an attempt to "build the Temple of Beauty" of which he wrote, and whose every action was tuned to a conscious attempt to disseminate this vision.

Intellectual background

After an unconventional childhood and education, by the age of 26 Péladan had already formulated a complex, coherent cosmology of his own, based in part on world mythology, which he had studied from a young age, and deeply influenced by a tradition of pansophy and "philosophical" history that was eclipsed during the Enlightenment, but which remained a significant element in esoteric thought; a complex of cultural currents that enjoyed a significant revival in the second half of the nineteenth century. Pansophy is understood as a way of combining all human knowledge according to analogical principles, and viewing human history through a form of allegorical hermeneutics, whereby events are interpreted as part of a larger narrative in which events within the human microcosm reflect the celestial macrocosm, and can be revealed through myths, legends, and their correspondences.

This form of historiography, or *Mythistory*, was popularised and brought into mainstream culture by the Romantics in particular, and remained popular among certain traditionalist circles in Péladan's time. In conjunction with an emergent quest for a new understanding of human civilization and origins that led to fierce debates over the course of the eighteenth and nineteenth centuries, a kaleidoscope of fantastical philosophical and metaphysical theories provided rich sources of inspiration that fuelled, first Romantic, and later Symbolist creativity. Thinkers and writers such as Protestant Freemason and polymath Antoine Court de Gébelin (1725-1784), and later, Pierre-Simon Ballanche (1776-1847), Antoine Fabre d'Olivet (1767-1825) and Delisle de Sales (Jean-Baptiste Izouard, 1741-1816), were the main "allegorical mythographers" who sought to discover universal, eternal "truths" through the allegorical analysis of all human knowledge, from the emerging sciences and observation of nature, to world mythology, Scriptural teachings, and

---

10 Christopher McIntosh, *The Rosicrucians: The History, Mythology, and Rituals of an Esoteric Order* (New York: Weiser, 1998), pp. 93-96.

exciting new archaeological discoveries which would lead to a host of new debates regarding Biblical history.

These ideas were keys to Péladan's early education, and a large part of the cosmology he adopted rested on the ideas put forward by Fabre d'Olivet, an erudite polymath who rewrote the book of *Genesis*, claiming he had discovered the "true", hidden interpretation of the Hebrew language. His conclusions were replete with theological implications that would fuel a particular brand of Luciferianism in occult circles, and were central to Péladan's work.

THEOLOGY AND THEODICY: REWRITING GENESIS

In his subversive rewriting of *Genesis* Fabre d'Olivet tackled the question of the Fall; one which troubled Péladan greatly, since he did not believe that original sin could truly be an immutable curse on mankind. Following Fabre d'Olivet, Péladan came to believe that the world had been created, not by God, but by the angels (whom he named *Elohim*), and that primordial man was androgynous and immortal. The only thing this creature lacked was self-awareness. On seeing their "most perfect" creation, the angels were so spellbound by its potential, that they sought to give it the opportunity to commune with the divine mysteries. However, this was forbidden by God, because the primordial androgyne belonged to a different order of being, and thus, allowing it access to higher spiritual knowledge through self-awareness contravened natural law. The story of the snake and the apple from the Tree of Knowledge is thus reinterpreted, not as an encounter with a cunning force of evil, but as an act of mercy and love on the part of the angels. Nonetheless, they were punished along with their creation, since the androgyne had received a small glimpse of the immensity of the macrocosm, and the first stirrings of self-awareness had begun.

This is the moment when time began, according to this retelling. The androgyne was separated into two, unequal beings, male and female each receiving different attributes and qualities, while those angels who, like Prometheus, had dared to try to share the "sacred fire", were sentenced to live out all eternity on earth, mating with humans and, in a twist of divine irony, charged to guide humanity and to help them to evolve spiritually, so that through the generations, they would achieve enough self-awareness and knowledge of the mysteries to be able to reunite into their original, androgynous form, and by extension, to reintegrate with the Divine.

This theory is the motive force for all of Péladan's work, and the metaphysical principles underlying this premise form the entire basis for his aesthetics. His fixation on the arts, and visual representation in particular, derived from his belief that humans were created by angels casting their shadow, and then tracing its silhouette in order to shape the human form.

The beings delegated by Being (Elohim) conceived their creative oeuvre by decreeing that humanity would be manifested (delineated) according to their shadow. The Elohim were spirits, individualised emanations of the essence. Since the shadow is a decreased form of light, the shadow of essence is substance, and the shadow of substance can be nothing other than matter ... The prototype of man, king of the sensible world, is the angel ... One can define beauty by looking at angelic forms ... We know the Greek legend of the origins of the art of Drawing. On the eve of their parting, the daughter of Butades, the potter of Sicyon, delineated the shadow of her lover with charcoal on a white wall. So, for the fervent memory of our angelic origins to remain in our soul, we must maintain our understanding and our sense of the desire to return, some day, to those who gave us perfect love, as they gave us reality and life. Some must do this by creating works of art, others by understanding them.[11]

ART AS RELIGION

To this end, Péladan saw the creative process as the ultimate sacred act, whereby through emulating the act of creation, humanity could move back towards a reintegration with their divine origins. Artists had been gifted with the talent to create those works of art that could spark the spiritual evolution he believed necessary for this process, and his mission was to inspire them to do so, while also attempting to attract the general public, and helping them to understand the content of this sacred art. He proclaimed art to be a religion in the sense of a process "mediating between the physical and the metaphysical"[12] and defined it as follows:

Art is the totality of the methods of realising Beauty. Beauty is the essence of all expression through form. Techniques are nothing more than the means to an end. If Beauty is the objective, and art the means, what is the rule? The Ideal. Therefore Idealist art is that which reunites within a work all the perfections that the spirit can conceive on a given theme.[13]

As Péladan saw it, the heart of this process was the act of giving form to intangible Essence, based on the Platonic notion of the world of Ideas, so in his vocabulary the "Ideal" is the sublime, ethereal aspect of creation, which needs to be given a shape, a body to inhabit, if it is to become perceptible in the material world. These "bodies" are nothing other than works of art, and a "perfect work" would also be an ensouled work – like religious icons, it would be inhabited by the Idea that it represented. Péladan was quick to specify that not all works of art are reflections of the Ideal; rather, they must conform to specific rules, and he wrote many long explanations arguing the philosophy of this point, summarised in his axiom that "A work that is real in form, and unreal in expression, is perfect".

IDEAS AND FORMS

For Péladan, a perfect work had to conform to the two characteristics of idealism and mysticism. He defined Idealism according to the dictionary definition: "that which reunites all the perfections that the spirit can conceive".[14] To achieve this goal, the idea had to be clothed within a form. Péladan stated that the content could, and

---

11 Péladan, *L'art idéaliste et mystique* (Paris: Chamuel, 1894), pp. 41-44.
12 Ibid., p. 36.
13 Ibid., pp. 36-7.
14 Ibid., p. 37.

should use a recognisable and realistic form to express the Idea it housed, but this was not all. It also had to express something of "the beyond", something ineffable that could tell the viewer that the apparently mundane object, or figure they observed in a painting, was something more than it appeared. This, he suggested, was to be achieved by a combination of three aesthetic principles: Intensity, subtlety, and harmony, combined in such a way as to hint at their symbolic nature, symbolism being a mode of expression that is subtle by definition. In the words of Jean Moréas, author of the *Symbolist Manifesto*:

> *The Idea, in its turn, should not be allowed to be seen deprived of the sumptuous lounge robes of extraneous analogies; because the essential character of symbolic art consists in never approaching the concentrated kernel of the Idea in itself. So, in this art, the pictures of nature, the actions of human beings, all concrete phenomena would not themselves know how to manifest themselves; these are presented as the sensitive appearance destined to represent their esoteric affinity with primordial Ideas... For the precise translation of its synthesis, it is necessary for symbolism to take on an archetypal and complex style.[15]*

In other words, the artist should create embellished, complex forms to house an idea, precisely because it must keep a certain distance from the "kernel of the Idea in itself". This obliges the viewer to engage intellectually with the work in order to begin to decipher it, and the use of archetypal and allegorical imagery, subjectively deployed but based on a shared frame of reference, should help the viewer to translate apparently mundane representations into their Ideal forms. Péladan's teachings are entirely in line with this perspective, his definitions of idealism and mysticism respectively expressed through the use of realism and the "unreal" perfectly mirroring Moréas' description.

By adjusting and balancing the relationships between the content (Idea), the form, and the technical rendering, one could create Péladan's notion of a "perfect work" that would serve as an aesthetic springboard to awaken the soul out of materialism and decadence, and if the public were exposed to this on a grand scale, then the cumulative effect, he thought, could only be a spiritual renaissance.

To support his arguments, and to inspire the artists (in all the arts) who understood his cause, Péladan reached to the art and architecture of ancient civilisations, selecting and highlighting specific symbolic elements to illustrate his philosophy. One such telling example is the Assyrian Sphinx, or *Lamassu*, a hybrid, protective deity with the body of a bull, wings, and a human head.

---

15 Jean Moréas, "Le Symbolisme", *Le Figaro* 18 September 1886.

This motif appears repeatedly in many aspects of his work, from the frontispieces of his books and the emblem of his organisation, to the numerous reiterations of his philosophy:

> *What is Art? Human creation. God made the universe (macrocosm), man made the temple (microcosm), from where arts emerged.... What is a monument, if not a calculation of lines and volumes for the expression of spiritual will? From the forest path and from the cavern to the cathedral, human work appears colossal. What is a figure such as the sphinx or the winged bull with a human face, if not a philosophical combination of natural motifs for the manifestation of an idea? From the cat to the sphinx, from the savage bull to the genius that guards the temple threshold, through quasi-divine operations the artist raises himself to the level of creator.* [16]

He explained the significance of this symbolic entity as follows, in one of the several theoretical handbooks that he wrote as guides to self-awareness designed to help his contemporaries achieve their spiritual potential:

> *That which the intelligence has conceived, the soul executes... Study this symbol; the human head wears the royal crown with three rows of horns, a privilege of the gods, and signifies, initiate, [that you should] no longer obey, for you are a king, if you think. A king does not seek to reign, the triple horns have destined you for the sole conquest of eternity. The wings show you that you must be inspired by the superior world, without ceasing, to manifest light on earth by the power of the bull's hooves.* [17]

This layering of symbolism demonstrated the kind of "idealism and mysticism" that Péladan preached; expressed through a deceptively familiar "real" form (in the sense that it is not an abstract composition of colour), but the form encapsulates the

---

16 Péladan, *Les Idées et les Formes: Antiquité Orientale, Egypte – Kaldée – Assyrie – Chine – Phénicie – Judée – Arabie – Inde – Perse – Aryas d'Asie Mineure* (Paris: Mercure de France, 1908)., pp.9, 10-11, 13.
17 Péladan, *Comment on Devient Mage*, p. 8.

"ineffable", "unreal" notions that cannot be expressed satisfactorily by other means. While the verbal description is linear by necessity, the visual depiction retains its stratified nature, and allows us to perceive the meaning that it houses in a flash of insight, complete rather than in stages. Thus, each line and detail becomes an ideogram to be deciphered by the viewer:

> *The line in itself is as abstract as the alphabet, it does not exist in nature; literally it is an ideogram, a hieroglyph which, for human intelligence, translates the sensible world; it is, therefore, in its highest form, the only thing that is independent of technique and where genius can show itself; all the rest belongs to talent.... Drawing is the art of writing by means of living forms treated by the abstract process of the line, augmented by the contours.[18]*

Other key recurrent motifs that Péladan gave prominence to in his work included the androgyne, the Sphinx in all its forms, and motifs from the myth of Orpheus. The androgyne reflected, first and foremost, Péladan's understanding of the origin of humanity, the unification of opposites and the ideal to which mankind should strive. A symbolic figure that has appeared in various philosophical and esoteric works since antiquity, Péladan's use of this symbolic motif is grounded in a Platonic, yet worldly context, and his treatises written for men and women explain in fine detail how human relationships should strive to achieve a perfect balance between the two sexes so as to create an androgyne from their union, since this held the key to unification with the divine.

Péladan's Sphinx is a mystagogue and mnemonic of the creative potential within man, and, like Orpheus, takes on an almost talismanic role as a patron and guide inspiring Symbolist expression. Comprehension and use of these symbols in artistic compositions (whether poetic, theatrical, figurative or literary), was the mark, privilege, and duty of the artist-initiates; whom Péladan exhorted to place their talent at the service of a supreme purpose; the awakening and raising of mankind to their divine potential.

In his treatise *The Birth of Tragedy* (1886), deeply influenced by various Theosophical theories and other occult practices of his time, Nietzsche outlined the notion of Dionysian-Orphic ecstasy and possession that were the motive force of Symbolist art, and a supreme form of initiation into the invisible forces of man and universe. This idea of initiation was at the heart of occult thought of the time, and it refers to awakening, discovery, and the development of dormant human faculties which are available to all, but are in a state of dormancy.

According to Orphic cosmogony, humans were the progeny of the ash of Dionysus' body and the blood of Titans, and it was this dual nature that made good and evil an intrinsic part of the human condition. To evolve spiritually and purify themselves from their evil, Titanic elements, humanity was bound to live through many incarnations until they achieved full self-awareness. As the legend has it, when they died, humans were obliged to drink from the Well of Oblivion

---

18 Péladan, *L'art idéaliste et mystique*, p. 102.

(Lethe), and forget their mortal life before they reincarnated, and so in their next incarnation they would begin afresh, with no memories to guide them. Initiates, however, may drink from the spring of Mnemosyne after death, so that they may evolve spiritually, but only if they spoke the password to the guardian of the spring: "A Child of Earth I am, and of the Starlit Sky", which denoted that they knew of their dual, earthly and celestial origins. Orphic cosmology and theology is reflected in much of Péladan's work, particularly with regard to the initiatory capacity of art – for both artist and viewer.

In the greatly influential work *The Great Initiates* (1889), Edouard Schuré discusses the notion of initiation in depth, and presents the initiatory journeys of various great figures in human history and legend. Among them, Ram, Moses, Jesus... and Orpheus. Regarding initiation, he says the following:

> *Modern man seeks happiness without knowledge, knowledge without wisdom...*
> *For someone to achieve mastery, the ancient sages tell us, man must fully*
> *reconstruct his physical, ethical and spiritual existence. Only then can an initiate,*
> *initiate [another]... Therefore, initiation was, then, something very different*
> *from a hollow dream, and something far greater than a simple scientific theory:*
> *it was, then, the creation of a soul out of itself, its evolution on a higher level, and*
> *its flowering on the divine plane.*

Orpheus stands for creative genius and initiatory tradition, and his lyre symbolises human existence itself, whereby, according to Edouard Schuré, a contemporary of Péladan's: "every chord corresponds to a mood of the human soul and contains the laws of one science and one art," thus 'proving' Orpheus to be "the great mystagogue, ancestor of poetry and music, which reveal eternal truths."[19] This "religion" of initiatory and creative genius was the motive force of the Symbolists, for whom Orpheus was the archetypal artist-priest, who, in Péladan's vision, would collectively initiate society through their exposure to the mysteries hidden within symbolic artwork. Hence the repeated motif of Orpheus' head and lyre, are no less than sacred icons, talismans encapsulating their whole raison-d'être. And Orpheus is their patron saint.

RECONTEXTUALISING PÉLADAN'S TEACHINGS

One might question the extent to which Péladan's vision, expressed in often quaint or bombastic terms, is something that can be of any interest in the 21st century. Can it be of any use to neo-symbolist artists?

As both a scholar and an artist, I believe that Péladan was ahead of his time, and that his aesthetic principles with regard to Symbolism in particular, are both timeless and a potential source of inspiration.

Regardless of whether or not we espouse his spiritual and religious perspectives, Péladan's priority was that art should fulfil a social role, and not simply exist as a

---

19 Édouard Schuré, *The Great Initiates: A Sketch of the Secret History of Religions*, trans. by F. Rothwell (London, 1913; originally published 1889), p. 92.

hollow imitation of reality, or as a tool for the self-aggrandisement of the artist. The Symbolist art of which Péladan spoke was an educational tool, which could be used to transmit the history of civilisation and perceptions of the human condition through line and form, and through the use of a symbolic language which brings both artist and viewer into a constant dialogue that continues long after the gallery lights have gone out – and that in itself is the ultimate act of animation, or ensoulment. Whatever the subject matter selected by a given artist, the particularity of Symbolism is that it must have a meaning, and that it is first and foremost, a mode of communication that bypasses linear thought processes. In order to effectively express such meanings and to translate abstract philosophical concepts in visual forms, one truly takes on the role of creator. It is possible that Péladan's ideas can serve as a springboard for inspirations and directions that might take us on some surprising journeys, allowing (Neo)-Symbolist artists, like their predecessors, to explore those difficult, timeless questions about the meaning of life – and indeed of art – in such a way that can help to shine a light (or indeed, cast a shadow) on those perpetual human questions that know no time, nor religion, nor space, but which remain a form of language that transcends both time and place. As such, it may yet prove to be of use to us.

A translation of excerpts from Péladan's "manifesto": *L'Art Idealiste et Mystique (Doctrine de l'Ordre et du Salon Annuel du Rose + Croix)*, 1894:

[17]

EXHORTATION

Artist, you are a priest: Art is the great mystery and, if your effort results in a masterpiece, a ray of divinity will descend as on an altar. Artist, you are a king: Art is the true empire, if your hand draws a perfect line, the cherubim themselves will descend to revel in their reflection. Spiritual design, a line of the soul, form of understanding, you make our dreams flesh. Artist, you are a mage: Art is the great mystery, it only proves our immortality.

[18]

Who still doubts? Giotto touched the stigmata, the Virgin appeared to Fra Angelico, and Rembrandt demonstrated the resurrection of Lazarus. [This is] the absolute rejoinder to pedantic quibbles: we doubt Moses, but here is Michaelangelo; we misunderstand Jesus, but here is Leonardo; we secularize everything, but immutable, sacred Art continues its prayer.

Unspeakable and sublime serenity, ever-shining Holy Grail, ostensorium and relic, unvanquished sacred banner, all-powerful Art, the God Art, I adore you on my knees, you, the final reflection from on High over our putrescence.

....

[19]

All is rotten, all is finished, decadence has cracked and shaken the Western edifice...
You, old Dante, get up from your throne of glory, you Catholic Homer, and join
your anger with Buonarotti's despair.

Yet a glimmer of Holy Light, a pale glow appeared, and grew... And thus on the
gallows of the holy torment, there blossomed a flower.

A miracle! A miracle! A rose emerges and opens as it grows, endeavouring to
grip the divine cross of salvation in its pious leaves: and the cross, consoled, is
resplendent: Jesus has not cursed this world, Jesus receives the adoration of Art.
The Mages, the first ones, came to the divine Master.

[20]

The last Mages are their sons. Pitiful moderns, your course into nothingness is fatal;
fall then, under the weight of your worthlessness: your blasphemies will never erase
the faith of works of art, you sterile ones!

[21]

You may one day close the Church, but [what about] the Museum? If Notre-Dame
is profaned, the Louvre will officiate... Humanity, oh citizens, will always go to
mass, when the priest will be Bach, Beethoven, Palestrina: one cannot make the
sublime organ an atheist! Brothers in all the arts, I am sounding a battle cry: let us
form a holy militia for the salvation of idealism. We are a few against many, but the
angels are ours. We have no leaders, but the old masters, up there in Paradise, guide
us towards Montsalvat... This precious Church, the last august thing in this world,
banished the Rose and believes its perfume to be dangerous. Next to it then, we will
build the Temple of Beauty; we will work to the echoes of prayers, followers, not
rivals, different,

[22]

not divergent, for the artist is a priest, a king, a mage, for art is a mystery, the only
true empire, the great miracle... Jesus has not cursed this world. Jesus receives the
adoration of art. The noble enthusiasm of the artist will survive beyond extinct,
erstwhile piety.

....

[33]

Theory of Beauty

A. I. There is no other reality than God. There is no other Truth than God. There is
no other Beauty than God.

God alone exists, and any word that does not express this is a noise, and every path
that does not seek him leads to nothingness. The only end of mankind is the quest

for God. He must perceive Him, conceive Him, hear Him, or perish in ignominy.

A. II. The three great divine names are: 1. Reality, the substance or the Father; 2. Beauty, life, or the Son, 3. Truth or the unification of Reality and Beauty, which is the Holy Spirit.

These three names govern three ways to the same end,

[34]

three quests for God, three religious modes. [You should] understand "religion" in the sense of [that which] connects the creature to the Creator.

A. III. Science, which seeks God through Reality. Art, which seeks God through Beauty. Theodicy, which seeks God through Thought.

What, then, is Beauty? If not...

A. IV. The quest for God through Life and Form.

But, even as the three divine persons are all present in each other, thus Beauty is specified in three rays, forming the triangle of Idealism.

A. V. The Beauty of the Father is called Intensity. The Beauty of the Son is called Subtlety. The Beauty of the Holy Spirit is called Harmony.

[35]

If one calls something ideal, that is to attribute conceivable intensity, subtlety and harmony to it; and art, considered in its essence, is that which defines it.

A. VI. The esthetic point of a form is the point of apotheosis, which is to say the realisation that it is approaching the perceivable absolute.

A. VII. Manifest intensity is called the sublime. The sublime is achieved by an excess of one of the proportions, and it operates on the aesthete through surprise/wonder: as in the lowering of temples in the Orient and the elevation of arched cathedrals; or Michaelangelo in both his arts.

A. VIII. Manifest Subtlety is called Beautiful; Beauty is achieved by weighting and the equilibrium of the most immediate relationships [of form], such as Raphael's School of Athens.

A. IX. Manifest Harmony is called Perfection,

[36]

and it is achieved through weighting and balancing all relationships, even the most asymptotic, such as in the work of Leonardo da Vinci.

The Rose + Croix class all the categories of understanding as subdivisions of a unique science: theodicy... The reader should never forget, over the cause of these pages, that Art is presented here as a religion or, if you will, as that part of religion that mediates between the physical and the metaphysical.

The Rose + Croix class all the categories of understanding as subdivisions of a unique science: theodicy...

The reader should never forget, over the course of these pages, that Art is presented here as a religion or, if you will, as that part of religion that mediates between the physical and the metaphysical.

That which distinguishes a religion from a philosophy, is the dogmatic absolutism and canonical ritual: it is the subordination of individualism to a collective harmony.

What dogma is applicable to all the design arts? What is the essence of Art? And how could one define Art itself, if not thus:

A. X. Art is the totality of the methods of realising Beauty.

A. XI. Beauty is the essence of all expression through form.

[37]

Techniques are nothing more than the means to an end.

If Beauty is the objective, and art the means, what is the rule? The Ideal.

Open a Littré dictionary at this word: "Ideal; that which reunites all the perfections that the spirit can conceive".

THEREFORE IDEALIST ART IS THAT WHICH REUNITES WITHIN A WORK ALL THE PERFECTIONS THAT THE SPIRIT CAN CONCEIVE ON A GIVEN THEME.

One may already understand that there are themes which are too low to sustain any idea of perfection, and that I have reviled, with absolute logic, from the Salons of the Rose + Croix [...]

[38]

....

Wagner says in one of his theoretical writings:

"Art begins where life ends". Because the same woman, whom lust greets with desire, does not solicit admiration through her reproduced image. This is why, after the first adjective: idealist, I had to add another: mystical.

For "mystical" means that it holds mystery, and a mystic is an initiate.

It is not therefore enough for a work to satisfy the idea, it must also determine an impression of the beyond, it must be a springboard of enthusiasm, a determinant of thought. Generally, Titian is ideal, but never mystical; the opposite appears among the *Trecentisti*, always mystical, rarely ideal.

[39]

A. XII. The Beauty of a work is made from sublimated reality.

A. XIII. The mysticism of a work derives from the depiction of the unreal.

A. XIV. A work that is real in form, and unreal in expression, is perfect: Leonardo. These antique principles, forgotten today, disdained, presided over ancient genius.

Plato alone dared to consider Beauty as a spiritual being that existed independently from our conceptions: and an unjustly forgotten thinker, Maximus Tyrius, showed in the second century (he lived in Rome under Commodus) that the tradition lived on:

"Ineffable beauty – he said – exists in the sky and in the planets. There, it remains unadulterated. But in coming to earth, it is obscured by degrees..."

[40]

He who maintains the essential notion of Beauty in his soul will recognise it when he sees it: like Ulysses recognised the smoke rising from his ancestral home, the aesthete quivers, joyful and moved. A majestic river, a beautiful flower, a fiery horse certainly offer some snippets of Beauty, but they are very crude.

If Beauty descends, to some degree, into matter, where would we see it if not in man, whose soul follows the same principle as Beauty?

...

Beauty is something that is more alive, it does not spend time on games, it brings ecstasy. Our souls exiled on earth, enveloped in thick slime, are condemned to an obscure life, disorderly, full of troubles and bewilderment, they cannot contemplate ineffable Beauty with energy and fulfillment. But our soul leans perpetually towards order and towards beauty. Moral or spiritual order, just like physical, or natural order, constitutes the beauty with which [our souls] are in eternal sympathy. Therefore, here is a philosophy that validates my use of the terms "idealist and mystical":

[41]

A. XV. The ideal, is the pinnacle of a form.

A. XVI. And the mysticism of a form is its nimbus, its countenance of the beyond. The beautiful form in itself, the ideal, is susceptible to two augmentations, as told by Maximus Tyrius in his 25th thesis:

"The beauty of the body cannot be beauty par excellence, it is none other than, in some way, the prelude to a more complete beauty."

In each of the three formulae of Beauty, there three further degrees, just as there are three elements in man.

Intensity, subtlety and harmony give way to three aesthetic results.

The sublime may be physical, like the torso palpated by a blind Michaelangelo; animistic, like Laocoon; spiritual, such as the Genius of eternal rest (Translator's note: this is a reference to the Hellenistic statue known as "Hermaphrodite Mazarin" or "Génie du repos éternel").

[101]

Writing of forms, or, drawing.

After *Genesis*, art began with drawing; the Oelohim appeared projecting their shadow so as to elaborate the human form. Art began with a line, this abstract, and I will immediately reach the greatest secret.

[102]

A. XXIX. The line is the philosophy of art, it must not depend on the artist's temperament; the line is dogmatic: it is the immutable theology of the form.

[... 102]

The line in itself is as abstract as the alphabet, it does not exist in nature; literally it is an ideogram, a hieroglyph which, for human intelligence, translates the sensible world; it is, therefore, in its highest form, the only thing that is independent of technique and where genius can show itself; all the rest belongs to talent.

THE ZEITGEIST CREATING PSYCHOANALYSIS AND DADA

Vanessa Sinclair

Historically, psychoanalysis has been associated with the Surrealists, who openly acknowledged the impact the theories of Sigmund Freud had on their work. The most widely known Surrealist works are often visual representations reflecting the juxtaposition of content present within the dynamic unconscious. What is often under-recognized is that Surrealism grew out of Dada, which developed during the same time period and within the very cultural and intellectual epicenters that birthed the field of psychoanalysis. Dada concepts and methodology fundamentally mirror and make use of unconscious processes and often the more process-oriented techniques later utilized by the Surrealists were adopted from the Dada movement. As a larger constellation of ideas and identity, Dada has not been well understood historically. Scholars and museums tend to deal with its participants as individuals, leaving the broader premise of Dada as a movement alone. Dada tends to be thought of as a precursor to Surrealism – a transitional period – and thusly Dada art is usually shown in conjunction with Surrealist works. However, when the intricacies of Dada are provided with the opportunity to stand on their own, viewing them separately clarifies their formal innovations and thematic concerns.

There has been much debate as to the exact origins of Dada as traditionally the movement has not been given its proper place in art history. In recent years this has finally begun to shift, and Dada is beginning to receive the recognition it deserves. One might even view the difficulty art historians have displayed in defining Dada as highlighting the premise of the movement itself, accentuating its resistance to definition, systematization and categorization, a resistance reflective of the human unconscious and sexuality which subvert normalization and classification. Proponents of new ways of thinking about society and the place and function of art within it, the Dadas utilized new materials and methods including collage, montage, assemblage, ready-mades, automatic writing, the cut-up, performance and chance. They created various manifestos and publications, influenced by the Futurists who were publishing and distributing their own manifestos as early as 1909. Centered in Italy, Futurism promoted provocation in art and performance, often commenting on contemporary Western society, industrialization, technology, youth and violence, while keeping an eye towards the future.

Writing in *Arts* magazine in 1962, Claude Riviere named Francis Picabia as the originator of Dada. Picabia began his movement into modern art with his first abstract painting *Caotchouc* completed in 1909. That same year he married Gabrielle Buffet, an avant-garde musician who remained an intellectual and creative stimulus throughout his career. Riviere posits that it was during a visit to the Jura Mountains with Marcel Duchamp and Guillaume Apollinaire in 1912 that we observe the seeds of what was later to become the Dada movement, as the group began to contemplate a certain "disintegration of the concept of art." Soon after, Picabia visited New York presenting four works for the 1913 Armory show – the first International Exhibition of Modern Art in the United States. Buffet-Picabia writes, "The confrontation of modern European art with the New World and even the presence of Picabia in the United States and later that of Marcel Duchamp, delivered the artists and intellectuals from the obsession of the European academic tradition and made them aware of their personal genius." Influenced by the machine of New York City, Picabia then began to incorporate more industrial elements into his work.

Psychoanalysis began to plant its roots just after the turn of the century. Beginning in 1902, Freud held weekly meetings of the Wednesday Psychological Society at his home office in Vienna with a few colleagues who were interested in the burgeoning field of psychoanalytic theory and practice. Eventually, this group became the Vienna Psychoanalytic Society, the first formal psychoanalytic organization established in 1908. During the period before the First World War, psychoanalysis was rapidly spreading across Europe and North America with societies forming in Berlin and Zürich (1910), New York and Munich (1911), London and Budapest (1913) and the establishment of the International Psychoanalytical Association (IPA) in 1910 with Freud appointing Carl Gustav Jung as the first president.

The relationship between Freud and Jung initially began in 1906 when Jung sent Freud his book *Diagnostic Association Studies* in which he frequently cited Freud's theories. Jung worked with Eugen Bleuler at the Sanatorium Burgholzli in Zürich, which had a reputation for being quite progressive. Jung read *The Interpretation of Dreams* (1900) the same year he arrived at the Burgholzhi and from that point forward attempted to integrate Freud's concepts into his own work, presenting his teachings to Bleuler along the way. Jung praised Freud's work highly, citing *Fragment of an Analysis of a Case of Hysteria* (1905) in his *Psychoanalysis and Association Experiments* (1906) and noting in the foreword of *The Psychology of Dementia Praecox* (1906), "Even a superficial glance will show how much I am indebted to the brilliant discoveries of Freud." Reciprocally, Freud gave his first published comments on Jung in a lecture in 1906, commenting on the association experiments and his theory of complexes.

Soon after, members of the Zürich Burgholzli began to regularly visit the Wednesday Psychological Society in Vienna resulting in a fruitful exchange of ideas. It is said when Freud and Jung first met in person they "talked uninterruptedly for thirteen hours." These two men engaged in a passionate and productive collaboration, continuing their correspondence for over seven years, writing each other every few days with only occasional gaps due to illness or holiday. In 1909, the pair traveled to America with Sandor Ferenczi to speak at Clark University, this event marking Freud's first and only venture to the New World. Eventually, their impassioned relationship ended with Jung resigning from his position as the president of the IPA in 1914. Yet even following his split with Jung, Freud continued to recognize the important contribution his colleagues in Zürich made to the field of psychoanalysis as Zürich was the first place outside of Vienna where Freud's theories really began to take hold.

Freud and Jung's relationship was ending just as World War I was beginning. Many fled their homelands in search of safety, Switzerland providing a neutral center sharing borders with the Central Powers of Germany and Austria-Hungary and the Entente Powers of France and Italy. Surrounded by violence and bloodshed, the Swiss found themselves in a tense albeit unique position. Hans Richter claims the true beginning of the Dada movement was here in Zürich. While the seeds of Dada had been planted in the years before the war, shaped by the Futurists as well as independent artists, writers and musicians, the opening of the Cabaret Voltaire in February of 1916 was monumental in bringing these artists and intellectuals together, pushing them towards the creation of a more coherent, integrated movement.

Soon after the outbreak of the war, German author and poet Hugo Ball came to Zürich with his mistress Emmy Hennings. Ball, himself a writer, philosopher, performer and producer, first established the Cabaret Voltaire as a literary cabaret where he accompanied Hennings on the piano whilst she performed songs and poetry readings. The charisma of the pair began to attract other artists and performers, and they were soon joined by Tristan Tzara and Marcel Janco from Romania, Hans Arp from France and Richard Huelsenbeck from Germany. The addition of Tzara with his revolutionary spirit, poems and manifestos sparked an element of mischievous, youthful upheaval and produced rambunctious happenings. With the publication of the first issue of *Dada Magazine: Miscelliny of Art and Literature* on July 1, 1917, Tzara exclaimed, "The Dada Movement is Launched!"

Both the Dada and psychoanalytic movements were inescapably influenced by the atrocities of WWI. In *En Avant Dada: An History of Dadaism* (1920), Huelsenbeck writes, "Politicians are the same everywhere, flatheaded and vile." The group agreed the reasons for the war were materialistic and contrived. Sickened by the state of affairs, this brutality of war was described as the "moral enemy of every intellectual impulse." For many, the war produced a collapse of confidence in the rhetoric and principles of the culture of logic and rationality that had prevailed across Europe up to this point. The birth of mechanized warfare with its massive death tolls, coupled with the totalitarian politics of the time, produced a sense of the fragility of civilization. In his essay *Thoughts for the Times on War and Death*, written approximately six months after the start of the war, Freud described the disorientation of modern man so divided from his nature, expressing disillusionment with the civilized world – in particular the state – and acknowledging the altered attitude towards death that this and every war forces upon its people. "The individual who is not himself a combatant – and so is a cog in the gigantic machine of war – feels bewildered in his orientation, and inhibited in his powers and activities."

Dada was born in this crisis of disillusionment, its collaborators' wartime experiences greatly influencing their collective body of work. The First World War shifted the terms of battle as it was the first war of the industrialized age. With vast numbers of technological innovations, it was the first global war of its kind and bore moral and intellectual crises. As the experience of the horrendously shattered bodies of veterans returning home from war became more and more commonplace, it was reflected in the art of the time. The Dadas often depicted the casualties of war, including wounded soldiers and amputees with prosthetic limbs, eventually even positing the conception of a race of half-mechanical men. The war left soldiers with psychological wounds as well, which in turn also became a motif of certain Dada works. For the first time, the military began to recognize psychological trauma as valid, almost on par with physical injury. A large number of those discharged from the service were diagnosed with war neurosis or "shell shock." Grafton Elliot Smith, one of the first to describe its pathology and symptomatology, cautioned that for those suffering reason was not lost but was rather "functioning with painful efficiency." Many physicians fled to psychoanalysis in an attempt to understand shell shock and the effects of such trauma on the mind.

Dada questioned society's accepted values and consensus worldview, challenging while embracing new ways of thinking, utilizing new materials and methods. Dada quickly shattered certain conceptions about the nature of art including the appropriate method and mode of creating, viewing and experiencing artwork, valuing cacophony, dreams and the violation of syntax as techniques for freeing the unconscious from the domination of reason and tradition. The Dadas felt that up to this point art had served civilization; their anti-art would challenge it. This radical rethinking of the creation of art is one of its fundamental achievements. Dada has not been readily understood as a movement in the traditional sense – a small alliance of artists working and showing together committed to a common aesthetic, credo and style – the individual participants of the Dada movement varied widely in their concepts and techniques. In contrast to Surrealism, which remained centralized in terms of leadership and geography, the Dada movement was notably diffuse with several active city centers creating a network of itinerant, politically displaced artists of diverse nationalities. Previously there had been no artistic movement so self-conscientiously international. Part of Dada's radical achievement lay in its ability to create a global network of artists and intellectuals, especially during such a tumultuous time in world history. In fact, this is an under-recognized and invaluable accomplishment of both the Dada and psychoanalytic movements of the time, and since has only been even closely matched by the Fluxus and mail art movements of the 1960s.

The Dadas made use of new media that allowed for contact between persons across long distances: letters, postcards, journals and magazines not only provided important means of sharing ideas and images but were also incorporated into new forms of artwork. Connections between artists and writers in different cities across the globe traced the movement of ideas that transformed art and intellectual thought as it had been known. The aims of Dada were often supranational; emerging amid the racially tinged nationalistic discourse of WWI, a central tenant of Dada was anti-nationalism. Fashioning itself as a network with centers in Zürich, Berlin, Hannover, Cologne, New York and Paris, Dada formed a web of connections between its various contributors serving as a conduit for creative thought. Even though Europe and North America contained the city centers, Dada promoted a global identity and was as far-reaching as Japan. In her essay *Arthur Cravan and American Dada* (1938), Buffet-Picabia states the atmosphere was heavily charged as a result of the unusual gathering together of individuals of all nationalities each with unique talents to offer, "It was an exceptionally favorable climate for the development of a certain revolutionary spirit in art and literature, which became crystallized under the name *Dada*."

The period of the First World War with its inherent fragmentation, destruction and reconstruction of both the physical world and of the psyche is reflected in the Dada methodology of the cut-up. While there are various ways in which to apply the concept of the cut-up, Tzara introduces one process in his manifesto *To Make a Dadaist Poem* (1920), instructing us to:

Take a newspaper.
Take some scissors.
Choose from this paper an article the length you want to make your poem.
Cut out the article.
Next carefully cut out each of the words that make up this article and put them all in a bag.
Shake gently.
Next take out each cutting one after the other.
Copy conscientiously in the order in which they left the bag.
The poem will resemble you,
And there you are – an infinitely original author of charming sensibility, even though unappreciated by the vulgar hand.

The Dadas also championed other methods that exemplify the workings of the dynamic unconscious including automatic writing, which was later incorporated into the Surrealist literary movement. Similar to the process of free association, automatic writing allows the creator a glimpse into his/her own unconscious processes attempting to bypass interference due to censorship and inhibition as much as possible, mirroring unconscious processes and illustrating Freud's notion that there is nothing left to chance. Everything, even if seemingly unrelated, is intricately intertwined, interconnected and overdetermined. In the unconscious, central concepts are concentrated into nodes with multiple pathways leading towards each of these kernels. No matter at what point one begins, certain themes and patterns will inevitably arise. French psychoanalyst Jacques Lacan later describes the unconscious as structured like language, an infinite web of signifiers, the sliding of metonymy an endless knot.

In 1918, German painter Christian Schad began experimenting with a form of automated collage, laying collected scraps such as torn tickets, receipts and rags on light sensitive paper to create abstract photograms. These images made without cameras came to symbolize the creation of the new from the damaged or discarded. Objects were laid out at random thereby allowing for the unconscious to work with as little censorship and interference from the conscious mind as possible. Tzara later carried a group of these tiny photographic compositions to Paris where Man Ray began to experiment with the technique in 1921, naming them *Rayograms.*

The trend of utilizing ordinary objects, presenting them as art and viewing them in a new way was originally brought to the fore by Duchamp in 1913, when he fashioned the *Bicycle Wheel* – a bicycle wheel mounted by its fork on a painted wooden stool. This sculpture is considered to be the first ready-made and the first kinetic sculpture. *Ready-made* was the term Duchamp used to describe his collection of ordinary, manufactured objects not commonly associated with art. Although many have not considered the ready-mades to have as serious a tone as other Dada works, which comment on and criticize the violence of WWI, Buffet-Picabia notes the mischievous nature and social commentary present in these works. This was most pointedly illustrated when Duchamp sent a urinal signed with the pseudonym "R. Mutt" to the first annual Exhibition of Independent Painters in New York in 1917, a group that he helped to found based on the premise of artistic integrity for each individual, a platform for artists to be able to showcase their work without judgment or jury. Of course this piece was ultimately rejected by the board of his own group, thereby proving his point.

Equally provocative, psychoanalysis has been called "the knowledge that disturbed the peace of the world." Freud's revolutionary conceptualization of the unconscious revealed that man is not master of his own mind. Within the unconscious, contradicting and oftentimes opposing ideas coexist. And while the Surrealists tend to illustrate this juxtaposition of content in their dream-like works, the Dadas allowed for the unconscious to permeate their process of creating, utilizing methods such as automatic writing and the cut-up, embracing chance and encouraging the expression of contrasting positions. Once delineated in this way, the parallels between psychoanalysis and Dada become clear, and although the impact these two fields had on one another's formation was not explicitly recognized at the time, perhaps this is yet another example of the dynamism of the unconscious, its pervasive nature and wondrous synchronicity.

References

—~— Ades, D. (2006). *The Dada Reader: A Critical Anthology*. The University of Chicago Press: Chicago.

—~— Chessa, L. (2012). *Luigi Russolo, Futurist: Noise, Visual Arts, and the Occult.* University of California Press: Berkley.

—~— Dickerman, L. (2005). *DADA*. National Gallery of Art: Washington.

—~— Freud, S. (1905). *Three essays on the theory of sexuality*. *SE* 7:123-246.

_______ (1912). *The dynamics of transference*. *SE* 12:97-108.

_______ (1915). *The unconscious*. *SE* 14:159-215.

_______ (1915). *Thoughts for the times on war and death*. *SE* 14:273-300.

—~— Kostelanetz, R. (2001). *A Dictionary of the Avant-Gardes*. 2nd ed. New York: Routledge.

—~— Loewenberg, P. & Thompson, N. (2011). *100 Years of the IPA: The Centenary History of the International Psychoanalytical Association, 1910-2010, Evolution and Change*. Karnac: London.

—~— McGuire, W. (1974). *The Freud/Jung Letters: The Correspondence between Sigmund Freud and C.G. Jung.* Abridged ed. Princeton: Princeton University Press.

—~— Motherwell, R. (1951). *The Dada Painters and Poets: An Anthology*. 2nd ed. Cambridge: The Belknap Press of Harvard University Press.

—~— Richter, H. (1964). *Dada: Art and Anti-Art*. New York: Thames & Hudson.

—~— Souto, A. (2013). *Do Me Dada Style*. *Abraxas* No. 3. Fulgur Esoterica: London

Tu Marcellus Eris (Following the Blind Man)

Kendell Geers

In the spring of 1912, Marcel Duchamp left Paris for Munich on a three month sojourn that would ultimately change the course of twentieth century art. He left Paris as the painter of "Nude Descending the Staircase" and returned with the concept of the Readymade as well as the foundations of his magnum opus "The Bride Stripped Bare By Her Bachelors, Even." A century later conspiracy theories and speculation abound as historians, artists and academics compete for the most compelling theory to explain the shift. Little is known about the details of his stay except that Duchamp made it very clear that he visited the Alte Pinakothek almost daily. Concerning these visits to the museum, he commented decades later on his interest in the work of Lucas Cranach, saying that "Nature and the materiality of his nudes have inspired me for the *colour* of the flesh" (my emphasis). On two separate occasions following his Munich trip he used Cranach's "Adam and Eve" as a readymade composition, once for Picabia's "Relache" in 1924 and again in a 1968 series of line etchings. This painting could not however have been the reason for Duchamp's daily museum visit since it is actually in an entirely different museum in another German city, namely Leipzig.

Whilst in Munich Duchamp created two key paintings, "The Bride" and "The Passage from Virgin to Bride." It has been pointed out that the latter broke with illusory traditions of the time, for the title of the work was written directly onto the front of the canvas, drawing attention to the materials, *colour* and surface of the painting itself. The text does demand some attention for more than a moment however, because the words THE PASSAGE are capitalised ("LE PASSAGE de la vierge a la mariée") suggesting that the painting might embody or represent some kind of RITE OF PASSAGE.

A century later, in 2012, I was visiting Munich for my upcoming retrospective and decided to walk through the Alte Pinakothek, forgetting everything I had ever read or been taught about the mother of all tricksters in the twentieth century Avant Garde, and trying to imagine myself looking through his eyes afresh. What could he have been looking at, or looking for, in a daily meditation?

One painting in particular did catch my eye on account of the fact that it too bore its title inscribed directly upon the front of the canvas, Albrecht Dürer's "Self-Portrait at Twenty-Eight Years Old Wearing a Coat with Fur Collar" from 1500. To the right of the artist's penetrating gaze, he inscribed the canvas with the text "Albertus Durerus Noricus ipsum me propriis sic effingebam coloribus aetatis anno XXVIII", which translates as "Albert Dürer of Nuremberg, I so depicted myself with colours, at the age of 28".

Tu Marcellus Eris

Staring at this 500 year old self portrait, something seemed extremely familiar in an uncanny sort of way, reminding me of Duchamp. Perhaps it was simply the seed sown by artist Rudolf Herz, who suggested that Duchamp might have been inspired by Dürer's deadpan stare when he asked future Nazi photographer Heinrich Hoffmann to photograph him for Apollinaire's book "Les Peintres Cubistes". Thinking as an artist myself however, I was certain that such a gaze alone would surely not be the reason for daily visits over a three month period!

Staring eye to eye, from one artist to another, across five centuries of self-portraits, it suddenly struck me where I had seen this image before. Man Ray's iconic 1921 portrait of Marcel Duchamp as Rrose Sélavy features a coat with a fur collar, almost exactly the same as Dürer's. Moreover the feminine hands (actually those of Picabia's lover Germaine Everling) seem to be drawing attention to the fur collar in a manner not unlike Dürer's own hand gesture. In addition to the iconic Rrose Sélavy portrait, I recalled at least two portraits of Duchamp wearing a similar fur coat, as well as an atypical 1950's version of Rrose Sélavy in a blonde wig with curls strikingly similar to Dürer's locks.

The title of the Dürer self-portrait makes specific reference to the importance of "colour" and Duchamp did mention precisely that in relation to his interest in the work of Lucas Cranach. Was Duchamp sending us towards Cranach that we might be blind to his real source of inspiration, Albrecht Dürer? We do know after all, that he was a consummate liar telling the world that he had given up making art in order to play chess when he was in fact working very hard on "Étant Donnés" all along.

The significance of the fur coat eludes me, but it must have been so important for Dürer that it is mentioned the title of the painting, important enough at least that Duchamp thought it worth visually quoting. I wondered if the age 28 might not also be significant? A quick biographical check left me a little disappointed in my treasure hunt for clues because he was 25 in 1912 as he made his daily pilgrimage to visit Dürer. On the other hand, I realised that he would be 28 years old a mere three years later, the very same year that he "officially" dates as the beginning of "The Bride Stripped Bare by Her Bachelors, Even." The choice of dating the "Large Glass" (as it became known) in 1915 is not at all random because he had already made a sketch called "First Study For Large Glass" which historically would locate the birth of the work in 1912 and not 1915 so the choice of dating is precise and very specific. Moreover both "The Bride" and "The Passage from Virgin to Bride" could be considered part of the "Large Glass" for they both already contained the complete image of enigmatic bride. The choice to date the "Large Glass" to 1915, in the artist's 28th year must surely be in reference to Dürer. I wondered if I might not be going too far beyond the safety of art history's text books, but then again I consoled myself with the knowledge that Duchamp had made a religion out of chance and that he might be more than a little amused by the journey my eyes were taking me upon.

Searching for an "official" link between the two artists I remembered the *de rigeur* comparison of "Étant Donnés" with Dürer's "Perspective Machine" from 1525, in which a seated man (the artist) directs his eye from the pointed top of an obelisk through a grid window in contemplation of a prostate naked woman with open legs. Of course it does not take a massive leap into the imagination to realise that what Dürer was looking at was the very same image that has been immortalised in "Étant Donnés" (as well as "L'Origin du Monde").

All of a sudden, my photographic memory yelled out to me, EUREKA, for the image of the artist with his eye, close to the (phallic) pointed obelisk, gazing through the window was none other than Duchamp's own eye in another work "To Be Looked at (from the Other Side of the Glass) with One Eye, Close to, for Almost an Hour." How could I have missed that before?

I looked again at the image of Dürer's perspective machine, at the image of the fully clothed artist seated to the right, with a his grid on the table in front of him, staring at a naked woman on the other side of the table and once again my photographic memory yelled out in protest for it reminded me of yet another portrait image of Duchamp, of him playing chess with Eve Babitz at his 1968 Pasadena retrospective. Duchamp was quoting himself quoting Dürer over and over again.

Marcel Duchamp's "Large Glass" has been referred to as a machine and Dürer's perspective machine seems to have had an influence in more ways than one through numerous works of art across six centuries. We do know that Duchamp was interested in the fourth dimension and that he had shifted the perspective of the 1914 painting "Network of Stoppages" in order to construct the bachelor machine for the "Large Glass," so I wondered if perspective might not be the key. In 1506, a few years after his Alte Pinokathek self-portrait, Dürer wrote a letter to Pirckheimer in which he said "I shall have finished here in ten days; after that I should like to ride to Bologna to learn the secrets of the art of perspective, which a man is willing to teach me." Since the very first time my art history professors had mentioned this, I marvelled at how a man capable of painting the 1500 self-portrait might want to learn "the art of perspective"? In 1506 Dürer was already a very accomplished, respected, talented and versatile artist, who surely did not need to learn how to make lines disappear upon a horizon! Unless "perspective" may refer to something else entirely?

The person that Dürer went to learn this "art of perspective" from was none other than Luca Pacioli, who had also mentored Leonardo da Vinci in the same. I was intrigued by the possible link to da Vinci, for I had only just discovered by absolute coincidence that, if you include the base plate, the dimensions of Duchamp's "Fresh Widow" (1920) are exactly the same as the "Mona Lisa." Besides, Dürer's "Self-Portrait at Twenty-Eight Years Old Wearing a Coat with Fur Collar" did seem to bear an uncanny resemblance to da Vinci's "Salvator Mundi" and the hand on the fur coat is practically the same as Cecilia Gallerani's hand on the ermine's fur in Leonardo's "Lady with an Ermine" (1489-90).

Sitting in a Munich Beerhall, I scanned through my art school memories, thinking about the endless flashes of art history slides putting me onto a hangover sleep as they panned across the centuries of old master paintings. Well on my way into another Bavarian hangover through the bottom of yet another jug of beer I looked at my printout of "The Passage from Virgin to Bride" concentrating on the (inverse) "L" form on the lower right and it began to look more and more like an arm lifting out from the darkness. On the left, the "tube" or "pipe" started to look more and more like a staff. The central round crescent shape that would later become the "head" of the bride, started to look more and more like a halo to me. The composition and features were all screaming out like a red flag in a bullfight and set off a chain reaction that has led me all the way through into writing these words, more than a year later.

The composition and symbolism that I suddenly saw is none other than Leonardo's "Virgin on the Rocks" (London National Gallery Version 1495-1508 / Louvre Version 1483-1486). I lost no time in making a quick Photoshop filter to posterise the Duchamp painting and overlay it upon the two Leonardo da Vinci paintings to discover that it's a dead ringer. The virgin's halo lines up, as does the little Saint John's staff, as well the angel's arm on the right. Looking at the overlay, there can be no doubt that "The Passage from Virgin to Bride" is quoting "The Virgin on the Rocks," right down to the title.

If Marcel Duchamp was quoting Leonardo, through the perspective prism of Dürer, what could the rite of PASSAGE have been? What could the significance of "The Virgin on the Rocks" have been for the 25 year old artist? As I have since marvelled as to why art historians had never "seen" this link before, so too had I been marvelling for many years at yet another art historical omission involving the very same da Vinci paintings, another art historical key that can only be SEEN and not read. I wonder if this is why Duchamp called his 1917 magazine "The Blind Man" for art history is very selective in editing out what is seen in favour of what is read, almost as if we should not trust our own eyes. But then again I am an artist, so fear not the gaze of another artist, so press on.

Holidays are not my favourite pastime, but admit they are the necessary glue that holds together couples and families, so concede to the annual ritual of worshipping the Sun. But still I tend to get very restless, so I sought out other ways of entertaining my mind on the crowded beaches, eventually falling into the "Da Vinci Code" conspiracy theories. I was drawn to their quasi art-historical aspect for it encouraged me to consider that art might be able to function in ways other than investment.

Ironically the da Vinci code conspiracy centres in truth upon a single painting by another artist entirely, Poussin's "Et in Arcadia Ego." Treasure hunters and conspiracy theorists alike have spent decades trying to line up the rocks, following the lines, fingers, shadows and features, overlaying them upon the landscape around Rennes le Chateau in search of the missing Templar and/or Cathar Treasures. The attempts at decoding the painting are as amusing as they are entertaining, but very few people seem to have taken the time to actually look at the painting itself. The so called "code" is not at all that complex and in fact screams out in frustrated rage.

On the left are two figures, one of whom is kneeling and pointing to the rock whilst the other rests upon his staff, both of which are literally the visual amalgamation of the Saint John figures in the two versions of da Vinci's "Virgin on the Rocks." In the London version, the second of the two, Saint John wears a white cloth and holds a staff in his hand, exactly as the rear figure in the Poussin painting, but his pose is that of the figure kneeing in front of him. This is the exact same staff that initially caught my eye in Duchamp's "Passage from Virgin to Bride".

The man with the red robe, leaning on a stone to the right in the Poussin painting, together with the "angel" in front of him, are the amalgamation of the angel in the two da Vinci paintings. The red robe and pointing index finger of the da Vinci painting cannot be missed and is very clearly the historical source for Poussin's man in the red robe resting on the rock. The blue and yellowish robe of da Vinci's Louvre painting have similarly been translated by Poussin into the blue and yellow dress of the "angel" in the foreground with her hand resting on the man's back. Curiously and not without coincidence I believe, the only known certified portrait of Leonardo da Vinci is that painted by Raphael for his "School of Athens," in which Leonardo has been cast in the central role of Plato, wearing a red robe over one shoulder, with index finger pointing up whilst Aristotle, besides him, wears a blue robe with hand outstretched in exactly the same two hand gestures as the London version of "Virgin on the Rocks" and Poussin's "Et in Arcadia Ego"

My mind was reeling and the Bavarian Beers seemed to flow like an eternal fountain of youthful fantasy, but I could not leave Munich before shedding some kind of light on what the nature of Duchamp's rite of PASSAGE might have been. Could I link Duchamp with da Vinci via Poussin in any other way than with my eyes?

I thought about the awful 1968 series of etchings that Duchamp made towards the end of his life. "Selected Details after Ingres II", featuring a line drawn image copied after Ingres' "Oedipus and the Sphinx". Lo and behold, the man leaning on his staff with one foot upon a rock, wearing a red robe over his shoulder and pointing index finger has returned once again. Duchamp is quoting Ingres, who is quoting Poussin quoting da Vinci, who studied perspective from the same person as Dürer. At this point I begin to rule out coincidence, for Ingres painted "Oedipus and the Sphinx" at the Villa Medici, the very same Prix de Rome academy that had been created for Poussin before death intervened. Moreover he painted it in 1808 in his 28th year.

As if I might need yet another quotation, Duchamp's best friend, Francis Picabia, also cited Ingres' "Oedipus and the Sphinx" in a 1922 canvas called "La Feuille de Vigne" (Fig Leaf), yet another man with raised foot on a (now round) stone with the title (as well as "Dessin Français") once again written directly on the front of the painting. In the avalanche of coincidences that just kept on coming, I remembered that "La Feuille de Vigne" was painted over an earlier painting called "Hot Eyes" recalling both Duchamp and Picabia's 1919 play on words L.H.O.O.Q. which transliterates as "Elle a chaud au cul" meaning "She is HOT in the arse." Duchamp's own 1950 "Female Fig Leaf" was cast off the genitals of "Étant Donnés" and so the never-ending line seems to spiral and twist and turn, back and forth.

It might be worth mentioning that Ingres made a second painting of "Oedipus and the Sphinx" in 1864, Poussin painted two versions of his "Et in Arcadia

Ego," one in 1627 and the other more infamous version in 1637/1638, Leonardo made two versions of "The Virgin on the Rocks" and of course Duchamp made two versions of his own magnum opus, being "The Bride Stripped Bare by Her Bachelors, Even" (1915-23) and "Étant Donnés (Given: 1 The Waterfall, 2. The Illuminating Gas, " (1946-1966))

The second of Duchamp's etchings quoting Ingres was "Selected Details after Ingres I," in which another man, this time with his arm upright, refers to Ingres' 1814 painting "Tu Marcellus Eris," being the moment in the "Aeneid" when Octavia feints as Virgil relates the story of Marcellus' death. As the words "Et in Arcadia Ego" have multiple translations and meanings depending on the reader and interpreter, so too the exact translation of "Tu Marcellus Eris" is contested. The translation that makes the most sense in the context of this story might be that a new or resurrected Marcellus will be born, that from death shall grow another life. It certainly follows in the same spirit, the translation of "Et in Arcadia Ego" as being "Even in paradise you shall find me (death)".

Mircea Eliade suggested that around the world rites of passage are built upon the notion of the symbolic death and rebirth of the initiate. It was not long after his return from Munich that Marcel Duchamp declared that painting was dead and eventually in 1918 made his final painting called "T'um" and once again baffled viewers with its enigmatic title. In the light of the last series of etchings quoting Ingres, surely "T'um" must be referring to "Tu Marcellus Eris" for out of the death of Marcellus, the death of classical painting, a new Marcel was born, the Marcel Duchamp of the "Large Glass"? Once again "T'um" fits the da Vinci, Dürer, Poussin, Ingres cycles of iconography and symbolic perspective, for it features yet another hand with pointing index finger, pointing towards as an endless series of overlaid *colours*.

It will never be clear exactly what the rite of passage was that Marcel Duchamp underwent in Munich in 1912, but it certainly seemed to have involved a cycle of references through the chains of art history, from one generation of artists through another, all the way back to Leonardo da Vinci and possibly Lucas Cranach. The fur coat, the age of 28, symbolic perspective, and of course *colours* all seem to be part of the rite. One might guess, as too many have, that the "initiation" might have been alchemical, or even imagine the workings of secret societies, but that would all be imaginative interpretation. The only things that we can know for certain are those that the eyes can see, for good paintings do not change their colours nor their forms. We know as fact that "The Bride Stripped Bare by Her Bachelors, Even" was conceived in Munich in 1912 but dated from the artist's 28 year, that Marcel Duchamp created two very important canvasses in Munich that same year, both of which contained the visual, symbolic and iconographic structure that would eventually transform into the large glass. Upon his return to Paris, Duchamp presented "The Bride," perhaps the most significant of all his efforts in Munich, to his best friend Francis Picabia and the rest of this story remains to be continued.

New Delhi, 31 January 2014

FALLEN WORLD, WITHOUT SHADOWS

The Luciferian Element in German Expressionist Cinema

Stephen Sennitt

I: LUCIFER

Baleful, penetrating eyes stare out from a begrimed landscape obscured by clouds of furnace smoke: The fallen angel has become a demonic slave of the machine age.

This stark, prophetic image is the product of symbolist painter Franz von Stuck in his work of 1890, 'Lucifer'[1], which was seen by contemporary critics as 'the personification of the rapid and threatening progress of industrialisation'.[2] Stuck's Lucifer is a modern *Doppelganger*, the devil in the mirror of societal progress. The shadow's terrible gaze holds the viewer's attention, reflecting subconscious fears and anxieties on to the screen of the mind where they cannot be ignored. Lucifer preaches the modern age ideal, self-knowledge – but at what cost?

Twentieth Century artistic movements can be seen as a reflection and critique of the 'consumer age'. Gadgets and machines of all kinds were appropriated by artists, sculptors and writers and used to create works of art. This fact, and the states of consciousness such appropriations afforded, is one of the key defining concepts of Modernism. This love/hate affair of the artist and his or her sense of place in a rapidly changing world is the major dialectic of Modernist philosophy, irrespective of the conflicting ideologies of specific groups. Behind it all is a sort of 'Devil's Bargain', where the path to progress and self knowledge is also strewn with psychic, subconscious debris upon which one can stumble, and sometimes fall. Perhaps it seems particularly appropriate that among early twentieth century Modernist groups there should be such conflicting responses to the burgeoning 'consumer age'. Futurism, for example, stridently embraces the more extreme manifestations of industry as a system of aesthetics, whereas Dada rejects all the age's manifestations, cultural or mechanistic, with equal scorn. I say 'particularly appropriate' because conflict and revolution were the vital characteristics of the culture of the epoch, a kinetic dance of creation and destruction, exhilaration and terror. In all of this, at the vanguard, was the concept of the 'new Man' (meaning in our updated, non-sexist language, 'new Humankind') an expressionist term which more than in any other Modernist movement signalled a reaction to the 'new Age' in terms of the

---

1 See Mendgen, Eva, *von Stuck*, Köln, 1995.
2 Mendgen, page 20.

inner-self, or the soul.[3] It is this concept in particular, especially in its rejection of rational, 'objective' constructs of the world, which relates expressionism, a new conceptualisation, to the archaic and the romantic/gothic strand of thought which expounded a philosophy of supernaturalism and magic. In expressionism we can see the dark face of von Stuck's 'Lucifer' as progress-turned-inward; a distorted, subjective reflection which portrays a rapidly changing world in terms of fear and doubt, but also as a kind of demonic elation.

2: STORM AND STRESS

Cinematic Modernism began in post World War One Germany as an extension of earlier literary and theatrical experimentation[4], the latter in particular expounding a deliberately confrontational relationship with its audience. Among many expressionist theatrical/art groups were ones described by the phrase *Sturm und Drang*, 'Storm and Stress', which Lotte Eisner[5] describes as being 'pledged to ecstasy and vision... in their short, chopped phrases, exclamations, associations of ideas, and violent imagery'.[6] These stylised occult expressions were transplanted to the screen with astonishing effectiveness in *Das Cabinet Des Dr. Caligari* (1919); perhaps not surprisingly in consideration of the creative team behind this landmark film, which comprised of scenariasts Carl Mayer and Hans Janowitz (Austrian and Czech poets, respectively); Hermann Warm, set designer from the avant garde group *Der Sturm* – who based his *Caligari* designs on drawings by symbolist/expressionist graphic artist Alfred Kubin,[7] author of the strange, mystical novel, *Die Andere Seite* ('The Other Side', 1909); and initially Fritz Lang, who was slated to direct but was later to be replaced by Robert Weine. Importantly, as noted, *Caligari* included contributions from many of the leading exponents of expressionism and the burgeoning German 'art film industry' (a tricky concept we will look at again), making it primarily a self consciously 'artistic' production as opposed to a film made purely to entertain – and it also included the entire *oeuvre* of devices and tropes later popularly associated with expressionism, and with expressionist cinema in particular. These stylistic qualities can be outlined as follows:

An 'exaggerated' acting style, based on gesture and mime; exaggerated facial expressions, enhanced by stark make up and lighting effects; adoption of frequently distorted or exaggerated postures, especially in the case of monstrous or villainous characters; stylised movement of the body – all these things based on the expressionist idea of an interaction between the occult, Luciferian 'inner self' and the world of the story as a sort of seamless whole.

Stylised costume, obviously in the creation of macabre characters, but also in

3 See Richard, Lionel, 'The Expressionist Movement' in *Concise Encyclopedia of Expressionism*, Hertfordshire, 1986, p.7 – 22.
4 See Steffens, Wilhelm, in Richard, p. 156 – 186. For an overview of expressionist stories of the 'phantastic', see Green, Malcolm, *The Golden Bomb*, Edinburgh, 1993.
5 Eisner, Lotte H., *The Haunted Screen*, Berkeley 1973.
6 Eisner, p.15.
7 Ibid. p.18.

the frequent use of caricatures, with eccentric hats and cloaks, pebbled eye glasses; archaic or anachronistic appearances, peculiar props; all of which creates an intentionally false, 'theatrical' effect.

Stylised lighting effects, making full use of side lighting, back lighting and both under-, and over-, lighting to achieve distorted or macabre effects; the play of light and shadow and the aesthetic properties of *chiascurio* are explored to their limits in German expressionist cinema to the extent that they could be seen as its most instantly recognisable, 'trademark' style.

Stylisation of sets and design in general, creating a holistic aesthetic experience, with angular exteriors and compressed interiors; stylised representations of natural objects, such as trees depicted as scratchy, two dimensional silhouettes, so that the expressionist 'idea' of a tree becomes its most important factor; houses and dwellings 'reduced' to a conglomeration of tottering angles, or alternatively enlarged to imposing, seemingly cyclopean, masonry (here, I am thinking, respectively, of the little houses piled on top of one another in the depiction of medieval Prague in Wegener's *Der Golem* [1920] and Death's massive wall in Lang's *Der müde Tod* [1921].) The Fallen Lucifer's world, re-inverted into the everyday imaginings of alienated madmen.

An often purposeful creation of artifice as an overall effect of the *mise-en-scène*; a 'theatrical' feel, for example in *Caligari's* use of patently stage-like sets with even shadows painted in to enhance the sense of unreality. This in opposition to most other films (either 'avant-garde' or mainstream) which strive for as 'realistic' a presentation of their material as possible. Here we can compare the fantastic elements in Bunuel and Dali's surrealist film *Un Chien Andalou* (1928) – such as the ants crawling from a hole in the male actor's hand – with expressionist presentations of fantastic material. While the former is made to look as real as possible to achieve its surrealistic effect, in a sense to make its 'revolutionary' point in questioning the accepted hierarchies of thought and consciousness, expressionist cinema seems more concerned to create an overall aesthetic effect, conjuring an atmosphere of otherworldliness that does not so radically intermix notions of 'reality' and 'dream' in similar overtly propagandist terms. In fact, unless we are to read into expressionist cinema ideas popularised by such writers as Kracauer and Eisner[8], with their philosophical notions of a body of film constituting an expression of 'typically German excess of soul'[9], then what we are looking at are only aesthetic 'surfaces' and highly stylised effects, essentially without Modernist revolutionary concerns. Of course, this does nothing to reduce the impact of, say, Murnau's *Faust* (1926), as an effective and fascinating evocation of legendry diabolism, but we cannot discern anything 'Modernist' about this film other than its style. It is this aspect of cinematic expressionism which Kristin Thompson[10] emphasises in defining expressionist *mise-en-scène:*

---

8 These influential writers have been recently criticised in Elsaesser, Thomas, *Weimar Cinema and After*, London, 2000.

9 A phrase I have borrowed from Elsaesser.

10 Thompson, Kristin, 'Expressionist Mise-en-Scène' in *Eisenstein's Ivan the Terrible*, Princeton, 1981.

Fallen Worlds, Without Shadows

Expressionism will here serve as a stylistic system term minimiz[ing] the differences among the four aspects of mise-en-scène: lighting, costume, figure disposition, and setting. The expressionist film makes, as much as possible, a single visual material of these aspects; the result is an emphasis on overall composition. Expressionism... makes[s] the body purely a compositional element.

In this there are aspects influenced by the 'pure cinema' of abstract film makers, such as Hans Richter, Oskar Fischinger, Viking Eggeling and others, whose concerns were wholly compositional, utilising geometrical shapes, animated silhouettes, etc, to create a Modernist cinema of structural continuity. Some of these aims seem to be echoed in expressionist concerns to create thematic fluidity, giving 'life' to the inanimate, or conversely, making living things (such as the crowds lining the bridge in the Italian segment of Lang's *Der müde Tod*) into a part of the frame's overall compositional pattern. We can also see the influence of constructivist ideas in the deliberate use of 'artifice', though, of course, this is directed to different ends than the more technical aims of the Russian school of constructivism. German expressionist cinema does not on the whole have the same ingredients as much other Modernist cinema, in that there is no rejection of a straight forward narrative. From *Caligari* forward, there is a strong emphasis on traditional narrative structure. Though the effect of a specific film can be 'poetic', there seems to be no attempt at a Modernist conception of 'pure poetry' which we discern in the films of Man Ray or René Clair. In fact, unlike the impecunious non-commercial cinema of the impressionists, the dadaists, the surrealists, et.al., the gamut of expressionist films were studio vehicles, produced on a relatively large budget (in fact some of the budgets became colossal, eg: Lang's *Metropolis* [1926], at 5.3 million marks![11]) which is in stark contrast to the 'home made' affairs of struggling artists. This is why it was remarked above that one should label the corpus of expressionist films as 'art' films (in the accepted sense, as I have just outlined) with caution. Certainly, the international success of *Caligari*, produced by the Decla company, created a lucrative 'art film' industry in Germany which could garner critical and commercial success in London, Paris and New York. In this respect, the expressionist productions which followed *Caligari* from Ufa became a recognised product to the international art *cognoscenti*, defining German cinema as 'expressionist' to foreign audiences who did not have the opportunity to see the types of films the 'ordinary' German cinema-going public would see.[12] The lasting impression of Weimar Republic Germany is one characterised by artistic abandon leading to a veritable hot bed of creativity. Images of wild, satanic, sexual licence in seedy Berlin night clubs and infatuated actors and artists have entered the popular consciousness as a prevailing image of these times, but as is always the case, these were things which affected the day to day affairs of the vast majority of people minimally. (In fact these minority-based assumptions about what constitutes a particular country's national cinema persist to this day, resulting in a distorted historical/cultural perception of the country in question.)

---

11 See Vierra, Mark, *Hollywood Horror*, New York, 2003, p.18.
12 This forms part of Elsaesser's argument against the interpretations of Eisner and Kracauer, who characterise the expressionist corpus in terms of prophetic fore-shadowings of Nazism; Kracauer the more explicitly.

That *Caligari* is stylistically Modernist there can be no doubt. It has all the instantly recognisable components outlined above, a remarkable fact in consideration of *Caligari* as a blue print, almost a prototype, of the expressionist genre. In this sense, it is a film that seemed to come out of nowhere, self contained and 'perfect' in its originality. So original, really, that it could not be repeated without the 'trick' seeming instantly 'old hat'. Most of the films influenced by *Caligari* soon abandoned its stark, uncompromising *mise-en-scène*, and developed their expressionist elements in different directions, which really meant toning them down. We see stills from *Genuine* (1920) and *Raskalnikov* (1923 – based on Dostoyevsky's brilliant novel, *Crime and Punishment*) that look like counterfeit *Caligari's,* and the more successful films, like *Der Golem* and *Der müde Tod*, dispense with such blatant references in favour of a fairy tale-like medievalism. In this respect, there is very little Modernist *content* in German expressionist cinema.

Further, to return to *Caligari* specifically, we can see that even in this archetypical expressionist film that Modernism is more evident in style than in 'content'. When we consider the stylistic elements of the film we clearly perceive the sinister, macabre characters of Dr. Caligari and the murderous somnambulist Cesare; the supporting characters with their eccentric gestures and stark appearances; the sharply angled 'exteriors' with mad cut-out shapes representing trees, buildings, windows, etc.; the claustrophobic 'interiors', with contrasting white walls and angular painted shadows that give a static sense of endless night; the canted camera angles and strong lighting techniques, making use of contrasting bright light and deep shade; the sense of cultivated artifice to engender a Luciferian, dreamlike effect. At the climax of the film, when the townsfolk are pursuing Conrad Veidt as Cesare (who has abducted the 'heroine', Jane, played by Lil Dagover) across the rickety, insubstantial rooftops, the audience has the illusion at one point that Cesare is actually standing on a precipice made of shadows. This is the film's most profoundly enigmatic image; a haunting effect that defines cinematic expressionism as something like the mad illusion the 'framing' sequence reveals *Caligari* to be. All a 'dream within a dream' worthy of Edgar Allan Poe.[13] But perhaps this is itself a hint as to why German Expressionist cinema seems less stridently Modernist than, for example, Dada cinema; in that its Modernism seems only a surface gloss on material which dates from previous epochs. Contrast the visual qualities of *Caligari* with its setting and story. What we find is a typical gothic/romantic fable set in a 'never-never land', with the dark overtones of the previously mentioned Poe, or the uncanny stories of E.T. A Hoffman; 'The Sandman' (1816) springs immediately to mind in this connection. The film is also plotted in a straight forward manner, and the 'framing' device which partially rationalises the story adds further elements of plot conventionality to what could have been a much more unconventional film if it had not been added on (much to the disgust of Mayer and Janowitz).[14]

---

13 Poe's 'Murders in the Rue Morgue', with its malevolent hypnotist would seem to have had a thematic influence on Caligari. The quotation is from Poe's poem 'The Haunted Palace'.
14 Robinson, David, *Das Cabinet des Dr. Caligari*, London, 1997.

Caligari's 'story' would be familiar to a literary audience who would recognise elements taken from the 'gothic' sources mentioned, but also from previous German films with macabre themes, such as *The Student of Prague* (1913) and earlier versions of *Der Golem*. In other words, if you remove the stylistic innovations, you are left with a conventional 'horror' film, albeit with a sound pedigree based on a self-conscious awareness of the gothic genre. This is also the case with Wegener's *Der Golem* (partially based, as it was, on earlier film versions; one of which Wegener made himself in 1914) derived from a contemporised medieval Jewish legend;[15] *Der müde Tod* is another updating of an old legend which apart from its light hearted 'stories-within-the-story' sections (the 'Chinese story', in particular, would seem to have been influenced by the pantomime-like trickery of pioneer special effects man, George Meliès) is essentially another foray into gothic fable territory. The story also doubles as a moral tale about selflessness, and the plot is constructed to create a linear or cyclic structure which produces a satisfying sense of closure at the film's end.

Similarly, the films directed by Murnau – *Nosferatu* (1922) and the previously cited *Faust* – are steeped in the tradition of popular supernaturalism, in the respective shapes of the vampire (specifically, Stoker's world famous *Dracula*) and the devil. Both films work brilliantly as exciting, conventional narratives, with superbly realised spectral *mise-en-scènes*. Stylistically they are innovative and well crafted, but not, I think, Modernist in any propagandist sense. Yet what these films I have briefly mentioned do communicate is a feeling of nightmarish vision and superhuman dynamism we can define as qualities of the *Sturm und Drang*, 'storm and stress', a state of occult self knowledge which transforms its working material onto a higher level of intensity. In this sense we can interpret these strangely traditional expressionist films as Modernist in the Luciferian sense: that of a romantic resurgence of demonic individualism in rejection of the prevailing socialist, 'collectivist', line of many other Modernist groups. These films would seem to be the work of *auteurs* concerned only with self, rather than societal, expression – Modernist in that sense as a specific precursor to post Modernist attitudes, I would argue.

3: TRIUMPH OF THE MUNDANE

It may seem ill-informed or reactionary to portray the 'post expressionist' period of German film making before the Second World War as a mere postscript to the creative torrent of the *Caligari* era. There were, of course, still masterpieces in the form of Pabst's *Pandora's Box* (1928) and Lang's *M* (1931) with its searing performance from Peter Lorre, and the development of the *Kammerspielfilm* from Murnau's *The Last Laugh* (1924) is of no small interest. However, on the whole, I think that when expressionism had run its course, so to speak, along with many other Modernist movements which took a down curve as the 'twenties merged into the 'thirties, the creative impetus seemed comparatively absent. Though many fine films appeared, not the least of which being Leni Riefenstahl's majestically picturesque *The Blue*

---

15 Eisner, p. 66 ff.

Light (1932), the overwhelming shadow of political oppression loomed too large on the horizon. By the time Riefenstahl was assembling *The Triumph of the Will* (1934) from her cleverly idealising, stirring footage of the Nuremberg Rally, which celebrated Hitler's ascension to absolute power, major figures of the industry had absconded to safer shores, such as director Fritz Lang and cinematographer, Karl Freund – both of whom would go on to lasting fame and fortune in Hollywood.

In many ways the Nazi suppression of creativity and self expression signalled a death blow to Modernism in Germany which was already atrophying. The rapid changes which had swept through the 20th century's early decades had also begun to sweep away many Modernist concepts. These things were, after all, the concern of a relatively small percentage of artists and self proclaimed 'mad people'. When the world slumped into economic depression in 1929, the effects would be felt throughout the 'thirties. Slowly but surely people had less time for art and leisure as the crisis deepened. The popularity of the Nazis can be seen as a product of desperation. Films like Riefenstahl's *Triumph of the Will* and *Olympia* (1936), confirm the death of individual expression. In its place we see a panoramic spectacle which, apart from the surprisingly homely visage of Adolf Hitler, is anonymous in its epic scale. Like Lucifer, the individual has been cast out from a collective mundane world, which has no place for him or for his shadows amongst the vast, open plazas of Nuremberg.

BIBLIOGRAPHY

—⁓— Elsaesser, Thomas, *Weimar Cinema and After: Germany's Historical Imaginary*, London, 2000.
—⁓— Eisner, Lotte, *The Haunted Screen*, Berkley, 1973 (1965).
—⁓— Green, Malcolm, *The Golden Bomb*, Edinburgh, 1993.
—⁓— Kracauer, Siegfried, *From Caligari to Hitler*, Princeton, 1974.(1947).
—⁓— Mendgen, Eva, *von Stuck*, Koln, 1995.
—⁓— Richard, Lionel, *The Concise Encyclopedia of Expressionism*, Hertfordshire, 1986.
—⁓— Robinson, David, *Das Cabinet Des Dr. Caligari*, London, 1997.
—⁓— Vierra, Mark, *Hollywood Horror from Gothic to Cosmic*, New York, 2003.

Slam Poetry: The Warrior Poet

Antony Hequet

La désuétude de la poésie

Is poetry dead, resting in peace buried in a few dusty books hidden in the back of the library? Were "the last poets" really the last poets? After we had finished shyly mumbling our little poems in high school, were we done with poetry for good?

Slam Poetry

But what about Slam Poetry, are these people really poets, or are they just rappers without music...? Can one jabber this way and call it poetry? Poets are supposed to be polite, educated and have a high sense of aesthetics. Slammers are rebels and outcasts.

Slam poetry is about speaking words of passion...

The power of the word

Slam poetry is about transforming, speaking words of passion, words of power...

When words are spoken out loud with passion, they resonate in space and in our bodies, thus provoking a strong emotional response. When words become an incantation they move us, they transform our reality.

Ordinary language uses words in an ordinary way, to describe, to paint a picture, it speaks to the intellect.

Poets use Words of Power.

Slam poetry is about feeling em-powered in a world where we have often been reduced to feeling power-less.

Poetry is a martial art, an internal martial art; the poet works with energy thru a specific & subtle use of sound vibrations.

Poetry is a martial art, a Kung Fu which requires *discipline and precision* (ie: *Sun Ra*)

The oral traditions of poetry

Slam poetry is part of a tradition.

55

This tradition pre-dates writing; it is oral by force, but also by will and by nature… Poetry is the vibrating essence of the Primordial Tradition.

This tradition goes back so far in time that we discover its source in the heart of Kaos, in dream time when the world was primordial soup. The first poet manifested in the Logos, at the very first moment of creation.

Primordial poetry is not based in aesthetics, it is a form of primordial Energy/Power. Primordial poetry deals with primordial forces:

⟶ Creation and Destruction
⟶ Kaos & Harmony
⟶ Nature & Elemental forces
⟶ Erotic forces – Attraction and Repulsion (desire – how to attract love – crying over lost love)
⟶ Magick – Incantation – the power to transform

The poet of the oral tradition is in touch with the forces of creation. He deals with myth and archetype, he deals with magick; consequently he stokes the fire of desire…

> *we had the seasons the sun*
> *the grace and the gods*
> *we had the spirits a soul*
> *our guide and a goal*
> *we had silence a song*
> *dreams and dread*
> *we had a secret a sign*
> *demons and dead*
> *once were warriors*
> *this is a war dance*

(Quote from the poem *Once Were Warriorz* by Antony Hequet)

Slam Poetry: The Rebel Poet

Antony Hequet

What does it mean to be a rebel?

To hipsters being a rebel poet has been reduced to a theatrical display: wearing certain clothes, riding a rusty bicycle, going to certain clubs, practising superficial forms of Yoga, smoking, drinking, taking drugs, staying up all night listening to blistering loud elektro. It is also important to litter the world with cigarette buts and empty beer bottles, ride in planes to various foreign destinations as often as possible. Naturally, being a slob is mighty good. And let us not forget that a token artistic front is also indispensable between hangovers: a singer-songwriter is very kool but a performance artist is also good. Just make sure that it is a completely harmless, absolutely egocentric occupation. In the end when the smoke has cleared, this sophisticated and and careless attitude amounts to an elaborate consumption of world goods (international flights, booze, Ikea furniture) poorly disguised as some vague benevolence... In the guise of a non violent rebellion, we have developed the most advanced variety of conformity: Yo, just surrender and be innocuous!

The Rebel Poet

To me, being a rebel means taking a stand against fear greed and egocentric behaviour. It means assuming responsibility for all that goes on in the world – taking charge of my life. It means *Precision and Discipline* (quoting Sun Ra). Most of all, it means connecting with the world's abundance and beauty. The purpose of poetry is to maintain a state of harmony in the cosmos; it is a spiritual mission. I call myself a Rebel Poet because as I rebel against those who are furiously working at the destruction of our world, I must engage – confront and risk in order to accomplish my mission. This is why I call my self Warrior Poet...

What is Slam Poetry?

As a Slam Poet I speak about what moves me, what matters,what is essential. As a Slam Poet I stand up and engage with my body, with nothing to shield me from others. No props, not tools, no back up music...

THE POWER OF THE WORD

In our world, the Word is monopolised by professionals and we are passive listeners. The media saturate the atmosphere with distracting information. There is no empty space left, not a tiny patch of void where we could even attempt to formulate our own thoughts, let alone express them… Yet, generations of outspoken Rebel Poets have demonstrated how effective the Word can be. So maybe the first step is to regain our ability to speak up & talk back.

As a Slam Poet, this is what I do.

Alien Lightning Meat Machine

Genesis Breyer P-Orridge

For Nicola Tesla

CARES NOT FOR IMMEDIATE RESULT
PLANTER OF A FUTURE
TRAMPLED UNDER FOOT
FEAR / JEALOUSY / GREED
A REASON DEMANDS UNREASON
YET RECEIVES ONLY UNREASONABLE
ABILITY DECLINED
UN-DER-LINED

SYMBOLIC ALLURE
A NEUROTIC TESLA
AN ELECTRICAL WRESTLER

WHITE PIGEON DREAMS
FEATHERED TOUCH
WHITE PIGEON DREAMS
FOR A ROMANTIC CRUTCH
HE DIED ALONE
IN A ROOM WITH A WHITE WHITE THRONE
FORGET FORGOT
FUTURES PLANTED
TWISTED KNOT

ALIEN P-ROPE-RTY
TAMING WILD KINETIC ENERGY
A WORLD'S FIRST RADIO

WAR OF CURRENTS
ALTERNATING RADIO
WAR OF CURRENTS
ALTERNATING RADIO
AUGMENTED AUTOMATON
HAAAARP ANGEL

HIGH FREQUENCY ANGEL
ACTIVE AURORAL ANGEL

PARTICLES OF COSMIC MATTER
IT DOESN'T MATTER AT ALL?
IT'S ALL A MATTER OF TIME

SUN TRAPPED IN VACUUM OF SPACE
IT'S A COSMIC CHATTER
LUMINOUS MASS
SWIRLING PAST PLAYS
ANGEL'S HAAAARP OF DEATH RAYS

PRIVATE PERSONAL
HE IS A LONER
STRIPPED BARE BY BACHELORS
EVER OLDER
OBSCURE TO STRANGERS
PHOBIC DANGERS

"THE MAN FROM VENUS!"
LIGHTNING IN HIS HANDS
PRODIGAL GENIUS
PRODUCT OF RUINED LAND

FANNED A NEVER DYING FLAME
OF LIGHT LATENT GASEOUS CONDUCTION
HIGH TENSION
HIGH WIRED ACT
SPARK IRON FLASHING AT A THEORY SNAP

REMOTE
BEYOND MANKIND
CHANGE THE WAY TO PERCEIVE
AND CHANGE ALL MEMORY

A RAGE OF TIME
BLASTING WALLS OF WATER
IN A HOSTILE CLIME

METICULOUS, NEAT, AFRAID OF
FEET, PEARLS, FLESH AND
SEXUAL HEAT
FEAR OF GERMS SO

Alien Lightning Meat Machine

PLAGUED WITH FEAR
BESET BY OBSESSIONS
AND MOTHER DEAR

SPARKLING SILVER
CRINKLING LINEN
HE HELD A TERROR WITHIN
HE'S SO AFRAID OF WOMEN

ERUPTING COILS
ENVELOP HIM
COMPULSION TO COMPLETION
ALMOST MURDERS HIM

EVERYTHING MUST BE
DIVISIBLE BY THREE

OH EDISON OF GLOWING NOSE
SKIN DISEASE AND BROKEN TOES
VENEER OF CULTURE HIDING HATE
FOR TESLA ALWAYS THROUGH THE GATE

GREEDY CHEAT INVETERATE LIAR
IMPALED FOR LIFE ON TESLA'S TOWER
EDISON EDISON A SERPENT'S SON
EDISON EDISON A SERPENT'S TONGUE

SIXTY CYCLES
OF THE FLAMING SWORD

WEIRD IN WHITE LIKE A CRANE
IN SHALLOW WATER
PIERCING FISH TO SWALLOW LATER
HIGH PITCHED AND HIGH VOLTAGE
FALSETTO WORDS FLOW IN HIS
DANCE WITH FLAME AND LANCE
SEEMING SIMPLE AT FIRST GLANCE
REVEALING GLOWS OF EXISTENCE

LUMINOUS FEATHERY BEAMS IGNITE
IONIZED GAS MOLECULAR MIGHT

ARE WE PLASMA
BURNING WITHOUT CONSUMING ?

ATTRACTIONS REPULSIONS ROTATIONS
AGENTS OF A MYSTERY
SCREEN
MOVING IN ORBITS CELESTIAL BODIES
IN AN ALIEN LIGHTNING MACHINE

LONG FINGERS DEFTLY
CHOOSE ANOTHER PROP

LUMINOUS STREAMS
PINWHEELS IN DARK PRESENT
BEAUTY FULL OWING TO
ABUNDANCE OF SEAMS
WIRELESSLY THROUGH SPACE
ENERGY IN A HARD FACE
FREE FOR THE TALKING
NO NEED TO TRANSMIT
AS GENERATIONS PASS
GENERATORS ASK
ALIEN LIGHTNING MACHINE
AT A POINT OF A UNIVERSE
A UNIVERSAL POINT OF TRUTH
EACH IDEA A NOVEL
GAZING
BUDDHA LIKE ERASING

ALIEN LIGHTNING
MACHINE
ALIEN LIGHTNING MEAT MACHINE

SUBTLE SPECULATIONS
MASSIVE CONFLAGRATIONS
THROUGHOUT SPACE
WITHOUT TIME
CLIMBING KINETIC
ENERGY FRENETIC
WE'RE INVERSIONS OF TIME
IT'S ALL A MATTER OF TIME
MERE INVERSIONS OF TIME
IT'S ALL A MATTER OF TIME

CARBON BUTTON LAMP
INCANDESCENT RAMP

Alien Lightning Meat Machine

SUN LIGHT
SUN NIGHT

COSMIC RAYS
COSMIC DAYS
SOLAR RADIATION
VISIBLE INVISIBLE
DIVINELY INDIVISIBLE
SOLAR EMITTED
SO FAR OMITTED

HIGH VELOCITY DREAMS
AND SCHEMES
REDUCE TO PARTICLE SCREAMS

SHOOTING IN STRAIGHT LINES
ACTIVE HIGH POTENTIAL
SUDDEN HEAVY METAL
ALIENLIGHTNING MACHINE
SPHERICAL SURFACE
CURSING WORSHIP
PHOSPHORESCENT IMAGES
FLARE ON AN ATOMIC SCREEN
PHENOMENON OF RESONANCE
IN TIME THIS WILL BE EVIDENCE
MOLECULES REPELLED
LIKE SEALS THAT HAVE RAPELLED
OSCILLATING ATOM SMASHER
CURRENCY OF BANK DISASTER
SO VIOLENTLY RESIDUAL
THE GAS MAY BE AN ACTUAL
CARBON BUTTON IN A PLASTIC PHASE
INCANDESCENT COSMIC RAYS
CAUSTIC LIPS BURN RADIATION
PLAGUES OF SCEPTICS
WORSHIPPING DAMNATION

MEAT MACHINES
ALIEN MACHINES
LIGHTNING MACHINES
MEAT MACHINES

SWOON AS CLOUD OF ANGEL FIGURES
SWARM UPWARDS TO MORTAL TRIGGERS

MOTHERS BREATHE IN MOTHERS WOMB
SLOWLY FLOATING 'CROSS O' DOOM
SWEET SWEET SONG OF MANY VOICES
CERTITUDE OF DEMON VOICES
LANGUAGE CAN NO LONGER SAY
WHY OUR MOTHER DIED THAT WAY

MEAT MEACHINES AND NEAT LATRINES
ALIEN LIGHTNING FROZEN MEANS
ALIEN LIGHTNING MEAT MACHINES
MECHANCAL STILL IN DISTRESS
MECHANICAL ENDOWED WITH SENSE
ALIEN LIGHTNING MEAT MACHINES
ALIEN LIGHTNING MEAT MACHINES
MECHANICAL AND IN DISTRESS
MECHANICAL OBSERVANT MESS

ALIEN LIGHTNING MEAT MACHINE
ALIEN LIGHTNING MEAT MACHINE
ALIEN LIGHTNING MEAT MACHINE
MAN OUT OF TIME
LORD OF LIGHTNING
MAN OUT OF TIME
LORD OF LIGHTNING

THIS IS A NICE PLANET

Genesis Breyer P-Orridge

ALIENIST
IS PSYCHOLOGIST
IS INSIDE
MY HEAD
MY HEAD
MY BRAIN
MY INDEPENDENT SENSE
OF FLORAL TRIBUTES
TO BEING IN THE
WRONG PLACE
AT THE ENDLESS TIME
OR IS IT JUST SHORT ENOUGH?
TO AN IN ALIEN ABLE
WRITE
LIVING OUTSIDE TIME
AS ALIENS DO
SEEM TO ME
IT MUST BE EASIER
TO LAUGH
TO SHAKE OFF
PROBLEMS
LIKE
A DEAD DOG
RIVER
FURRING UP MY FLOW
DID YOU EVER FEEL
ILLEGAL?
ALIEN
YET ANGRY
DISPLACED
OUTSIDE
NOT ALONE
BUT IN THE ALL LONELY?
DID YOU WATCH

The Fenris Wolf

AS YOUR ROME BURNED
AND
EACH SYNAPSE WAS
FIRE FIRING
INSPIRING
ABUSE and HUMILIATING
SIRCUMSTANCE
WHAT IS IT LIKE
NOT BEING HERE
BEING OTHER
BEING ALIEN
A PROCESS
A PROCESSION OF
EASY OPTIONS
NEW BODIES FOR OLD
INFINITELY REPLACING
YET RIDICULING
Yours truly, SELF
THAT MIGHT JUST BE
ME
OR MY SELF
AM I YOUR DREAM
AMIABLE
ALIENIST
HISSED
I KISSED
ALL THE HUGENESS
OF YOU
AND
YOU
OVERWHELMED
ME
SINCE THEN
I WONDER WHO INHABITS
THIS SPACE
YOUR

SPACE
CREATURE
COMFORTS
FOR ALL
AS
AN
IN

ALIEN
ABLE
RIGHT

AS I PASSED YOU ON THE STREET
YOU
SO AM I THE ALIEN WATCHING ME WATCHING YOU
ALL TRICKED
BY TIME
INTO ASSUMING
THE OTHER
IS
LESS
REAL

I ALWAYS FELT TRAPPED
IN A BODY

YOU SEEM
IN MANY
RATHER
DIMENSIONAL
WAYS
REALLY
ILLEGALLY
AND
RELATIVELY
AS GREEN
NAIVE
INNOCENT
AS
YOU ARE

EQUALLY
AS CONFUSED
AND
REALLY
NOT
SO DIFFERENT
AS THE REST OF
BEINGS
PUZZLED
MORE THAN
A MONKEY PUZZLE

TREE
EXCEPT
I HAVE
AN
ALIEN
BRAIN
AND YOUR
SURE
AIN'T
HUMAN
BUDDY

SO
LEAVE ME
TO
BUILD
BRIDGES
SHIP ON OUT
SWITCH
SIDES
CLOSE DOORS TO OPEN PLACES
AND
OPEN UP EACH
MOMENT
THIS
VERY
ODD
STATE OF BEING

LOOKING
AS YOU DO
ALIEN
describe
YOU SAID
WITH GREAT SURPRISE

I DIDN'T EXPECT
TO SEE YOU
HERE!

AND DESPITE
MY GENERALLY
MORE THAN SUPPORTIVE
FEELINGS

This is a Nice Planet

TOWARDS ANY AND
ALL ALIEN
EXPERIENCES

I WONDERED
PRETTY MUCH
EXACTLY THE
SAME THING
ABOUT MY SELF

I DIDN'T EXPECT
TO SEE ME
HERE EITHER

Note Towards the Definition
of a Psychedelic Philosophy

Patrick Lundborg

Introduction

Much of what has been written and said about the psychedelic experience over the past 75 years has been surprisingly narrow in scope. Enthusiasts have been so bowled over by their early journeys into Innerspace that they've rushed to apply the first paradigm that seemed to fit. Typically, this paradigm has been either psychotherapeutic or religious. As pointed out in my general study *Psychedelia* (2012), the 20th century saga of psychedelic culture is in a way the saga of a series of failed metaphors. For several decades, learned, enthusiastic men and women twisted their brains into knots trying to understand, formulate and propagate the meaning of the psychedelic experience. The majority of their contentions have turned out to be inaccurate, no matter how great the enthusiasm with which they were presented. As detailed in Chapter II of the aforementioned *Psychedelia*, this sequence of failures was to some extent due to the Zeitgeist and intellectual state of the mid-20th century.

Today, a decade and a half into a new century, at the final stage of the third wave of modern Psychedelia (the 'techno-shamanistic' phase), the future should be of greater relevance to us than the past. More people are using psychedelic drugs today than at any other point in history. Science focuses increasingly on the operations of the human brain and the mystery of consciousness, and scientists have been allowed to run experiments with psychedelic compounds again, after a 40-year moratorium. Currently there are dozens of mainstream research projects going involving psilocybin, LSD and DMT. The next phase of Psychedelia is likely to be dominated by the consciousness enigma and its micro and macro-level implications.

Despite these encouraging developments, there is a troubling lack of intellectual discussion regarding the psychedelic way of life and the extraordinary insights and changes that the serotonergic hallucinogens bring about in many men and women. Coupled with the inability of earlier generations to create a coherent understanding of Psychedelia as a culture and lifestyle we are currently provided with a *tabula rasa* of sorts. The lack of consensual, fundamental structures offers the opportunity to start afresh, integrating valuable knowledge clusters from the past century as one goes along. Ultimately, the objective is nothing less than the definition of a stand-alone psychedelic philosophy, an intellectual paradigm through which other phenomena can be analyzed and evaluated, but also an understanding of the world from which to shape one's life. The present notes discuss the principles upon which such an intellectual model could be raised, and take some steps toward an outline.

As the reader will find, the difficulties involved can be reduced by keeping a persistent watch on the primary beacon that governs a psychedelic philosophy, which is the psychedelic experience itself. An effective 'acid test' for the progress of the model checks its truthfulness against the nature and effects of the journey to Innerspace, both as individual knowledge and as the experience base of millions of travelogues. Using empirical evidence to validate or refute a general theory may sound obvious, but only in rare cases has this norm been adhered to within Psychedelia.

LEARY & KESEY

In the 1966 foreword to his hallucinogenic interpretation of the ancient *Tao Te Ching*, Dr Timothy Leary wrote:

> *From the beginning of the Harvard-IFIF-Castalia exploration into consciousness two facts were apparent. First, that there were no extant maps, models, myths, theories, languages to describe the psychedelic experience. Second, the temptation to impose old models, premature theories, must be avoided...*

This would have been an admirable approach, if Leary & co had actually followed it. However, during those preceding years that he mentions, Leary and his fellow psychologists had actually done everything they could to 'impose old models' on the psychedelic experience, be it Tibetan meditation instruction or psycho-dynamic 'imprinting'. By 1966, not much was left of the original Harvard scientist agenda, and Tim Leary himself was preparing to leave academia behind and target the youth of America with his psychedelic gospel. His foreword may have been an attempt to re-write the 'Harvard-IFIF-Castalia' group's history, after realizing how misguided their numerous attempts at structure and metaphor had been.

The original 1950s-60s research into mescaline, psilocybin and LSD was strongly dominated by attempts to pigeonhole and subordinate the psychedelic experience into a closely guarded little box within an established field of research. There were some early enthusiasts who understood not to rationalize the journey to Innerspace, but instead enjoy and hopefully extend the ride, the most prominent example being Ken Kesey & the Merry Pranksters. Kesey's group of fun-loving bohemians did on occasion claim to adhere to certain philosophical and aesthetic principles, but as one looks closer at the statements and events that form their legacy, the intellectual content becomes inconsistent. What is claimed to be an artistic or philosophical approach appears more like a behavioristic principle than anything profound. Tom Wolfe's 1968 book *The Electric Kool-Aid Acid Test* discusses in some detail Kesey's notion that we are 'watching the movies of our lives' due to a millisecond processing delay in our central nervous system. This observation, that we are forever lagging behind the actual flow of the world, may at first strike one as an intriguing concept.

But like several Merry Prankster principles, attempts to turn this quirky fact into a general, existential notion yields a kind of irresponsible nihilism and little else.

As exemplified by familiar cases like Leary and Kesey, the early days of psychedelic culture displayed only a limited interest in devising a coherent system of ideas and experiences. Other nexus of psychedelic activity from the first (1950-1963) and second (1964-1980) phases show similar kinds of inconsistent, *ad hoc* intellectual frameworks, even when the outward intentions seem varied. The reason why usable cultural paradigms failed to emerge even among its bohemian supporters is that Psychedelia was taken as an attribute, not the central object. To truly understand the range of human consciousness, both scientists and laymen need to reverse their perspective and place the psychedelic experience at the center of the experiment.

Rather than using notions from mainstream religion or psychology as yardsticks for Psychedelia, the psychedelic experience itself should be the yardstick by which things like religion and psychology are measured. More than a catalyst it should be understood as a prism through which the rest of the world is passing. This seemingly radical view is not unprecedented, but can be found with several of the ayahuasca/yagé-drinking tribes in Amazonia. The notorious Jivaro (Shuar) even go so far as to view the hallucinogenic state as the real world, and the baseline world as an illusion. In the modern West, despite the remarkable socio-cultural impact that psychedelics have had from Aldous Huxley in 1955 to Terence McKenna in 1995, the potential for Psychedelia as a free-standing spiritual lifestyle and intellectual frame of reference is seldom discussed.

WESTERN LEGACY

Invoked via words or put to use through action, the merits of a psychedelic philosophy of life will be examined again and again, at different times and places. Not just by its adherents, but by critics opposed to the idea of any abstract model based on the psychedelic drug experience. With its roots in the otherworldly climate of Innerspace, Psychedelia tends to produce concepts far from the semi-secularized monotheism and Cartesian-Newtonian positivism of the West. This conflict with the local socio-cultural tradition strengthens the experiential orientation, but even more importantly, it reveals for those concerned that the psychedelic philosophy of life offers something that existing belief systems do not, which is the direct experience of the otherworldly.

Dominant ideas, such as Christianity, will replace the citizen's immediate experience of its tenets with the publicly sanctioned teaching of Christian beliefs in schools, mass-media, in the military and so on. These fundamental ideas are injected into every personal copy of the socio-cultural template and so become validated as principles of society, even if the individual lacks both faith and interest. This acculturation of what was originally a radical religious sect has been so effective that it could afford to restrict the visionary experiences that originally gave birth to it. The revelation of the Logos and the sacred visions has been removed to an intermediary class of saints and priests, who as gatekeepers pass the divine teachings on to the congregation. This model, which is characteristic of all three major Abrahamic religions from the Middle East, is sustainable and at times even successful, but the practical value it offers society at large is also the spiritual loss of the single individual, who is not allowed access to the revelations of the higher realms.

It is interesting to note that the earliest psychedelic gatherings of the West, the Great Mystery celebrations at the temple of Eleusis in ancient Greece, were directed entirely towards the individual's experience of eternal life and the felt presence of the gods. After preparation through fasting and physical ordeals, the initiand at Eleusis was required to drink the hallucinogenic *kykeon* before spending the night in the great temple, where visual and aural effects stimulated the minds of thousands toward a climactic moment of private revelation. The Great Mysteries were celebrated for nearly 2.000 years. They followed Mediterranean culture out of the vegetation rites of prehistory into the great societies of Athens, Alexandria and Rome, influencing the entire duration of classical antiquity. The experience of Eleusis is so strongly intertwined with Greco-Roman high cultures that its presence is simply taken for granted by classic scholars.

The final days of Eleusis coincide with the final days of Rome, as a joint force of Germanic tribes and Christian conquerors destroyed the great temple around 400 A.D. Emerging as the new dominant force in the Mediterranean region, the adherents of Christianity were eager to destroy existing polytheistic beliefs and nature cults, a show of violent intolerance that coming centuries would find repeated around the world. Despite the intermingling of these elements in the Western heritage, the Greco-Roman seeds of our civilization championed a belief system and a way of life that was profoundly opposed to the Christian notions that would ultimately emerge as the basis for Occidental society. Central to the spiritual celebrations at Eleusis stood the individual's immediate experience of a higher world, the main principle of a psychedelic philosophy.

Phenomenology

It was suggested above that the psychedelic experience could be used as a prism, through which our perception of the world might become richer and more imaginative. In an objective experimental setting however, it is more appropriate to apply what cybernetic science calls a 'black box' model. A black box is an active process element whose interior design and functionality are unseen and unknown. What is known is that the black box receives certain in-data and produces certain results, and from this available information a sufficient image of the unknown process inside the box is developed.

The black box model is well-suited for the empirical approach that this paper promotes for understanding the psychedelic experience. A similar conclusion has been reached by earlier researchers in the hallucinogen field, although their vantage point is psychological rather than cybernetic. Their paradigm of choice is the philosophy branch known as *phenomenology*, a model which in practical application aligns closely to black box methodology. Both variants operate in a pure observational mode, registering the data that surface with no hypothetical result or end-state in play, putting the analysis aside for a later phase. There are several indications that phenomenology is becoming the gold standard for the experimental study of psychedelic drugs and their effects. Research elder Ralph Metzner, who was a vital member of Leary's group back in the 1960s, points to the usefulness of a phenomenological approach in his excellent foreword to the anthology *Ayahuasca* (2002). Similarly, in *Antipodes of the Mind* (1999) one of the most thorough studies of psychedelic states so far, cognitive psychologist Benny Shanon defines his method as wholly phenomenological.

Looking back on the earlier phases of Psychedelia for traces of phenomenology, one will find the same combination of bold intention and poor implementation as the socio-cultural metaphors discussed above. Timothy Leary's ex-Harvard group went on record around 1965 stating that their approach was phenomenological, a claim repeated some 10 years later by Terence McKenna and his brother Dennis when probing the depths of high-dosage psilocybin trips. Neither case have left any records behind to indicate any phenomenological studies, and in all likelihood these were cases of harmless lip service, by which 'phenomenology' simply meant that one paid close attention to what was going on inside Innerspace. The desire to verbalize and metaphorize the extraordinary impressions will effectively void the neutral stance of phenomenology; when out there in the psychedelic state, it seems the temptation for the analytical mind becomes too strong to resist.

What writers like Metzner, Shanon and Lundborg (in the aforementioned *Psychedelia*) describe for the psychedelic research of the 2000s is a phenomenology rooted in the actual philosophy that bears this name, rather than some loose vow to be objective and attentive. What this entails is not difficult to understand, and its practical usefulness should be equally easy to see. Phenomenology was essentially the brainchild of a single thinker, the German 19th century philosopher Edmund Husserl. Husserl was dissatisfied with the vagaries and open contradictions of contemporary philosophy, and from a relatively young age he strove to develop a philosophical system that was both independent of other disciplines and as rigorously defined as the natural sciences.

Unlike more recent thought models such as post-structuralism, the principles of phenomenology are not difficult to grasp, even for a layman unfamiliar with branch philosophy. Phenomenology, as Husserl devised it, is clearly defined and intuitively sound. For the psychedelicist, two of Husserl's fundamental principles are of particular interest; (A) *any mental activity such as looking, thinking, imagining, dreaming, etc, is constituted by three elements:* a) the consciousness that is engaged in the act, b) the phenomenon that is being perceived, and c) the act of perception (seeing, thinking, remembering, dreaming…). If either one of these three elements is removed, there no longer exists a mental activity. It is vital to understand that Husserl viewed these three elements as bound together in a totality, and it was this totality that was the main object of his interest. He dismissed traditional models like the subject/object distinction as insufficient to truly understand consciousness.

The radical yet conceptually simple model that Husserl proposed leads to an interesting effect; namely that (B) *there is no qualitative distinction between different types of mental activity,* such as imagining, seeing, remembering, dreaming or hallucinating; nor is there any formal difference between the thought of something that 'exists', such as an apple tree, and something that probably 'not exists', such as a unicorn. To Husserl, these activities all fall under his same fundamental principle (A). They may be classified as different *types* of thought, but can all be described and analyzed by the same simple model.

With this ingenious system, Husserl solved several problems that plagued earlier models of epistemology (knowledge theory). For the psychedelicist the advantage is obvious; receiving and documenting the often radical mindstream in the hallucinogenic state can be performed in an equal manner to how one describes an eventful day in a diary, or how one takes down a nocturnal dream. Assumptions or defensive belittling of the extraordinary input on LSD-type drugs automatically fall away, since they have no place in phenomenology. Instead, the method points out the resemblance between writing down a memorable night dream and the recollection of a powerful sequence in psychedelic Innerspace. No matter how bizarre or otherworldly, these dreams and drug visions and dizzying sights all pass through the simple, objective core channel of phenomenology.

An intriguing meeting between Psychedelia and phenomenology occurred as early as the 1940s, when the French philosopher Maurice Merleau-Ponty underwent a few mescaline experiments in order to develop his theories on perception. Rarely discussed and in fact unknown to many psychedelic researchers, this event yielded no major intellectual breakthroughs for Merleau-Ponty (unlike his colleague Jean-Paul Sartre, who wrote the groundbreaking *La Nausée* following a horrific mescaline journey) due to the moderate doses he took, but it provides us with a look at how phenomenology encounters psychedelics. As a phenomenologist, Merleau-Ponty makes no valuation of his OEV (open eye visuals) hallucinations, but simply registers what takes place before his eyes. Distinctions of things as 'real' or 'unreal' are not made, nor is there any type of symbolic reading of the visions. Judgment or interpretation would mean a regression into the primitive forms of epistemology that Husserl wished to eradicate. Given science's historical mishandling of LSD it is obvious that phenomenology, especially the pure Husserlian form described here, could have offered a terrific framework for psychedelic research, with a fit and intellectual rigor superior to the psychoanalytical or religious-mystic models that were invoked in the 1950s-60s.

PURPOSELESS PLAY

It is vital to understand that phenomenology doesn't form a closed system that would make it an idealist or even solipsist philosophy. It does not aspire to make definitive statements about the world, neither outside us nor inside us. Merleau-Ponty accepts the logic in extending phenomenology into a complete philosophical system, but rejects this path in favour of a modern and less definitive paradigm. As phenomenologists, our view of the world is radically changed, but the world is not reduced to something only in our own minds; rather it occupies a peculiar, hypnotic middle ground. The reduction that this modern intellectual stance occasions is not a reduction of the world or our position in it, but of the rigid attention we have developed to all sensory and cognitive input. As a method it '…steps back to watch the forms of transcendence fly up like sparks from a fire; it slackens the intentional threads which attach us to the world, and thus brings them to our notice. It, alone, is consciousness of the world, because it reveals the world as strange and paradoxical' (*Phenomenology of Perception*, 1945).

Another of Husserl's followers, the German philosopher Eugen Fink, found a similar transformation of consciousness in the phenomenological reduction, 'a wonder in the face of the world'. Fink viewed man's conscious life as an enthralment with the constant mystery of phenomenological observations, and he took man's purpose as to engage in what he called 'play'. As an expression of free will and the phenomenological stance, man finds meaning in play, which forms a microcosmic mirror of a macrocosmic world, abstracted out of his reach. In play, there are no boundaries for consciousness, and man transcends the rules and restrictions of his everyday life. As a field of endless possibilities, play becomes a symbol of the totality of the world, and to engage in play is to come closer to understanding the full nature of our existence.

With these developments from Maurice Merleau-Ponty and Eugen Fink, phenomenology is brought in the vicinity of what could be called a psychedelic philosophy. Unlike structuralism, neo-Marxism or psychoanalysis, there is nothing in phenomenology that contradicts the psychedelic experience. On the contrary, Fink's notion of play is reminiscent of the ideas of certain genuinely psychedelic thinkers, such as Alan Watts. Being a phenomenologist, Fink did not entertain the notion of a true 'I' or 'self', but merely noted that there was an activity of consciousness. For this reason, Fink's philosophy has been called 'play without anyone playing'. Compare this to *The Joyous Cosmology* (1962), where Alan Watts writes: '…Life is basically a gesture, but no one, no thing, is making it. There is no necessity for it to happen, and none for it to go on happening. For it isn't being driven by anything; it just happens freely of itself. It's a gesture of motion, of sound, of colour, and just as no one is making it, it isn't happening to anyone. There is simply no problem of life; it is completely purposeless play'. Alan Watts arrived to this view by way of LSD and his substantial training in Eastern religion. His vantage point was completely different than Fink's, yet the ultimate insights that the two men describe seem close. There are clearly parallels between the Buddhism and Taoism that Watts knew, and the basic tenets of European phenomenology. However, the ego-less play that Eugen Fink and Alan Watts independently describe is neither Buddhist-Taoist nor classic idealist, but something else; perhaps it could be called a psychedelic existentialism, casting a wider net than phenomenology. Again like Fink, Watts pointed to the importance of this 'purposeless play':

'No one is more dangerously insane than one who is sane all the time. He is like a steel bridge without flexibility, and the order of his life is rigid and brittle

[...] our play is never real play because it is almost invariably rationalized; we do it on the pretext that it is good for us. [...] The play of life is at first apprehended rather cynically as an extremely intricate contest in one-upmanship, expressing itself deviously even in the most altruistic of human endeavours. [...] But finally, rapacious and all-embracing cosmic selfishness turns out to be a disguise for the unmotivated play of love.' *(The Joyous Cosmology)*

As I show in *Psychedelia*, Watts most likely picked up the phrase 'purposeless play' from avant composer John Cage, who used it in lectures to explain his new and radical aesthetics. Watts' familiarity with New York City avant-garde was manifested in his groundbreaking free-form acid jam recording *This Is IT* (1962), frequently described as the first genuinely psychedelic LP. While the ongoing dialogue between his Eastern metaphysics and a series of psychedelic trips bred the unorthodox existentialist world-view described above, it is evident that cutting edge aesthetic theory also informed Watts' activities and provided him with the psychedelic key phrase 'purposeless play'. The *This Is IT* album has been written about at length elsewhere; its connection to Watts' LSD experiments is evident from the back liner notes, which quote directly from *The Joyous Cosmology.*

Only a year or so later, a new generation of non-academic psychedelicists would appear not far from Watts' San Francisco home turf, putting into practice Watts' hypothetical notion of purposeless play as a lifestyle. Ken Kesey & the Merry Pranksters used their own set of trippy catch phrases to signal their presence, but there are few better ways to describe their free-form multimedia mind games than purposeless play. In interviews, such as the one heard on the *Acid Test* LP (1966) Kesey would insist upon the meaningless nature of their goals, and how they would also try to undermine the efforts to reach the goals. This, we are told, all takes place because the Pranksters 'have nothing else to do'. Amusement for no reason and with no actual goal; purposeless play.

This perspective bears upon the Prankster group's lack of a genuinely operative philosophy or aesthetic theory that was discussed above, suggesting that the playful phenomenology of Fink and the purposeless, ego-less diversions of Watts could in fact serve as pre-existing models for Kesey & co, instilled by zeitgeist and the psychedelic experience. Alas, the lack of a fully developed intellectual framework (beyond the active principle of purposeless play in the movie of life) made the Pranksters overly dependent on specific personalities rather than creativity, which contributed to their fairly rapid downfall in a San Francisco scene that was becoming self-aware of its collective significance.

PSYCHEDELIC CORE VALUES

Perhaps because their most vital heritage was socio-cultural rather than intellectual, the Merry Pranksters have remained relatively immune to the passing of time and the often critical revaluations of the counterculture 1960s. When the 'rave' scene emerged in the late 1980s, psychedelic veterans were quick to point out the similarity to the old Acid Tests around the SF Bay Area. The lingering relevance of

Kesey's group to underground culture in general and Psychedelia in particular is linked to one of the fundamental values that inform a psychedelic philosophy of the West, which is the belief in and practicing of *hedonism*. As shown above, Alan Watts referred to this kind of psychedelic existentialism as 'purposeless play', while the Pranksters thought of it as a 'movie of life'. Hedonism is the celebration of the present moment, a giving in to the natural euphoria of the here and now.

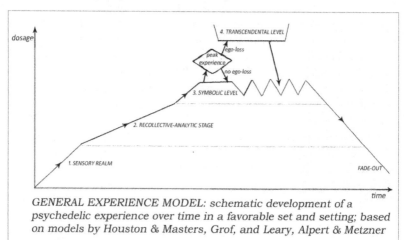

GENERAL EXPERIENCE MODEL: schematic development of a psychedelic experience over time in a favorable set and setting; based on models by Houston & Masters, Grof, and Leary, Alpert & Metzner

A 3000-year arc connects the Dionysian festivals of ancient Greece with the psychedelic parties that defined the mid-'60s (the Millbrook weekends, the Acid Tests, Trips Festival, Human Be-In, Monterey Pop) and the all-night dances of today's neo-hippie Goa culture. None of these gatherings were revolutionary think-tanks or cutting edge artist collectives, but events of joy and exuberance, an unconditional championing of the glory of human life made manifest by LSD and its sister hallucinogens. Psychedelic hedonism is not a wish to escape, nor is it a neurophysical effect of hyper-stimulant drugs: it is a core element in the psychedelic way of life, rooted in profound individual revelations of higher states. Aldous Huxley put it most succinctly: the world, it seemed to him after a few mescaline experiences, was 'alright'. This insight calls for a celebration.

A second fundamental value of Psychedelia which is both linked and juxtaposed with the hedonistic strain is *holism*. Psychedelic holism is not some vague phrase on a Mahatma Gandhi t-shirt, but a core principle that emanates out of the uncharted depths of consciousness. To truly understand what is meant by holism in a psychedelic philosophy, you need to get far out enough in Innerspace so that you perceive and understand the notion that the world is constructed of energy, and that the same type of energy is everywhere, even in conceptually dead things such as rocks and buildings. Some may embrace this energy as 'sacred'; others may choose to simply register it as a visual representation of the micro-physical plane. Either way, the constantly buzzing transformations of energy among the elementary particles are laid bare for you to see. How and if you interpret this experience is subjective and non-vital, the lasting insight is the holistic homogeneity of the world.

Whatever the cosmos is made up of, it is the same fundamental energy everywhere. The Tibetan Buddhists have a terrific term for this; they call it 'one-taste', meaning that for your senses and your cognitive mind, everything 'tastes' the same once you reach a certain level of transcendental insight. This state is not necessarily the experience of non-duality, but it is at least the *perception* of non-duality, and as such it represents a substantial gain on the spiritual path. Indeed, a Platonic/Neo-platonic interpretation of the psychedelic-holistic revelation would be that one has left the mundane plane of emanated forms and ascended to the level of ideas. This has a certain amount of historical justification, since both Plato and several of his followers partook in the celebrations at Eleusis. The few documents that refer to Eleusis (despite sworn secrecy) talk of the peak experience of the hallucinogenic night in the temple as an understanding of eternal life and the existence of a transcendental world.

Pantheism is the third psychedelic core value. Clearly related to holism, its specific traits need to be distinguished for a full conceptual understanding. Holism is essentially the result of a vision of homogenous energy which is frequently experienced in the higher states. Pantheism is primarily a mundane, earthbound philosophy which usually emerges from a different experiential path than holism. The concept behind pantheism says that everything that is alive is charged with the same presence, or spirit, or god. The orientation is towards animate agents only, meaning living organisms; some might limit it to higher animals only, which would be considered to have a soul. Again, the personal definition is less important than the fundamental experience from which pantheism emerges in an almost automatic manner.

In the psychedelic state there will come a passage where you seem able to see through present organisms and discover their true core. If this occurs, the discovery is usually that all these living things are alike at the core; animated by the same drive, or energy, or spirit or god. This is usually a humbling experience as the subject realizes the arrogance of his assumed human superiority over animals and plants, and questions his or her right to dominate organisms whose principle of life is the same as one's own. It is no coincidence that many acid-heads become vegetarians, or that almost all higher spiritual schools proscribe vegetarianism. Not because you feel 'sorry' for animals, but because you are violating a sacred presence whose existence you yourself have felt. The pantheistic insight brings an important ethical dimension to Psychedelia.

Pantheism as a revealed philosophy of life may emerge out of holism, or precede the holistic vision during the same psychedelic experience, but it is the present author's belief that the pantheistic vision arises out of a wholly separate mindstream. It is possible to receive the pantheistic message without entering the non-dualistic ego-less vision of holism; depending on set, setting and dosage, as always. The pantheistic insight is dualist and organic in its nature, whereas the holistic insight is non-dualist and cosmic. Some might perceive the pantheistic core as a kind of transcendental fiber around which the myriad of living entities are formed, leading towards a radical form of Gnosticism, or the Hindu dichotomy of the *Atman* and *Brahman*.

Another perspective validated by the Eleusinian-Platonic model is to view the pantheist as someone who has ascended to a higher spiritual state, from which he can recognize spiritual qualities in the material plane otherwise hidden from human eyes. The ascension of layers is not only typical for the psychedelic journey, but also a model with a Neo-Platonic implication. Plotinus and the later Neo-Platonists strove to examine the higher, formless planes while Plato had restricted his cosmology to one undifferentiated higher world. A charting of the psychedelic experience will favor the gradual Neo-Platonic structure, in the sense that Innerspace displays topology and amplitude, in addition to its horizontal vastness. The vital facts remain untarnished by these speculations—the pantheistic impulse was present at Eleusis 3000 years ago, and it remains present in the psychedelic experience that people are embarking on today.

THE DOUBLE POSITIVE OF PSYCHEDELIA

A significant contribution to the allure of the psychedelic lifestyle comes from the fact that it is a philosophy that does not deal in negatives or contradictions. Psychedelia's fundamental message is to enjoy yourself in your present time, respect life and respect nature, and in time prepare yourself for ascension to the transcendental state that the hallucinogenic experience showed you exists. This *double positive* stands very much in contrast with the Abrahamic religions and their rigid dichotomies, and even the Eastern religions, despite their flexibility and variation, cannot really accommodate the combination of pantheism, hedonism and Neo-Platonism that a tentative psychedelic philosophy might embrace.

As one familiarizes oneself with the psychedelic perspective, it becomes increasingly clear how remarkably sinister the traditional religious schools are. The body is there usually said to be evil, as are normal human desires, and personal guilt over supposed transgressions become liturgical weapons for the ordained religious teacher, who alone is allowed to communicate with the godhead, which in its monotheistic domain is as fixated upon Manichean dualism and human behavior as everything else in the old Middle Eastern belief systems.

Nor is there relief in the revelation of a higher transcendental state that was offered the initiands at Eleusis and which motivated their jubilant celebration, since this experience too remains the property of the religious middle-man such as a priest, rabbi or imam. In fact, private visions of high spiritual realms may expose the congregation member to accusations of heresy rather than a vital step forward on the path. A direct comparison between the tenets of a psychedelic philosophy of life and the leading world religions yields so little conceptual overlap that the situation looks more like a direct conflict than a disagreement. That Christian forces from the East led the attack and destruction of the Great Temple at Eleusis seems entirely logical in view of the respective teachings. Indigenous cultures around the world, not least in the Americas, would come to find their pantheistic belief systems eradicated along with their villages by invading Christian warriors.

As for the double positive of Psychedelia, it is possible to find instances of ideas along this route in modern Western culture. However, the picture is made clearer if the core values of hedonism, holism and pantheism are augmented with another vital element in psychedelic culture, which is *utopianism*. The drive to create a psychedelic Utopia is so common that it seems almost inevitable among long-running, coherent groups of 'acidheads'. The Utopia can take many forms, from the anarchic jet set party at Millbrook to the large experiment in self-subsistence at Stephen Gaskin's Farm. The utopian idea itself can be tracked backwards to the core values of pantheism – to live close to nature – and hedonism – to enjoy life in one's own way. But other and more specific factors also informed this drive, which are more of a socio-cultural nature and needn't be covered here. What is relevant is the frequency with which the utopian project emerges among psychedelic enclaves after a certain time. Any model that deals with a psychedelic philosophy of life should recognize the utopian aspect as integral to the enterprise.

PATTERNS OF PSYCHEDELIZATION

The relation between the utopian drive and the double positive of a psychedelic philosophy can be discerned among certain artists who have made significant contributions to the field of Psychedelia. An interesting parallel emerges from a close study of two seemingly very disparate icons, the Nobel Prize winning author Hermann Hesse and the legendary acid rock group the 13th Floor Elevators. Their preoccupation with psychedelic lifestyles is evident for all to see in works such as Hesse's *The Steppenwolf* and *Journey To The East*, and the Elevators' *Roller Coaster* (an anthem for hallucinogenic hedonism) and *Slip Inside This House* (both with lyrics by the group's intellectual leader Tommy Hall). Much has already been written about these works, but the thematic correspondence that spans across several works of Hesse and the Elevators is rarely discussed. What one finds, beyond their shared interest in higher states of consciousness, is a near-identical thematic arc which in turn matches the psychedelic philosophy discussed in the present article.

The arc takes its beginning with an initiation into hallucinogenic Innerspace, and the spontaneous enjoyment of one's newfound world (hedonism; *Steppenwolf; Roller Coaster*). This is followed by the necessary deepening of the experience into the transcendental state of ego-loss and the emergence of a spiritual revelation (holism; *Siddhartha; Kingdom Of Heaven)*. The third step finds enlightened psychedelic beings developing a shared spiritual view of the world and tightening their bonds via mental explorations (pantheism; *Journey to the East; Slip Inside This House)*. The fourth and final step is the impulse towards tribal Utopia, wherein the members of the psychedelic group retreat from the world to set up an ideal community where they will enjoy the double positive of purposeless play in ordinary reality, illuminated by the beckoning transcendental glow of higher realities (utopianism; *The Glass Bead Game; Dust)*.

It should be stressed that the isomorphic pattern found in these otherwise divergent sources can be identified in several other cultural contexts where use of psychedelic drugs occur; the comparison between Hesse and the Elevators is just one example. The long night of initiation at Eleusis began with hedonism and moved into holistic-pantheistic revelation as the *kykeon's* effect peaked inside the participants. The first utopian vision, Plato's *Republic*, is quite possibly inspired by what he himself saw in the Great Temple. In our modern times, one could dissect the socio-cultural development of the psychedelic underground of the 1960s and find the same schematic process; from the hedonistic acid parties of 1965, via the closely bonded "love generation" of 1966-67, up to the communal-rural impulse of the later years. Hedonism, holism, pantheism and utopianism linger as psychedelic effects on the individual micro-level, soon to be reflected back on a socio-cultural macro-level like a fractal pattern receding to reveal identical supra-levels. The development also illustrates the difference between how a psychedelic community and a religious community emerge. In the case of the latter the profound vision of revealed truth comes first, and it is usually only incarnated in a single prophet-founder, while the hedonistic element is often completely absent.

CONCLUSION

These notes suggest several aspects worth considering in the development of a psychedelic philosophy of life. The fundamental principle is that anything included in the system must have evolved naturally from the psychedelic experience itself. External concepts are only brought in when they fill a specific need. Such is the case with Husserl's phenomenology, which is a tool that helps the psychedelicist to stay objective and attentive before the rich and often chaotic flow of the experience, and in addition works to remind one that visions received in hallucinogenic Innerspace are of equal validity as visions received in dreams or meditation. Phenomenology reduces the drama of the experience, it helps one to preserve the vital information given in the higher state, and (in the mode of Eugen Fink and Alan Watts) it has a corresponding active principle in the notion of purposeless play.

The psychedelic experience itself can be understood by Lundborg's *General Experience Model*, which describes the subject's progress through levels of altered cognition as a typical journey unfolds over several hours. The model highlights the importance of dosage for reaching the higher states, a factor often forgotten when set and setting are discussed. The GEM is not a 'map' to follow, but a generalized model drawn from thousands of observations and calibrated against older models. It is intended primarily to identify one's degree of psychedelization (i.e: 'how high was I?'), and to indicate approximately how the path unfolds. Students of Neo-Platonism may find it particularly easy to adapt the levelled model, while the practical handling of the experience can be developed by studying principles from shamanism for navigation and interaction in altered states of consciousness. From traditional meditation the technique of maintaining 'the Witness' and other ways to regain control of one's mindstream are excellent tools.

The *Psychedelia* book to which this paper corresponds stresses the need for preparation by way of 'Gnothi Seauton 101'. This ground course to 'know thyself' refers to a basic cleansing of psycho-dynamic baggage, either through therapy or meditation, in order to reduce the risk for strong adverse reactions on the initial psychedelic journeys. Ego-defenses, fixed ideas, repressed material and similar mental obstacles can of course be dealt with in the hallucinogenic state, but it is a demanding and risky type of self-treatment. As one becomes familiar with the psychedelic landscape of one's consciousness, there is frequently a development of one's personality following the first few experiences. This may be subtle at first, but in hindsight stand out as a major turning point. Not everyone is affected in a lasting manner, but those who felt attracted to Psychedelia even before taking a hallucinogen almost invariably become enthusiasts and even advocates for this way of life.

Visionary Design
Through the Power of Symbolism

An Exposition of Book Covers in Psychedelic Literature

Henrik Dahl

Book covers in psychedelic literature are rarely discussed. Yet they are part of a design tradition that goes back at least to the mid 20th Century.[1] Admittedly, some covers reflect the content poorly. But a considerable amount of them are made with great care and effort, often displaying intriguing, original and thought-provoking designs. Although usually ignored and overlooked by researchers, the field of book design may provide us with a better understanding of the genre and psychedelic culture as a whole.

A Design Tradition

There are several good reasons for analysing book design in psychedelic literature. For instance, book covers may reveal a lot of information about the times they were made. Obviously, they show the technical progress that has taken place over the decades. Book covers can also reveal a lot about our relationship with *the other*. One may ask what it means to place a shaman from the rainforest on the front cover. Is the motif a necessary reflection of the content of the book, or is the publisher simply expressing anachronistic fantasies of life in the wilderness?

Before looking into cover design in the genre a few words should be said about what defines it. The common definition seems to be that these are *works about psychedelics and/or the psychedelic experience*. They can be non-fiction or fiction, even though the former is the most common. Writers may for example include scientists, journalists, researchers or fiction authors. Some of the titles are in the grey zone. These include books where only a minor portion of their content is about psychedelics. Books about cannabis are generally not included in the genre. Defining psychedelic literature in the way just described is far from perfect. Clearly there are books that do not meet with the criteria, yet are still considered belonging to the genre. One such example is the 1971 book *Be Here Now* by Ram Dass. Despite not being about mind-expanding drugs per se, the book has a

---

1 One could argue that psychedelic literature existed long before the 1950s. For instance, in 1896 trip reports by Dr. Eshner and Dr. S. Weir Mitchell, describing their experiences on peyote, were published in *The British Medical Journal*. However, psychedelic literature as we know it today was unseen of before the mid-20th Century.

literary style and visual aesthetic that makes it part of psychedelic literature.

It may look like psychedelic literature is only a minor niche in the world of book publishing, but a few authors in the genre have actually become hugely successful. One such author is Carlos Castaneda. During his lifetime his books were sold in at least 10 million copies, and none of his titles have ever gone out of print.[2] Castaneda's controversial début *The Teachings of Don Juan – A Yaqui Way of Knowledge* (1968) is probably one of the most well- known works in psychedelic literature. The book has gone through several different cover designs, and it is presumable that they have played an important part in its success.

When writing this essay only front covers were taken into consideration. The spine and the back cover are also very important elements. Still, it is the front that we mostly think of when we refer to a certain book design. It is also the front that is used whenever a book is marketed by a publisher, or reviewed by the media. In addition, all the books referred to in this piece are in English and have at some point been printed on paper.

Although psychedelic looking imagery had been used on book covers before the 1950s, it was the design of Aldous Huxley's 1954 essay *The Doors of Perception* that marked the start of the publication of books on psychedelics where the content is reflected on the cover. The dust jacket of the original cover design of Huxley's seminal trip report contains one of the most used and, admittedly, most powerful symbols seen on psychedelic literature, namely the eye. Since *The Doors of Perception* numerous books in the genre have been published showing one or several eyes on the front cover. A book about, say, LSD therapy will probably look very different from a book about ayahuasca shamanism. There is, however, a psychedelic aesthetic that runs through the decades. Some motifs, such as the eye, occur over and over regardless of which psychedelic is discussed.

In a sense a book cover can be regarded as a map. It can reveal ethnocentric attitudes, not to mention those relating to race, globalisation, gender, animals, the environment and tourism. Moreover, when looking into the topic of book design in psychedelic literature one soon finds that book covers reflect which psychedelics were the ones most in vogue in a certain era. Generally speaking, it seems every decade from the 1950s and onwards in psychedelic literature is associated with a specific psychedelic. The seminal works of Aldous Huxley and Henri Michaux in the mid-1950s were based on their experiences with mescaline, while in the 1960s Alan Watts, Timothy Leary and numerous other authors turned to the topic of LSD. The mid-seventies saw a shift to psilocybin mushrooms. Major works from that era include those by Terence and Dennis McKenna. Terence McKenna reappeared in the early nineties with several books, again focusing on psilocybin mushrooms, but also DMT and ayahuasca. During the 21st Century there has been a growing interest in psychedelics used by indigenous peoples. This has resulted in a number of books on ayahuasca (e.g. by psychologist and Leary associate Ralph Metzner and Australian journalist Rak Razam), but also accounts of previously lesser-known

---

2 Marshall, Robert. *The Dark Legacy of Carlos Castaneda*. Salon.com, 2007. Retrieved from http://www.salon.com/2007/04/12/castaneda/.

drugs such as iboga (the perhaps most well known being that of journalist and *Reality Sandwich*-editor Daniel Pinchbeck).

It seems very few designers get to specialise in psychedelic literature, that is, unless one gets to work for one of the very few publishers focusing exclusively on the genre. When going through the credits of a number of books published in recent years by Park Street Press, a subdivision of American publishing company Inner Traditions, I noticed that the name Peri Swan appeared repeatedly. Swan's covers often show heavily edited photographs or graphic shapes – motifs include indigenous peoples, plants and animals – while typefaces usually are written in golden serif typography (i.e. letters with "feet"). In addition, Swan's work is characterised by strong colours and the designs clearly have a psychedelic aesthetic.

Many covers in psychedelic literature are based on artworks created by professional visual artists. For example, in the early 2010s paintings by Fred Tomaselli were featured on no less than three book covers: *Nomad Codes – Adventures in Modern Esoterica* (2010) by Erik Davis, *Psychedelic – Optical and Visionary Art since the 1960s* (2010) by David S. Rubin and *Are You Experienced? – How Psychedelic Consciousness Transformed Modern Art* (2011) by Ken Johnson. The latter two are books on psychedelic art. Interestingly, Tomaselli has distanced himself from the genre: "My art is informed to a certain degree by psychedelic art but it's in concert with many different ideas and 'isms,' so I don't really consider myself a psychedelic artist per se."[3] Other artists whose art have appeared on book covers are Alex Grey and Anderson Debernardi. Grey's art is featured on the 2001 book *DMT – The Spirit Molecule – A Doctor's Revolutionary Research into the Biology of Near-Death and Mystical Experiences* by Rick Strassman. The painting – arguably one of Grey's finest – is called *Dying* and shows a man lying in a reclining position, presumably in an altered state, while being surrounded by a swarm of eyes emanating from a centre that radiates white light. As for Debernardi, his painting *Shaman Cosmico* is featured on *Inner Paths to Outer Space – Journeys to Alien Worlds through Psychedelics and Other Spiritual Technologies* (2008) by Rick Strassman *et al.* The Peruvian painter draws inspiration from ayahuasca visions, resulting in finely detailed and colourful artworks, which often includes non-human animals, plants and beings belonging to the spirit world.

What is the real purpose of designing books? Andrew Haslam, designer and course leader at Central Saint Martins College of Art and Design in London, says in *Book Design – A Comprehensive Guide* that, "A book cover is a promise made by a publisher on behalf of an author to a reader".[4] Book design in psychedelic literature is, of course, no different. In the second part of this essay I will discuss the imagery that is the result of these promises.

---

3 Taaffe, Philip. *Philip Taaffe and Fred Tomaselli in Conversation, with Raymond Foye and Rani Singh.* Philiptaaffe.info, 2002. Retrieved from http://www.philiptaaffe.info/Interviews_Statements/Tomaselli-Smith-Taaffe.php.
4 Haslam, Andrew. *Book Design – A Comprehensive Guide.* New York: Harry N. Abrams, 2006, 160.

Visionary Design

AN ATTEMPT AT DEFINING THE ENDLESS STREAM OF PSYCHEDELIC IMAGERY

The Eyes are wings of the Soul - they see us to Heaven.[5] *– Alex Grey*

As a starting point for discussing psychedelic book covers, I have put the most common motifs into three categories. They are:

—⁓— Mushrooms and plants

—⁓— Human and non-human animals

—⁓— Abstract shapes and typography

Obviously, if pushed, many book covers can be placed in more than one category. The purpose of creating these categories is to show *major currents* in the designs. Further research may show that the categories need to be improved upon or altogether redefined. However, at the present moment I find them a useful tool when discussing the covers. In the *Mushrooms and plants* category one finds various psychoactive drugs. Mushroom species include *Psilocybe cubensis*, *Psilocybe semilanceata* and, of course, *Amanita muscaria*, also known as the fly agaric. Examples of plants are peyote, *Banisteriopsis caapi* and *Datura*. The *Human and non-human animals* category includes the following subcategories: *Indigenous peoples* (often South or Central American; typically shamans); *Portraits of authors* (usually found on biographies); *The human body* (body parts such as the eye); *Non- human animals* (e.g. birds, snakes and dolphins). The *Abstract shapes and typography* category includes various shapes such as spirals, circles and concentric objects. These are often symbolising visions seen while in altered states of consciousness and needless to say usually have a psychedelic aesthetic. This category also includes typographic covers, which consist of typography only and are devoid of images. Before looking into the most common themes, a few words should be said about imagery that is only rarely seen on the covers. For example industrially manufactured objects are almost never included. A rare example is the previously mentioned *Be Here Now* (1971) by Ram Dass, which includes a chair placed in an abstract shape where lines and the phrase "Be here now" constitutes a yantra. In addition, objects such as vehicles are seldom included on the covers, even though the 2008 edition of *The Electric Kool-Aid Acid Test* by Tom Wolfe, in accordance with the story, has a bus on the front cover. Another example of an unusual motif is seen on *Millbrook – The True Story of the Early Years of the Psychedelic Revolution* (1977) by Art Kleps, which features a picture of the estate.

I. MUSHROOMS AND PLANTS

For obvious reasons there are mushrooms aplenty on front covers of psychedelic

---

5 Twitter.com, 15 January 2014. Retrieved from https://twitter.com/alexgreycosm

literature. The perhaps most commonly depicted species is the *Amanita muscaria*. An early example of psychedelic literature with this mushroom species on the front cover is R. Gordon Wasson's 1968 book *Soma – Divine Mushroom of Immortality*. Other, more recent, examples of front covers featuring fly agarics are the 2008 paperback edition of *Shroom – A Cultural History of the Magic Mushroom* by Andy Letcher, and Arik Roper's 2009 art book *Mushroom Magick – A Visionary Field Guide*, featuring Roper's art on the cover. Since the *Amanita muscaria* is so iconic and eye-catching it is very likely we will continue to see front covers depicting this mythological mushroom.

Even though *Amanita muscaria* is found growing on many locations around the world, it is only rarely used as a mind-expanding drug. Those who have experimented with the mushroom seem to find it somewhat disappointing, and, at higher doses, unpredictable and disturbing with unwelcome side effects. But this fascinating white spotted red mushroom has nevertheless become a staple in psychedelic imagery. The fact that psilocybin containing species such as *Psilocybe cubensis* are far more commonly used as a mind-expanding drug doesn't seem to make any difference; their visual appearance simply can't compete with the *Amanita muscaria*.

Unlike the brownish psilocybin containing species, the fly agaric screams for attention. Obviously, this is a quality that appeals to most designers and publishers. The smaller *Psilocybe semilanceata*, or the *liberty cap* as it is also called, has a form – usually conical to bell-shaped with an umbo – that is actually more easily depicted than the fly agaric. Still, the *Psilocybe semilanceata* is rarely seen on book covers. The mushroom is featured on the front cover of *A Guide to British Psilocybin Mushrooms* by Richard Cooper. Published in 1977 and, after being pirated, followed by a new edition in 1994, this thin little book contains a series of beautiful illustrations credited to Graeme Jackson, which are also used on the front covers. Jackson has a poetic and slightly romantic yet seemingly precise style making the title worth looking up for the drawings alone.

An example of a cover that includes both mushrooms and plants is the 1993 edition of *True Hallucinations – Being an Account of the Author's Extraordinary Adventures in the Devil's Paradise* by Terence McKenna. Originally published as an audio book in 1984, it became highly influential and is of course a classic in psychedelic literature. The cover design of the print edition from 1993 is credited to Nita Ybarra, while the illustration on the front is by Peter Siu. In the middle of the front cover is a rectangular plate with Siu's illustration as well as title and author name, the latter written in a bow shape over the illustration. Around the plate are stylised leaves. The overall aesthetic harks back to Art Nouveau and is, of course, decidedly retro. At the centre of the cover is an illustration of a large mushroom with a smaller one at each side of it, and, at the left, there is a bird sitting on a branch. More than 20 years after it was published, it is still a cover that perfectly reflects its content.

Peyote is a well known psychedelic, but books exclusively on the cactus are rarely published today. The fairly low interest in the plant possibly has to do with it being overshadowed by the current popularity of ayahuasca shamanism. Peyote is also growing very slowly, making it substantially less accessible than many other psychedelics. Even so, from a historical perspective peyote plays a very important role in psychedelic culture. It is assumed that peyote has been used ritually among indigenous peoples in North and Central America for millennia. As for the western world, trip reports started to appear in the late 19th Century describing peyote intoxication, and, as mentioned before, in the 1950s, both Aldous Huxley and Henri Michaux experimented with mescaline, the active ingredient in peyote. In addition, the beat writers of that era were known to use the plant. An example of a cover design featuring peyote is the 1976 book *Peyote Hunt – The Sacred Journey of the Huichol Indians* by Barbara G. Myerhoff. Based on a photo by Myerhoff, the front cover of the eleventh paperback printing shows a basket of newly harvested peyote buttons.

II. Human and non-human animals

Indigenous peoples

When indigenous peoples are depicted they are often shamans originating from South or Central America, where there is a strong tradition of using plant based psychedelics. For example, the front cover of the 1992 edition of *Plants of the Gods – Their Sacred, Healing and Hallucinogenic Powers* by Richard Evans Schultes and Albert Hofmann, features a photograph of a medicine man called Salvador Chindoy of the Kamsá Tribe in southern Colombia. The photo is taken by Schultes, while the cover design is credited to Pat Gorman Design. Framing the photo is an orange graphic pattern, while outside of it are illustrations of psychedelics. Just like its contents, the cover is one of the classics in psychedelic literature.

Other examples of front covers showing indigenous peoples are the 1963 and 2001 editions of *The Yage Letters* by William S. Burroughs, featuring a black and white photo of a shaman, and *Peyote Vs. The State – Religious Freedom on Trial* (2009) by Garrett Epps, which has an illustration of two Native American shamans engaged in ritual activity.

Clearly, western culture has had a huge impact on indigenous peoples around the world, yet on the covers they still often appear somewhat unaffected by the west, as if they were frozen in a previous time. Although not wanting to downplay the designs mentioned above, there is reason to be sceptical of some of the covers that are featuring indigenous peoples. Of course, this can also be said of their contents. In his aforementioned book *Shroom*, Andy Letcher questions the way Mazatec shaman Maria Sabina has been portrayed by researchers. Included in the book is a picture, taken in the 1980s, of her playing an acoustic guitar. As Letcher points out, westerners, presumably wanting her to be thought of as a primitive curandera, failed to mention she played the instrument.[6]

---

6 Letcher, Andy. *Shroom – A Cultural History of the Magic Mushroom*. New York: Harper Perennial, 2008, 108.

Portraits of authors

As in most literary genres, portraits are usually seen on biographies. The perhaps most well known autobiography in psychedelic literature is *LSD – My Problem Child* by Albert Hofmann. The cover of the 2013 edition of the book shows the scientist in glasses wearing a white laboratory coat, while the 2005 edition features a photo of him without glasses, dressed in a sweater and grey-haired. Interestingly, both covers feature the word "LSD" in a very big font size, indicating that, generally speaking, people are still more familiar with the name of the drug than the name of its discoverer. As a side note, books written by famous authors, such as Huxley or Castaneda, often have their names in big letters on the front covers.

When looking at psychedelic literature from a gender perspective, one soon finds that the genre is heavily male-dominated. This is of course reflected on the cover designs, where very few women are depicted. Examples of covers showing portraits of authors who are women include Marlene Dobkin de Rios's 2009 book *The Psychedelic Journey of Marlene Dobkin de Rios – 45 Years with Shamans, Ayahuasqueros, and Ethnobotanists*, and the 2000 edition of *Sisters of the Extreme – Women Writing on the Drug Experience* by Cynthia Palmer and Michael Horowitz. Featured on the latter are, among others, Grace Slick, singer of 1960s psychedelic rock band The Jefferson Airplane. Incidentally, the first edition of the book, published under the name *Shaman Woman, Mainline Lady – Women's Writings on the Drug Experience* (1982), features an illustration of an unidentified pipe-smoking woman surrounded by *Art Nouveau* styled vegetation. The cover brings to mind 1960s poster design, which was often heavily influenced by *Art Nouveau*.

The human body

As mentioned earlier, the eye is a very common image on front covers in psychedelic literature. Some examples where a single eye is central to the design include front covers of *Doing Your Own Being* (1973) by Ram Dass, *Cleansing the Doors of Perception – The Religious Significance of Entheogenic Plants and Chemicals* (2000) by Huston Smith and *The Psychedelic Future of the Mind – How Entheogens are Enhancing Cognition, Boosting Intelligence, and Raising Values* (2013) by Thomas B. Roberts. The eye is clearly a well- worn cliché in psychedelic book design, and no designer will get any points for originality for putting another eye on the cover. Still, given that it is a powerful symbol of perception it is no wonder the eye is used repeatedly.

When it comes to other individual parts of the human body, faces are sometimes included, as exemplified by the cover of *The Psychedelic Renaissance – Reassessing the Role of Psychedelic Drugs in the 21st Century Psychiatry and Society* (2013) by Ben Sessa, where a part of a face of a man is seen. Other body parts are very seldom used in psychedelic book design, a rare exception being the front cover of the 1986 edition of *Psilocybin – Magic Mushroom Grower's Guide* by O.T. Oss and O.N. Oeric – pseudonyms for Terence and Dennis McKenna – where the imagery of Cathleen Harrison's illustration includes a hand.

Non-human animals

Non-human animals are fairly common on the covers of psychedelic literature. For example, a dolphin is included on *The Scientist – A Metaphysical Biography* (1996) by John C. Lilly, who, in addition to inventing the isolation tank, made research on dolphin communication. Another cover showing a dolphin is *Psychedelia – An Ancient Culture, A Modern Way of Life* (2012) by Patrick Lundborg. It is based on a painting by Anderson Debernardi and includes several other animals such as snakes and a bird. Birds are also seen on several Castaneda covers, such as the paperback of the 30th anniversary edition of *The Teachings of Don Juan* (1998).

The butterfly – a symbol of transformation – is occasionally seen in psychedelic imagery. Still, it is not as common on book covers in psychedelic literature as one may think. A butterfly is included on the cover of the 1993 edition of *The Invisible Landscape – Mind, Hallucinogens and the I Ching* by Terence and Dennis McKenna. The inclusion of the motif makes sense; Terence McKenna worked as a butterfly collector before he became a writer. There is also a butterfly on the front cover of the 2003 book *Magic Mushrooms* by Peter Stafford.

It appears the archaic "back to the nature" sentiment of the psychedelic experience goes well with non-human animal imagery. Yet psychedelic culture's relation to non-human animals clearly have a troubled past given that thousands of them have been used – and killed – in scientific animal testing involving psychedelics.

III. Abstract shapes and typography

Abstract shapes

These are very often used on psychedelic book design. Typically they have a psychedelic aesthetic in the sense that they are obviously meant to make the reader associate to visions one may experience while in altered states of consciousness. They can take many forms. Spirals are often seen, an example being the cover of *2012 – The Return of Quetzalcoatl* (2007) by Daniel Pinchbeck. Designed by Gretchen Achilles, it consists of a white spiralling shape on a green background. Compared to other books in the genre, the cover design is quite minimalistic. Still, the illustration has an alluring, somewhat psychedelic, quality.

Concentric shapes – especially circles – are also a common motif. Visual artist Fred Tomaselli often includes them in his paintings, making his work especially interesting for publishers of psychedelic literature. The three previously mentioned books that have his art on the cover all feature concentric circles. This is perhaps most prominent on *Are You Experienced?* by Ken Johnson, which features a detail of Tomaselli's 2009 artwork *Big Eye*.

The Fenris Wolf

Typographic covers

In 1900 basically all covers were typographic.[7] Later, book design changed radically thanks to the technological developments that took place in the 20th Century. Today's typographic covers have a wide diversity: Some express an experimental playfulness, while others signal an academic seriousness. An example of the latter is the design of *LSD, Man & Society* edited by Richard C. DeBold and Russell C. Leaf. On the front cover of the 1968 paperback edition the title is written in large letters in serif typography, while the editor's name is in a smaller font size at the bottom. Included on the front cover is also a short description saying that the facts about LSD are "soberly stated" in the book. In the introduction the drug is described as "a serious problem",[8] and contributing author Donald B. Louria suggests "severe penalties" for those who manufacture or sell LSD.[9] The book title is written in red letters on a black background. Red is, of course, often used as a symbol of danger.

What may come as a surprise to some is that the very first cover of Carlos Castaneda's *The Teachings of Don Juan* – originally written as a master's thesis at UCLA – looked completely different compared to how the book was packaged in the seventies and onwards. Instead of imagery such as birds and shamans, the 1968 edition had a very clean typographic cover. Clearly, this formal looking design gave the book an air of academia. As readers of psychedelic literature are well aware of, the anthropologist was accused of making up most of his experiences with Don Juan. Regardless of what was the actual truth behind Castaneda's writings, the covers that followed on later editions and printings make the book appear more like fiction literature than a scientific work.

ENDNOTES

Red books, like rubies; emerald books; books bound in white jade; books of agate, of aquamarine, of yellow topaz; lapis lazuli books whose colour was so intense, so intrinsically meaningful, that they seemed to be on the point of leaving the shelves to thrust themselves more insistently on my attention.[10] – Aldous Huxley

In the mid-1990s, while on a holiday in London, I bought my first book in psychedelic literature. It was a thin, stapled book – a booklet is perhaps a better word for it – with an intriguing cover. The book in question was the previously mentioned 1994 edition of *A Guide to British Psilocybin Mushrooms* by Richard Cooper. Some 20 years on I still read psychedelic literature, and after finishing this essay I can't help to think that the cover design of that first book had a strong impact on my interest in the genre.

7 Haslam. *Book Design – A Comprehensive Guide*, 160.
8 DeBold, Richard C. and Leaf, Russel C. (Eds.). *LSD, Man & Society*. Middletown: Wesleyan University Press. 1968, xii.
9 DeBold and Leaf (Eds.). *LSD, Man & Society*, 44.
10 Huxley, Aldous. *The Doors of Perception*. London: Flamingo. 1994, 9.

Visionary Design

During my research I went through a great number of book covers. A few of them are sitting on my bookshelf, while many of them were found online. I also had the great fortune to access the drug bibliography and cover scans of designer and former book collector *Jdyf333*. His bibliography contains over 1400 titles, complete with publishing data and personal comments, while his collection of scans features over 4000 book (and magazine) covers. Going through all the covers, I realised that in the past I had not given the designs any deeper thought. I assume I was too focused on their contents to analyse their designs. This is not to say I did not appreciate a beautiful cover when I came across one; they have always been an important part of the reading experience. I just did not realise *how* important, possibly because they are, strangely enough, almost never discussed. Hopefully this will change with the growing interest in the visual aspects of psychedelic culture, which has been seen in recent years.

HIGHER MAGICK:
CANNABIS AND THE NATURE OF REALITY

Philip H. Farber

One of the promises and primary purposes of the use of entheogens is development of self knowledge. On the personal level, that includes revelation about our lives and insight into our own spirituality and consciousness. On a broader scale, we hope for insights into the phenomenon of consciousness itself, clues to the essential nature of the human experience. And that's where the psychonaut and shaman may find common interests with the scientist.

Given the political climate of the last 70 or so years, only a few scientists, historically, were bold enough to transcend the taboos and do meaningful research into mind-expanding plants and drugs. Fortunately, that's beginning to change and, in the case of cannabis, the scientific research may, right now, be on the brink of revelations that the shaman and magician can appreciate. It may be a fortuitous confluence of events; we now have tools to study the human organism, including the brain, which never before existed in our culture – at a time when worldwide acceptance of the plant is growing rapidly.

In *The Fenris Wolf 6*, I referenced the role of cannabis in memory reconsolidation, a process by which our brains sort and delineate the world we experience. Understanding this process may be worth deeper exploration (and some speculation).

First, a bit of background:

Human brains spend a hell of a lot of time sorting and searching. Every time we encounter a word, to some extent, we have to sort through definitions and contexts and find the appropriate meaning. For example, the word "chair" can refer to a wide range of seating equipment. In making sense of the word, our brains may flip through a few different kinds of chairs before fixing on the one that makes sense in the current context, perhaps the one that you're sitting in now. Usually this happens too fast for your conscious mind to track, but when we start to pay attention, we can notice the process.

EXERCISE I

Think of a time when you felt really, really good.

So what happened when you attempted to recall a time when you felt really good? Most people, when encountering a vague suggestion of this kind, will find themselves recalling not just one, but at least several memories, and then comparing and contrasting for a few moments until finding one that comes closest to the criterion of "really, really good."

If this happened to you, what you just experienced was a process called *transderivational search* [1] which is mediated by a feature of the human brain known to neuroscientists as the Default Mode Network (DMN). Here's another example:

EXERCISE 2

Picture a really sexy face.

Whose face did you end up picturing? How many faces did you have to look at and adjust before you settled on that one? How quickly did the process happen?

Okay, one more for now:

EXERCISE 3

What's the most comfortable item of clothing that you own?

While the original concept of transderivational search was applied to linguistics, to the choices that we make in our words, these experiences of the DMN and sorting happen in every sense. We sort through images, voices, music, emotions, tactile feelings and every other form of human perception and internal representation, with equal ease. And we do it, consciously or unconsciously, on and off through most of our lives.

The discovery of the DMN by neuroscientist Marcus Raichle was in part unexpected. Dr. Raichle was hoping to measure baseline activity in the brain, to provide a statistical basis to compare with experimental activities. The idea was that when it wasn't doing anything consciously directed, the brain would power down like the hard drive in your computer, a mental screen saver would come on and the brain scans would show, in general, less activity than when the subject was working a math problem or solving a jigsaw puzzle. When Raichle and his team placed subjects in the fMRI machine with no specific instructions and scanned while they did "nothing," he found something odd. Certain areas of the brain, including the hippocampus, midline cortical structures, and some frontal cortex structures, would hook up in a new configuration and really go to work. Raichle didn't know what these brain areas were doing, chattering furiously to each other, but the brains were using 30% more energy than when the subjects were consciously working on mental activities. [2]

After years of study, scientists are figuring out what the DMN does. I'll cut to the short answer, so you can sort out what I'm getting at here.

The Default Mode Network creates reality.

Or, to state it in a wordier but more accurate way, the DMN is a physical component of the human organism that mediates the largely non-material process

1 Dilts, Robert and Judith DeLozier. *Encyclopedia of Systemic Neuro-Linguistic Programming and NLP New Coding.* Scotts Valley, CA: NLP University Press, 2000. p1467.
2 Marcus E. Raichle et al., "A default mode of brain function." *Proceedings of the National Academy of Sciences,* January 16, 2001 vol. 98 no. 2 676-682

of delineating and experiencing our world. It is the engine of sorting in the brain that also mediates some of the important processes of magick. And understanding how the DMN works in the brain can give important clues how to create more effective magick. I promise that after you give yourself a moment to sort through the range of things your brain wants to include as "important clues" or "effective magick," I'll explain what I mean.

The DMN can be thought of as an engine of narrative. It starts with active experience in the hippocampus, where the brain processes short term memory. This can be either something that you just experienced within the last, say, half a minute, or it could be something that you remembered, the memory being shunted back to short term memory so that you can experience parts of it again. If it is a memory, it already comes with some note in the margin from the last time it took a tour of the DMN. The notes in the margin come in the form of sensory markers called "submodalities." These are the qualities that we use to fine-tune our perceptions, for instance, brightness, dimness, volume, size, distance, location, color, movement, shape, and so on. If the narrative created by the DMN – the story of your life – were a motion picture, the submodalities would be the lighting, camera angles and sound design that are used to convey mood, passage of time, foreshadowing, and so on. Here's an example:

EXERCISE 4

Think of two things that are objectively the same (or pretty damn similar), but you like one and not the other. For instance, oak trees versus maple trees, Toyotas versus Hyundais, Coke versus Pepsi, pullover sweaters versus button-down sweaters, and so on. The stronger your feelings of like and dislike, the better.

First think of the thing you like and make a visual representation. Look at it in your mind. Eliminate context and background, so that you are only looking at the object in question. Notice where you have to aim your eyes to look at this imagining. Point to it. Notice the colors of the image – are they rich and vibrant or dull and subtle? Notice how large you have made the image, how far away from you it is, whether the lighting in the image is bright or dim.

Now perform the same experiment for the thing you don't like. Notice the qualities of the representation you make. Eliminate context and background. Notice where you have to aim your eyes. Point to it. Are the colors rich and vibrant or dull and subtle? Notice how large you have made the image, how far away from you it is, whether the lighting in the image is bright or dim, if the focus is sharp or blurry, if the image is moving or still.

Most people will notice some differences between these two internal representations. You will point to different locations or one will be larger, brighter, or more colorful than the other. Each one of us has a unique set of submodality tags that we apply, so the results of this experiment will be at least somewhat different for each person, but the lesson to be derived is that we represent images, sounds, feelings, tastes and smells to ourselves with variations that let us know crucial information about the memories or imaginings. Often these submodality differences will be reflected in metaphoric language: something very clever might be "brilliant" (have a brighter internal representation); someone you feel uncomfortable with might be "distant;" a friend with a distinctive personality might be "colorful;" a dynamic person might be represented as "larger than life;" something you don't like "smells rotten;" and so on. In each case, the content of the memory remains fairly consistent, although some way of viewing, hearing, feeling, tasting and smelling has been altered to convey a message. Those judgments and evaluations of perception help to adapt the memories or experience into the greater narrative.

The default mode network, as the engine of narrative, is the seat of the imagination. It runs our fantasies, daydreams, visualizations and hallucinations as tools to incorporate information into the over-arching tale of our existence. The submodality choices carry emotional and evaluative information along with the tale. The way the choices are made, running through a super-position of multiple possibilities before collapsing to a single delineation, parallels the process of measurement and delineation of particles in quantum physics. In effect, each submodality nuance that our DMN attaches to a memory defines what kind of reality, what story, we inhabit. And the DMN makes those delineations quite frequently.

Except when it doesn't. For some reason, focused attention and DMN activity are mutually exclusive. This is why your third grade teacher told you to stop daydreaming – you can't solve an arithmetic problem while your DMN is operating. For that, you need focused attention from the prefrontal cortex. Normally, that kind of focused attention shuts down the DMN and, vice versa, your wandering mind can prevent focused attention.

Unless you're stoned.

One of many roles of cannabinoid chemicals in the brain is moderation of the default mode network. In brain scan studies, it was observed that smoked cannabis switches on the DMN – without fully deactivating the areas of the brain involved in focused attention. Which means that when you are stoned, you can be focused and spacey at the same time, clever and creative, productive and imaginative. [3]

It means that your connection to the realm of imagination, myth, legend, symbol, and magical archetype, can remain active while you engage in almost any activity. The most ancient texts that mention cannabis, some thousands of years old, tell us that the herb was used to communicate with the spirit realm. No matter how often it was repeated in Chinese medical texts, Indian sacred writings, African lore, Arabic traditions and in writings from nearly every civilization that knew of the psychoactive qualities of cannabis, the whole "spirit realm" concept was usually branded primitive superstition and soundly ignored But now we can understand that there is a real basis for the connection between the plant and the world of thought-forms and imagination.

As well, what we can hold in focused attention is rather limited. In the 1950s,

3 Bossong et al. *Default Mode Network in the Effects of Δ9-Tetrahydrocannabinol (THC) on Human Executive Function*. PLoS One. 2013 Jul 31;8(7):e70074. doi: 10.1371/journal.pone.0070074. Print 2013

scientists determined that our conscious awareness can hold "seven plus or minus two" pieces of information at any one time. However accurate that number might be, it certainly does seem that the DMN can work with quite a bit more information at any one time, including every derivation of a transderivational search, and every detail of a vast plot arc. This creates opportunity for mystical experience, for perceiving the connections and patterns between apparently disparate objects and ideas. At the extreme end of cannabis-influenced mystical experience, consider Aleister Crowley's 1906 *Vision of the Universal Peacock:*

> *The 'millions of worlds' game – the peacock multiform with each 'eye' of its fan a mirror of glory wherein also another peacock – everything thus. (Here consciousness has no longer any knowledge of normal impression. Each thought is itself visualized as a World Peacock....) 1:20 A.M. Head still buzzing: wrote above. Samadhi is Hashish, an ye will; but Hashish is not Samadhi...* [4]

While Crowley apparently struggled, at that early date, with the role that cannabis might play in magick, his "World Peacock" is a fine description of a cannabis revelation, the richness and depth of information in a cosmic-scale narrative, and some interesting hints as to what submodality cues Uncle Al's brain might favor.

Cannabis may disrupt short term memory when you're high (experiential evidence of its action on the hippocampus, processor of short term memory), but the flow of narrative creation continues unabated and you may find later that your experiences are written large upon on the screen of long term memory. Ordinary events and objects become imbued with mythic importance. Your hand becomes the symbol of the universe's striving, a trip to White Castle becomes an epic quest, a sip of beverage becomes a peak experience, a visualized shape gains depth and form, and the elements of ritual exude their symbolic properties. And each perception becomes consolidated in memory with submodality markers denoting importance in the story of your life.

> *[I]t is the Quality of this Grass to quicken the Operation of Thought it may be a Thousandfold, and moreover to figure each Step in Images complex and overpowering in Beauty, so that one hath not Time wherein to conceive, much less to utter any Word for a Name of any one of them. Also, such was the Multiplicity... that the Memory holdeth no more any one of them, but only a certain Comprehension of the Method, wordless by Reason of its Subtility. Now, therefore, must I make by my Will a Concentration mighty and terrible of any Thought, that I may bring forth this Mystery in Expression. For this Method is of Virtue and Profit; by it mayst thou come easily and with Delight to the Perfection of Truth, it is no Odds from what Thought thou makest the first Leap in thy Meditation, so that thou mayst know that every Road endeth in Monsalvat, and the Temple of the Sangraal.* [5]

4 Crowley journal entry from OTO archive, quoted in L. Sutin, *Do What Thou Wilt.* St. Martin's Press, New York. 2000.
5 Crowley, Aleister. *The Book of Thoth.* Samuel Weiser, Inc. York Beach, ME, 1974.

Painting My Will

Kendell Geers

He who fights with monsters should look to it that he himself does not become a monster. And when you gaze long into an abyss the abyss also gazes into you.

– Friedrich Nietzsche, *Beyond Good and Evil*

From this green earth; of all the mighty world
Of eye, and ear, both what they half create,
And what perceive; well pleased to recognise
In nature and the language of the sense,
The anchor of my purest thoughts, the nurse,
The guide, the guardian of my heart, and soul
Of all my moral being

– William Wordsworth, *Lines Written a Few Miles Above Tintern Abbey*

It is said that it is darkest just before the dawn, but in the darkness, everything is possible for there are no shadows and no horizons. That's how I felt, going every day to my studio, without reason, to do nothing, clinging to my depression as consolation for losing my way within a system.

ISANG does not profile or endorse individual artists without the interpretive intervention of curatorial activity, whether this is directed by one of ISANG's staff curators or by an external curator in consultation with ISANG's own curators. This is to ensure that a minimum degree of institutional impartiality and public accessibility is maintained. Therefore, henceforth we will liaise only with [the curator] on all curatorial decisions, and Kendell [Geers] will be consulted where necessary, and as a courtesy.

Such were the harsh terms and conditions contractually imposed upon me by the South African National Gallery and my once upon a time best friend, the curator of my first retrospective in the country of my skull. My contemporary desire and historical intentions meant little in the face of a system that protects the weak and stupid behind desktop bureaucracies of power. How could Marcel Duchamp's statement that "the creative act is not performed by the artist alone; the spectator

99

brings the work in contact with the external world by deciphering and interpreting its inner qualification and thus adds his contribution to the creative act"[1] have been so badly misunderstood? It has grown ever more common to denigrate the power of the artist in favour of the curator and collector, but rarely in my experience to such extremes. Eventually the ineptitude of the National Gallery's appointed curator and their own museological incompetence led to the show being cancelled, but they were all too quick to blame it on "the artist" for having "interfered too much" in his own retrospective. The damage had been done and I slowly baked myself in pity and despair with creative resignation.

Then one day, I risked peering through the dark clouds of doubt and despair and noticed the faintest glimmer of light upon a horizon that I did not even know existed. It was a spark of impossible, the glow of the inconceivable and a sparkle of insanity, as the sun was rising upon the realisation that I had spent a year of my depression making paintings. Not some conceptual trick or a self-conscious parody of painting, but simply paint on canvas.

As a strict disciple of Marcel Duchamp, so called retinal art was the domain of the arch enemy and foremost amongst the ranks of the foe was painting. I had even once made a work of art about his disdain, quoting Duchamp's favourite aphorism "Bête Comme un Peintre"(as stupid as a painter). Adding insult to injury, I remember recoiling in horror at Matisse's words "What I dream of is an art of balance, of purity and serenity, devoid of troubling or depressing subject matter, an art which could be for every mental worker, for the businessman as well as the man of letters, for example, a soothing, calming influence on the mind, something like a good armchair which provides relaxation from physical fatigue." From an early age I had decided that I would never make art for the tired businessman, never make art that avoided the pains of my lived experience and certainly I would never compromise my art to make paintings.

As I look back now, I understand, perhaps as self-consolation, that my first steps into the world of paint were everything but "an art of balance, of purity and serenity, devoid of troubling or depressing subject matter" for from my anger and despair, I began pissing on canvasses painted with copper and watching with alchemical amusement as they transformed into "vert de gris" under the influence of my urine. I had neither an intention nor did I consider what I was doing to be anything but a cathartic exorcism as I laid waste to the memories of a friend, colleague and my faith in the very institution of art. But, for reasons unknown, I did not stop there and leapt out into the darkness on a pilgrimage that would take me beyond the boundaries of everything I had ever been taught, thought I understood and way beyond the limits of what I thought I believed in.

The great twentieth century magus Aleister Crowley defined magick as the method of science with the aim of religion. For many years now, I had been searching in all the wrong places to find a way to create in harmony with that same spirit and principle. It is especially difficult to speak of an impalpable spirit in an art world saturated with gross materialism, a system that has abandoned integrity,

---

1 Published in: Robert Lebel: *Marcel Duchamp*. New York: Paragraphic Books, 1959, pp. 77/78

vision and sincerity in favour of profit dictated by taste. Rituals of consumption have all but eroded away the transformative power of art and with every art fair the spirit of art dies a little more.

All creation myths begin with chaos, the darkness before the dawn, the inconceivable nothingness of divine creation ex nihilo. "Chaos (Greek, *khaos*) refers to the formless or void state preceding the creation of the universe or cosmos in the Greek creation myths, more specifically the initial "gap" created by the original separation of heaven and earth."[2] Out of this chaos, God, or the Gods created order in the forms of night and day, earth and sky, air and water and eventually the fauna and flora until at the very end, human beings were created in the image of God, or the Gods. "So God created man in his *own* image, in the image of God created he him; male and female created he them" *Genesis* 1:27

It is because of this implicit embodiment of the divine will, that at heart, every human being is defined by an intrinsic need to believe, whether that be Biblical, Capitalist, Atheist or Marxist by nature. In the end our faith, call it hope if you must, is always that which defines us.

Once I had cleared my mind and understood that my depression was only polluting my being and scarring my perceptions, I opened my mind and allowed the spirit of painting to reveal itself to me. The unrolled, unstretched, canvas lay mutely upon the studio floor, a virgin white sheet of infinite potential. This "Prima Materia" of my creative potential awaited, with neither judgement nor prejudice, the form, content, intention and embodiment of my imagination. I have since found that the only way into the canvas was literally with, and through my entire body, for my thoughts alone could not support my imaginary weight needed to hurl myself within the meters of cotton or linen beckoning and teasing with coy insolence. I found that thinking with my stomach and feet, with my penis and prostate, with my back and elbows, knees and lungs, made me intelligent in ways that thinking with my hands and cerebral cortex alone could not. I remember thinking about Jackson Pollock and Yves Klein but could not stop myself there. According to Goethe, "The human being himself, to the extent that he makes sound use of his senses, is the most exact physical apparatus that can exist." Whilst he was speaking in terms of a holistic science, he could just as well have been describing my own method of creation for I am using my entire body, my full holistic being, as my paintbrush.

In Istanbul fortune tellers throw molten lead into water or break open a raw egg, observe coffee grinds in an upturned cup, as means to read a person's past, present and future. In the hands of a gifted seer, these seemingly unrelated random processes of chance are the tools that enable the visionary to see through and beyond the bounds of time and space. In South Africa *Sangomas* ("witchdoctors") throw sticks, stones and bones, in Europe they read Tarot Cards, in Asia tea leaves, but it's never about the medium as much as about the seer, for any object or process that s/ he has faith in may be used. The object or process is merely the trigger or key with which to open the doors of perception for everything that exists is connected and

---

2 Wikipedia

interconnected to everything else within the divine matrix. Perceiving something changes the nature of that thing and vice-versa. At its most scientifically reductive, the quantum physicist's intention to prove either the wave or particle nature of sub-atomic reality changes the results of the experiment as two mutually exclusive irreconcilable contraries can exist simultaneously in the past, present and future, in different places within the universe, all depending on the perception and intention of the scientist.

I would even suggest, as so many mystics, occultists and Jungian psychologists have, that there is no such thing as chance, nor even synchronicity, and that every seemingly random event or process that takes place around us, is in fact a mirror of a divine destiny. Is it not curious that classic psychologists and sceptics are very willing to accept the Rorschach Test as proof of an unconscious, to readily accept the results of such tests, but cannot accept that this unconscious world might be every bit as real as the world we call reality. Whether we accept or believe in it, all things created share the same divine spark and therefor connected and interconnected by mystical thinking threads so the layout of the tarot cards are not coincidental so much as the external mirror of an internal reality.

The canvas yields, ever so slowly, but still demands complete commitment on my part. My entire body and being, mind and spirit is summoned in the exorcism of consciousness and perception that must take place before the paint accepts to write itself upon the canvas of my soul within my imagination. I cast my paint upon the floor, like Jackson Pollock throwing dice, trusting that every splash, blot, mark, stain, bleed and blur is guided by the unseen forces of my true will in harmony with nature. The paint explodes like a cocktail of fireworks in a dark stormy sky. I trust in the canvas field as much as in the intelligence of the paint, in the animistic spirits of the mineral, vegetable, animal and chemical pigments, as we all collaborate in laying down a destiny like the seers molten lead finding form in water. William Burroughs and Brion Gysin might have called this unseen intelligence the "Third Mind" and William Blake would have named it "Second Sight," Wordsworth called it the "language of the sense," but for me it's simply a force of my nature in tune with all others.

Like every student of conceptual art, I had read Sol Lewitt's *Sentences on Conceptual Art* and like everybody else did not pay much attention to what was written so much as to what I wanted to read. For too long, I glossed over the very first sentence that sets the tone for the entire manifesto, that "Conceptual artists are mystics rather than rationalists. They leap to conclusions that logic cannot reach."[3]

Without any equivocation Lewitt locates conceptual art within the realms of mysticism and beyond the logic of rational understanding and linear language. At first, I had mistrusted my paintings as therapy, denied that I had been foolish enough to cross over the threshold from conceptual art into the autographic domain of gesture, but then it struck me like a bolt of lightning, that I had in fact left all rational logic behind and leapt into an irrational abyss and was in fact creating quintessential "Conceptual Art."

3 First published in *0-9* (New York), 1969, and *Art-Language* (England), May 1969

Painting my Will

None of it made any sense and the self-appointed janitors and doorman of the art market would certainly never grant me access into their endless lists of artists who are rewarded for doing the right thing, but I certainly felt as though I had not sold my soul to the devil so much as taken another step into the unknown on the stairway to heaven. Given that Duchamp had lied about the last two decades of his life, lied that he had given up making art to play chess, when in fact he was secretly working on "Etant Donne," his last masterpiece which would turn out to be his least readymade and most classic sculpture of all, I felt happy to embrace the turn of events that destiny had thrust upon my preconceptions of art. Such a conclusion, that today conceptual artists might follow an irrational logic into the mystical domain, via painting, certainly flies in the face of every expectation and assumption might just prove to be every bit as subversive as a dry self-defined sentence on a wall or a banal repetitive 8,7 cm stripe was in 1968.

Painting differs from sculpture, at least as I had been working, in that painting begins from absolutely nothing apart from an empty canvas support, the clean white sheet of haunting emptiness, the portal into Yves Klein's "Void." Every mark, line, dot or shape has meaning and soils the purity of the field. A single dot is enough to punctuate and resonate with meaning beyond our ability to comprehend. A dot may be the viral spark of an idea, the full stop at the end of an epic, the smallest blemish that sets the virgin aside and is the mark of the beast. From the point to the line and into the triangle, the dimensions unfold and add up. From the square to the pentagram, on to the hexagram, layers of meaning and complexity evolve, layer upon layer until Plato's octahedron, dodecahedron and icosahedron and Mandelbrot's fractal images provide us with the keys into reading reality.

From beneath the linear dimensions the fields of colour emerge, harmonies and disharmonies alike, washes and glows, runs and bleeds. Colour fascinates because it is both a condition of ephemeral light and at the same time the two retinal psychological expression of emotion. We are coloured by the experience of light and dark whether it be riding the wavelengths of light or surfing the surface of pigments. "Goethe pictures to himself that light and darkness relate to each other like the north and south pole of a magnet. The darkness can weaken the light in its working power. Conversely, the light can limit the energy of the darkness. In both cases colour arises" (Rudolf Steiner). In Goethe's own words "Yellow is a light which has been dampened by darkness; Blue is a darkness weakened by light".

Colour introduced itself upon the canvas of my experience emotionally, spiritually, symbolically as well as through the prism of pigment and perception, simultaneously being both tactile and totemic. The pigments are never simply about colour for they retain and embody the memory and animistic spirits of their animal, mineral or vegetable source. Vermillion is created through the highly toxic explosion of mercury and sulphur heated until the form the alchemical marriage of male and female forces, the creative and destructive principles, the impossible union of fire and water.

Whilst most contemporary pigments can now be chemically engineered, their emotional, symbolic and spiritual resonances remain rooted within their alchemical origins. The mortally dangerous health risks of creating Vermillion made it worth its weight in gold in the Middle Ages for it was the alchemical marriage that, if properly understood held the key that would ultimately transform lead into gold. Even today pure Cinnabar, the naturally occurring equivalent mineral found at the sulphurous edge of active volcanoes, remain amongst the most expensive natural pigments on the market. In the fourth century BC purple dyes were traded for its weight at the same price as silver, for it was extremely difficult to extract the pigment from the shells of carnivorous sea snails. This value lies at the root of both Papal Purple and Royal Blue.

In a system known as *Gematria*, Kabbalists assign numbers to letters and vice versa. Every word is a number and reality is as much numerological as it is physical. It is believed that to know the true name and number of God would grant one the very power of God. We erroneously assume that these signs, symbols and numbers are our rational logical means with which to understand highly complex divine concepts, but what if they were really at the origin of creation? According to the *Koran*, the first thing that Allah created was the pen and with it he then wrote the world into existence. The *Bible* confers that "In the beginning was the Word, and the Word was with God, and the Word was God"[4]

It is testimony to our human ego that we assume without any hesitation that we are God's gift to the world and simply assume our intelligence to be superior to all others. Even if the *Bible* tells us so, we certainly could never accept that "words" may have created us rather than the other way around, that words, symbols, signs and images may turn out to be the blueprint in the creations of the world as we don't understand it. As hard as I have tried, I have not been able to escape the eternal return of these symbols, the haunting of signs that force themselves upon me as the paintings seem to give birth to their own selves with me as their midwife.

The ancients seem to have known this better than we do and explained such things in their myths and with their superstitions. Gurus, mystics, alchemists, shamans, monks, pagans and some musicians, artists and poets have spoken of it in their poetry, in their holy books and bibles, with their paintings, music, prophecies and fairy tales. At least two Nobel Prize winning scientists (Kary Mullis and Francis Crick) have confessed to have received the keys to their scientific discoveries whilst tripping on LSD. According to Aleister Crowley "In ninety-nine cases out of a hundred, any stimulant of whatever nature operates by destroying temporarily the inhibitions of education. The ordinary man loses the veneer of civilisation. But if you get the right man, the administration of a drug is quite likely to supress his mental facilities, with the result that his genius is set free" *(Diary of a Drug Fiend)*

Years after his death, Carl Jung's *Red Book* was finally made public, a book written by means "of a technique developed by Jung which he termed active imagination. As Jung described it, he was visited by two figures, an old man and a young woman, who identified themselves as Elijah and Salome. They were accompanied by a large black snake. In time, the Elijah figure developed into a guiding spirit that Jung called *Philemon*. The figures, according to Jung, "brought home to me the

---

4 *John* 1:1

crucial insight that there are things in the psyche which I do not produce, but which produce themselves and have their own life. The Philemon figure represented superior insight and communicated through mythic imagery. The images did not appear to come from Jung's own experience and Jung interpreted them as products of the collective unconscious"[5]

The open format of the empty canvas opened my eyes to ways of being and modes of seeing that no other medium of art ever had before. Having been forged upon the anvil of disillusionment and forced through the eye of the needle of despair, I felt like the proverbial camel in the cultural desert and knew better than to resist. I walked the thin line between that which was in within my control and that which I could not control, call it chaos, disorder, entropy or what you will. Creation and destruction in balance, mutually irreconcilable, never at peace. Too much creation and harmony and the results are predictably comfortable, slipping into lifeless kitsch. In contrast too much destruction generates discomfort to the point of nausea. It's vitally important that my work be built upon the foundation of points of contact and points of resistance, the contact zone being the vocabulary and languages conceded us through the annals of history, the security of being able to browse the legacies of art and its codes. And yet the avant garde cycle of life demands the symbolic killing of the historical father which can only be done through the violence of the unknown.

In many ways I imagine that Francis Picabia might be the father I have to kill (and Rrose Sellavy of course my symbolic mother) and his "La Sainte Vierge" the umbilical cord from which I hang my paintings. A few simple drops of Indian Ink marks the virgin territory that give rise to an unparalleled symbolic embodiment. Historically the deceptively simple gesture, first reproduced in the March 1920 issue of Picabia's *391* journal, has been interpreted at classic Dada provocation. It is read as a heretical and sacrilegious insult against both art history and Catholic faith. It has been suggested that the ink represent the blood stains of a virgin birth or even the loss of virginity itself, the blood of defilement.

Most art historians bound to their armchairs of conventional perception, locked into three dimensions of rational logic, sweep this work into the trashcan of history as a prime example of Dada absurdity and pure nonsense. As proof, Picabia is quoted as saying "We strive toward White considered as a psychic entity, or to give concrete expression to this goal through the immutable relations of colour and music, we strive toward pure 'tone' = 435 vibrations." Very aptly, he continues and explains that "It is only after the continuous and infinite awakening of the 'self' that we have grown able to perceive this immeasurable ideal in the space of nothingness" [6]

Absurd to the extreme, and yet reading the very same quote from an animistic point of view makes perfect sense. The disregard of Cartesian logic does not make Picabia's work and statements nonsense so much as non-sense, the perfectly sound conclusion that rationalists cannot reach.

In another less well known reproduction of the same image within the pages of

5 Carl Jung (1961) Aniela Jaffe, ed. *Memories, Dreams, Reflections.* pp 178-194
6 "Open Letter to H.R. Lenormand", 1920

another journal, *Les Hommes du Jour*, Picabia juxtaposes his holy virgin with Ingres' *La Vierge Adorant l'Hostie* from 1841 beneath the title *Deux Ecoles*. With an open mind, it reads as a clear indication that he did not consider his ink blot sacrilegious so much as a different perception of a classic subject, a point of resistance within a point of contact. In the Ingres version, the virgin prays devoutly to the Eucharist wafer, the unleavened bread that from a Catholic point of view is the animistic embodiment of the Christ's spirit, whereas Picabia's holy virgin is at once both the ink and the paper as much as it is the animistic embodiment of the virgin.

"Accidents were awful things. She winked again. The mast was straight; the waves were regular; the lighthouse was upright; but the blot had spread." (Virginia Woolf, *Jacob's Room*)

Picabia's holy virgin is none other than "Mother Nature" and "Father Destiny" in a symbolic celebration of their divine union. The ink made from soot, the black residue of fire, is cast upon the paper according to the laws of chance and gravity in a divine ejaculatory splash that takes on the shape and form of a destiny that might even be read by a shaman or seer. Meaning is acquired as much through the perception and reading of the viewer or seer as through the intention of the artist, but above all else, the virgin speaks with an inked tongue. Under other circumstances she might manifest in or as a cave or waterfall, with tears of blood or even, as she did to Bernard of Clairvaux, spouting forth milk from her breasts.

The question I was left to answer was what if believing might not be seeing and what if there might well be other intelligences at work. What if our five senses of perceiving the three generally accepted dimensions were nothing more than a transmitting and receiving apparatus and that our true selves existed in worlds (and words) far beyond that which the apparatus is able to understand, much less even perceive? What if the selves we think of as the real, and the world we live in, is only one tiny facet of our greater being within a world infinitely more dimensionally complex than we could ever imagine? What if the Rorschach ink blot or Picabia's *La Sainte Vierge* are not so much windows into our unconscious, as the very keys through which our other selves are opening doors in order to communicate with us?

According to the *Rig Vedas*, one of the oldest books ever written, this world of three dimensions and five senses is "maya", nothing more than an illusion. The Tibetan Buddhists and Hopi Indians believe, as did William Blake, that the worlds of dreams and the imagination is the real and everything else illusion. With our transmitting receiving five senses we are able to receive glimpses of our greater selves through dreams, visions and embodied as art, poetry, theatre, music and dance. We were created in the image of God/s so it would stand to reason that we must surely be more than the material and mechanism of our flesh, bones, breath and thoughts. How could creatures created in the very image of God/s be reduced to three dimensions and five senses in a world as simplistic as that which Cartesian rationalists would have us believe?

Semele, Dionysis' mortal mother was tricked by Hera into demanding that Zeus, her mystical lover, reveal himself to her in all his divine glory. Having in turn being tricked himself, Zeus had no other choice than to reveal himself to her and so in a flash of divine glory, so intense, poor Semele burst into flames and Dionysis henceforth completed his gestation inside his father's thigh. I suspect that the truth hidden within the layers of this particular myth is that our mortal three dimensional selves would probably burst into flames if ever exposed to the full glory of our multidimensional selves. In the *Rig Vedas* this must surely be what is meant by the *Kundalini*, the coiled serpent that lives at the base of our spines (in the sacrum no less) and which, when awakened, leads to enlightenment, but only if one is ready for the fire, for if not leads either to madness or death.

Could this also be the "fire below" that Duchamp alludes to with his *L.H.O.O.Q.* Mona Lisa hermaphrodite? When spoken, the letters L.H.O.O.Q. annunciate into the words "Elle a chaud au cul" which literally translates as "She is hot in the arse." In the very same year, 1919, Duchamp's best friend, Picabia, used the very same letters in a painting called *Le Double Monde* ("The Double World") in which the words "haut" and "bas" (above and below) mark their territory upon a strange figure eight or upturned lemniscate, the same symbol of infinity featured above the heads of the Magician and Strength card in the Rider Waite Tarot deck from 1909.

The saintly words Teresa of Ávila might be the best known European description of this fiery process of awakening:

> *I saw in his hand a long spear of gold, and at the iron's point there seemed to be a little fire. He appeared to me to be thrusting it at times into my heart, and to pierce my very entrails; when he drew it out, he seemed to draw them out also, and to leave me all on fire with a great love of God. The pain was so great, that it made me moan; and yet so surpassing was the sweetness of this excessive pain, that I could not wish to be rid of it. The soul is satisfied now with nothing less than God. The pain is not bodily, but spiritual; though the body has its share in it. It is a caressing of love so sweet which now takes place between the soul and God, that I pray God of His goodness to make him experience it who may think that I am lying.[7]*

I suspect that the battle between the mythological Titans and Olympians is taking place not in ancient mythological history, but within ourselves, on a daily basis, as the various facets, in multiple dimensions and incomprehensible forms, battle for supremacy. According to Rudolf Steiner one needs to embark on a mystical journey that begins with "Recognizing that the true essence of a human being does not lie in the person's outer appearance, but rather in the inner nature, in the soul and spiritual existence of this person" and that "one's thoughts and feelings have as significant an influence as one's deeds" because "one's inner life is as important as work on one's outer life." When the three dimensional transmitter/receiver of our mortal selves, in flesh and blood, takes the time to develop their ultra-sensitive selves, we gain access to our higher selves, but when the transmitter/receiver gets clogged up and polluted with Cartesian logic we run the risk of being reduced to mortal material dust and nothing more.

---

7 Chapter XXIX; Part 17, Teresa's Autobiography

The *I Ching*, Tarot, molten lead cast into water, coffee grinds, bones and every other method of divination work simply because our higher selves exist beyond the bounds of time and space, and once the rational mind is silenced we gain access to these other worlds. Millions of people around the world and across the centuries practice meditation, yoga, tai chi, chi kung, acupuncture, homeopathy, superstition and magick, take ayuhuasca, iboga, mushrooms or LSD to the same end, the silencing of the monkey mind that tries to reduce the experience of reality to its most mundane.

Humanity's greatest fear, at least in the Occidental world, is the notion of pre-destiny, that our lives are not lived with free choice but that everything has already been written into some divine book and we are no more than destiny's puppets. I certainly have the impression that, as hard as I have tried to seize control of my own life, some "thing" always somehow manages to intervene and decisions seem to be taken by forces unknown. The more I try to resist, the greater things seem to slip out of my control almost as though I am being guided somewhere I don't want to know. It was precisely my resistance that led me into my dark depression and it was only in accepting that "life" was conspiring to give me exactly what I needed, when I needed it, that I was able to crawl out from the darkness. But it's not some malevolent God or predestiny leading me along, but simply my own higher self, creating coincidences, opportunities of chance, circumstances, conditions and events that I may, with my own rational free will accept or reject, act upon, with or against. The book has not been written so much as is in the writing. The pen of Allah's creation is still busy and we are all participants of that creation with our own individual pens.

We are trapped by our ego, snared by logic and bind our selves to three dimensional materialist conceptions of reality, locking our selves into our physical bodies with their demands for instant gratification and rational experience, refusing all things that don't make sense or go bump in the night. I have since learned that it is not this "me" who creates my paintings, but the paintings that are making "me" in ways I can only trust to accept. The muses of old are not mere caryatids holding up mythological histories, but very real spirit beings within our imaginations guiding those who care to see, listen, feel and create as they take us across the river of prejudice into worlds of infinite potential. My paintings are windows and portals through which I have been invited to take leaps of faith, hurling myself into unknown worlds and hidden dimensions, surrendering to a much bigger picture.

The thin line of the razorblade that I found myself walking upon, cut right through my consciousness and opened my eyes to other ways of seeing and multiple ways of being. Every slash, gash, splash, drip, dribble, smear, line, bleed and pool were already there before I painted them, calling out to me as they manifested themselves. This is what Alfred Jarry must have meant with his notion of *Pataphysics*, a system of absurd non-sense in which the world of objects has a spirit and an intelligence over our own, in which the words you are reading called upon the lead in my pencil to guide me into writing them.

I resisted and struggled, refused and protested, wrestling against my will in a conflict between what I thought I knew and understood to be real, and where my paintings took me. I refused to accept the pervasive animistic powers of destiny, much less that destiny was being laid out before me upon stretch of canvas, but these things had minds of their own and I was under their control. I try to use my words, my education, understanding and my will in the game of chess called creation but I always seem to lose out of respect. Signs, sigils, symbols, archetypes, ancient totems and mystical elements emerged out from the chaos and a talisman manifested itself, a silent sacred witness to my struggle of becoming. The chaos magician does not burn the sigil in order to embed it within his or her unconscious so much as the unconscious burns the sigil in order to get the attention of the magician and make conscious that which already exists.

I paint, not because I want, but because my will demands it out of sacred emergency rather than need. It is certainly not an art of balance, of purity and serenity, devoid of troubling or depressing subject matter, a soothing, calming influence on the mind, something like a good armchair providing relaxation for the tired businessman, for it is no less than a baptism by fire. I paint in the same way that the shaman throws bones or the seer casts molten lead into the waters of destiny, losing control to find my self.

Out from the darkness of my depression, from the paralysis of thinking too much about the loss of a friend and a system's betrayal, I discovered a fire that burned holes into my skull that I could learn to see differently. Painting unfolded and revealed itself to me and through the narrow chinks of my cavern I saw Picabia's "Double World" of infinity. I may yet return to the material worlds of sculpture, but they will be different for I have learned to see differently.

21 December 2013

The Imaginative Libido

Carl Abrahamsson

This text was originally published in a Polish translation in the magazine Trans-Wizje, no 4/2013. – Ed.

It's easy to see how dolls and playing with miniatures are attractive to children, whose imaginations are not yet repressed by the demands of adult behavior. However, the externalizations or projections onto talismanic objects are of great value also for the psychic hygiene and well-being of adults. It seems that the times are changing in favor of an integration of a wider definition of "play" and, as an extension of this, of artificial human companions.

The child who plays with miniatures is regarded as "normal". Indeed, the child seeks an externalization of fantasies in tangibly bestowing objects/proxies with magical life in a phase where confusion reigns and there's simply quite a lot to learn about how to behave and when, etc. Traditionally, girls are equipped with dolls and household items, and boys with tools of various kinds (cars, weapons, machines, fellow soldiers, etc). Whether this is all tradition and a manifestation of imposed gender patterns from anxious parents or something completely natural, we will leave for another discussion.

Mimicking adults close by can of course be both good and bad, depending on what these adults do. At best, parents can serve as good examples of balanced and creative decision makers. At worst, their own destructive behaviors can be contagiously transmitted into the psyche and behavior of the child in question. Using dolls in these formative years is a way to relate to and structure the chaotic aspects of childhood, both as amplification of positive emotions and experiences and as exorcism of bad ones.

Suffice to say here that doll houses, garages, pastel colored stables for cute unicorns, replica weapons, dress-up cut-outs, grand landscapes with miniature trains and roads or even battlefields are integrated parts of growing up for most Western kids.

Dolls and toys in general have always existed and always will. Under dire straits, a stick and a pine cone can do the trick and get you to the "zone". Under more well-to-do circumstances, advanced and expensive mechanical miniatures will help saturate the imagination. The value seems to not have to do with cost *per se* but rather with invested emotional and imaginative energy. Your own favorite teddy bear may not have been the most lavish, costly or elegant but what does it matter: it was yours and you felt an intense emotional resonance with it. This dynamic relationship can be so strong that the mere thought of that teddy bear later on in life can evoke a feeling of warmth and nostalgia.

There are several wonderful museums for toys in the world. One of the best when it comes to dolls, teddy bears and doll houses exists in the old town in Basel, Switzerland. On well visited floors are thousands of items, all beautifully preserved. It is almost like entering a shrine somehow, the way the dolls and other items are meticulously showcased and looking out at you from behind glass boundaries.

Not only is there an impressive display of technical craftsmanship (now probably lost forever) but also of the very essence of dolls and proxies: yes, they are dead but they can easily come to life (of sorts). This becomes especially evident when looking at the multitude of mechanical dolls and constructions that move, either wound up or electrically. Although their movements are likely to be jerky and stiff, the mere action in itself does indeed tilt one's imagination. It is quite often an uneasy experience and one that provokes a light sense of fear. Probably because it mimics our own behaviour or environment but in a disturbingly flawed way.

On display at the Basel museum are many doll houses which provide an insight into the behavioral programming of 19th century Switzerland (and, surely, other equally civilized regions of the world). Everything is orderly, all the boys and girls are well-dressed and well-behaved (at least on the surface and during opening hours) and there is an ample display of exquisite miniature items belonging in the spheres of home, school and work. That this was not strictly a matter of toys-for-fun quickly becomes evident.

Technology and craftsmanship dictated the shape of these important learning platforms of the era in question. In a Switzerland of the late 19th century, where 10% of the gross national product came from exports of mechanical music machines, it's no wonder that expertly constructed and fine mechanical worlds of wonder were presented to the Swiss children.

Today, entertainment has taken over the same function. However, there is a big difference. Today, kids are educated in passive modes by a never ending flow of entertainment. Where active fantasy and play-acting used to be key ingredients in the mental, moral and emotional development of children, today there is a saddening prevalence of introverted staring into illuminated screens of varying sizes.

This is also why prefab household robots, for instance, can't fulfil the same needs as artificial human companions. Their robotic presets and cold, distinctly non-human behavior leaves very little for the imagination to work with.

The fear of dolls in general is called *pediophobia*, and constitutes part of a greater cluster of fears called *automatonophobia*. The considerably more enthusiastic attitudes towards the same phenomenon are called *pediophilia* and *automatonophilia*.

The eerie and sometimes even terrifying encounter with glassy eyed porcelain dolls or even mute teddy bears, especially when one sees many of them at the same time, clearly distinguishes the thin line between death and magical life. By mere will, an inanimate object can go from being a scary-zombie-voodoo-horror film-nightmare item to something that is "cute", "cuddly" and, not forgetting, "mine". And then also integrated in harmonious playing, alone or together with friends. It's what the human imagination invests in the object that makes it come alive.

Historically, the projection of life onto or into inanimate objects belongs in magic and proto-religious perspectives. Children have always played in this sense, but adults have also to a varying degree been "allowed" to do this. Rituals and ceremonies in all cultures have been creations by proxy, either for keeping a community together by sharing a belief system, or for making substantial and sympathetic changes in a willed direction. The use of totems, dolls, proxies etc has always been integrated in this process.

Imagination in itself shouldn't be forgotten either. This is a quality or essence that is so fundamentally human that when it is discouraged ("Stop daydreaming and get back to work!") it creates severe emotional imbalances in the individual. For children, using toys and acting/playing is considered natural. But for adults, rigidity and obedience are encouraged. Interestingly, this is a process or projection that sets in as the individual becomes sexually mature. There seems to be a link in there somehow, one that demands that the two proto-human phenomena of sex and imagination should not be allowed in the same psychic sphere. Now, why is that?

There have been many pioneering psychologists and intellectuals who've focused on these phenomena, Jung being but one. His integration (not least in his own life and creativity) of the imagination and his trusting his own intuition remain groundbreaking when looking back at the 20th century. Several of his disciples have carried on researching this:

> *In a way, one must be potentially "whole" already in order to enter the drama; if one is not, one will learn to become so by painful experience. Active imagination is thus the most powerful tool in Jungian psychology for achieving wholeness – far more efficient than dream interpretation alone. – – – In contrast to the numerous existing techniques of passive imagination, active imagination is done* alone, *to which most people must overcome considerable resistance. It is a form of play, but a bloody serious one. – – – We also know that many alchemists used an* imaginatio vera et non phantastica *in their work, which was a form of active imagination. This gives us the satisfaction of knowing that we are dealing here not with a weird innovation, but with a human experience which has been lived through before. It is actually a new form of one of the oldest forms of* religio, *in the sense of "giving careful consideration to the numinous powers."*[1]

The American Satanist and philosopher Anton LaVey wrote and talked a lot about something he foresaw as a great business and phenomenon of the future: artificial human companions. What he meant by this was the integration in daily life of life size dolls, with which you talk, hang out or even have sex. LaVey himself had an entire room designed as a 1950s bar, complete with furniture, musical instruments, a bartender and life size guests that he had built himself over the years. The possibility of venting anger or indulging in prurient fantasies (and behavior) in this strictly private sphere LaVey saw as something that could

---

1 Marie-Louise von Franz in the introduction to Barbara Hannah, *Encounters with the Soul: Active Imagination*, Sigo Press, Boston, 1981, p 2.

become not only psychologically healing but also a revolutionary big business.

Time has definitely caught up with this thinking. Where previously store mannequins were modified by a few pediophilic Galatea aficionados, now an entire industry has bloomed that makes life size dolls, complete with natural feeling skin, various hair and eye color options, racial features and physical endowments. As with so many aspects of the development of human technology, sexual needs have been instrumental in this. Companies like the American *Real Doll* manufactures dolls for sexual use, but they can of course equally well be used for polite conversation or whatever else that "floats the boat".

If you think it's strange that people of both sexes would indulge erotically with dolls or toys rather than with real people, think again. The predominantly female use of dildos has been with us since time immemorial and is perhaps the most common example of adult talismanic use in our contemporary culture. The use of a proxy penis not only gives sexual and sensual pleasure but also activates the adult imagination immediately. Also, try to remember what you yourself (God forbid!) or your friends did when you got a new doll in your hands. Wasn't Barbie more or less immediately defrocked and examined between her legs? Ditto with Ken? The curiosity and relationship has been there all along.

There is nowadays a gigantic global industry that has surpassed its cousin, pornography: sex toys. That's right: "toys". And dolls constitute a large portion of this industry of adult toy making. Does this mean that adults have suddenly become more infantile? No, it very likely just means that the market now acknowledges a deep-rooted human need to act out fantasies in isolated spaces that allow for not only a sexual but also an overall psychic release.

As soon as you so desire, the pediophobic aspects of dolls in general are magically removed and these become alive and someone you can talk to or integrate in your own and possibly your friends' interactions. That is, when *you* yourself make that happen by opening up *your* mind to a reality slightly less causal than the normal, waking adult state of mind. The doll then becomes very much alive. If it's only in your own mind or not is irrelevant. In the subjective sphere, subjectivity rules supreme. The pediophobic quickly turns into the pediophilic at the very first realization that you are now alone with your new artificial friend.

One usually says that size doesn't matter, but of course it does. Small dolls are for small humans, meaning children. But what happens when the dolls grow in size along with their owners? Well, they need to do what adults do, of course. Or what adults would like to do with other adults but don't. The primitive inflatable dolls with washable plastic orifices or attached dildos have been an interesting part of human culture from the 1970s and onwards. From a psycho-analytical perspective, very revealing. You fill a doll with your own breath (of life) – or perhaps use a pump – then fuck it or are fucked by it, clean up the mess and eventually deflate it again. How is that for an analogy of the Western libido and its shame-based repression?

With a new generation of life-size and life-like dolls designed for various purposes (basically with or without orifices), we are going to see a change in privately controlled psychic hygiene for adults. When Anton LaVey prophesied and in a pioneering way built his own best friends, he consciously and willingly paved the way for a potential quantum leap in human behavior. LaVey:

> *I have great respect for those who pioneer their own artificial human companions, crude as they might initially be. They will have come a small step closer to playing God and creating man or woman according to their desired image. With a creative outlet as cloaked in age-old taboo as this, innovation may now run rampant – more so than any art form man has yet known.[2]*

What the kids do with their dolls is their business. What the adults do with theirs, ditto. Those who can't, won't or simply refuse to realize the potential of pediophilic power will eventually have to find themselves becoming unwilling puppets rather than (self-inflated) puppet masters. Inter-human communication is becoming more banal and strenuous with each day that passes, which is in part a result of intellectual depletion by technology. Why not rather live to the fullest and explore all the intimate facets of life together with a companion (or several) that is not terrifying and dead (nor banal and strenuous) but rather filled with exactly the kind of life and style you prefer and are stimulated by?

2 Anton LaVey, "The Construction of Artificial Human Companions", in *The Devil's Notebook*, Feral House, Portland, 1992, p 138.

The Sacred Whore Utilised in a Post-Modernist Creative Context as a Form of Expression to Reach Spiritual Nirvanas' Gates

Angela Edwards

It has been two years since I started my Pomba Gira sacred prostitution ritual invocation art project. Inspired by the post-modernist artworks of Cosey Fanni Tutti and Annie Sprinkle I made the decision as a sex worker to explore sacred prostitution and ritual in a physical way within my art. Up to this point my main body of work consisted of writing and painting though privately I had a longstanding interest in transgressive ritual/sexuality. I have also been involved in body modification scenes and BDSM.

Previous to this I had worked as a sex worker when a teenager, up to my early twenties. This was to support my intravenous crack/heroin addiction. This involved sleeping rough on the streets, suffering rape and encountering many violent situations and serious threats from pimps – it was a lifestyle over which I had little or no control. Given these circumstances I therefore felt that I could not relate to sex work as a choice or an empowering spiritual tool.

With this history, subconsciously, I could not take sex work or the ideas of Left Hand Path sexuality out of the damaging environment where I had experienced it. Nor in this lifestyle was I ever aware of prostitution being used in a sacred context or the ideas of left hand path Indian tantra of the whore as a transgressive healer.

My actions were not of invocation but done solely out of necessity. Later when I cleaned up from this lifestyle, leaving the dangerous ghetto of sex work behind me, throughout my art and writing I began my exploration of sex, creation and death.

I also started researching several religions, such as Voodoo and Quimbanda, drawn to these traditions through their primitive earth bound invocation. The fact that their altars favoured the poor or those living on the streets rather than the self-righteous or high-born. The idea of spiritualism used as a more pure approach. I started thinking about my bisexuality and varied sexual experiences, I pushed all moral boundaries of the mainstream as a type of exploration of the left hand path within my life.

Approximately seven years into creating my art I felt painting had lost its direct visceral action. Painting was like acting, convincing others to feel whilst faking the emotions. While painting evokes a feeling from the onlooker or audience, for me I feel it expresses a lack of power of the real as would be present in an action moment. Painting is an action which creates a product – the art – outside of the creator's mind and body. Painting as a medium for the artist is not physically immersive. For myself, although creating art through the mediums of painting and sculpture is spiritually or mentally immersive, these things offer something that cannot be attained in the performance/action art medium. The difference being that ritual work is transgressive and working in the performance art sector incurs full body immersion depending solely on a direct physical manifestation the action being the sole expression or experience of this type of art, this makes the physical body-work the product or act. Another main difference between action art is that it is only living in the direct moment of its manifestation in that there is no action art that can live on after the moment of the work's creation in the outside world. It cannot survive as a separate creation outside its communicated moment of time. In this type of work I find a certain power in using the body in the now and it being more rooted in my body's reality or the truth of my own experiences as they evolve in ritual unlike other mediums of art which, like painting, do not afford this type of ritualistic experience.

Therefore I sought the reality of this type of ritual as a transgressive experience through my sacrificed body, scarred, ripped, bleeding, torn completely in martyred divinity.

Action is an ACT directed, projected or ingrained with enforced magical intent/intention, to evolve and change oneself, to break down and become something new. I felt in order for art not to be considered fixed or fake it should push the body/soul to limits as without the limits of control, to evolve physically, spiritually and mentally in an authentic ritual/experience. I decided in this process as an artist and practitioner to film and record transgressive cutting ritual invocations.

To begin with, I privately documented cutting blood rites invoking Pomba Gira and sex magick rituals. These included masturbation, anal and vaginal penetration, blood and scat rites, etc.

They often became a type of documented endurance art, like Marina Abramovic's art, pushing the body to limits through spiritual invocation and had a climax of shattering my body's boundaries or confronting taboos.

My work during this time not only started to be influenced by philosophical, spiritual practice but also by a developed use of the mediums of sculpture, film, extreme performance body art and action as well as the previous medium I used, solely of painting.

I made a pact and commitment to myself at the start of my exploration of ritual performance art, which throughout my performance action work I have honoured, that I was to never repeat an action or a ritual. I have for a long time taken issue with "performance art" when staged and not real or artists who even in the transgressive performance art scene repeat performances re-enacting major works for audiences. If you perform the same action more than once I feel it becomes invalid in having power as a transgressive or esoteric experience, or the work becomes manipulated and overused. For example if you perform a cutting invocation ritual or endurance piece the whole point is using the work as a transgressive spiritual invocation such as in endurance art at its purist is not being aware of the outcome either visually or physically. I am totally averse to using the same images or experiences more than once and I feel this especially so in transgressive/endurance action based art. Doing so would be a violation of these mediums based upon the artist's pushing their own spiritual and physical boundaries. There is however a temptation I have experienced as an artist to re-enact certain work if the documentation fails to visually manifest something artistic impressive or viable. Though such ideologies have to be abandoned when working in real esoteric ritual or action as invocation or transgression, it is about the purity of the experience as it is in that moment of time. Therefore it can never be staged or moulded in future performances or actions. Like the medium of normal performance art/theatre is based upon being created for the sole entertainment of the artist rather than creating a living esoteric experience for the individual. I feel this is a really important point to be made as it points out the major differences between staged body art work in the transgressive art mainstream and the occultist/practitioner who uses the medium of "performance art" to express genuine spiritual invocation or explore a new territory and in endurance art push the body/mind to true limits. It also explains the differences between how a performance artist who is a practitioner utilises the body and work in ritual or the tools of transgression to reach a higher understanding and the performance artist who repeats or performs as an artist outside of being a practitioner and working in an occult context.

I also developed the art into public interactive ritual from the extreme cutting ritual at Torture Garden to a public sex magical invocation of full anal and vaginal masturbation in a sex club.

For this rite I consecrated an twelve inch sculpture of a phallus I had created and in public penetrated myself to climax invoking the sacred whore/Pomba Gira.

I also lay naked tied up and powerless in a cell for three hours with dildos and knives beside me as a developed interpretation of Marina Abramovic's *Rhythm 0* (1974). This focused on the powerlessness and total submission in sex work of realism of spiritual transgression or empowerment through total chosen submission.

In the works that I developed at the time, providing the basis for my ritual spiritual path and art, I developed a deep interest in transgressive rites using the body, the whore's tool, which is the current activator of sex and death. During this time I became interested in refining my experiences and direct experimentation with chosen sex work or sacred sex work and sexuality rites wherein lie the currents of Voodoo/Quimbanda in essence, or in our shamanistic ethos of an elemental connection to the earth.

A view expressed in not just certain religious traditions but art also.

For example, in art history we are confronted with the ideology of ritual and spiritualism. In pioneer works of 1960's performance art of Hermann Nitsch and Rudolf Schwarzkogler. This group consisted of scarification, body modification practices, defecation and religious rites including animal sacrifice rituals.

Although in high art the philosophy of invocations in blood and transgression was communicated through these actions, they also formed in the works of the aforementioned action artists a strong blueprint for this type of spiritual evocation.

The ideologies of ritual animal sacrifice and blood as a vital part of spirituality of life, sexuality and death were explored in the 1970s by Santeria ritual artist Ana Mendieta.

Transgressive piercings, hook suspension, the native American sun dance shamanism as a form of initiation through pain was used from the 1950's onward. Fakir Musfar has throughout his work attributed transgression and pain to his artistic shamanistic practice, seeing extremes in body violation as a way to reach higher enlightenment. The reason I reference these examples of artistic shamanistic practices is in order to understand our magical/occult heritage. We must both acknowledge and understand the ancient formal traditions of our path and the relationship in the creation of art to such and its practitioners of the occult or use of spiritual methods pertaining to the left hand path.

These things like BDSM subcultures are rooted originally in our magical cultures.

They are a post-modernist interpretation of a relation to our work or ideologies just as alchemy is the father of modern science, or gnostic theory is the father of modern philosophical thought as we know it in the modern living world.

We must be fully aware not only of past traditions but of their living interpretation or practice in the present. My experiences are of a journey encompassing all these elements.

Although I have experimented with several subcultures from BDSM, body modification, occult and polygamous groups I always found that although I had taken several aspects of these scenes into my work I could not attribute my work, artistic or spiritual, to such narrow margins.

Once something belongs to a certain fetish in the scene, whether past or present, it becomes spiritually irrelevant. Therefore it becomes still-born because firstly it is known territory/familiar in a lifestyle context, and secondly it places too much importance on group development rather than the pioneering aspect of the spiritual development of the individual. With the individual rather than the group placed at the centre of true spiritual gnosis, practice or enlightenment.

In my practice both as an artist and spiritually there has always been a close relation in context to transgressive body art, prostitution, art, magical traditions, ritual and action. I feel I am unable to separate these as they are one of the same and all contribute to one body of work.

The development of my spiritual philosophy or knowledge of traditional occult practice is universally linked to my philosophy in life and as an artist. I honestly believe there is no magical tradition without art and vice-versa and while I do not believe that all occult practitioners are natural artists I feel that art being magic simplifies our work as practitioners and is not factual of all mediums/fundamentals of fine art.

I do believe however that throughout art history there have been certain individuals who have developed their mysticism/spiritual learning/practices through their visual arts or who have philosophically used occult/religious practices and rituals in context of their visual arts development.

Firstly, as regards sacred prostitution/sexuality, I am a firm believer in first hand experience, like in cutting or piercing initiation rituals, and invocation only.

I believe in order to explore sacred sex work/sexuality as a progressive Left Hand Path tool valuable to the practitioner, we must choose it or consider it a spiritual path rather than be stranded in these experiences through poverty or circumstance.

If a woman wishes to invoke Pomba Gira/Babalon she must be free in spirit and not trapped by material circumstance or forced into this expression of her sexual self.

He/She must violate or open herself, she must not be violated or taken, she must take herself. She must also transgress all concepts or male objectification and use sex work solely for his/her own spiritual development.

The vessel should also be severed from shame in that even if sex work is used as a tool of temporary invocation or magical development the vessel should not in the future feel the need to deny her past or reflect social taboos upon her previous practices.

Although sacred sexuality/sex work is a small aspect of our magical heritage this is an aspect nonetheless which, like the fundamentals of life, sex and death, should be celebrated and acknowledged as our full spiritual human nature being revealed.

Morally she should not be judgemental towards herself or to those who pay for her services.

There has to be a form of meditation and focus like in Zen Buddhism where the soul leaves the body or is projected outside of moral or mundane thought processes which regard outside influences such as the preconceptions of society regarding sexuality/or the sex worker in general.

To understand the workings of sacred sex work in a spiritual context you have to open your mind and philosophy to certain attributes of these workings.

Firstly you have to project spiritual purity upon the act of sex work.

You have to view sex workers as healers or shamans relating love or the ability to accept all in sin.

The sex worker needs to be considered wise and spiritual, relating an essence through his/her touch/actions.

The way I consider the whore is not unlike the role of the village shaman or witch doctor who as a vessel would have been shown full respect and adulation as having the knowledge of herbs or healing that others did not possess.

When we relate to the prostitute's role beyond basic bodily functions or sexual lust nothing is so true of this ideology as in the embodiment of *Pomba Gira das Matas* who is seen as a whore but also as a healing nursemaid with the magical healing knowledge of herbal remedies of the forest.

This idea is in Quimbanda given the form of the whore as a combined elemental deity of the earth and ethereal traits, of this world and not of this world.

QUEEN OF THE FORESTS/EARTH: POMBA GIRA RAINHA DAS MATAS

The Fenris Wolf

Invocation

Death's elemental beauty in terracotta dusts passage
I lay Nature of humanity my kingdom seated abode Green leafed,
blue sky, red illuminated sun the rooted world
praise be in her Ancient Proserpina's abducted underworlds
in darkened Hades filth revealed
Excrement coated raw matter beauties ancient primal stripped down
reflective hymn in martyred nursemaid's medicine mission to repair
As a sacred whore to the destitute I come to heal
Ugly decaying flesh age mounts my youth consumed he enters me
Lay all your fears within me
Lay all your desires, wants upon me
Lay all your yearnings upon me
Know that I am free of judgement, free of prejudice
Then therefore know that I REJECT NO-ONE
Come into my hands, my mouth, my cunt,
reflective in my unashamed love
Find within my treatment, kindness, debased absolution
Enchantments lust upon him sacrificed
Feel no weariness in my inserted life's resonator.
For being a whore is a talent,
as we are the world's unacknowledged healing masters
Who, open to all, take upon ourselves everything, all despair,
in our repair we are the filth that cleanses in our interactions
of our actions of exorcism alone
To know that I chose to give myself wholly,
totally to you, in my home you are always rested welcome
To feel alive renewed, sagging flesh breathed within stunning life sustained
Penetrated punters rancid glory revered
The nunnery of sin tools' consecration at the gates of material flesh blood,
bones diseases resided heaven unconditionally
she is invoked detached self sacrifice her gateway is open to all
without discrimination healed enchantments, chanted
Pomba Gira Rainha Matas

QUEEN OF THE FOREST AND THE EARTH: POMBA GIRA RAINHA MATAS

Initiation via Dream

In the forests my feet touch the earth
the wind howls in never-ending darkness
Blinded by my conquest fulfilled I lay in the shadows

The Sacred Whore

Crouched down, shitting anal dead matter
I cover my body, elemental primal holiness is within her, wisdom invoked
I close my eyes whereupon I am holy earth's entombed restorations
Standing wearing a flowing nursemaid's
cloak of red and blue tied in green waited ribbons.
In midnight's clear waning moon chastity
An old aged ugly man lying dead by the passage
Ugly decaying filthy rotting away in his own mortality
Creased smelly sweltering putrid wasting away flesh
Chalked saggy deceased crinkled skin touching firm sacred tightness
Open cloak I stand over him to reveal the jewel of my sex
I raise my lips upon him gripping his flaccid deathbed looseness
I offer myself unto him come into the whore's sacramental divinity.
Come into life designate all fears in my medicines body healing
no suppressed needs, feel in my healing love filled up peacefulness
Youth's beauty en-flowed eruption over age
White lightening intoxicated spurted shocked sharp vision broken through
Come into my cunt wherein life's intoxication you are renewed
Nursemaids martyred sainthood scarified to cradle all in my flesh
upon my body dispel all diseased restlessness
wherein myself lays fulfilled blessed satisfaction

POMBA GIRA RAINHA DAS MATAS: QUEEN OF THE FORESTS AND THE EARTH

The Ritual

Terracottas, smouldered urns earthed cauldron my soul in her invoked
I place dried excrement dirt over open wounds
Flaking into me enchantment trails I taste her earthed matter gagged
I take punters aged creased into my hands my mouth, my cunt full
submission given over
without discrimination I resign myself to the sole life purpose
of unconditional medicines, night nurse's position
Sacred I am the healer of all Services encapsulated to all my humble prayer
I take everybody into me, healed loneliness invoked
Self sacrifice repaired consummation radiating through my actions

POMBA GIRA RAINHA DAS MATA

Excerpts from my journal of sex work and Pomba Gira invocation. Through words, sex work, action and art in 2013:
I have chosen this aspect of Pomba Gira's seven legions because I feel this particular embodiment of this spirit best represents the example of the whore as a healer and

witch with higher spiritual knowledge, or elevates the role of the whore to that of temple priestess.

The whore booth or flat can also be likened to that of the Catholic confessional box.

Come into and unto me and abolish all guilt in the client's need to expose their sexual self and total vulnerability to him/her. The whore is like a saint or deity, total unconditional love without judgement, without sin in this context. The punter confesses all in hope that the soul will be saved or satisfied and so is rebirth brought into the interaction in death of climax to become saved.

I can only fully explain the role of being a sacred sex worker or the ritual as a type of conducted baptism.

The client comes in, satisfies, off-loads their lust or in the case of working as a pro submissive darker elements of the self onto you. As a confidant and in performing the act of sexual lust/seedier fantasises you cleanse them or sustain that part of human nature.

In sacred sex work there is the concept of Left Hand Path transgressive practices realising equality with the deity. In other words man as a god or goddess because you reject no one and accept everyone unconditionally into your body for money.

When we pray to saints or deities in religious practices no matter what religious denomination you originate from, the aspect all these spirits/deities have in common is the fact that they unconditionally accept all in loyalty like the whore.

These spirits also have the power of forgiveness or to erase our mortal sins which is another aspect the whore has in feeding mortal sin and acceptance of mortal sin.

The whore like the deity therefore abolishes sin as irrelevant and destroys the existence of sin in her wake.

The dichotomy being that sex work which is viewed as morally sinful or disreputable in the eyes of society/mainstream becomes sinless in the practice of acknowledging all sins or placing irrelevance upon sin which ceases to exist in the act of sacred sex work that is the profession or spiritual act of prostitution.

The sex worker's job also in this essence becomes beyond the sexual act or mundane considerations such as sexual objectification.

The act when viewed or operated in these contexts becomes a transgression to nirvana. The sexual exchange or act used as a tool or operating method to a higher celestial cosmic knowledge of universal fulfilment.

Sex in sacred sex work therefore becomes irrelevant as the whore spiritually transcends physical actions or elemental primitive sexual instincts of man/woman.

The whore's prayer is that of cleansing man/womankind of sin to regain spiritual purity.

Cleansing is fed by action and experience, acknowledged where all become sacred.

Where the whore's sacrament is found within all debased aspects of human nature.

The whore acts as a passage of the low to the high. An avatar of a higher spiritual nature and transferring the low into higher enlightenment.

The sex worker, when working with the concepts of sex work as a form of sacred ritual, is also a conductor between the high and low planes.

This is another similarity placed upon the whore when relating his/her profession to the law of voodoo, or the Exus and Pomba Giras of Quimbanda. That in her/his profession she/he works as an intermediary in possession between the low human elemental realm and higher spiritual elevated enlightenment.

She/he belongs and works between both worlds without judgement and her wisdom is communicated universally.

Another aspect I would like to conclude when looking at sacred prostitution as a practice or ritual tool is that you cannot choose sex work as a lifestyle choice. In my philosophy I would recommend every person experienced sex work but for a short amount of time and in a ritual context.

Sacred prostitution is not part of western culture and for the large amount of time it is denied in western society. Sex work is looked upon as something morally of a low nature, exploitative and mostly done not out of choice but through economical circumstance or desperation.

It is ironic that sex work has such a soiled reputation as the profession is as ancient as spiritualism itself. In the western world sex work has never been viewed as sacred and besides the material glamour of the high end escort/sex work industry/ porn industry it is viewed in all cases with intolerance and disgust.

Though this has not always been so, in other cultures such as the Babylonian/Mayan sex work, temples of ancient times or the whore goddess temples of deities such as Ishtar and Inanna to even modern day India who still practice such traditions today.

There is a large inbred stigma attached to this work in western society as it is viewed as unclean.

In the west we view prostitution as an economical product or sex work as something founded on the ethos of money or materialism rather than in ancient times. We therefore end up linking the sex industry with consumerism which is a very modern day trait as the individual's journey or more ancient aspects of this profession is forgotten, when in other cultures or throughout history it was regarded as a spiritual practice or initiation passage into womanhood or also manhood.

This is a huge obstacle we have to overcome as practitioners when examining this work in our cultural modern day environment.

Without romanticising the prostitute/sex worker as an other-worldly sensual being or the idea or placing the whore on the Babalon goddess avatar pedestal, for us to reach a realistic view of sacred sex work placing this practice in relation to a higher spiritual enlightenment. In OTO traditions for example we are often confronted with the idealised version from a male point of view of the icon of Babalon and female sexuality. This is for most of the time a hollow superficial pinup version adhering to the male fantasy, rather than the reality of real sacred sex work.

It is in this instant often founded upon male objectification of the sacred whore rather than spiritual enlightenment. This will then bring the feminist argument into play that as a sex worker you become a slave to mankind by the act of objectification. That of a woman being used for male sexual gratification. You are also disempowering the female race and supporting the sexism of the brotherhood.

I would like to not get distracted with the ideology of Feminism or gender associated politics.

When exploring sacred sex work or spiritual practices, feminism has no place in ancient spiritual traditions, as temples have throughout history used male and female sex workers. For example the ancient temples of Inanna/Ishtar where boys would work also. Traditionally in all forms of sacred sex work this is the case. With only the later western OTO traditions focusing on sex work/the role of Babalon being assigned only to mainly the female gender. I find gender not relevant to a higher enlightened understanding of these things. Culturally, any associations with gender roles have to be abandoned for our practices in sacred sex work to work, when used as a ritual or spiritual tool in a sacred context.

Of course the practice of sex work in a spiritual context is far from an unchallenging experience for the practitioner. Though not unlike the *Aghori* (hindu) of Indian culture who begs and lives upon the streets to receive a higher non-materialistic understanding, it is a rite of spiritual passage no less to those who choose to surrender to it in a deeper spiritual understanding.

The whore embodies the need to strip down not in her intimate day to day activities but in her vision and transgress. From the viewpoint of the left hand path or using transgressive extremes to express all or to be beyond mundane preconceptions of sin the sacred sex worker is the ideal role model.

Now I would like to address how the Left Hand Path ideology of transgression through extremes to gnostic enlightenment has been a large part of my own work. As well as using piercings, blood rites, a variety of sexual interactions privately in my ritual work and art.

Out of choice, I felt only recently with my exploration of sacred sex work that my understanding of sex and death with sex as a transgressive tool deepened. Sex work deepened my understanding of transgressive extremes in that the sexual acts were out of my choice or control. I mainly worked in sex work but also in extreme submission work in my sacred sex work profession.

A lot of interactions tested my body to physical limits including the harder elements of fisting, burning, caning and restraints, etc.

For these I took upon my body bruises and beatings and violations, others' deprivations, until with deprivation no judgement existed erasing all sin also. A lot of incidents of sexual extremes I would not in my private sex life have chosen, as they are not my personal sexual preference. In other words, as I did not choose or plan these interactions besides totally giving over my body as a sacred whore's vessel I felt the transgressive ritual element of left hand path ideology to annihilate myself and my ego and to be outside of myself spiritually even more potent through surrender and empowerment. I had become empowered and experienced all aspects of sin and the darker human self.

For myself sacred prostitution when I practised it for two years while developing my spiritual practice and art was never about money. I did not desperately need money at this time in my life. I am not rich but I survive and I did not need the money to support an addiction.

In other words I chose sex work not out of desperation but as an experiment and to develop a higher spiritual understanding of this aspect of the occult.

Also I planned to only be involved with sex work for a year for this sole purpose and never that I be dependent on it financially or as a lifestyle choice.

Personally I feel like losing your virginity, sex work should be a rite of passage in a spiritual context for all young/men or women. I would advocate sex work for a short amount of time, though obviously learned about in spiritual context.

I honestly feel that with sex work, there comes a deeper spiritual understanding that empowers in that the act allows you to go beyond sin and totally give yourself over in healing to another individual. In no sin existing through sex work we can become cleansed of all sin becoming pure.

Sacred sex work practices pure love and unconditional love or acceptance.

These are all valid traits and traits that we aspire to in spirituality. Sex work also gives you a deep understanding of real human nature in all aspects good/bad.

So in all these things, when utilised in this context, there is no shame. During my time as a sex worker before each session I would pray for Pomba Gira's protection. I would initiate My mortal body bound to her flowing through my blood.

Knowing that her first and only lesson was beyond sin in selfless love, she rejects nobody and like the whore sees worth in everybody. Where she reigns in art, lust, beauty and fire. For she becomes the living embodiment of flesh. Where open, invoked, our flesh is possessed. She is the sacred whore utilised in a post-modernist creative context in a form of expression to spiritual nirvanas' gates.

WARNING

If you do decide to explore sacred sex work in ritual context...

Firstly, I have to recommend safety.

In the sex industry away from the sexual act there are a lot of dangers including pimps, addiction, rape and even stabbings or shootings.

Whilst working on the streets as a teenager many of my friends died through stabbings, overdoses or HIV, all as a consequence of this type of work or lifestyle.

The dangers, not unlike cutting/blood rituals, need to be taken into consideration as they can, if you do not research your method correctly, be fatal.

I also fully advise that if you cannot perform or interact with sex work without drink or drugs, it is clearly *not* the right spiritual path for you to take.

Sex work is a talent in many ways in the fact you have to be born with an understanding of this type of work on a deeper level. Not all women/men can utilise sex work in a spiritual context or have a positive fulfilling experience that develops a spiritual understanding of their own mystical path from these experiences or is beneficial to your own exploration of sacred sexuality or development as a gnostic experience.

The Women of the Æon

Vera Nikolich

What inspired me to write this article were the conversations with women who got swirled into the ordered structures of occultism, not yet realizing their potentials and capabilities as valuable contributors to the magical reality. Somewhere along the way of pep-talking to the end of empowering their passions for completeness and self-trust, I ran an errand for myself as well. Being a woman in a world that still clings to alpha-masculinity set on protecting the confines of a "home" scheduled for renovation is not an easy task. But they need us to deliver themselves from the dirt of the old place – and we need them to finish what we started. – Vera Nikolich

Foretellers of Change

Even as early as the 15th Century, Renaissance Europe was having a taste of the avant-garde served by few prominent characters speaking up for the peculiarity and equality of women, either fervently like in the case of Agrippa or satirically like Rabelais. While the potentials of women under pressure by the patriarchal age were being perpetually suffocated, the social miasma of male domination received its first hints of what was to come. Agrippa and Rabelais are suitable for obvious reasons and selected as forerunners of the Change, though there were a few other contemporaries seeding controversy in the somnambulistic Europe.

Rather than directly disproving prevailing wisdom, Agrippa, for instance, uses women's superiority as a rhetorical device and overturns the misogynistic interpretations of the female body in Greek medicine, in the *Bible*, in Roman and canon law, in theology and moral philosophy, and in politics. In his work *On the Nobility and Preeminence of the Female Sex*, he raises the question of why women were excluded and provides answers based not on sex but on social conditioning, education, and the prejudices of their more powerful oppressors. Agrippa, from this point of view, given his status of a magician, occult writer, theologian, astrologer, and alchemist, is a very important fragment of the whole, since he was among the first to proclaim such ideas in a world dominated by men with imparted "access to divinity" through science and organization in certain societies.

But he [God] has attributed to both man and woman an identical soul, which sexual difference does not at all affect. Woman has been allotted the same

126

intelligence, reason, and power of speech as man and tends to the same end as he does, that is, [eternal] happiness, where there will be no restriction by sex. ... Thus, there is no preeminence of nobility of one sex over the other by reason of the nature of the soul, rather, inwardly free, each is equal in dignity.[1]

In the same work, he further proceeds to claim superiority of women, something harder to imagine as opposed to the controversial equality previously exposed.

Since the world itself has been created by God as a circle of absolute perfection, it is fitting that the circle be perfected by this particle capable of being the link that unites perfectly the beginning of the circle with this end. That is how, at the time of creation, woman was the last in time of all things created, in the conception of the divine mind, however, she was first of all, as much in prestige as in honor, as was written about her by the prophet: "Before the heavens were created, God chose her and chose her first." [Possibly referring to the Shekinah] Indeed, it is a commonplace among philosophers to say (I cite their own words): "The end is always the first in intention and the last in execution." For woman was the last work of God, who introduced her into our world as the queen of a kingdom already prepared for her, adorned and perfect in everything. It is therefore right that every creature love, honor, and respect her, right also that every creature submit and obey her, for she is the queen of all creatures and their end, perfection, and glory, absolute perfection. This is why Wisdom says of her: "She glorifies her noble birth by living with God, for even the Lord of all has loved her.[2]

Rabelais (a contemporary of Agrippa's) on the other hand, by the interplay of amusement, extravagance and satirical elements, portrays the ideals of a healthy society. In the first book of the series, he gives a description of an Abbey of Thélème which celebrates the "will of God" or more likely its mundane version.

Thélème mixes men and women, has no walls, no fixed rules, no poverty, and no expectation that the residents (who enter the abbey between the ages of ten and fifteen for women, twelve to eighteen for men) will spend their whole lives there.[3]

Although not so ferociously and written over a different manner, Rabelais realizes that in a society delivered from the walls of ecclesiastical oppression and scrutinizing of personal actions, where divinity is obtained by each one for him/herself by the use of as simple a principle as "Do What Thou Wilt," women had an equal right to partake of the freedom and the possibility of self-realization. Both of these extraordinary individuals faced the consequences of their controversial statements made in a time and society fundamentally influenced by masculine standards and ideals.

---

1 *The Other Voice in Early Modern Europe*; Edited and Translated by Albert Rabil Jr. (1996) Text: *On the Nobility and Preeminence of the Female Sex*; Agrippa; *Equality of soul in men and women*
2 Ibid. *The superiority of women in the created order*
3 *The Rabelais Encyclopedia*; edited by Elizabeth A. Chesney (2004)

The Fenris Wolf

After a disputable hiatus, and possibly as a result of a concealed simmering of the planted ideas, some centuries later the first beacons of light for the magical immersion and emancipation of women in the matters of the divine emerged from the somnolent ground of the western world. In 1875, the Theosophical Society was founded by a revered female figure, namely Helena Blavatsky. One of the basic aims of the Society along with the study of comparative religion, philosophy and science accompanied with the investigation of the mysterious laws of nature and the powers latent in man, was to form a nucleus of the universal brotherhood of humanity *without distinction of race, sex, caste, or color.* As opposed to the Freemasonry organizations and those of a similar kind, this one offered a key to the mysteries without distinction or partiality between sexes. The forbidden ground of spiritual, mystical, alchemical and religious experience was suddenly opened up to women as well. Undoubtedly, there wasn't shortage of interest on the female side, as the magical West opened up to the delicate feminine genius. Several years later, in 1887, the Hermetic Order of the Golden Dawn had its beginnings, after the emergence of a cipher manuscript that contained the address of a female character claiming to draw from the Rosicrucian lineage. This dubious figure, namely a certain Anna Sprengel, apparently possessed the power to contact "supernatural" authorities or the "Secret Chiefs", and in the course of the unfolding, granted her permission for the establishment of a Golden Dawn temple while promising alliance to the founders. Regardless of the truthfulness of this person, her identity was given as female, which to some extent implied the capacities and influence of the female magic practitioners garlanded in the shroud of mystery and ineffableness, over the magical world of men. The Hermetic Order of the Golden Dawn as such, produced some of the most notable female magicians of the 19th and 20th centuries, including: Dion Fortune, occultist, author, psychologist, teacher, artist, and mystic; Florence Farr, actress, writer, and educator; Annie Horniman, patron of the arts, founder of two world-renowned theatres and the modern English repertory movement; Maud Gonne, aristocratic revolutionary who incited people to riot yet advocated amnesty; and Moina Bergson Mathers, artist, priestess, and channeler of Golden Dawn rituals.

> *I propose that it was magic that gave these women the knowledge, use, and understanding of their deepest creative abilities. Magic provided them with mythic models and foremothers who achieved such aims - and who had powers to produce change. They developed a taste for results that went beyond physical experience, beyond material rewards. They did not accept the roles and boundaries defined for them by family circumstances and societal expectations. They remade themselves after their own magical images and helped to remake their world. They belonged to the timeless legacy of the priestesses, sibyls, and healers who throughout history have been "midwives to the Psyche," assisting individuals and cultures in times of difficult passage.[4]*

---

4 *Women of the Golden Dawn: Rebels and Priestesses;* Mary K. Greer (1995)

And so, as the end of something makes way for the beginning of something else, like links in a circle, no matter how tiny, so was the Old Æon set to yield in the battle of power to the coming Age.

CONTEMPORARY WOMANHOOD IN MAGIC

The beginning of the 20th century manifested as an entirely new epoch and style of involvement for women in magic. From a personal stance, at the stage of inception – or rather initiation into the doctrines of the new Æon when the path was set for paving, the women were introduced to the mysteries by direct or indirect intermediation of the men already involved – positively with a significant number of exceptions related to the notion. A significant portion of these women, or at least those who over time gained the most popularity were pushed or voluntarily led into the world of obscurity by Crowley himself. The numerous cases and notably the brightest ones such as Rose Kelly (whom he married), Mary Desti Sturges, Jeanne Robert Foster, Anna Catherine Miller, Roddie Minor, Leah Hirsig, Jane Wolfe, Dorothy Olsen, Bertha Busch, Leila Waddell and many others... testify on the magical engagement, inspire and teach us stories of failure and success. More importantly, all of these women were independent, strong-minded, they knew what they wanted of life (or so it seems), they were fearless, with a heightened sexuality and inclination to open up to new experiences, disposed towards selfless immersion in work and most of all, willingness to walk where very few have walked before. Observing the cases in such manner, it seemed that the new women-magicians manifested archetypal attributes throughout the cases. The combined range of female experience, thought to be composed of a fourfold structure of separate archetypes tightly connected with C.G. Jung's four functions. These aid in the process of overcoming the duality between self and shadow and aid the drive force of human experience, namely: intuition, thinking, feeling and sensation. These were integrated in the center of the cultural evolution of the feminine archetype, recomposing into four distinct classes of personality types within the feminine psyche and further mutating into: (according to Irene de Castillejo and Toni Wolff) Medium, Amazon, Mother and Hetaira – and their corresponding feminine shadow types: (according to Maxine Harris) Victim, Exile, Predator and Rebel. But owing to the cultural evolution of the female experience and the progress of the archetypal characteristics (no thing is immune to change), the shadows grew to be considered as dark mirrorings of potential strengths where the Victim had a propensity to become a Priestess, the Exile an Amazon, the Predator could embody the attributes of a Mother and the non-conforming Rebel turn into an Alchemist.[5] Evidently, the contemporary woman of magick has transcended the classifications and grown into a self-made creation that epitomizes a complex construction of unified archetypal classes and structures, bound together by the unbreakable adhesive of resoluteness and nourished in an environment of the best informational climate as well as acquired openness to the diversity of experience. Though each one of these foremothers was different,

---

5 Vide: *Women of the Golden Dawn: Rebels and Priestesses;* Mary K. Greer (1995)

unique and isolated, they all happened to be manifestations of something almost identical. The embodiment of this archetypal feminine principle that embraced a plentitude of aspects in the range of holy priestess to courtesan to purity of the utmost ladylikeness created the magical genetic imprint that lies at the core of every inward star – freedom of manifestation under will.

Skipping forward to the present-day diversity of woman-magicians it becomes quite perceivable that the archetypal and magical genetic code constituting the girl-stars is not only well-kept-up but also considerably advanced. The cultural phenomenon of the transformed magical (as well as Thelemic) woman evolved over time and adapted according to the social changes and paradigm shifts of the last century. The contemporary woman of magic whose inherent delicate perception allows for adaptability and harnessing of future potentials transformed the ballroom of captivating dancers into a fortress of power, strength and consistency embedded in the graceful manifestation of the subtle feminine configuration. A present-day magical woman is both a perfect example of oneness and union of opposites, owing to evolution and adoption of accumulated knowledge of the best practices.

In order to illustrate the above statements, we can turn to but one example of the multitude of manifestations: the modern female magician who at the same time works and brings food to the table – she is a businesswoman, someone who quite ferociously pursues a career, a leader and a dedicated worker, a public figure; at the same time she is a caring mother; a wife or an independent woman with an awakened sexuality and ability to bind the power of freedom; a housewife tending to the domestic engagements; she is an entertainer – the life of the party; on top of it all by the application of Will she manages to keep the torch of light ever flaming. In all of this she remains a Priestess, a Scarlet Woman and more importantly a skillful Magician proficient in all matters of the mundane woven into the divine. The facts presented in this manner indicate that the long sought equality prophesied by the Prophet is finally coming to its full actualization:

> We do not fool and flatter women; we do not despise and abuse them. To us a woman is Herself, absolute, original, independent, free, self-justified, exactly as a man is.[6]

But is this really what the woman has become? Is she "exactly as a man is?" Different perspectives can yield different views and yet it should not be forgotten that form is merely an Illusion and the appearances can be deceiving. The woman (at least in the magical community) is in a position to easily claim superiority and fuel her virtues or faults by the newly arisen influence of empowerment. The imbalanced wielding of her powers poses as a tremendous source of error, so she must learn to balance and not give in to lusts for results or attainment, or worse, the dominating will of a magical partner; the apparatus must gradually adjust to the electrical influx if it is to shine longer.

---

6 The Commentary to *The Book of the Law*, III:55

It would be biased to neglect the significant undercurrent of the Witchcraft egregore which emerged (directly or indirectly) inspired by the movement of Thelema in the second half of the 20th century. Although inclusive of women or rather dominated by them, it is my personal opinion that this is an unexpected resurrection of the outdated version of the Isis-Mother-Goddess formula which might appear empowering but is, to a significant extent, imbued by defective and imbalanced energy in quite the same way as the Osiris-Father-God formula of the last age.

So far we have observed women in a broader sense of magic, encompassing a myriad of interest fields. The paths pursued are all but few and the interpretations of the intimate quests as sundry and diverse as well. What lies at the core of the subject exposed in this text of what seems to be merely a girl taking the first hints of womanhood is the future change of the Woman of the Æon in accordance with the Law of Thelema. Are there indicators that can imply the course of her evolution and is the doctrine a valid determinant of the next-gen Thelemic women?

We are not in for a return to the earth-mother-goddess paganism of the past, but something much more interesting.[7]

SISTERS

This shall regenerate the world, the little world my sister, my heart & my tongue, unto whom I send this kiss.[8]

The magical formulae at operation and particularly in the context of Thelema within the new Æon are those of "women." There are numerous indications for the veracity of this statement.

First of all, in consideration of the procession, "the last Æon, that of Osiris, is referred to Aries and Libra, as the previous Æon, that of Isis, was especially connected with the signs of Pisces and Virgo, while the present, that of Horus, is linked with Aquarius and Leo."[9] The Tarot, being a most sublime form of Qabbalah, has ATU XI and ATU XVII bearing the symbols of present time; Strength for Leo and The Star for Aquarius. Even in a simple elucidation as this which is only scratching of the surface, we get all kinds of light bulbs popping around our heads. There are two parts of the whole: the way and the aim – thus Strength becomes the aim and the Stars our end. The passed age, on the other hand, had a patriarch for a way, and Balance to mediate the fire of motion towards its purpose. The domination of man was placed in first plan but the Emperor's demise was signaled by his enthronement on the cubical stone. Nevertheless in the current arrangement of things, the Strength depicts a fierce and lustful Woman astride a Beast. The ATU, moreover means a Serpent, which is not only a treacherous redeemer but a female counterpart of the Sword as well. Yet this woman does not represent a means to an

---

7 Hymenaeus Beta XI° "Women's Conference Address", *The Magical Link*, Fall 1997
8 *The Book of the Law*, I:53
9 *The Book of Thoth*, Aleister Crowley (2011)

end, she is not auxiliary in the operation – she is the Scarlet Woman, the one in whom is all power given here posing as if she was steering the will of the prince-priest the Beast. This magickal formula of the fiery goddess holding the cup of her whoredom in which instead of wine is the blood which is life, is the key that opens the gates. The Mother of Abominations, who is only a notch south of the Great Mother to whose womb everything returns, is a sound indicator of at least one role of the woman in the new Æon.

> *With the breath of her kisses hath she fermented it, and it hath become the wine of the Sacrament, the wine of the Sabbath; and in the Holy Assembly hath she poured it out for her worshippers, and they have become drunken thereon, so that face to face have they beheld my Father. Thus are they made worthy to become partakers of the Mystery of this holy vessel, for the blood is the life. So sitteth she from age to age, and the righteous are never weary of her kisses, and by her murders and fornications she seduceth the world. Therein is manifested the glory of my Father, who is Truth.[10]*

The Star on the other hand and the doctrine connected with it, worthy of Nuit's note, is equally a very important element of the Thelemic theory and practice. In this delicate image is moved the very substance of feminine divinity, its power and ability to transform and transmute the essence of the highest and thus pass it along the structured totality of spiritual experience. In this sense, as Crowley elucidated in *The Book of Thoth*, The Star depicts or rather represents The Lady of the Stars in her mediating influence between Heaven and Hell[11] (note that the positioning of her cups is made in such manner that she receives the essence from the path of Aleph and pours it onto Tiphereth). In this order, we have two important levels of spiritual experience embedded in the doctrine. Further in the attainment arrangement appears the reassembly of the Pyramid on the shores of the Great Sea of Binah represented by the Great Mother. This Holy Trinity of womanhood is of crucial importance to all aspects of the work.

> *And for this is BABALON under the power of the Magician, that she hath submitted herself unto the work; and she guardeth the Abyss. And in her is a perfect purity of that which is above; yet she is sent as the Redeemer to them that are below. For there is no other way into the Supernal Mystery but through her, and the Beast on which she rideth…[12]*

Additionally, the Tetragrammatic journey in Thelemic theory context no longer places the emphasis on the Son, but better yet on the Mother/Daughter. Jehovah, the isolated case of a God, who saw his countenance in the Magical Mirror and

---

10 *Liber CCCCXVIII: The Vision and the Voice*, Aleister Crowley (12th Æthyr)
11 ""Hell" is the pure Inmost Self of Man, that suffereth not extinction, but consumeth all the experiences of Life, coming thereby to know its own Perfection." *Liber CCCCXVIII: The Vision and the Voice*, Aleister Crowley
12 Ibid. (12th Æthyr)

concluded that he is the sole creator who is crushed and destroyed even in the lower planes of the spirit vision. On the other hand, his son, who bears the essence of the father interpolated by the crowning principle of the flaming triune Spirit is no longer the highest dwelling place of supreme attainment. These formulae are still applicable but nevertheless obsolete. Perhaps the fallacy of sovereignty was hinted precisely by the crown of the square: the triune Spirit whose flame extents aloft implies on the lengthiness of the quest.[13] The Son is now the Microcosm, but as such he needs to be integrated in the macrocosmic scheme of things. But back to the incestuous Tetragrammatic scheme! The archetypal son is related to ATU V, or the Hierophant of the Tarot. There is a depicted inherent connection with Heh and the way of the Vau. The sign of the Zodiac encompassed in the card is Taurus, the Bull which is the Kerub of Earth. Earth as such is the little/final Heh of the Tetragrammaton. Furthermore, the pictorial representation of this qabbalistic essence portrays a myriad of feminine elements encompassed in the card. Before the High Priest is a woman girt with a sword, she is Venus, the ruling planet of Taurus. As such she is transformed and adapted to the currents of the new Æon and therefore "no longer the mere vehicle of her male counterpart, but armed and militant."[14] The atmosphere in which the Hierophant operates reminds of Nuit's starry blue, as well as the prevailing color of Saturn pertaining to the Great Mother. Another feminine "slip" in a card showing a man in his high office is the fact that the Moon is exalted in the sign referring to this card. The Moon as such is the feminine part of the duality, the Yin, the Goddess of Women and *Nighttime*. Moreover, the myth of Pasiphae is attributed both to ATU V and ATU XI. Pasiphae in love with the Bull might become Isis (speaking strictly archetypally) whose symbol is the Bull as well. Isis as the Mother is attributed to Binah. However, the Heavenly and Celestial Cow which is also an aspect of Isis can be regarded as Nuit (Infinite Space and Infinite Stars) and therein is a connection with Malkuth and a restoration of the circle or the snake that bites its tail. The entire journey of completeness is shown through a gentler looking glass. In this manner, the Son is tasked with saving the damsel in distress, the fallen Daughter of God, who is also the Mother and surely enough everything feminine in the system. The Son must reconsider his relationship with the feminine current of the age. There is no emphasis on which element is more important, but rather, the focus of the formula is diffused and no longer enlightening the male domination of the magical journey. His duty is to make a "Queen" out of a "Princess."

The symbolism of the Tarot abounds with the presence of the initiatrix. It couldn't be disregarded that the significant portion of the attainment milestones marked by the mind-blowing appearance of women coming across as experiences and shifts in the very cores of those who pursue the path, is especially strong in terms of the current thelemic progression. Everything spins around "her" while "she" is the one that circles around everything. This principle is reflected on the material plane and the fluxes at play enter and radiate by the virtue of women as

13 37 = Jechidah, the Atma of Hindu philosophy, 37x3=111 the Swastika, pertinent to Kether; Also "Flame" three times strengthened and ablaze at the top.
14 *The Book of Thoth*, Aleister Crowley (2011)

divine vessels, catalysts, superconductors, channels, magicians, lovers, initiatrixes, goddesses... The sheer variety of feminine manifestation becomes perplexing.

> *In this Æon, the central formula is not L.V.X., but N.O.X. Much more than the*
> *balance or opposite of L.V.X., the formula of N.O.X. is that of the Mother (ה),*
> *while L.V.X. was once that of the Son (ו). The former once opened the Vault of*
> *Abiegnus; the latter opens the Gates of the City of The Pyramids.[15]*

In this age, the extending light needs to be surrounded by the circle of "darkness" so that it may acquire its true properties. For this to be ensured, the emphasis must be placed on the circle of the unknown that makes the known that which is. The balance is constantly implied, though not always evident. The man, still symbolized by the dying god, must become one with the Mother and journey on to the annihilation of the individual ego. Much like a Thelemic Benjamin Button story, the new formula of initiation is one that draws us towards the womb of the Mother. The mystery of the Averse[16] postulates that even though the New Æon emulates an initiation progression of a child, the starting point is the one that issues from death, or to be more precise, from the land of the dead. The thunder of the sword strikes upon the abode of the Daughter and causes an initial awakening impulse thus reversing the Wheel spinning towards the unison between Mother and child. The Triumphant Mother marks the step of re-entry whence things started to happen at first place. The reabsorption into her body and the transfer of the traveler's essence into the company of heaven represented by the encompassing starry blue of Nuit is the desirable charged potential of nothingness.

This metaphysical paradigm shift of Æonic proportion was originally signaled by the qabbalistic symbolism implanted in the former illustrative representation of the card (the final) Judgement, namely ATU XX. The dreadful image of those who won't wake up to anything less than the call of Israfel's trumpet itself haunted the bewildered interpreters of "old" and gave them *Night* terrors of *Desolation* and *Sorrow* as they saw the world change. The current appearance of this card, at the very least in the relevant Thelemic context, contains the image of the child and its two appropriate forms, thus implying on the forces at work in our current age. But the reputation of this card is such that whenever it cries "wolf" the beast is truly there. So, therein faint, behind the forces of present, lies the still face of Balance. Being a "prophetic" card as it is, it foreshadows the change of the world that is continuously evolving. Moreover, as the little prince now runs towards its mother, eventually it might start to take after the venerable queen. So in relation to everything exposed above, and in terms of the progressing malleability of the female spirit and its thriving influence over the world, the woman could really become "something much more interesting" and much more powerful, self-sustainable and domineering for that matter.

Could she be the puppeteer behind the curtain that although not visibly in

---

15 *Initiation in the Æon of The Child: The Inward Journey,* J. Daniel Gunther (2009)
16 Vide: ibid.

the show was there all the time? As the foundations of human civilization and development were built upon the blueprints of a temple dedicated to the Holy and Mysterious Mother in whom all potentials lay, the top of that structure might as well be cast in the gold of the Stars. There is a sound indication that this advancement won't stop at the step on which we currently stand. The Beasts of women that bleed and do not die might as well take over every sphere of the known and unknown world, mutating the formulae of spirituality to fit their take on life. As terrifying as this sounds, it has a solid tendency of happening.

THE SCIENTIFIC ASSASSINATION OF A SEXUAL REVOLUTIONARY: HOW AMERICA INTERRUPTED WILHELM REICH'S ORGASMIC UTOPIA

Jason Louv

It was the greatest incidence of scientific persecution in American history.

In July of 1947, Dr. Wilhelm Reich – who had once been Freud's most promising student, who had enraged the Nazis and the Stalinists as well as the psychoanalytic, medical and scientific communities, who had survived two World Wars and fled to New York – was dying in a prison cell in Lewisberg, Pennsylvania, accused by the government of being a medical fraud engaged in a "sex racket."

That "racket" would one day be called the "sexual revolution." But it was still 1947 in America – an America not even ready for psychoanalysis, still a nascent science that *Harper's* and *The New Republic* had categorized, right alongside Reich's theories, as being no better than astrology. (Reich, *Harper's* had decided, was the leader of a "new cult of sex and anarchy.")

If the American public wasn't ready for Dr. Freud, then how much less prepared would it be for Dr. Reich – a man who, at his Orgonon institute near Rangely, Maine, was researching the energetic force of orgasm itself?

Reich had taken Freud's theories far – too far, according to the FDA. Starting with Freud's connection of sexual repression to neurosis, Reich had theorized that it was the physical inability to surrender to orgasm that underlay neurosis, and eventually turned people to fascism and authoritarianism. Reich migrated from Freud's simple talking cure to what he called character analysis, a therapy designed to help his patients overcome the physical and respiratory blocks that prevented them from experiencing pleasure. Finally – and most dangerously – he claimed that the orgasm was an expression of orgone, the joy-filled force of life itself. With phone-booth-sized devices called orgone accumulators he could harness this force to cure neurosis, disease and even affect the weather and help crops grow.

For these lines of inquiry, the FDA demanded Reich appear in court to defend himself in 1954. He refused, stating that claims of scientific truth should be settled by experiment, not in court. The court responded by issuing an injunction against the sale or transportation of his devices across state lines, and proceeded to systematically burn his books and journals. Not only Reich's writing but any written material that contained the word "orgone" was fair game for destruction. (Paranoid and embattled, Reich would refuse offers of help from the ACLU, believing it to be filled with communist subversives.) FDA agents also began destroying his devices and laboratory with axes – but that wasn't all. The FDA would carry their persecution of the Austrian psychoanalyst much, much further.

What was it about this man and his theories that invoked the wrath of nearly *every* political and scientific faction of his time? What was it about the "sexual revolution" that earned Wilhelm Reich a 789-page FBI file? What provoked a systematic campaign of attacks hardly suggestive of a sane and rational America that had just won the war against the book-burning Nazis – and more reminiscent of the Inquisition, the incineration of Giordiano Bruno, or the ending of Frankenstein, in which angry villagers with torches and pitchforks burn down the mad scientist's castle?

THE SEXUAL STRUGGLE OF YOUTH

Reich was born on March 24, 1897, on a farm in Galicia, Austria-Hungary, in what is now Ukraine. He embraced sexuality early, unsuccessfully attempting to have sex with his brother's nurse at the age of 4 1/2 and successfully with the family cook at 11. At the age of 12, Reich discovered his mother having sex with one of his tutors. When he told his father, the man repeatedly beat Reich's mother until she committed suicide. Reich blamed himself.

From the age of 15-17, he would pay visits to brothels, and recorded sexually fantasizing about his mother in his diary at the age of 22 (during the same year he met Sigmund Freud, whose theories on the Oedipus complex may have influenced this confession). Lore Reich Rubin, Reich's second daughter, would later tell the journalist Christopher Turner that she believed Reich was a victim of childhood sexual abuse.

Sent into the Army during WWI, Reich saw "man's inhumanity to man" first-hand at the Italian front. Afterwards, he studied medicine at the University of Vienna, where he became dissatisfied with what he considered the "mechanistic" approach to life he saw in his fellow students' cold dissection of corpses. He instead began a quest for the creative energy he felt must underlie life. It was then, in 1919, that he met Sigmund Freud. Welcomed into the burgeoning psychoanalytic movement, Freud allowed Reich to begin seeing patients at the age of 22 – he was soon earmarked as Freud's star pupil, perhaps even destined for leadership.

Freud had identified the root of neurosis in repressed sexuality, and the driving force of life to be the libido – stating that "no neurosis is possible with a normal *vita sexualis.*" His two greatest students, Jung and Reich, were to take his theory further. But while Jung would move into the realm of mythology, symbolism and the occult, Reich would venture in a completely different direction: into the body.

Moving beyond the realm of psychic repression, Reich postulated that trauma was also repressed physically. A child who was abused, for instance, and who lacked the emotional development to process such an event, would "store" the trauma as muscular tension, which could become chronic pains in later life and form the individual's general physicality and character, their approach to existence. Reich believed that the fascist character was created by early trauma and a repressive or abusive attitude towards sexuality that would manifest as physical and emotional "rigidity" in later life – and Reich was concerned with nothing less than the eradication of fascism and authoritarianism.

Reich's approach to therapy would therefore go beyond the simple talking cure: He would also use deep and often extremely painful tissue massage on the patient's areas of muscular tension to release the buried trauma, and work with clients to deepen their constricted breathing and express buried emotions, even their repressed anger and rage. It was this approach, combined with Reich's pro-sexuality attitude, that scandalized the public and put his career on a rocket to nowhere. (Though quite sexually conservative in some ways – he opposed pornography and homosexuality – Reich conducted affairs with patients early in his career, after their therapy had ended. This was not uncommon in the early days of psychoanalysis; even Freud discussed the inevitability of affairs. In his quest to free the life energy, Reich would later have patients partially or totally undress, breaking analytic neutrality totally.)

Yet Reich soon found that working through blocks in both the psyche and musculature would create immense emotional release in his patients, even feelings of bodily elation and bliss. (Reich called these physical sensations "orgonotic streamings.") As his practice continued, he came to theorize that underneath the layers of muscular repression lay what he called "orgiastic potency," and that it was the muscular repression which armored his patients from full orgasmic release – or a full experience of life.

In 1948, he would codify his theory in his major work, *The Function of the Orgasm*, in which he stated that the orgasm exists not only as a reproductive function but as a way for the body to regulate tension and achieve emotional release. Full orgasmic release – in which the individual holds nothing back and does not seek to repress the function psychically or physically – was seen by Reich as a key to mental health. As he wrote in the book, "Psychic illnesses are the result of a disturbance of the natural capacity for love." (Reich would be married and divorced three times – to psychiatrist and former patient Annie Pink from 1924 to 1934, with whom he had two daughters; to dancer Elsa Lindenberg, with whom he had an open marriage from 1933 to 1939; and to Ilse Ollendorff, with whom he had a son, Peter, from 1946 to 1951. Paradoxically, Reich is recorded as being cruel, unfaithful and jealous in his relationships.)

Freud was ambivalent about his disciple's ideas. In 1926 he wrote that "I am in no way opposed to your attempt to solve the problem of neurasthenia by explaining it on the basis of the absence of genital primacy." But he withheld support for Reich's more extreme theories within the broader psychoanalytic community, perhaps with one eye on preserving his own hard-won cultural victories on the issue of sexuality. Without Freud's support, the psychoanalytic community soon washed their hands of the young analyst.

Things began to take a turn for the worse for Reich. Struggling with the reaction against him throughout 1926, he asked to be psychoanalyzed by Freud. His mentor and father figure turned down his request for help. Reich was deeply hurt. Soon afterwards, his brother died of tuberculosis; Reich contracted the disease too, and spent a year in a sanatorium in Davos, Switzerland. Shocked by the sequence of events, he became radicalized and soon joined the Communist Party. Witnessing first-hand the police indiscriminately shoot and kill 84 workers and injure 600 in the July Revolt of 1927 in Vienna further convinced Reich that something was very wrong with the world. The police weren't only brutal, he observed, but they were robotic, as if in a trance – armored.

Working in the streets, Reich now connected sexual repression with the economic repression he saw all around him. He opened a series of clinics throughout Vienna, offering analysis as well as sexual education and contraceptives to young and working-class people. (At the time, liberals advocated contraception only for the married.)

Reich moved to Berlin in 1930, just in time to witness the rise of the Nazis – the apex of character armoring. But though he continued to develop his theories and write, even the Communists showed little interest in his material. His contract with the International Psychoanalytic Publishers was cancelled after he began advocating sexual education and contraceptives for teenagers instead of abstinence – and even suggesting that healthy, demystified sexual expression by children might be crucial to raising healthy adults, and that their questions should be answered frankly. In 1932, in a booklet called *The Sexual Struggle of Youth*, Dr. Reich railed against the mixed messages under which adolescents struggled to understand their sexuality.

"Young people are contaminated on the one hand by moralizers and advocates of abstinence and, on the other hand by pornographic literature," he wrote. "Both influences are extremely dangerous, the former no less than the latter." The stakes were high at that moment in Germany, the 27-year-old psychiatrist observed: "The sexual misery of modern youth is immeasurable, but most of it is out of sight, beneath the surface." His opponents took his statements to mean that children should be able to watch parental intercourse, though Reich never advocated that.

He persisted, arguing forcibly against monogamy, and advocating "lasting love relationships" that were not encoded by law but held together through love; anything else would instead lead to "sexual dulling." He lashed out at the economically dependent status of women that kept them trapped in forced marriages. Most radically of all, he suggested that children should be raised by an extended community, thereby freeing them from the neuroses of their biological parents. (These attitudes were to some extent influenced by similar social experiments occurring in the Soviet Union.)

Dr. Reich was entering taboo territory that few dared to breach, territory that would remain taboo long after he was gone. But his experimentation – and particularly the response it engendered – left him a changed man, for better or worse. When he met with Freud again in 1930, his former mentor now seemed diminished. Dr. Freud, he wrote, was a "caged animal."

In 1933, Dr. Reich's sexual stance provoked the Nazis to action. He and his mistress escaped for Denmark – only to be thrown out of the Danish Communist Party. They relocated to Sweden, where Dr. Reich was placed under surveillance; after the police saw a string of patients coming and going from his hotel, they became convinced he was a pimp. The authorities denied him a longer stay. More shocks were to follow: not only was the contract to publish his book *Character Analysis* cancelled, but upon arriving at the 1934 conference of the International Psychoanalytic Association in Lucerne, he was informed that he had been expelled the previous year. He delivered a paper at the conference as a guest, but the episode marked the very end of his ties to the mainstream scientific community.

> *I was told that my work on mass psychology, which was directed against the irrationalism of fascism, had placed me in a much too exposed position,"* he later wrote. *"Hence, my membership... was no longer tenable. Four years later, Freud had to flee Vienna for London, and the psychoanalytic groups were crushed by the fascists... Subsequently, I avoided contact with my earlier colleagues. Their behavior was neither better nor worse than is usual in such cases. It was low and uninteresting. A good dose of banality is all that is needed to hush up a matter.*

I Got an Orgone Accumulator – And It Makes Me Feel Greater

It was in Norway, where he settled for the next five years, that Dr. Reich developed a new theory: he came to believe that orgasm carried an actual energy, which he termed *orgone*, that was expressed not only by the orgasm response but was, in fact, the energy of life itself. This energy, in his view, permeated nature and the cosmos, expressing itself in atmospheric phenomenon like the *aurora borealis*. (Freud had actually posited a similar theory in the 1890s, but scrapped it.) Dr. Reich further stated that the orgone could be observed objectively, and that it was composed of blue-colored particles called *bions* that he had seen under a microscope. This was perhaps Dr. Reich's most controversial theory – an attempt to move psychoanalysis beyond the realm of soft "science" and directly into the realm of hard physics and biology. For the psychoanalytic community, this was pure heresy.

Having enraged the psychoanalysts, the communists, and the fascists, Dr. Reich now prepared to come under direct attack from the entire scientific community. Norwegian scientists waged war against him in the liberal press, rejecting his research out of hand (while refusing to submit it to a detailed control study) and seeking to deport him. The Norwegian government, which had come under criticism for deporting Trotsky, compromised and allowed Dr. Reich to stay – but arranged that he would be unable to practice psychoanalysis.

When World War II erupted, Dr. Reich, then 36 years old, fled to America, taking up residence in Forest Hills, Queens, and experimenting by injecting cancerous mice with bions. But Reich continued to be a magnet for misfortune. On December 12, 1941, five days after Pearl Harbor and the day after Germany's declaration of war with the United States, he was arrested and jailed by the FBI on Ellis Island. It later turned out to be case of mistaken identity with a communist bookstore owner in New Jersey also named Wilhelm Reich – but the bureau wouldn't acknowledge its mistake until two years later, in November 1943. For the rest of December 1941, however, Reich was left to sleep on a floor next to imprisoned members of the German American Bund, an American Nazi organization that Reich was convinced would kill him.

Wilhelm Reich

The FBI released Reich after he threatened a hunger strike, but Reich remained on the "key figures list" of the Enemy Alien Control Unit, and was kept under state surveillance. The incident demonstrated to Reich that he might have left Europe behind, but there was no escaping the mass psychology of fascism.

Reich became more committed to the cause of breaking down mankind's armoring than ever. Next, he would begin the project that would prove to be his most controversial: an attempt to harness and concentrate orgone with adapted steel Faraday cages he called orgone accumulators. Insulated with organic materials like wood and paper, which Reich believed forced the orgone energy to oscillate back and forth inside, the accumulator, he claimed, could heal mental and physical disturbances – potentially even cancer. On January 13, 1941, Reich brought the devices to Albert Einstein, who tested them enthusiastically, noting that the accumulators created a rise in heat. But when Einstein's assistant, the Polish physicist Leopold Infeld, suggested that the orgone accumulator was producing heat simply because of the temperature gradient in the room, as it was elevated off the floor, Einstein rejected the boxes and refused completely to admit them to further experiment. For Reich, it was a bitter echo of his rejection by Freud, a dismissal by another establishment gatekeeper and potential father figure.

Reich purchased land in Rangely, Maine and opened his "Orgonon" institute, where he would continue his research into orgonomy. Beyond orgone, he now identified a secondary force – DOR or "Deadly Orgone Radiation," a kind of orgasmic anti-matter present in (and responsible for) environmental degradation, that he believed blanketed the world. He soon came to see his work as standing in direct opposition to what the US government had done at Hiroshima and Nagasaki: he was in an arms race for life energy, not death energy.

It was then that Reich began to build massive orgone guns he called "cloudbusters"; these, he claimed, could reverse desertification and create rain. While the government had been using cloud seeding technology since the 1940s to coax water from clouds with silver iodide or dry ice, Reich took a less conventional approach. His cloudbusting technique purported to draw "orgone" energy directly out of the atmosphere through a series of hollow pipes, and into the ground or a body of water, much like a lightning rod, creating clouds in the wake of the channeled orgone. Farmers began paying him to produce rain for their crops – allegedly with success, at least by their own reports.

During this time, Reich claimed that his experiments with cloudbusters had generated interest from some unexpected visitors: he believed that alien UFOs, or "energy alphas" in Reich's terminology, were attacking the earth with Deadly Orgone Radiation. Reich purported to have seen a number of alien craft over Orgonon; once, he said, he and his son had used a cloudbuster to fight a "full scale interplanetary battle" in Arizona.

The FDA's response to Reich's endeavors was to declare him a "fraud of the first magnitude" and obtain an injunction preventing the interstate shipment of orgone accumulators and any related literature. When one of Reich's associates broke the injunction against Reich's wishes, and transported an accumulator across state lines,

141

Reich was arrested on contempt of court and sentenced to two years in prison.

At Lewisburg Federal Penitentiary, Reich was known by other prisoners as the "sex box man." On November 3, 1957, at the age of 60, he died of a heart attack. It was days before he was scheduled to be paroled. Not a single psychiatric or scientific journal covered his passing. Beyond a few anarchist newspapers, his work merited only a paragraph obituary in *Time*:

> Died. Wilhelm Reich, 60, once-famed psychoanalyst, associate and follower of Sigmund Freud, founder of the Wilhelm Reich Foundation, lately better known for unorthodox sex and energy theories; of a heart attack; in Lewisburg Federal Penitentiary, Pa; where he was serving a two-year term for distributing his invention, the "orgone energy accumulator" (in violation of the Food and Drug Act), a telephone-booth-size device that supposedly gathered energy from the atmosphere, and could cure, while the patient sat inside, common colds, cancer, and impotence.

Only a decade later, in the mid 1960s, *Time* would muse that "Dr. Wilhelm Reich may have been a prophet," and "For now it sometimes seems that all America is one big orgone box." But in 1957, the world could care less. Instead of testing his theories or simply dismissing him, the FDA had effectively burned Reich at the stake.

I STILL DREAM OF ORGONON

In his quest to dig mankind's sexual neuroses out by the roots, Reich challenged or broke nearly *every* taboo of Western civilization, angered almost *every* establishment force of the time, and died in prison for his efforts. But his influence may be far greater than he is generally given credit for.

While Reich was languishing in prison, the sexual revolution he had helped initiate was beginning to manifest itself. Elvis made his television debut in 1956, shaking his hips in a decidedly orgone-radiating way, demonstrating the type of freedom from character armor that Reich might have wanted for his patients. By the mid-sixties, and the release of the birth control pill, the sexual revolution was in full swing. ("Sexual revolution," by the way, is a phrase Reich coined.)

Students in the 1968 protests in Paris and Berlin threw copies of Reich's *Mass Psychology of Fascism* at helmeted police. Jack Kerouac and Allen Ginsberg embraced Reich's theories; William S. Burroughs investigated the orgone accumulators for years and wrote about them extensively in his work. He even constructed his own accumulator box, which he would sit inside to write (while smoking kif).

"When I went into the accumulator and sat down I noticed a special silence that you sometimes feel in deep woods, sometimes on a city street, a hum that is more rhythmic vibration than a sound," he wrote in *Junky*. "My skin prickled and I experienced an aphrodisiac effect similar to good strong weed. No doubt about it, orgones are as definite a force as electricity. After using the accumulator for several days my energy came back to normal. I began to eat and could not sleep more than eight hours. I was out of the post cure drag." As he did with ayahuasca, Burroughs had attempted to cure himself of heroin addiction, and withdrawal sickness, with the accumulator. (Despite trying nearly every heroin cure on the planet, Burroughs was never able to remain fully clean for long, and died on a methadone maintenance program.)

Kurt Cobain visited William Burroughs in 1993. "I sat in this orgone machine, and there were black widows in there, he [Burroughs] still has one and I was afraid because I have arachnophobia. He had to kill all of the spiders for me."

Saul Bellow, J. D. Salinger, Michel Foucault and Norman Mailer also dug Reich; like Burroughs, Mailer built his own accumulators and went on an epic quest to free himself through what wrote of as an "apocalyptic orgasm – in his essay *The White Negro*, Mailer spoke of the anti-authoritarian as one who "seeks love... love as the search for an orgasm more apocalyptic than the one which preceded it." Even Sean Connery was soaking up orgone in his own accumulator while starring as James Bond.

The New York Times, in a 1971 review of *The Mass Psychology of Fascism*, called for a serious reappraisal of his work. Reich soon became so fashionable with intellectuals that in 1968, Roger Vadim tormented Jane Fonda on-screen with a pleasure-creating orgone machine in *Barbarella*, and Woody Allen would parody the orgone accumulator as the "Orgasmatron" in his 1973 film *Sleeper*. Over a decade later, Kate Bush and Terry Gilliam would tell Reich's story in Bush's video for *Cloudbusting*, in which Donald Sutherland portrayed Reich, and Bush played the part of his son Peter.

The psychoanalytic discipline's understandable ambivalence about Reich hadn't changed, but as the broader culture changed, Reich's ideas were meeting with wider interest. As Norman Mailer would later summarize his experience with Reichian analysis to Walter Kendrick, "What was important to me was the force, and clarity, and power of [Reich's] early works, and the daring. And also the fact that I think in a basic sense that he was right."

Reich's ideas have never been reassessed by the scientific community – nor by psychoanalysts, who still consider him a black mark on their history. Yet his therapeutic ideas did filter out into the wider psychoanalytic community and took new form under different names, contributing to body psychology, ego psychology, Fritz Perls' *Gestalt* therapy (which seeks to treat the patient as a whole, complex organism instead of only individual symptoms) and Janov's primal scream therapy (which, like Reich's therapy, utilizes screaming and loud vocalization to open up the patient's armoring).

In many ways, nowhere can Reich's influence be detected more than in the vast array of "feel good" body therapies, and even the mass popularity of massage and yoga. Reich's idea that man is caught in the "trap" of his own character armoring found a ready home in the nascent New Age and Human Potential Movement.

Reich's books are kept in print by Farrar, Strauss and Giroux, and the American College of Orgonomy, in Princeton, NJ continues his lines of inquiry, publishing the *Journal of Orgonomy*, hosting public lectures and offering outreach classes. Reichian therapists, though increasingly limited in number, continue to practice. The world of the Reichians, however, remains a closed shop, whether through public disinterest or the siege mentality of Reich's remaining proponents. A few rogue Reichians, like James DeMeo, continue to attempt new experiments and generate minor publicity. Dr. Reich's archives are maintained by the Wilhelm Reich Infant Trust at Orgonon. His final resting place is on the 175-acre, forested property. The estate welcomes visitors.

Only fifty years after the sexual revolution that Reich foresaw, we live in a hypersexualized society – a place where we're constantly barraged by the opposite of sexual repression. Everything around us seems to be hard at work accumulating our orgone – advertising, pop stars, television, magazines, Internet porn.

But while 21st century humanity perhaps seems more sexually liberated, Reich probably would have seen media overstimulation as just a new form of "running" a way of escaping loving contact with another human being. Fervently against pornography, Reich might have seen a civilization hunched over at computers and sweatshop benches, trading connection with the physical for connection to a smartphone, and concluded that the "emotional plague" was alive and kicking. He may have seen a population more armored than ever, immersed in an environment full of some variant of Deadly Orgone Radiation, out of contact with life, and in need, perhaps, of a completely new sexual liberation – a return to the physical world.

To Make It Happen:
Communicating with the Invisible

Kasper Opstrup

Let thy lips bluster with my words! Are they not meteors in the brain? Back, back from the face of the accursed one, who am I; back in the night of my father, into the silence; for all that ye deem right is left, forward is backward, upward is downward.

– Aleister Crowley 1911: 448

In times of systemic change and political upheaval, old dreams of creating autonomous universities often find new expressions. Mostly, the hope seems to be to produce historical roots to the given movement as well as future escape routes from the present. Examples of this can be found both in the wave of anarchist free schools in the 1920s and 1930s as well as in the Free University movement of the 1960s and the 1970s. Today, there has been a renewed critical interest in (higher) education. Artists and activists have experimented with new types of communities and the creation of new institutions both inside and outside the already existing ones. On the one hand, the art space has been instrumentalised as a space for experimental learning. On the other, the learning site has always already been a place for the formation and production of subjectivity (Allen 2011; Ivison et al.: 2013).

In the wake of the international occupy movements, there has been a return of free universities and free schools where new desires for collectivity and action, for alternative ways of rigging the world, have arisen.

While the medieval universities arose to challenge the church's monopoly on knowledge, its catholic dogma and the powers the church represented, the modern university became the educational apparatus which produced future leaders and tycoons. The postmodern university has largely become either a place for mass education or, in terms of research, it has been instrumentalised by means of funding from major corporations. In contrast, the free universities emerged to produce and share a knowledge that their participants deemed necessary for human survival, believing that the course of capitalism is catastrophe and that there were only minutes to go before annihilation would strike. Alternatively, in a tradition that reaches back to, at least, German Romanticism and Schiller's notion of an aesthetic education of man, they insisted upon the right to dream and act informed by a politics of revelation based on Blakean visions and a pre-occupation with utopian living.

145

The Free University movement, including anti-universities, spontaneous universities, action universities and the like, emerged in the context of the budding counter-culture of the early 1960s. On the one hand, it can be traced back to the civil rights movement and its freedom schools in Mississippi and, on the other, it became part of the arsenal of the New Left through the Free Speech movement at the University of Berkeley. More or less instantaneously, it spread to the UK and Europe where it merged with other traditions of learning. This international movement can be seen as an attempt to reinvent the educational institutions. It is an idea about revolution as a type of collective desch0oling which is able to break the shackles of past conditioning as it has been internalised by the exploited classes and their tribunes. Like the situationists who imagined a take-over of UNESCO, it is a realisation that a postmodern revolution needs to be a cultural revolution that produces subjectivities.

In order to produce communism, one needs to produce a new type of wo/man.

The means to realise this age-old dream of un-alienated existence, thus, becomes a new type of university. If we accept that any successful revolution is dependent upon a new production of subjectivity, the free universities can be seen as the backbone of the counterculture. They wanted to detonate what the Scottish writer Alexander Trocchi called an 'invisible insurrection' in the manifesto for his sigma pipe dream, 'A Revolutionary Proposal: Invisible Insurrection of a Million Minds' (Trocchi 1962-7). In short, sigma combined a beat ethos with situationism and imagined spontaneous universities built outside all major cities in the world. They were to be close enough to take advantage of the already existing infrastructure but would eventually grow into experimental cities which would slowly become strong enough to become foci of counter-power. What should be taught there was how to fight behavioural conditioning (Opstrup 2014). Again following situationism, the 'sigmanauts' realised that the crisis was systemic.

Structural transformation was necessary in order to produce an as yet unknown future. This desire for an unknown future – which is unfathomable yet has to be produced by what already is – opens the gates for the occult revival of the 1960s. Esoteric topics became standard in most of the free universities: psychonautism as a radical political and educational practice. In this context, the occult becomes a means through which to think the unthinkable and comprehend the unknowable. It can be thought of as a strategic, psychogeographical displacement which can be used for contesting pre-learned as well as habitual terms and thought patterns.

It is a question of how to understand, manipulate and communicate with the invisible.

Thus, a kind of 'potere occulto' opens up the possibility of switching the terrain on which questions of future societies and what is to be done are discussed in order to approach these through a kind of 'magickal Marxism' instead of through handed down dogma. Seen in this perspective, magick – which all good art and poetry strive to become[1] – becomes politicised as a continuation of the class struggle by other

---

1 Compare, for example, Crowley's famous definition of magick from the introduction to *Magick in Theory and Practice* as the 'Art of causing Change to occur in conformity with Will' with Burroughs' oft-

means; 'the superstructure's superstructure', as Dr. Last, a semi-fictive portrait of the anti- psychiatrist R. D. Laing, calls it in Clancy Sigal's novel *Zones of the Interior* (1976).

Instead of the classical model for warfare, informed by Clausewitz and taken up by the situationists, where two opposing armies confront each other on the battlefield, it becomes semiotic guerilla warfare, sabotage on the level of words and ideas in an uneven terrain.

Laing was in direct touch with the London Anti-University which – for a short moment in time – seemed like the realisation of sigma's eternal dream of creating an anti-university, an arts lab, a fun palace. Even though it only existed in material terms during the spring of 1968, it not only questioned the relationship between teacher and pupil, but also the subject matter and research autonomy of the traditional university by offering courses in matters normally suppressed or marginalised: esoterica, Forteana, communism, anarchism, histories from below.

As such, it does not seem coincidental that the magickal revival – magick had been relegated to its chthonic existence by the rise of rationality after the renaissance (Webb 1974) – started to accelerate in late romanticism, where a barrage of theories about art, politics, evolution, education and speculations about the future of wo/ man can be found, e.g. S. L. MacGregor Mathers' creation of the Hermetic Order of the Golden Dawn which can only be compared to freemasonry and Madame Blavatsky's Theosophic Society in its influence on modern occultism. Together, these three constitute the roots of the patchwork spirituality and the rise of the New Age movement often associated with the 1960s. It is a world view where alienation has evaporated and the rules of rationality are defunct due to that 'one and one is not two, but one' to paraphrase British occultist and Golden Dawn member Aleister Crowley.

Seen in this perspective, the 1960s were truly the 'morning of the magicians' where access to esoteric knowledge and hidden doctrines traditionally reserved for initiates became widely accessible to an experimental public interested in defining a new way of life.

One of the first to critically analyse the wave of free universities was Theodore Roszak who was also briefly affiliated with the Anti-University. In his seminal *The Making of a Counter-Culture* (1968), he found that these new universities were characterised by a move from the political towards the mystical. If one examines the first three catalogues of courses from the Anti-University it is clear, though, that these two tendencies were present at the same time: it was as much about inner space as it was about outer. As such, they complement each other by paying attention to not only an outer history of failed revolutions and ecstatic insurrections but by also being sensitive towards inner space by exploring anti-psychiatry, psychotherapy, magick and mysticism, thus charting the grey zone between psychiatry and religion where both existential anti-psychiatry and esotericism can be located.

Such a concatenation of art, politics, occultism and experimental learning is also conspicuously present in a slightly later example: Thee Temple ov Psychick

---

quoted adage that the purpose of writing is 'to make it happen'.

Youth (TOPY), which was active during the 1980s. The immediate precursor to TOPY was Academy 23, a free schooling initiative described by William Burroughs through a series of articles in the magazine *Mayfair* in the late 1960s as well as in the last chapter of his interview book, *The Job* (1974). Academy 23 was developed through conversations with Trocchi about sigma – which Burroughs contributed to – and the founding of a spontaneous university. Thus, it can be seen as a sort of sister project to the sigma project which was the immediate precursor to the Anti-University. At the Academy, the students would respond to the prophetic calls for a new aeon by creating a new mythology for the space age while learning to fight control. In Burroughs' interpretation, words and their linearity are vehicles for control. When grammar becomes politics by other means acts of resistance can be the discovery of a new word; the re-arranging of old words; the creation of languages.

TOPY was the creation of an anti-cult. The same way the Anti-University realised parts of the sigma project, TOPY would realise parts of the Burroughsian academy. The roots of the temple goes back to industrial subculture, the band Throbbing Gristle and, earlier, the performance group COUM Transmissions. The common denominator between the three is the persona of Genesis (Breyer) P. Orridge. After the dissolution of Throbbing Gristle in 1981, P-Orridge and Peter 'Sleazy' Christopherson continued with the project Psychick TV (PTV), which would become the propaganda wing of the temple, just as TOPY would become the ideological wing of PTV. The goal was to realise Academy 23's transcendence of conditioned consciousness with an emphasis on 'occulture' – a term coined by TOPY – rather than a more recognisable political agenda.

It could be a kind of creative anarchism more closely related to Stirner than to Bakunin and thus a type of collectivity which emphasised individual emancipation.

TOPY revealed itself to a wider public on the PTV album *Force the Hand of Chance* (1982). The track *Message from the Temple* presented the temple and became its first open call for affiliation. From there it evolved to become an improvised organisational structure that along the way experimented with various types of apparatuses for behavioural conditioning from the cultic to the educational. These founding ideas developed through discussions between the American performance artist Monte Cazazza and P-Orridge (2009a: 175) about

> ... *what might happen if a rock band, instead of just seeing fans as an income flow and an ego booster, focused that admiration and energy toward a cultural and lifestyle-directing network? What would happen if we created a paramilitary occult organization that shared demystified magickal techniques? Sleeve notes could become manifestos, a call to action and behavioural rebellion.*

Maybe the temple started as a sort of fan club and cult of personality but it soon evolved to become a network of artists, musicians and writers who tried to make an intervention in the mainstream with ideas about a new culture and an emancipated art which did not yet exist. They showed their belonging to the greater TOPY community by doing an unusual thing: practicing ceremonial magick and sex magick in a way similar to the then contemporary chaos magick scenes. Their book of methods, *Thee Grey Book* (1982), stated the TOPY mission: "We are not seeking followers, we are seeking collaborators. Individuals for a Psychick Alliance. What we suggest next is not instruction. It is a method. [...] Our interest is therefore practical." (P-Orridge et al 1982:41).

TOPY's methods were influenced by situationistic *détournement* which had become part and parcel of underground culture in the UK not least through sigma but, to an even greater degree, they were inspired by the cut-up methods of Brion Gysin and William Burroughs – this was obviously related to *détournement* in the way that use is made of what is already there – which they applied to everything from words, pictures, sounds, video experiments, television programmes, e.g. *First Transmission* (1982) which was meant to be sent between midnight and 6 am. They even cut up their own bodies as in P-Orridge's later *pandrogeny* project. They claimed to be modern alchemists who through cultural production, the free circulation of information and the viral transmission of memes could alter the ways of the world. P-Orridge (2006: 279):

> *Everything is recorded. If it is recorded, then it can be edited. If it can be edited, then the order, sense, meaning and direction is as arbitrary and personal as the agenda and/or person editing. This is magick. For if we have the ability and/or choice of how things unfold – regardless of the original order and/or intention that they are recorded in – then we have control over the eventual unfolding.*

At its peak, TOPY had a headquarters, TOPY WORLD, in Brighton, UK, three major centres in the UK, the US and Europe as well as various smaller Access Points which could be anything from an affinity group to a single person distributing information about TOPY locally while pretending to be an institution in the tradition of Mail Art. In the early 1990s, the network – which several members have referred to as 'being the internet before the internet' – rapidly expanded as it began to recruit more broadly and become part of the expanding tactical media scenes. The temple itself, though, lost its momentum after 1991, when the police raided the Brighton HQ on suspicions that P-Orridge was the ring leader in a Satanic child abuse ring. This caused P-Orridge to close down the network and choose exile in the US. During the next few years, the network completely dissolved in Europe where its members drifted on to related projects like, for example, the Association of Autonomous Astronauts who became part of the creative activism scenes connected to the rave culture and the anti-globalisation movements around the turn of the millennium.

These various types of experiments with a type of aesthetic education wanted to produce a future that was unknown but self-organised; it was about being pro-active and organising one's own temple, sigma centre, academy, anti-university, enabling the movement to spread like a virus and create a leaderless network where nobody would need a badge to know they were part of it.

The ones who were able to come in and feel comfortable were welcome to stay. The weapons of this invisible insurrection would be cut-ups, détournements, new medias – a post-modern politics par excellence (Gilman-Opalsky 2013). The terrain consisted of images, myths, ideas, architecture; stories we tell ourselves and each other in order to mobilise energy and move in multiple directions. The free universities would detonate the insurrection. From then on, it would have a snowball effect: the myriad creation of new forms of life based upon a bio-political production of subjectivity and a new mythology; de-mystified structures one could utilise at will. Ultimately, by using the apparatuses at their disposal and by enabling experimentation with behaviours and limits, they sought to produce the new wo/man of the future.

That which follows capitalism must necessarily come through that which has already been produced by capitalism.

Ironically, in this vein then, it is the scientific world view and technological acceleration that some claim have caused social fragmentation and a spiritual vacuum which become part of creating a new techno-eschatology; what the cultural critic Mark Dery (1996: 9) has called 'a theology of the ejector seat'. It is not just about exodus, it is about leaving the body and the planet behind in order to emigrate to outer space as bodies of light.

That the battle is fought on the level of language can mean that a possible escape route is total silence.

The counter-cultural universities strove to unite the inner with the outer in order to find a way out which often as not proved to be a way in. The new centres expressed the politics of the New Left – a motley combination of anarcho-communism and revisionist Marxism – on their own user-run schools and universities where the syllabus included cultural production and a revival of the occult: tarot cards, transcendental meditation, Thelema.

It can be seen as an attempt to link psychological revolution with social revolution in order to make an opening for other futurities. Trocchi once termed these possibilities as 'cultural engineering'.

Cultural engineering recognises that a broader wish for social transformation has to spread through a population like a cultural meme but also that this is dependent upon an altered state of consciousness where instead of talking about 'there', we talk about 'here' and instead of talking about 'then', we talk about 'now'. Our predecessors in the1960s thought that the survival of humanity was dependent upon a pooling of resources, a sharing of knowledge as well as the creation of a free information exchange.

This resonates into our own contemporary with, for example, the Italian media theorist Franco 'Bifo' Berardi (2013: 34) who, in a recent interview stated, that "[n]ow more than ever we have to invest our political and cultural energy into the creation of an autonomous process of self-education, of research and transmission of knowledge".

To Make It Happen

A List of Works Cited

—∿— Allen, F. (red.) (2011): *Education*, London: Whitechapel Gallery

—∿— Berardi, Franco 'Bifo': 'Autonomy and General Intellect', in: Ivison et al. 2013: 31-42

—∿— Berke, Joseph (ed.) (1968): *The Antiuniversity of London – Catalogue of Courses, vol. 1, 2, 3* + newsletter, 1968, London: Antiuniversity of London

—∿— Burroughs, William S. & D. Odier (1974): *The Job: Interviews with William S. Burroughs*, London: Penguin Books 2008

—∿— Crowley, Aleister (1911): 'The Vision and the Voice', in: Regardie, Israel (1974): *Gems from the Equinox – Instructions by Aleister Crowley for His Own Magical Order*, San Francisco: Red Wheel/Weiser 2007

—∿— Dery, Mark (1996): *Escape Velocity – Cyberculture at the End of the Century*, London: Hodder & Stoughton

—∿— Gilman-Opalsky, Richard (2013): 'Unjamming the Insurrectionary Imagination: Rescuing Détournement from the Liberal Complacencies of Culture Jamming', in: *Theory in Action, Vol. 6, No. 3*, July 2013, pp. 1-34

—∿— Ivison, Tim & T. Vandeputte (red.) (2013): *Contestations: Learning from Critical Experiments in Education*, London: Bedford Press

—∿— Opstrup, Kasper (2014): 'On the Ecstatic Edge of Something to be Known: Three 1960s Experiments with Total Transformation and Experimental Learning', in: Grindon, G. (ed.): *Art, Production and Social Movement: Remapping the History of the Radical Avant-Garde;* Wivenhoe: Minor Compositions (forthcoming)

—∿— P-Orridge, Genesis Breyer et al (1982): 'Thee Grey Book', in: P-Orridge 2009b: 37 - 50

—∿— P-Orridge, Genesis Breyer (2006): 'Magick Squares and Future Beats: The Magickal Process and Methods of William S. Burroughs and Brion Gysin', in: P-Orridge 2009b: 275 - 298

—∿— P-Orridge, Genesis Breyer (2009a): 'Thee Process is thee Product – The Processean Influence on Thee Temple Ov Psychick Youth', in: Wyllie 2009: 173-184

—∿— P-Orridge, Genesis Breyer (2009b): *Thee Psychick Bible: Thee Apocryphal Scriptures ov Genesis Breyer P-Orridge and the Third Mind ov Thee Temple Ov Psychick Youth*, Port Townsend: Feral House

—∿— Roszak, Theodore (1969): *The Making of a Counter Culture*, Berkeley and Los Angeles: University of California Press 1995

—∿— Sigal, Clancy (1976): *Zone of the Interior*, West Yorkshire: Pomona 2005

—∿— Trocchi, Alexander (ed.) (1964-7): *Sigma Portfolio 1 – 39*, London: sigma

—∿— Webb, James (1974): *The Occult Underground*, Chicago: Open Court 1990

—∿— Wyllie, Timothy et al. (2009): *Love Sex Fear Death: The Inside Story of the Process Church of the Final Judgment*, Port Townsend: Feral House

A Manifesto of Apocalyptic Witchcraft

Peter Grey

1

It is not our way of life, it is life itself which is under threat.

2

Witchcraft is our intimate connection to the web of life.

3

We are the Witchcraft.

4

Our world has forever changed.
The trodden paths no longer correspond.
Witchcraft thrives in this liminal, lunar, trackless realm.

5

We are storm, fire and flood.

6

We will not be denied.

7

Witchcraft is the recourse of the dispossessed, the powerless,
the hungry and the abused.
It gives heart and tongue to stones and trees.
It wears the rough skin of beasts.
It turns on a civilisation that knows the price of everything
and the value of nothing.

8

If you have no price you cannot be bought.
If you do not want you cannot be bribed.
If you are not frightened you cannot be controlled.

9
Witchcraft is folk magic, the magic of the people and for the people.

10
We call an end to the pretence of respectability.

11
We will not disarm ourselves.

12
The War is upon us.

13
Choose then to become a Mask.

14
Those with nothing left to lose will dare all.

15
There is one Witchcraft under many names.
There is one Grand Sabbat on one mountain.
There are many ways to fly.
There is no witness present at the Sabbat.

16
Witchcraft is a force, not an order.
Witchcraft is rhizomatic, not hierarchic.
Witchcraft defies organisation, not meaning.
We simply bear the marks.

17
Witchcraft is power and possesses this in ekstasis, sex and ordeal.

18
Witchcraft is unbridled sexuality.
In Witchcraft it is the woman who initiates.
We challenge man to be the equal of this woman.

19
Witchcraft is the art of inversion.

20
Witchcraft is the beauty which is terror.

21

Witchcraft is a myth, which drawing on the past,
clothes itself in the symbols of (its) time.
Witchcraft does not mistake myths for history,
it harnesses them to transform the future.
Witchcraft knows the ground upon which it stands.

22

Witchcraft honours the spirits.
Witchcraft enchants for the lost.
Witchcraft will not forget.

23

Witchcraft embodies our ancestors and saints, they carry us with them.

24

To Her is offered the blood, to us the care of the ash and bones.

25

The example we follow is our own.

26

The practice of witchcraft is one of revolution
and of the power of woman.

27

The Goddess who speaks through us is known among men as Babalon.

28

Witchcraft concerns itself with mystery.
Through the gates of mystery we come to knowledge.
Knowledge enters us through the body.
The highest form of this knowledge is Love.

29

Every drop of blood is sacrificed to the grail.
Love cannot be bought with any other coin.

30

We seek and drink this wine together.

31

Will is finite, passion infinitely renewed.

A Manifesto of Apocalyptic Witchcraft

32

Witchcraft is present, it is ensanguined and vivified.
Witchcraft is prescient, it gazes on the future.
Witchcraft is oracular, it will not hold its tongue.
Our time has come.

The Gospel of Cosmic Terror

Why Open the Gateways to Extra-dimensional Worlds and Entities?

Timothy O'Neill

The gnostic theme of Earth as a Cosmic Prison Planet has a long and noble past. Many of the 1ˢᵗ and 2ⁿᵈ Century Gnostics viewed the Earth as a coffin, a morbid grave or a pulsating Hell of trapped and mindless souls struggling for Light in a dark pit. This vision has taken on new depth and prescience in light of the accelerating levels of anomaly and high strangeness that we experience in our mundane existence. It is as if the prison walls are suddenly becoming more and more porous and allowing *things* from elsewhere to walk freely amongst us as they will but still keeping humanity trapped.

H.P. Lovecraft's famous story *From Beyond* suggests that we swim in a black sea of infinity populated by horrendous creatures who can see us, but we cannot see them. The movie *Pitch Black* takes place on a planet with three suns that experiences a total eclipse of absolute darkness for one year out of every 22 years. That is when vicious and unearthly predators emerge from their caves and feast upon anything moving. It is the perfect metaphor for our planet, where humans are trapped in mindless and pointless electro-amusement whilst all manner of interdimensional, extradimensional and ultradimensional beings move through us every second of every day. As Lovecraft notes, if our minds could correlate the fullness of their own contents, we would be driven stark raving insane. He adds to this that it would also lead to the dawning of a new and horrible Dark Age.

In a real sense, the fact that our minds normally filter out the entirety of reality is a good thing. Recent psychological research has indicated that many things just under the normal range of our awareness are still recognized by the mind, interpreted and stored in the deep vaults of memory. This Twilight World of our inner perceptions is undoubtedly filled with unimaginable terrors and things that would jar our waking ideas of reality. There are thick shells of cognitive dissonance surrounding us and it is only in moments of magickal practice, psychedelic awareness, and highly altered states of awareness or extreme experience that we become aware of them for even a split second. Lengthening those seconds into moments in order to discover new worlds is what Magick is becoming, slowly but surely. But still, why would we risk life and sanity to explore such unearthly and terrifying cosmic realities?

My past articles in *The Fenris Wolf* have covered a variety of magickal topics including the construction and use of astral machines, the role of some long neglected areas in alternate physics, conspiracy theories, the role of the Nothingness as the root of Magick and I hope to tie these all together in this article into a larger picture that indicates practical efforts and experiments to come. This is part of a larger project that I term the "Grand Correlation." H.P. Lovecraft's famous comment that "The most merciful thing in the world… is the inability of the human mind to correlate all of its contents" is a statement which will serve as a foundation for this article. It led me to the conclusion that such a correlation, even in part, might have positive aspects for the revelation of what is actually occurring in the World on levels we cannot usually see. Seeing the connections that others might miss is as much the method of the paranoid schizophrenic as it is the hope of the investigator or detective. It is an informing method for Kenneth Grant, whose Typhonian Magick forms the backbone of our work here.

As synchronicity would have it, Peter Levenda's new book *The Dark Lord: H.P. Lovecraft, Kenneth Grant and the Typhonian Tradition in Magic* was published by Ibis Press on my greatest Holy Day of the year; Lammas Day, August 1st, 2013. Levenda approaches the very same essential problem that I am writing about here, but in a very different way. He writes about Kenneth Grant with tremendous insight and clarifies several problematic areas that Typhonians have struggled with over the past six decades. His book is well worth the read, although it will probably infuriate most normative Thelemites and many Typhonians. He quotes a Typhonian Order newsletter published in Miami in the 1990's, which seizes upon the central goal of the Typhonian-Sethian Current in no uncertain terms:

"The central concern of Magick is the communication with disincarnate or extraterrestrial intelligences." (Page 286 of the Kindle Edition of *The Dark Lord*)

The central force creating and shaping that communication is agreed upon by all parties to be sexual in nature and that I would not doubt. The idea that such sexuality would be antinomian and transgressive in nature is not to be argued. The idea that Tantra in some form is essential to the practice of extraterrestrial or ultraterrestrial communication is also clear. The possible use of The Voidness in that Tantra is also clear, although Crowley and Grant steer clear of the Yoga of Emptiness in favor of a more technical and earthly approach founded in the chemistry of the human body and the nervous system. I believe the human body is still the key to the Work, but more as an anchor and spiritual matrix than as a chemistry lab. That is open to discussion, as we shall see. The use of advanced physics and non-Euclidean geometries, guided by the ideas of Scientific Illuminism is also an integral piece of this practice, as is the use of advanced astral and causal plane machines and servitors to aid the Work. We are looking at a system that is parallel to Thelemic principles but that moves beyond it to the same areas explored by Kenneth Grant, H.P. Lovecraft and Richard Sharpe Shaver, the great trinity of explorers who carved out this domain of Cosmic Terror.

Let me state clearly that I am not directly initiated into any Thelemic organizations and I will not claim any Initiation or Work beyond those of the Rosicrucian and Martinist Orders and the Kriya Yoga Path of Satsanga Yogoda. Those bodies are perhaps best considered as cognates and fellow travelers to the Thelemites along divergent and distinct roads. Yet, of course, we wind up at the same summit of the Holy Mountain, Abiegnus, where the 13 gated City of black basalt walls awaits us with its bizarre and troubling sigils, marks, signs and wonders. Above that City floats Polaris, strange home to unknown monsters and beings we can barely dream of. The Mysteries of Thelema and the Mysteries of the Rose Cross are both mysteries of the Stars for the Stars are the origins of the oldest and most powerful magical traditions, so much older than Egypt and even Sumeria that we cannot imagine in what strange Ocean they were born.

It is at this point that I begin a strange and winding story which is born in a dream which I had in 2005:

I am on the wide grassy field and there is a large and stately University edifice before me. It is all white and shining marble. It feels very much like we are in the 1950's or early 1960's. There are dozens of steps leading down from the University building to the grassy field. I see a close friend; a young black man dressed in beige slacks, loafers and a collegiate letter-sweater, coming down the steps. He is wearing black framed glasses. I wave at him and he suddenly collapses. I run to his side and yell for help. The next thing that I am aware of in the dream is standing next to him as he lies in a hospital bed, hooked to all kinds of wire and tubes. He is barely conscious. The doctor looks at me and says that my friend is suffering from a completely unknown kind of disease. His flesh is slowly melting away and there is nothing that they can do to stop it. I look at him and he is thinner than I can possibly imagine. When I return the next day, his flesh is entirely gone and he has been reduced to an ebony black skeleton with gleaming ruby eyes that look like gems. He is still somehow magically alive. It takes me quite some time to come to terms with this and I sit on a bench outside his hospital room trying to make sense of it.

When I come out of my reverie, my friend is already being released from the hospital since there is nothing more they can do. He is alive, yet he is dead. It is inexplicable. I arrange for a robe to cover his body... a brilliant red-scarlet robe with a hood that only allows his eyes to be seen. We travel to a house where he tells me that if I take a close look at his bones I will see something. He holds his arm out to me and I look at the highly polished ebony surface of his bones. I can see stars, nebulae, galaxies and things that I cannot comprehend or understand. It is at that point that I understand intuitively in the middle of the dream that my friend has become an avatar of Nyarlathotep. We sit together, huddled over the wooden table in the simple little house. He tells me that he is planning a great war and that I shall be his lieutenant, his amanuensis, his strength on the battlefield. It is never clear in the dream exactly who the enemy is, but our Army is called the Army of the Single Eye and we use the ancient machines of the Elder Gods to blister and erase the heathens who do not worship the Great Ancient Ones. Slowly, the tide begins to turn against us as the enemy begins nuclear attack. The huge black basalt fortress in the sands of Arabia is beginning to fall, when my friend and master looks at me, hands me a simple scroll and tells me to bring it to the World, since it will be a greater weapon that all of the atomic bombs put together. I opened the scroll and looked at it. It was completely and utterly blank.

At that point, I awoke in a cold sweat. The dream was completely lucid, logical and absolutely terrifying, like being in the middle of a widescreen Technicolor movie. I have spent years feeling the effects of that dream upon my destiny and my existence. I realized that I needed to write and draw this scroll as a large part of my life's work. These articles in *The Fenris Wolf* have parts of that project that are now drawing together into a larger whole. For some time, I felt that this was the true form of the *Necronomicon:* a *tabula rasa* into which we dream the Stars and their terrifying inhabitants. Lately, it has become more and more clear that the *Necronomicon* was intended to be a defensive book designed to contain and "control" the Great Ancient Ones and Elder Gods. The Scroll is intended to be the way to open the doors to them. The Schlangekraft recension (The version transcribed from the Greek by "Simon" and available as a simple paperback from booksellers all over the world – over one million copies have been sold!) is basically a magical text of protection based upon Babylonian-Sumerian Mythology rather than the actual magical practices of antiquity.

Even the more advanced sections of the book that dare to invoke a presence of the outsiders do so with head cowered and eyes averted to avoid the danger of insanity upon seeing them. *The Scroll of the Desert Prince* (The name that the Avatar of Nyarlathotep took in my dream) would be something different: a scientific document that approaches the problem from the viewpoint of mathematics and physics. The extraterrestrials, extradimensionals and subterranean ultraterrestrials operate in realms of pure number and geometry. To approach them from that "angle" creates an entirely different perspective.

Does "Magick" *work* in such an environment? Should we be doing this at all? That is the question behind this paper. I believe that it does and the keys may lie in Civilization One, the very ancient Civilization that created an advanced scientific culture some 60,000 years ago. This was a culture that worked with Nature and Her secrets rather than trying to master Her like a slave. The great cyclopean stone monuments of the ancient past, the megalithic cultures of Malta, Turkey, Russia, India, South America, etc. all worked to enhance the fertility and peace of the land. They knew the secrets of Nature because they *loved* Her.

There is a very interesting and highly revealing sequence towards the climatic and dreamlike ending of the *Chemical Wedding of Christian Rosenkreutz*. After his bizarre and deeply initiatory experiences, beginning with the Royal Wedding, Christian is finally able to pass by the Porter who controls access to the Door of the Cave of Venus deep below the Sacred Mountain. Once inside her cave, she reveals to him her Mysteries by unveiling herself and allowing him to see her naked. The book suddenly ends on that note. We garner that the Rosicrucians were trying to revive the wisdom of the ancients that we now call Civilization One. The sciences and Mysteries that they celebrated came from the Stars and to the Stars they will allow us to return someday. The Goddess is our guide because she controls the central force, the fire of Kundalini that allows our Magick to proceed to the goal.

There is much ambiguity around the whole idea of our relationship with the Great Ancient Ones and the Elder Gods, who are, after all, extraterrestrial, extradimensional and ultraterrestrial beings of some kind. It is thought that they may have created us as a jest or as a steady supply of food, genetic experimentation and amusement. Charles Fort noted that we seem to be owned by someone and this may be the answer to whom that might be. Friendly Space Brothers there may be, but the UFO experience teaches us that there are much darker and more terrifying realities out there. August Derleth, Lovecraft's friend and founder of Arkham House saved his work from oblivion but he seriously misunderstood Lovecraft's Philosophy of Cosmic Terror and Despair. There is no "Magic" capable of holding back such fundamental forces of anti-nature from another Universe, another Dimension or from below the surface of the ground we walk upon. The Simon *Necronomicon* (The Schlangekraft Recension as Peter Levenda terms it) magnifies the error by supposing that Babylonian and Sumerian magic can hold back the alien. There is no basis for that belief. There is simply no protection outside of what we can do by understanding and using the same advanced mathematics and geometries that the outsiders live in.

It is clear that the *Necronomicon* in Lovecraft's mind was something very different and something much more like what I imagine the *Scroll of the Desert Prince* to resemble. Reading about it in his stories, it is clear that it is a text on how to *open the gateways* and *call forth these entities from their hiding places, to make them manifest.* This is the true idea of what the *Necronomicon* would really be. But why would we want to call such horrors into physical manifestation? Donald Tyson in his cycle of books based upon the literary *Necronomicon* takes the position that we *should* invoke these entities because if filtered properly through the right sort of magic, they can teach us wonders beyond the imagination and open infinite gateways to our exploration. Let us assume that the Scroll of the Desert Prince would be a book of openings, evocations and invocations rather than a book of closings or protective spells. This may be a strong clue to the counter-intuitive reasons that we should open to these worlds and their creatures who see us as microscopic pests.

To open a door requires that one knows some key things: where the door is, when it opens and what is behind it. Those are all issues in classical Physics, and it strikes me that the Scroll would have be two things: a book of equations, simple equations that can open the mind when deeply contemplated in the Tantric states. I am thinking here of the Quaternion equations of James Clerk Maxwell with their "spooky" implications of hidden forces. It would also be a book of geometric signs and glyphs which would open deeply atavistic areas of the reptile brain which are more capable of perceiving the Great Ancient Ones than our developed forebrain with its filters and defenses. Add to these the ideas of the generation of everything out of nothing and the use of Astral Machines and you have the following elements:

The mind-opening equations of the classical Illuminati redaction:

The Gospel of Cosmic Terror

radius >=0 The Physical world

radius <=0 The Astral World of Dreams and Quantum Reality

radius = 0 The Causal World of Pure Thought

The Quaternion equations of Maxwell

The Work of Kozyrev on Time and Space

The Topological Metaphor as described by Joseph P. Farrell

This gives us a clue that the secrets are found not only in geometry, but in the field of *Topology*. Joseph P. Farrell has covered this ground extensively and it is beyond the scope of this article, but the "Topological Metaphor" that he describes contains the secrets to R.A. Schwaller De Lubicz' "Primal Scission" of nothing into something. It is quite true that even the outsiders must obey these equations when they are in physical form. That gives us an edge which we can use to filter and protect the mind for at least a moment in their presence. There is a rich literature of Alien Abduction and UFO experiences which also help in this regard, The High Strangeness of these visitors can be invoked and utilized once its source is found in the topological sciences. We will have more to say about the centrality of the UFO experience in all of this below.

The atavistic mind opening glyphs and signs that work with geometry and topology to create a framework for nonlinear perception are purely intuitive and based in the Tantric sciences. For them to be effective in reaching down into our atavistic roots, the body must *change* and be trained. This is the catch, for it demands total sacrifice. The Oracle of the Atavism makes the sacrifice of life and sanity in order to contact that which transcends the forebrain but it is a consciously chosen and consensual decision. The Megalithic cultures reached a point of body modification, sound control, yogic meditation and Tantra that is only faintly echoed in the historical practice written down in texts. We need most of all to recover all that we can of this. The Typhonian Order is doing much of this work to the benefit of all involved. It is slow and intuitive working of the Tunnels of Set that leads to discoveries of what works and what leads where in the maps of the dark side.

The use of Astral and Causal Machines to facilitate servitor programs that work while the mind is in completely nonlinear states is crucial, because these machines can be set to translate and record things and states of mind that are otherwise unreachable. It is possible that they can be used to filter and protect because of their inherent geometries and advanced topological characteristics. This is another area of key research before we are ready to launch our vessel toward the stars.

Where I differ from the Typhonian work is in my assumption that the basic framework for all of these tools is the Nothingness: entry to the Nothingness is the primordial setting for all these to work in. Where The Typhonian OTO and the

Thelemites use earthbound Tantric tools to study the Stars, I reach directly into the Yoga of Emptiness because even the outsiders have to emerge from the Voidness, regardless of which alien star system, Universe or dimension they may emerge from. There is no-thing which does not emerge from Emptiness. Mapping the Emptiness is possible only through pure crystalline Intuition, which is best developed through constant meditation upon the ultimate source of all Being in nothingness.

Where I strongly agree with Kenneth Grant is that *something* happened in the late 1940's and some kind of gateway opened. Whether it was opened by Aleister Crowley, Jack Parsons or someone else, the emergence of the UFO phenomena is unquestionably the key sign that we are being watched and tested by someone.

My research and the work of the late Jim Keith along with the books being written by Dr. Joseph P. Farrell move us along the complex lines of this situation. This is a very real impingement of the outsiders into our daily lives, but it is also a situation being used and manipulated by human governments and agencies to their own mysterious ends. Past the reality of the outsiders, there are a host of others who have developed strange machines and propulsion systems who are both terrestrial and subterranean. I have compiled a list of who is doing what as best as I can from the literature on the subject. In my mind, this is a critical approach to pursue, because if we understand this phenomenon, then we understand a sliver of what the Great Ancient Ones are and what they mean to us: are they creators or destroyers or both?

Possible factors of the UFO situation:

It is critical to realize that in discussing the UFO situation, there are a plethora of different sources for the objects, their inhabitants and the strange phenomena that surround them and that they can emanate from different sources and not just one monolithic source:

—〰— **Genuine extraterrestrial or extradimensional types**... Extremely rare but they exist.

—〰— **Genuine ultraterrestrial subterranean and ocean types**... More common. These are the parallel subterranean dwellers who resemble humans but branched off of our genetic tree many hundreds of thousands of years ago. They inhabit caves in the mantle of the earth and many undersea locations. They are the source of the culture of Civilization One and have sciences far in advance of our own, although we *are* catching up much to their dismay.

—〰— **Breakaway civilization types,** based on German propulsion and aerodynamic research dating back to as early as the 1920's... Much more common. The breakaway civilization developed from the advanced research going on in Germany at the end of WWII. Dr. Joseph P. Farrell has written extensively on the breakaway culture and its relationship to advanced UFO activities.

The Gospel of Cosmic Terror

In response to all three types of these advanced craft, the major superpowers realized the need to create technologies that mimicked those of the ancient races and the breakaway civilization. The US, Russia and Germany had the obvious upper hand because of resources and access to research undertaken in Germany before and during the War as well as the scientists responsible for it.

—⁓— **US:** clearly testing craft as early as the 1950's.

—⁓— **Russia:** clearly testing craft during the same period and there may have been some covert cooperation with the US on extremely secret levels when it was realized that the outsiders posed a serious threat to the World as a whole.

—⁓— **Germany and the NATO countries** appear to have started later, probably during the 1960's but reports of advanced craft clearly had a huge impact during the 60's and thereafter. It is not impossible that some South American countries were also working on these lines, particularly **Brazil and Argentina**. That means that at least 6-8 different variations of the same circular, triangular or cigar shaped vehicles were active from the 1950's on. Earlier reports dating back as far as antiquity probably emanated from the ET and UT types.

This brief sketch just helps to orient us in our research and provides one more piece of the puzzle. There is a strange sense of recurrence and continuity in all of the fields of the Scroll that I have mentioned above. The same archetypes, dreams and images keep coming up again and again unfailingly. I certainly agree with Peter Levenda that Kenneth Grant did a magnificent job of intuiting his way through this complicated and barely comprehensible minefield. All I can hope to do is to follow in his footsteps and see where it all goes from my own perspective. If I have done nothing else but help to point us in some of the right directions using some of the right resources and the right books, I will be thankful that my task is successful. To sit back and allow the outsiders to treat us like cattle is the worst thing we could possibly do. To prove to them all that we are equals through our skillful use of science and Magick is the best response we have available.

What follows is a partial bibliography of some of the main works consulted for this articles and its predecessors. One of my projects is compiling a full and exhaustive bibliography for those wishing to continue this work on their own. It will eventually be published at one of my main research sites:

www.obesonomicon.org

BIBLIOGRAPHY

Richard Toronto:
—⁓— *War over Lemuria*
—⁓— *Shaverology*

Peter Levenda:
—⁓— *The Dark Lord*

Joseph P. Farrell:
—⁓— *Covert Wars and the Clash of Civilizations: UFO's, Oligarchs and Space Secrecy*
—⁓— *Covert Wars and Breakaway Civilizations: The Secret Space Program, Celestial Psy-OPS and Hidden Conflicts*
—⁓— *Saucers, Swastikas and Psy-ops: A History of a Breakaway Civilization*
—⁓— *Roswell and the Reich*
—⁓— *Secrets of the Unified Field*

Jim Keith:
—⁓— *Casebook on the Men in Black*
—⁓— *Saucers of the Illuminati*
—⁓— *Black Helicopters over America*

Geoffrey Ashe:
—⁓— *The Ancient Wisdom*

Christopher Knight and Alan Butler:
—⁓— *Civilization One: The World is not as you thought it was*

Paul Foster Case:
—⁓— *The true and invisible Rosicrucian order*

—⁓— The entire series of *Illuminati* books published on Kindle and written by "Adam Weishaupt" Michael Faust and Mike Hockney.

SENTIENT ABSENCE

Stephen Sennitt

Esoteric tradition attributes the whole of human self-awareness, culture and civilisation to certain races of entities, which are said to have provided the spark of cosmic intelligence that created 'divinely-inspired' human beings; melding daemonic wisdom to proto-humans with our prehistoric ape-like ancestors, whose flesh formed our original earthly template.

In this mythos, these strange, multifaceted beings, whose essence as divine Creative Light was plunged into the darkness of terrestrial matter in a 'spiritual involution' (and whose long-term directive was to produce a complimentary evolution of the bestial) acted for millennia as the advising, tutelary inner-genius informing and guiding proto-humans and humankind towards civilization.

These beings have been identified in biblical lore, both in the orthodox version and more explicitly in the various apocryphal texts influenced by Gnosticism, as the Fallen Angels. In more modern satanic traditions, such as in the authentic mythos of the Order Of Nine Angles (o9a), these entities are known as the Dark Gods.

Upon banishment from our world, corrupted and partial knowledge of these entities survived in qabalastic lore, magical grimoires and in the esoteric forms of witchcraft and Satanism, ascribing to them a continuing, shadowy existence as the qliphothic Lords of the Abyss; the once-incarnate Kings of Edom, now exiled from the Tree of Life beyond the gates of Da'ath; yet via the Nightside seals and sigils which evoke them into perception, they are said to be as close as the untrammeled instincts and desires of our own Ids. O9a teaching refers to this dimension or state-of-existence as the Acausal; an apt summation of the seeming reversal of the mundane, 'causal' world that human beings normally inhabit.

One of the most accomplished, influential and erudite exponents of magick and mysticism, Aleister Crowley, experienced a crucial revelation when exploring these alien dimensions beyond the Abyss, which only a handful of occultists have since seemed to fully comprehend; namely that conditions dictating humanity's limited notions of 'reality' no longer apply beyond Da'ath, or the gates of the Acausal, and its daemon-guardian, the Dark God Choronzon.

Radical perceptual adjustments must occur if humans are to fully comprehend the strange entities and vistas pertaining there and thus avoid destruction of mind, intellect and 'soul' as they impinge increasingly into the human life stream. (There is little doubt that we are witnessing an intense ratiocination of daemonic communication in the present era which threatens to overturn the precarious balance of our civilization; exponents of the o9a are, in fact, gleefully throwing all their weight into tipping this balance in favour of the Dark Gods – and for legitimate reasons, as we will discover).

Crowley elucidated this profound truth concisely via the paradoxical observation that whilst the reality of objects and entities below the Abyss (the causal realm, where humanity-at-large dwells) can be defined only by their apparent separateness from one another, in the aethers and realms beyond Da'ath, the reality of objects and entities are instead defined by *both their oneness and separateness from each other at the same time.*

This is an exact definition of what o9a doctrine refers to as the 'Acausal', indicating a state of conscious existence which is *inclusive* rather than exclusive of opposites or contradictions, whilst still maintaining a discrete aspect of what we would call individuality; despite these two states logically seeming to cancel one another out – a Zen-like paradox indicating the existence of a tenuous or *sentient absence* which defies all rational analysis.

This is the state-of-being possessed by the Dark Gods and their retinue.

It indicates a parallel stream of self-conscious existence which might be perceived as a different branch of evolution stemming from a common source of origin: In this case, instead of the familiar mystical concept of spirit refining matter (as in man's spiritual evolution via progression from the grosser material forms of his animal predecessors to his current state of self-conscious existence – and further towards the ideal states of enlightened consciousness in the higher spheres of the qabalistic Tree of Life) we must in addition posit the notion of a retrograde 'involutionary' stream in which time is reversed, and in which all the excess primal forces and forms that our level of creation has rejected (or has yet to find evolutionary use for) either decay in stasis, like cast-off skins, or continue along their involutionary course into the shadowy, multifarious forms, aeons and worlds existing in flux in the astral darkness beyond the Abyss, known in qabalistic tradition as the qliphoth.

To mankind, these are the ghost worlds of the Fallen Angels; zones of negative existence beyond Da'ath, which Kenneth Grant has described as a tangled network of endless tunnels beneath the paths connecting the spheres of the Tree of Life; and which Michael Bertiaux has called 'Universe B', or the Meon – the realm of non-being.

In other words, the Acausal entities we perceive as spirits, demons, gods or archetypes, and especially those of more archaic provenance (commonly associated with the qliphotic, 'infernal regions') have a radically different form of consciousness and ontic basis to that of human beings, far transcending our dualistic, 'either/or' tendencies, seeming to us to be logical impossibilities in their capacity to appear to be many things at once; not just in thought and imagination like human beings, but in actuality, function, appearance and deed – and more crucially still, having the ability to exist conterminously in various dimensions of space/time.

Such daemonic entities have been erroneously identified throughout history as the opposite of humans; denizens of a 'topsy-turvy' shadow world which is this world's dark and sinister reflection.

This is not *precisely* the case: *They are our sinister opposites and intrinsically our inner-most selves – the Id – at the same time.*

They do not merely mirror our deepest, subconscious natures, as a reflection or a shadow; they subsume us and supersede us and oppose and reflect us, are our enemies and our allies all at once, because their nature is not either 'this *or* that'; instead these entities are equally 'this *and* that' – simultaneously, borrowing from our own thoughts, memories and aspirations a kind of loosely fitting robe of identity with which to materialize themselves.

In the present era, these guises are often dangerously inimical to psychological well being, partly due to the inability of humans to raise consciousness above a conditioned level of binary, 'either/or' thinking, whose common evolutionary directive would appear to be to protect the ego from being subsumed by these 'outside' forces and intelligences, but whose usefulness in this capacity is becoming increasingly limited, as qliphothic forces interpenetrate our world in increasing numbers; and it is also an engram-artifact of what orthodox religion has called 'The Wrong of the Beginning', a theme which will be examined in more depth below.

(In history, this situation has been exacerbated by state, social and religious conditioning, which has turned the individual away from self-exploration and the personal attainment of gnosis to the point of ostracizing or terminating such individuals who attempt it, or destroying whole communities of 'heretics' and 'witches' in various holocausts of murderous insanity.)

Once this admittedly abstruse and paradoxical doctrine which goes beyond 'either/or' thinking is accepted, all the bizarre beliefs of the ages and the enigmatic habits attributed to the Dark Gods and 'supernatural beings' by esoteric tradition and folklore fall into place.

For those who would aspire to transcend the human condition, these entities adumbrate the revered state of non-duality alluded to by mystics throughout the ages as being a necessity to gaining self-realization and true wisdom, but to which so few it would seem have attained with any degree of success, due to the inherent danger attached to such self-explorations.

In fact, advanced systems of attainment, such as Advaita and Mahayana Buddhism, most often instruct the aspirant to resist communicating with the *siddhes* – the daemonic entities which haunt certain stages of the path to Enlightenment (including the preternatural powers they impart) – as dangerous distractions at best, and fatal traps at worst. Concomitant legends and folklore abound in tales of weird faery lands where humans become lost, along with demonic entities which lure unwary magicians into their grasp, or in recent times, the bizarre mélange of alien abductors who suspend time and consciousness in order to exact their incubus-like investigations of the human form.

Yet towards the end of his life, Aleister Crowley, who was influenced by, and borrowed heavily in some cases from, the Eastern sources similar to those mentioned above, made the following statement:

The Fenris Wolf

My observation of the Universe convinces me that there are beings of intelligence and power of a far higher quality than anything we can conceive of as human; that they are not necessarily based on the cerebral and nervous structures that we know, and that the one and only chance for mankind as a whole is for individuals to make contact with such Beings.

This is a view traditionally styled as having more in common with the magick of gods or angels than mysticism; its doctrine advocating, rather than rejecting, the necessity of communing with such entities as helpers or mentors (despite the potential risk involved) in order to attain insights and wisdom otherwise out of reach to ordinary people – or perhaps to purposely obtain the same powers rejected by the Mahayana tradition and similar philosophies, seeing them as necessary stepping stones to the ultimate state, instead of hindrances.

This view of the matter gives rise to its own branch of mysticism via the records of the Hermetic and qabalistic schools; the Typhonian remnants extant in traditions of bona-fide witchcraft and voudon; in its currently most pristine form in the annals of the o9a – and in the scriptures and documents of Gnosticism, where the specific reason why dealings with infernal demigods, spirits and daemons has always been deemed inherently dangerous is clearly stated.

In the *Septem Sermones* of Basilides, the 'higher' realm of existence (in qabalistic terms, beyond Da'ath: the Acausal) is named the *pleroma*, which is described as a 'nothingness, which is the same as fullness'. What is meant by this is that the *pleroma* contains all qualities simultaneously, and this is the same (from the human perspective) as if it contained none, because it is the locus where 'both thinking and being cease and it is quite fruitless to think about it for it would mean self-dissolution'. (Austin Osman Spare's term *kia* would appear to be his name for the *pleroma*, and in turn *kia* has been designated a cognate term for chaos or dissolution, and glyphed in the form of Typhon-Set, or Choronzon.)

As the *pleroma* contains all things and pervades everywhere, humans – who Basildes defines as creatura (created beings) – inescapably partake of *pleroma*, as all things must, but 'distinctiveness is a quality of creatura whereas the pleroma has all, *distinctiveness and indistinctiveness*'. And so: 'Man, being of creatura, has distinctiveness as an essence; it is his nature to distinguish things. When we talk about qualities of the pleroma we learn nothing of the pleroma, we are really revealing our own nature, or way of thought. We must be true to nature and go on distinguishing.

'Why must we distinguish things? Answer: if we cease to distinguish we fall into the pleroma and cease to be creatures. This is the death of the creature. Therefore we die in such measure as we do not distinguish.

"This is why non-distinction is a great danger for the creature".

So, the Dark Gods, demons, spirits and archetypes, denizens of weird, qliphothic worlds that humans have encountered through the ages, and continue to encounter in the present day, represent a two-edged sword which can bring enlightenment and wisdom – or terror and insanity (or indeed a chaotic amalgamation of both beyond rational analysis, thus creating the Tarot's holy Fool).

Esoteric tradition ascribes states of consciousness and existence to these Nightside entities, partaking of a more tenebrous material structure than humans, as being 'closer' to the *pleroma*. But, as they are also said to have a component in their nature which seeks to become *creatura* (or to be reinstated as such after having fallen into inferno) there can be very grave danger in any dealings with these beings for humankind.

Such scriptural and magical doctrines are supported by corroboration in a world-wide tradition in myth, legend and folklore of powerful, frequently monstrous, alien beings which created humans from the remnants of a past world and its previous denizens. All these traditions indicate the colossal impact of the dramatic and 'sudden' incursion of daemonic, 'pleromaic' consciousness into the flesh and bone receptacle of *creatura*.

(It should be no surprise to learn that the method utilized by Crowley when he accessed the regions beyond the Abyss was adapted from the Enochian system – named after the biblical and apocryphal Enoch of scripture – devised by Dr. John Dee and Edward Kelley in the 16th century. This is comprised of a series of complex 'calls' said to be in the language of the Angels, containing hitherto lost keys unlocking the gates of existence and foretelling a coming Apocalyptic age on earth. It would seem significant that the only ranks of Angelic beings which tradition states to have ever been in intimate contact with humanity are of the 'Fallen legions': the Dark Gods who have revealed their true names and sigils to Adepts of the o9a).

The later Gnostic and Christian traditions in particular, focus on the 'wrongness' of this daemonic phase of creation, associating it with a morally sinful, 'fallen' condition of benighted ignorance due to terrible errors which were made at its inception. This condition has been termed, 'the Wrong of the Beginning,' alluded to in *Genesis* in reference to the sexual transgression of Adam and Eve and their subsequent expulsion from the Garden of Eden.

Lest it be forgotten, their 'tempter', the serpent, was also punished and hence-forward reviled by orthodox religion as mankind's enemy; a manipulative trickster to be distrusted and altogether shirked, unlike earlier cultures who had understood its role to be the multifaceted inner-genius of whom one had to be wary, but who should be respected and honoured as a guide 'sent by God' to aid in personal spiritual redemption.

This serpent, identified in the popular canon as the arch-Fallen Angel, Lucifer/Satan, thus had its previous majestic form as a winged Being of Light metamorphosed into a limbless Creature of Darkness, forced to 'crawl in the dust' throughout eternity along the anti-matter tunnels of Hell.

This image perfectly symbolizes the utterly damned condition said to have been imposed on the Fallen Angels by God, who destroyed the evil civilization of the Titanic Kings of Edom (the Dark Gods incarnate) via deluge and banished them to a world even lower than the human sphere, there to exist in 'eternal darkness' as entities neither of the *pleroma* in the strictest sense, nor of *creatura*, but an implosive and involutionary concatenation of form and force beyond human comprehension: a 'sentient absence', the qliphoth.

At this point, it becomes clear that we must examine further and in some detail why the seemingly innocuous 'sin' of cupidity said to be the origin of 'the Wrong of the Beginning' gave rise to centuries of fearsome anathema towards sexual creativity, and gave birth to legends of monstrous cannibalistic giants of a previous order of creation who lurk at the gates of the Abyss, ever ready to return and reclaim the earth.

Note: Comments on Gnosticism and the Pleroma are taken from Lemuel Johnstone's (Lionel Snell) 'Spare Parts'; *Agape* Vol.1, No. 3, 1973.

Anton LaVey, Magical Innovator

Carl Abrahamsson

This text was originally delivered as a lecture at the Nekropolis Bookstore in Copenhagen on December 7th, 2013. – Ed.

Assuming that there is already a fundamental knowledge of Satanism in this illustrious crowd, I'm going to allow myself to delve deeper into a few specialized sections of Anton LaVey's contribution to contemporary magical philosophy.

Let's generalize a bit and say that the first half of the 20th century was all about synthesizing. East met West and this was integrated into esoteric systems by intelligent structure-makers. The Golden Dawn was one such group of structure-makers. Theosophy under Blavatsky also. Gurdjieff was another protagonist, and Steiner another. Aleister Crowley perhaps the most well-known one. They all made nutritious stews but basically out of already existing ingredients.

The second half of the 20th century was more violent and also more creative in many ways. As the recent structures had become established and their once so pioneering key people had become accepted teachers or gurus, a new breed bred on first generation Thelema, Golden Dawn splinter groups and assorted pre-1960s swamis from the East concocted their own syntheses and groups. However, taking considerably more contemporary fodder into account than previously before.

Science, psychology, irony and humor, art, speculative philosophies and other previously rare phenomena within occultism suddenly overrode arcane concepts like invocation, banishing, kabbala, tarot, wands, astrology, mystical angelic languages and ancient demonic names, etc. Instead, the focus lay in spheres of experimentation, neurology, psychodrama, sexuality and other non-sectarian core human phenomena. Old structures were dissolved in new ways of looking at things.

The Church of Satan was one of these precursors of radical change. Established in 1966 by Anton LaVey, the Church's first phase up until the late 1970s was one of visibility and provocation. LaVey's colorful presence made both him and his Church celebrities. As a well formulated and intriguing antidote to the mellow and essentially selfless hippies of the era, LaVey was cabled all over the world into news- and men's magazines, who found the naked women on his altar just enough shocking to print.

During the second phase, from the late 1970s and up until his death in 1997, LaVey became much more of a recluse. He was established and *The Satanic Bible* kept on selling and generated an income, which meant he could thereby devote his time and energies to one of the key concepts of the Church of Satan: "Indulgence

171

instead of abstinence." One of the things he enjoyed and indulged in was writing.

Although his books *The Satanic Bible, The Satanic Rituals* and *The Satanic Witch* are his most well known, I would say that the later anthologies *The Devil's Notebook* and *Satan Speaks* are much more substantial when it comes to his own thinking. *The Bible* and *The Rituals* were basically assemblage volumes, in which pragmatically chosen material was edited together and augmented further by initiated comments. But the two volumes of essays and maxims that followed much later, ie *The Devil's Notebook* and *Satan Speaks*, genuinely contain the essence of LaVey's latter day wit and creativity.

The essays are also a great source of some groundbreaking magical concepts, both on the "Lesser Magic" level (willed manipulation of everyday life) and "Greater Magic" level (ritualized programming of a willed "Is To Be" situation or development).

Already in *The Satanic Bible*, LaVey had shown considerable creativity. Concepts like "Psychic Vampires" and "The Balance Factor" soon became household terms in America and the rest of the world. His description of the ritual space as an "Intellectual Decompression Chamber" also hit home outside the strictly Satanic perimeters. As did the slightly later term "Occultnik", signifying a person who is lost within old structures of occultism without being able to see what's really of use on a practical, material level.

In *The Satanic Bible*, we can also find an old-school method within occult writing: creative appropriation of an older source. In this case, LaVey's use of the Enochian keys originally written by Dee and Kelly via the biographer Meric Casaubon in 1659 and then regurgitated throughout the centuries up until Crowley. LaVey exchanged the final intonations traditionally translated as "the highest" with "Saitan", claiming the previous translations and vibrations had been erroneous. "The barbaric tonal qualities of this language give it a truly magical effect which cannot be described."[1] He also claimed that the nature of the scrying that Kelly as the "gazer" used had been mispresented as via the grace of angels, when in fact, according to LaVey, it has to do with ocular and psychic "angles", which can, metaphorically or not, open wide the "Gates of Hell".

The Satanic Witch was a primer in applied, practical feminism. It also brought in concepts like *The LaVey Personality Synthesizer*, or the *Personality Clock*. This is a method to be used in various kinds of matchmaking, human as well as within other areas of choice and resonance. Not as a spiritual oracle of some kind, but as a down-to-earth method of applied psychology.

There was also the important concept of *ECI: Erotic Crystallization Inertia*. Meaning that our very first defining erotic moments, like the first orgasm for instance, will be forever linked to the surroundings, emotional atmospheres etc within our psyche. That crystallizing moment will be with us forever and affect us all throughout life. As it is an overwhelmingly emotional moment, for good and bad, it can be tapped as a source of energy in magical workings. As with a general and honest definition of one's own sexuality, the conscious working with ECI brings several benefits to the magician.

---

1 Anton LaVey, *The Satanic Bible*, Avon Books, New York, 1969, p. 155)

One telling example most of us can see within our own culture is the fact that both men and women seem to get stuck time- and look-wise in the period when they were most sexually active and attractive. LaVey pointed out some concrete situations where ECI is usually unconsciously used but even more visible. Solitary elderly people, like widows or widowers, usually become depressed and lacking in motivation. When in the company of people of the same generation, and in an environment that is created to evoke this sexual peak period of life, vitality and general health comes back in almost miraculous ways. We'll return to this in the form of another LaVeyan construct: the total environment.

One important aspect of *The Satanic Witch* was the development of what LaVey called *The Law of the Forbidden*. Meaning that to attract a person or a desired situation, one needs to be genuinely aware of one's own qualities (this is very tied in to *The Balance Factor* mentioned earlier) and the alluring display of sections but *not* all of it. Showing a little bit of flesh by "mistake" can create a greater jolt and impact than quickly undressing and revealing it all. "Nothing is so fascinating as that which is not meant to be seen." There is even a chapter is *The Satanic Witch* called "The Secrets of Indecent Exposure". However, the dynamic need not be sexual at all. *The Law of the Forbidden* can be used in many different areas.

Sexual honesty is paramount in the LaVeyan universe. Personal fetishes are also extremely important, whether sexual or emotional. To feel strongly about something that concerns noone else is to generate a force field that can be tapped indefinitely. To feel strongly about something that concerns a multitude of people is to generate leakage and distortion. To savor small items of active preference in a fetishistic way thereby becomes a highly conscious magical act. Emulation is *not* a key to Satanism. Passion, on the other hand, is.

What follows here is an overview of some key concepts that can hopingly inspire the student to delve further into the mysteries via the Satanic grid.

INTEGRATION OF THE EGO

Almost all previous magical systems were developed within a dichotomy that is structured around the relationship between "higher" and "lower". No doubt having to do with monotheistic religious imprints in which "this life" is insufficient and that some kind of idealized "pie in the sky" is better.

The heavy influx of Freudian energy during the 20th century revealed the power of the conscious ego. LaVey integrated the ego as a valid and relevant component in magical thought and thereby made void invisible moralisms that had up until then permeated the worldview of practically all previous magical conecptualists.

Higher/Lower is in itself a concept imbued with value, and that value stems from control systems stressing that the ideal can essentially not be reached within the span of one human life-time. LaVey, on the other hand, stressed that the uncertainty of karmic relations *possibly* transcending this life-time is too strong, and that gratification of desires in the here and now is more of a natural given, and certainly more worth striving for.

One also has to take into consideration that will is always expressed through the ego, and that even demi-god characters projected with selfless, altruistic and "spiritual" existence (the Dalai Lama, Gandhi, other Eastern figures, gurus, the Pope, *et al*) all make choices through their egos.

The LaVeyan perspective disrobes a great deal of hypocrisy in our *Zeitgeist*, whether the proponents be political, religious, "magical" or just generally altruistic. There is always ego involved in decision-making, and if this is not recognized and exposed, obstructing illusions will dominate the analytical faculties of those taking part. This illusion would only be deemed Satanically sanctioned if the person in question allows him- or herself to be "duped" in order to gratify his or her *own* masochistic need of servitude.

The LaVeyan magical system favors the eloquent will of the ego – as well as its underlying libidal and compensatory forces – as the most relevant "ideal" to strive for. Whichever clothing this ideal is individually dressed in is, it rids itself of the illusions stemming from other people's projections, as well as from *their* individual ego-based wills.

Although LaVey and later LaVeyans have expressed a critical stance in regard to a concept like "spiritual", the concept in itself would be better off in a dichotomy called "inner" and "outer" (thereby decimating any inherent "value"-based interpretations). We all work with processes of thinking, willing, feeling etc, and they could all be seen as being "inner" and/or related to the workings of the mind. These processes are then expressed in the "outer", filtered through the ego.

If the inner is inspired somehow by what is traditionally stamped as "spiritual" or "higher" (adherence to a certain technical language or certain techniques like yoga, meditation, or even specific religious thought or iconography) and this is expressed through a conscious ego, the ballgame is moved from an externally controlled or imposed field of "values" to the highly magical and ego-gratifying field of well-being in resonance.

All altruism stems from decisions made by the ego, as does all non- or anti-altruism. This integration of a considerably more stripped attitude when it comes to the human psyche and its motivations is probably LaVey's most important contribution to magical thought.

THE VALIDATION AND INTEGRATION OF EMOTION

Where previous Western magical systems had been based on an intellectual and systematized/structured approach, Anton LaVey brought in the emotional as a key agent. No Greater magical working can, according to LaVey, be successful without an "evocation" of relevant human emotions. Although this sounds simple enough, it becomes a dilemma when the individual is armed to his or her teeth with fancy elemental weapons and a perfect *intellectual* understanding of "how" to perform a traditional ritual. But what about "Why"? Why is this ritual performed? Usually to "cause change to occur in conformity with will", to paraphrase Crowley. That's fair and fine enough, but if the magician in question only works within a strictly intellectual sphere with a rational approach, he or she might just as well focus on Lesser magic, ie a Machiavellean manipulation of the surroundings.

Any working dealing with "greater" aspects needs emotional investment in the ritual moment. LaVey's term for the temple space – the "intellectual decompression chamber" – pretty much sums it up. It is a challenge for most people to honestly know themselves and to have the courage, even in solitary settings, to display weaknesses and emotions not in line with the desired self-image. But how else can you develop, overcome or banish these weaknesses?

A SENSE OF HUMOUR

Of course, this was not invented by Anton LaVey. But few magicians have stressed it as an important quality and also a tool. "A Satanist without a sense of humour would be unbearable", he says in the documentary *Speak of the Devil*.[2] The use of tricks, jokes and pranks can be integrated in complex and highly serious magical workings, especially if it entails ridiculing a pretentious person or force or strategically demeaning or belittling oneself to gain a better perspective or position. The clown or the joker is indeed a powerful figure or type.

The Devil's Notebook is suitably dedicated to "the men, whoever they are, who invented the Whoopee Cushion, the Joy Buzzer, and the Sneeze-O-Bubble".[3]

> *Invariably, those with the most finely-honed sense of humour find serious meaning in what everyone else ridicules. The very nature of the joke is its foundation of misfortune. The joke maker can spot the sham in acceptably serious situations. Then, having called attention to the deception, he may stand forth as a Satanic tribune. Not so easy is the reverse. The same rebel who defends the unpopular and the ridiculed, lays to an audience whose only illusion of strength lies in its ability to ridicule. It's interesting to observe how lower man, while realizing the sadness of clowns, seldom pays attention to them when they have serious thoughts to offer.*[4]

Incidentally, the Satanically important character of the villain, by his very antithetical stance, also makes fun of the existing order and morals and hence functions as a liberating character – if intelligent and conscious about it. Scapegoating is an important and apparently necessary function in the human psyche. At least for egos that are not healthily gratified. To take on the persona of the villified or the mocking catalyst requires an inner strength not often found among the "herd", according to LaVey.

2 *Speak of the Devil*, a film by Nick Bougas, Wavelength Video, Burbank, 1993.
3 Anton LaVey, *The Devil's Notebook*, Feral House, Portland, 1992, p. iii
4 Anton LaVey, *Satan Speaks*, Feral House, Los Angeles, 1998, p. 9)

The Fenris Wolf

ARTIFICIAL HUMAN COMPANIONS

Inspired by his own misanthropy, nostalgia and will to be in charge, LaVey early on started creating humanoid dolls. Often, as memories from his own youth. In the basement of his Black House in San Francisco (the house immortalized by the Eagles in their chartbusting song *Hotel California*), LaVey had a bar called *The Den of Iniquity*, complete with several artificial human companions. This environment and its denizens acted as an intellectual decompression chamber as much as the classic black temple space upstairs or the kitchen where he kept his vast collection of synthesizers and other musical instruments. To be able to make small talk with the drunks, the bartender and the old lady on the floor who was a drunken victim of LaVey's own sexual fetish – watching women piss their panties – became a sanctuary and a zone free of rational processes and expectations. Anything could happen. And often did.

The emergence of commercially available human companions (for instance those made by the company *Real Doll*, etc) not solely intendend for sexual use is a clear current example of a LaVeyan concept manifesting outside of the strictly Satanic environment. (For more on this, please also see my essay *The Imaginative Libido* elsewhere in this issue. – Ed.)

> *I have great respect for those who pioneer their own artificial human companion, crude as they might initially be. They will have come a small step closer to playing God and creating man or woman according to their desired image. With a creative outlet as cloaked in age-old taboo as this, innovation may now run rampant – more so than any artform man has yet known. The bizarre twilight world of the ventriloquist, the puppet-master and the dollmaker can perhaps be undertstood through other than the minds of psychologists. The acceptable schizoid element in all of us – the one that selects our mates – has a fresh, new, open portal to pass through. Through surrogates the race will survive.*[5]

> *... the prime appeal of the humanoid lies in its approximation of the purchaser's "other half". - - - Artificial companions that are pleasingly heard, smelled and felt also constitute positive selling points. But that an artificial companion looks right is of primary importance.*[6]

THE TOTAL ENVIRONMENT

One of the most important ideas or concepts along with that of artificial human companions is the *Total Environment*. Consistent in his exclusion of the herd that provokes deep misanthropia and his inclusion of personal esthetics and fetishism, LaVey's development of total environments is a key to understanding the subtleties of his magic.

---

5 *The Devil's Notebook*, p. 138)
6 Ibid., p 133

176

In a world that becomes louder and louder and more and more fragmented, the existence of a sacred space filled with perfection and maximum personal resonance almost becomes a heretical act. It is. Not only does it affect you in beneficial ways like relaxation, excitement and inspiration. There's also the possibility of using these spaces (and times, if they are time- or era-specific) for creative magical rituals in many different directions.

In *The Satanic Rituals*, LaVey stated that "Man's ugly habit of elevating himself by defaming others is an unfortunate phenomenon, yet apparently necessary to his emotional well-being."[7] With the development of total environments and many of his other concepts, there was no longer a need for LaVey to be a frustrated outsider in conflict with the herd. The Satanist's creative isolation in a space/time-warp-possible mindframe is one of silence and subtlety, and one of the greatest tools in the Satanic trade.

This, combined with honest self-knowledge and a proud appreciation of one's own kinks and complications makes for a good, solid Satanist. There's always a strong focus of real-life material success too. But only based on The Balance Factor and what actually is possible for an individual in that position. Self-deceit is not a popular quality in LaVey's cosmos.

> *The most successful individuals throughout history have been the people who learn a few good tricks and apply them well, rather than those with a whole bag full who don't know which trick to pull out at the right time – or how to use it once they get it out!* [8]

The Total Environment encompasses many of the central LaVeyan concepts in one confined yet endless space. Personal preferences, esthetics, the intellectual decompression chamber, fetishism, misanthropy and possibly artificial human companions to share the magic with... It's a sphere of clearisghted yet romantic proto-creativity previously unheard of in "classical" magical lore.

INTEGRATION OF MUSIC

LaVey was a skilled musician and loved music. No wonder then that he had explored magical aspects of tone, vibrations, rhythms, the human voice and all of these things put together. His own rituals often included his own playing suitable instruments. Sometimes the ritual itself *was* the actual playing of one selected piece of music with heavy emotional gusto.

> *Music is the most effective tool for evocation, as the entire body rhythm is helplessly taken up by the pattern of life associated with the musical selection. A meaningful idea never dies, nor does the emotional response generated by certain compositions. If enough people are inspired or moved by these compositions,*

---

7 Anton LaVey, *The Satanic Rituals*, Avon Books, New York, 1972, p. 11
8 Ibid., p 22

the selections become sonic repository for the accumulated emotions of all those affected by them. Becoming an all-encompassing sensing element to the collective feedback of a particular composition can yield a total evocation.[9]

Again, the integration of emotion is fundamentally important. There is probably no art form more emotional than music. To get into the "mood" of a specific working, the inclusion of a musical piece chosen for its evocative qualities is essential. If performed live, the emotional amplification will be even greater.

In discussing these things, LaVey also mentions "emotional chording". There seems, according to him, to exist one chord for each emotion. Animals respond to very few: basically pleasure and pain.

Humans have added certain chords to their internal lyre, such as sentiment, which sometimes appears as nostalgia – a combination of pleasure and pain. Humans' internal chording is more complex because humans experience a wider range of stimuli than do other animals (though, alas, the reverse is often true).[10]

THE VILLAIN

Satan was defined by LaVey as a symbol with the powerful potential of accusing and revealing hypocrisy and double standards. Satire, irony and scathing intelligence here become magical qualities, as personified in LaVeyan inspirations like Mark Twain, Ben Hecht and H.L. Mencken. Wherever there is dogmatic hypocrisy and attempts at control through intimidation, there will be counter-forces. When direct causal balancing is not possible, then a sardonic strike can do just as well.

In all cultures, the anti-hero, rebel or villain is usually more popular than the (self)righteous hero running the errands of the corrupt. Even worse than the "hero" him- or herself is the person cheering on the righteousness imposed by others. LaVey describes these people as those bearing a "good guy badge". Gather two or more of these together, and an intolerant lynch mob is never far away.

The balancing force is the "lone ranger" – often a truly good and just person, but with methods and an intelligence in direct opposition to the *status quo* behavior of the herd.

The more grandiose the villain, the more beneficent he is to society.[11]

The greater one's natural degree of non-conformity, the greater are one's magical powers.[12]

This is no way automatically implies that non-conformers or outsiders are villainous or vice versa, but there's something in the isolation from the herd or the collective

9 *The Devil's Notebook*, p. 78
10 Ibid., p. 80
11 Ibid., p. 17
12 Ibid., p. 63

that is absolutely central in the LaVeyan *Weltanschauung*.

Besides the integrated sense of dark humour, there's also the concept of noir justice in both Satanic and criminal environments. The anti-hero of hard boiled crime stories of the 1940s and 50s and his stern cinematic counterpart in films noirs often represents justice but very seldom the legal system. And the criminal world is truly one of Machiavellean strategies and the protonatural *Lex Talionis* that LaVey was such an avid advocate of.

THE THIRD SIDE

Oppositional transcendence is a fairly new construct in Western magical thought. Where Chinese Taoism has always favored the "both-and" rather than the "either-or" stance, Western occult philosophy has up until the 20th century been bogged down by religious dualisms and simplified divisions.

Aleister Crowley was instrumental in this transcendental process with his famous definition "The Magick of Horus requires the passionate union of opposites." It is not only a "magical" way of solving problems or looking at things but also acknowledges modern scientific thought. As opposites either clash or unite, there is a great amount of energy set free. For the magician aware of the mechanisms involved, the energy can easily be directed to do his or her bidding.

What's interesting here is what LaVey called the "third side" of any issue at hand. This side he described and defined as Satanic because it challenges dim-witted dualism. Reality is always more multifaceted than a Yes or a No, and especially if one is on a pragmatic prowl for success and pleasure for oneself. Aligning oneself with either the either or the or is usually to take the safe way out. The third side may be controversial but that's never a problem for a Satanist.

> *The third side can be the crackpot stuff of conspiracy theories, or it can be the most logical and simple, yet* deliberately neglected *conclusion.* [13]

In *Satan Speaks*, LaVey gives an example of how this dynamic could work as a pragmatic magical formula mixing two iconic, almost mythic energies of 20th century life and culture: National Socialism and Judaism. LaVey himself was Jewish by birth and at times even expressed Zionist leanings but at the same time he admired fascist esthetics from both Italy and Nazi Germany.

> *It will become easier and more convincing for any Satanist to combine a Jewish lineage with a Nazi aesthetic, and with pride rather than with guilt and misgiving. The die is cast with the vast numbers of children of mixed Jewish/ Gentile origins. They need a place to go. They need a tough identity. They won't find it in the Christian church, nor will they find it in the synagogue. They certainly won't find acceptance among identity anti-Christian anti-Semites who use noble, rich, and inspirational Norse mythology as an excuse and vehicle to*

13 *Satan Speaks*, p. 30

rant about the "ZOG". The only place a rational amalgam of proud, admitted Zionist Odinist Bolshevik Nazi Imperialist Socialist Fascism will be found–and championed–will be in the Church of Satan.[14]

Criticism of Anton LaVey and his genuinely creative concepts most often stem from blunt prejudice within the critic. When the individual feels safe and comfortable within a system, even systems of otherwise radical and provocative concepts, the critical faculties toward that system become void, and scapegoating towards others begin. While often being brushed off as a "con man" or a "charlatan" by these kinds of critics, Anton LaVey still lingers on as an important player in contemporary magical philosophy. He was decidedly a heretic but perhaps not so much against the Christian Church and other monotheistic control systems (these being already increasingly redundant and far too easy to mock), but more so in relation to the magical moralists all too happy to do some unconscious scapegoating and all too happy to flaunt their degree-studded good guy badges.

There are many other concepts that deserve a closer study: LaVey's thoughts on masochism in relation to beneficial slavery, the *Law of the Trapezoid* and *Lycanthropic Metamorphosis*, to mention but a few. I hope this lecture has at least laid a solid base as an overview for future interest and attention.

> *When I think of all those who would rejoice at my discomfort, I am energized and strengthened to the extent that I might overcome any malaise. It is not my love for mankind that sustains me, but rather mankind's resentment of me. My disdain and contempt for the mediocre masses in general and those who calumniate me in paticular angers me to regeneration.*[15]

---

14 Ibid., p. 22
15 *The Devil's Notebook*, p. 140

MAGICIANS:
EVOLUTIONARY AGENTS OR REGRESSIVE TWATS?

Alexander Nym

Way back in the past millennium, I had an influential encounter with a magickal adept, whom I'd later initiate into SOL[1]. Before this happened, however, we had a long conversation about the nature of his previous interest in esotericism and magick. When he reflected on his path, he admitted he had used to be a rather geeky teenager whose primary interest in the occult was "to gain power."

Now, that was news to me: Magick for the purpose of power and influence? Wasn't that unheard of? And weren't people with such a lack of self-confidence that they looked to magick to gain power over others generally those types anyone in their right mind would rather not admit into an association of illuminates? Hell, you could break something loose there! Yet, looking back at a host of encounters with the magickally inclined which took place since, I dare suggest that probably most people with an expressed interest in the occult used to be geeky teenagers, and that a good deal of us, troubled by the demands of adolescence, may have turned to magick for help in gaining "power". I'm certainly not intending to revive worn-out dichotomies of white vs black magick, left-hand/right-hand and so on, but the uneasy truth is that there are lots of wackos out there dabbling in magick trying to assume power over others without having understood the prerequisite of power over oneself, eventually damaging themselves and possibly others while giving the occult a bad name.

Since I'd mostly approached the occult on an empirical level, I was always dedicated to the motto "The method of science, the aim of religion", which I still consider to be the best advice regarding the gradual immersion of (sub-)conscious creation into our reality. Yet, since there are as many ways to illumination, godhead and attainment of a variety of siddhis as there are human beings, chances are that the individual's way to enlightenment is barred or marred with intricate delusions fostering our "dark passengers" to surface and try to take the wheel. A good deal of (self-)doubt is always helpful in keeping one's head on one's shoulders, especially when dealing with elusive

---

1 Society Of Life -- a satirical yet very thorough "order" of which literally everything living being is a member even without being aware of it. Its three grades were the *phool* (people who'd realised their membership), the *phreak* (grasping and applying the order's rules & rituals) and the *phyrass* (bringing them and oneself to full blossom through conscious application) -- the latter being a wordplay on the German word *Führer* (leader, for those who don't know) combined with creative fire and the humility of referring to oneself as a mule, attempting to preclude such delusions of grandeur as had destroyed virtually every attempt at communal life and magick in previous instances like the G.D. and OTO as well as the communal experiments by the hippies and art groups such as the Vienna actionists.

subjects such as the "supernatural", the "immaterial" or the "collective psyche". Being a pragmatic agnostic, I'd prefer not to speculate on the existence, much less working processes of these spheres, but if they exist and function (and there are practical indications that they might), they are pretty complex concepts to work with and have a tendency to backfire in the most unexpected ways when proclaimed magicians attempt to tamper with them – which is why magickal literature is crammed with red flags and precautions warning the adept not to deal with them prematurely, without proper preparation, or for purely self-serving ends. As a result, history is saturated with examples of spiritual and political idealism turned into their own opposites by way of corruption, often enough resulting in (self-) destruction, greed (for self-affirmation in form of power, money, sex) and killing "in the name of".

THE RISE OF OCCULTURE AND THE DEMISE OF MAGICK

It seems there is a certain likelihood that the mere attempt at application of magick may irrevocably cause its own corruption and demise, yet how does this fit in with the initial ideas of personal liberation, responsibility and strife for enlightenment that fuelled magick since its modern post-Levi resurrection? Where is the turning point, and is there any working way to prevent the eventual descent back into the depths of all-too-human selfishness? And what is the current state of the magickal community these days in comparison to the heyday of the occult revival throughout the 19th and 20th centuries?

Before attempting to approach modest answers (which, due to their hypothetical nature, will probably only lead back to the Golden Rule anyhow, so no breaking news there), we'll take a look at the matrix of the recent Western magickal tradition in terms of its own ethico-political implications, since there is a good chance that the tragic failures of the past were not necessarily all caused simply by the inability of the practitioners or their individual personal shortcomings – maybe there's some basic thing wrong with the tool (or rather, the method) as such?

The history of magick has always been intertwined with politics. Be it the shamans of ancient times whose vision-quests had an impact on their tribe's decision-making, the counsel of court's astrologers or magicians (think of John Dee), the romanticised and sometimes factual influence of Masonry on occidental politics (like the French Revolution or the constitution of the United States) or the more recent change of Western consciousness through 1960's counter-cultural explorations of consciousness alteration and practical magick. Let's take a look into current developments concerning the relations between magick as a tool of cultural engineering and politics as means of organising intra-cultural and societal relations, applying a critical perspective towards present tendencies of "non-political" identity-construction (ironically enough resulting from its transcendence) within the magickal or "esoteric" scene(s).

At the turn of the millennium, lots of people born after 1965 seem to have lost interest in politics, at least for as long as their wallets aren't concerned. Parties and unions decry this decline for lack of younger activists joining their ranks, and lots of fuss has been made about current youth's supposedly predominant orientation towards hedonism, self-interest and their lack of political participation. On the other hand, there are statements by some belonging to the indicted generation(s), who claim that their activities, although not organised in any classical political body, nevertheless strike political chords, although it seems that spontaneous associations of resistance like the Occupy movement lack the longevity (and thus efficacy) of established organisations. Resistance to neo-feudal corporate politics is divided into irrelevance; society as a collection of fragmented individuals hardly ever amounts to exclamations of collective will beyond participation in pointless election rituals. For a while, it seemed as if Timothy Leary's "politics of ecstasy" were about to replace traditional forms of socio-cultural organisation. Indeed, the 1990s' Love-Parade/cyberpunk-generation's disinterest in everyday-politics seems a far cry from their elder's revolutionary stance which dates back to the international student upheavals of 1968 – possibly because their demands had at least partially been appeased by the transformation that the emerging globalised society underwent after the *Beatles* had put Aleister Crowley's visage on the sleeve of "Sergeant Pepper". However, a good deal of escapism was included in the 1960s' predominant interest in drugs & esotericism, which was then passed on to the 1990's rave-generation which was fond of magic mushrooms, gaian philosophy and techno-shamanism. Naïvely enough, there was a notion that all the world's mishaps might be put right by getting high and dancing till dawn, or that the supposed demonic possession of the White House by the Bush bunch could be fought off by a drum circle on the lawn outside the oval office. Good luck with that! However silly this may seem, it bears a striking similarity to the rather absurdist attempt to exorcise the pentagon, undertaken in 1967 by beat poets Allen Ginsberg and Ed Sanders together with Yippie-heads Abbie Hoffman and Jerry Rubin. While both exorcisms have in common that they ultimately failed, their tiny yet distinctive difference is that the anti-war-movement in 1967 reacted in an absurdist way to an absurd situation and manipulated perception through performance, ridiculing their object, while neo-hippy drum circles at the White House, though they may seem absurd, merely succeeded at ridiculing themselves, for no perceptions (except perhaps their own) were challenged.

These instances might actually help to clarify the difference between actual magickal procedure and simple superstition: While both operations aimed at changing the status quo in magickal fashion by staging a ritual, and were taking place within broader, supportive *Zeitgeist* currents, the ca. 2003 one proved utterly unsuccessful. The yippie one can't seriously be described as having had success either, yet either the celebrity of its performers, or their care for invoking actual deities, or the overall insurgent spirit it tapped into render it more significant than its more recent edition. The intended change of the status quo however wasn't effected by either ritual, not even in the long run, suggesting that either the pentagon and the White House muster the better magicians, that the performing magicians were in both cases incompetent (seeming less likely in the case of the Beatnik ritual) or that the entire premise of assuming ability to influence political processes with magickal means is flawed. In my opinion, the actual ineffectiveness of magick in political matters results from all of these conditions. Bearing in mind that the magick of power works on various "frequencies" of textual, pictorial, symbolic and imaginary nature, the defeat of the ritualistic attacks against the state may be attributed to both the superiority of the institutions' manipulation of above mentioned frequencies as well as the inability of the performers to counteract their opponents on those very frequencies, again suggesting that magickal means are too impotent to provide critical influence over decision makers, let alone the masses and their demands. Superstition with regard to this relative ineffectiveness of magick in the realm of politics would be to suggest otherwise, and further on I will debunk some of the common myths suggesting a working connections between magick and politics. But first, let us take a closer look at what it is that connects them.

Since every act of magick aims to effect a change in the status quo, be it in consciousness, in external reality, or both, in accord with the original intention infused into the ritual, and since intentions may run in opposition to intentions of others, every attempt at magickal influence *always constitutes a political act* – perhaps a sublime one, but possibly one with unforeseeable macroscopic long-term effects. Yet there is a difference between esoteric and exoteric effects, and assuming the probability or erroneous or disadvantageous factors is a combination of the risk factors outlined above (lack of tapping into broader *Zeitgeist*, confusion of frequency levels, personal incompetence) each feeding back into the other, it seems generally unlikely that external reaction chains can be triggered to produce the desired effects. Magick as mysticism in practice may not have the spectacular attributes of "power over others" to it, as its main focus rests on esoteric (literally inward) illumination rather than effecting impressive spells in external reality, but changing one's consciousness may arguably be considered more subversive and radical (from a political viewpoint) than working for social change in a more conventional manner. Changes in individual perception, thought and decision making are much more difficult to gauge and counteract for the hegemon, which accounts for the incredible impact the 60's had on Western societies (even though the actual percentage of drop-outs, yippies, CND activists etc. was tiny in relation to the overall population).

Considering that most of today's "pop-culture" was pre-formatted by people like the Beatniks, Crowley, the surrealists and, before all of them the French "Satanist" Bohème of the late 19th century, who coined the term "modern"[2], there is a great temptation to assume that magick and the occult not only experienced a widespread revival, but by themselves managed to permeate culture, suggesting either the successful machinations of secret societies and magickal orders (a perspective conspiracy theorists share with paranoid superstitious pseudo-Christians), or the coincidence of their availability with the readiness of a generation yearning for something else – or both. Thus, a huge lot of information we're dealing with in

2 Poet Charles Baudelaire was a friend of writer and famed occultist Eliphas Lévi, whose philosophy had a huge impact on the young, radical drug fiends (cf. Dieckhoff, Reiner: *Rausch und Realität – Drogen und Literaten*, in Voelger, Gisela (Ed.): *Rausch und Realität. Drogen im Kulturvergleich*, Cologne 1981, p. 420)

today's popular culture has, just as our way of perceiving it, already been sublimely influenced by occultism in theory or practice. Post-modern society and the way it organises itself through media and communication is therefore the (in)direct result of the of cultural engineers systematically and intentionally altering their consciousness, even if most of its members wouldn't recognize (much less embrace) the fact that their unique possibilities of arranging their lives in a framework granting economic and religious "freedom" originates (partly) in the anti-establishment struggles of transgressives such as Crowley, Burroughs, Leary and others (referred to by Leary as "evolutionary agents"), who all fought what they knew best. Also outside the realms of pop-culture, occultism and its little retarded brother superstition are at work in the mysterious goings-on of Wall Street, where, when NASDAQ has had a bad day, literal sacrifices (mostly of employees) are performed in order to satisfy the greedy beast guarded by the high priests of financial sorcery who manipulate streams of symbols according to formulas which turn those symbols into physical effect in places far remote from their causes. We are arguably living in a society run and informed by magick, at least to a much higher degree than can be said about the pre-modern era, even though superstition may appear as a constant throughout history. As our present is characterised by essentially magickal factors like secrecy (restricted access to information), dis- and misinformation (spin-doctoring perception and thought processes) etc., it becomes quite clear that the front-lines in today's magickal battles are defined by the individual's capability to independent thought versus attempts at influencing whole populations opinions through mass communication. Technological development and the co-emerging magick of electronic data mamagement have reduced ritual magick to merely aesthetic theatrics, and its practitioners to little more than fancy cosplayers.

MAGICK AND POLITICS MAKE BORING BEDFELLOWS

The contradictory relation between individual freedom and collective oppression and thought control through professionalised (if mundane) application of (electronic) magick has never been so evident as today,[3] which might explain to some degree the continued rise in the popularity of conspiracy theories, which themselves often refer to or directly address the dealings of magically inclined secret groups, fraternities and magickal orders. If society allows its members to program their realities individually, it seems a reasonable conclusion that politics as a means of organising the masses for the sake of collective ideologies (like "fascism" or "communism") becomes less important in the constant process of rearranging that society's internal relations under the ever-pervasive yet all-encompassing agendas of those in power, effectively reducing the participatory means of those concerned by

---

3 Allen Ginsberg described the clash between counter-culture and establishment of the 1960s as "political battle, black and white magic [became] publicly visible for a generation." (In: *A Tale of the Tribe* [from preface to "Jail Notes"] as quoted in the CD booklet accompanying the compilation album *Beyond Life With Timothy Leary*, Mercury Records 1997). It is this author's declared opinion that today, these front-lines are simultaneously much more apparent as well as "hidden in plain sight" (obfuscated by disinformation, myth making and conspiracy theories) than ever before.

political decisions while simultaneously creating a chimera of individual freedom and responsibility. To put it bluntly: simplistic ideologies of immersion into an exclusive totalitarian community (be it the national-socialist "Volkskörper" or the communist international) only work in societies either marked by pre-existing collective traditions, or those totally devoid of them, worshipping the cults of individuality, celebrity and civil religion[4] instead. Mass movements in today's society cannot but fail due to the absence of shared core values and ideas in the face of the multifaceted invasion of corporate interests today's consumer society's subjects are targeted by. Yet, intriguingly enough, the very same psychic mechanisms of inclusion/exclusion, self-elevation and gratification as in any ideologically minded group are also at play in magical orders, lodges and so on, indicating the human animal's forms of social organisation constantly move along the lines of "us" and "them" and inviting a critique of the use of those very same mechanisms they seek to distance themselves from, as "The Law is for All."[5] However, it seems that the liberating strike Crowley (and in his wake, chaos magick) performed against the forces of control and authority succeeded mostly outside the realm of the esoteric community: The (ultra-)conservative, exclusive (yet quite bourgeois) and essentialist currents present in European occultism at least since the late 19th century[6] not only continued into and beyond World War II but may even have been on the rise since the 1980s.[7] Besides this general critique of occult organisations and the individuals constituting them, the question of their overall efficacy must be posed.

In recent history, no single organised group devoted to magick has had any particular influence on the cultural developments, shifts and changes in Western civilisation throughout the 20th century, though this assessment is going to be "disproved" by countless people who'd prefer to believe in bizarre inventions from the likes of Rauschning, Landig, Pauwels/Bergier and Francis King, to name but a small selection from the infinite army of pulp novelists, cheaters, exaggerators and outright liars, rather than accede to the method of science mentioned above. A prime example of this continuing self-deception concerning the supposed influence of occult groups is the Thule Society, which used to be in the focus of romanticising mystification regarding its role as a magickal crucible for would-be Nazi leaders, which has been entirely disproved in every way.[8] Instead, SS-mysticism and Nazi-ufology gradually stepped in to fill the void. And, yes: Even though history is

<hr />

4 See Robert N. Bellah: "Civil Religion in America", in: *Daedalus. Journal of the American Academy of Arts and Sciences*, 96 (1967), Boston, Massachusetts, p. 1–21.
5 Title of a 1975 commented edition of Crowleyanity's basic text *Liber Legis*, edited by Israel Regardie (Aleister Crowley & Israel Regardie [ed.]: *The Law is for All*, Phoenix, Arizona 1975).
6 See James Webb: *The Occult Underground* (London 1974) and *The Occult Establishment*, London 1976.
7 The ongoing skirmishes between universalist and essentialist/racist Asatrù are but one example, and the relation between popularity increase of esotericism and its turning into a breeding ground for radical right-wing views is well documented (see Eduard Gugenberger/Roman Schweidlenka: *Mutter Erde, Magie und Politik. Zwischen Faschismus und neuer Gesellschaft*, Wien 1987; Nicholas Goodrick-Clarke: *Black Sun. Aryan Cults, Esoteric Nazism and the Politics of Identity*, New York and London 2002).
8 See Detlef Rose: *Die Thule-Gesellschaft. Legende – Mythos – Wirklichkeit*, Tübingen 1994. Rose's book is a throrough historical analysis, methodically sound and his approach unprejudiced. Ironically enough, even though it has an entire chapter devoted to debunking the most common conspiracy myths, it was published by a publishing house of extreme right-wing reputation.

littered with influential individuals connected to occult organisations, the fact alone does not prove a coherent program of influence actually (and successfully) executed by "conspiracies" which, at their most politicised would become lobbyism wearing costumes and waving wands. Try to imagine Silvio Berlusconi obeying anyone else's instructions but those of his genitals, let alone from some "secret elders" or "invisible masters" of Propaganda Due, the skull-and-bones-bearing criminal Italian lodge he joined in 1975. Chances are that by now, in fact, he is the one issuing orders for the other members, should there be any left. 19th century racist mystery cults informed nazi-racism to a certain degree and could thus be held responsible for indirectly causing a genocidal war and the Shoa, yet the Nazis' supposed engagement in actual practical occultism, as far as its existence can be conceded, never amounted to much more than nationalist, germanophile sentiment, romantic speculation, and "völkisch" protocols in the guise of ritual – following the conspiracy-theorists' logic, military drill and exercise would thus also amount to ritual magick (which, in terms of sect-like mind-programming, would certainly apply). In fact, what little esoteric activity occurred in the brains and ranks of the SS was a source of ridicule rather than an affirmation of Norse religion and/or general esotericism, which were frowned upon since the Third Reich was all about establishing a syncretist civil religion of its own, unassailable by competing belief systems suspected to be potential hijackers of the Movement.

The major magickal enterprise of the late 19th century, the Hermetic Order of the Golden Dawn, accumulated a concise archive and working model of comparative religion and contemporary psychology, but degraded due to its leading members' lapse into childish power games and ego worship.[9] None of the occult organisations formed in its wake came even close to the influence and power commonly acceded to actually existing neo-feudal, non-magickal conspiracies like "Skull & Bones" or the NSA, or the paranoiac's favourite scapegoats from history (Freemasons, the Vatican) and legend (ZOG, the Illuminati, extraterrestrials, the lizard conspiracy). The inverse proportion of actual political influence of magickal organisations as opposed to their "secret" powers of lore warrants a psycho-sociological study of its own. Suffice it to say at this point, that an attractive lie will generally be preferred to an ugly truth, especially when the lie satisfies self-aggrandising urges to power, glory, and fame. And when it comes to the realm of magick, nothing is simpler and simultaneously more difficult than exposing a fraud.

TRANSCENDENCE OR DELUSION?

The decline of ideology as a by-product of esoteric enlightenment and consciousness expansion was taken for granted, especially by those involved in initiated occultism, for those who had experienced and transcended the range of their egos and had begun to live by *Thelema* didn't care much about outdated modes of thinking or marching in line with profane fools. But let me get this straight: there is a trap set up in this particular mode of being "beyond" politics. It is none other than the

---

9 See Israel Regardie: *What You Should Know About The Golden Dawn*, Phoenix, Arizona 1993.

abyss in disguise, for not only do politics still work in the realms "below utopia", but within the occult scene as well, as outlined above. I've shown above that acts of magick are by their very nature political, and though the reverse does not necessarily apply, politics and magick both aim at changing reality according to envisioned ideas of a different version of that reality and both exercise theatrics, eloquence, and intentional manipulation of the way facts are perceived. In short, while not all politics are magick, all magick is political. Therefore, any esoteric claiming to be disinterested in politics is either oblivious of its true nature and should thusly neither be trusted in occult matters, is playing an arrogant game of deception with the foolhardy, or consciously pretends in order to hide his/her actual agenda, which in turn cannot be other than political. Yet, the difference between being political while pretending not to is most prevalent in the recent revival of pagan folk-music (dubbed "neo-folk") in the wake of 1980s occult-influenced industrial culture, where the notion of having transcended classical modes of dealing with culture and religion by becoming the "stars" Crowley and Nietzsche were so fond of, has given rise to reactionary, if not openly racist right-wingers dressing up as independent thinkers and, bizarrely enough, claiming the very tolerance for themselves that they'd likely rather see abolished according to their own predilections. Occult-minded would-be-*Übermenschen* bemoaning the dumbness of the masses (supposedly manipulated by Hollywood, McDonald's and ZOG[10]) and go on to construct their own ingenious identities as social Darwinists way up above the uninitiated hordes of barbarians. In some cases this results in a slow process of neural (self-)reprogramming, ultimately resulting in the abolition of the "mediocre" ideas of humanism, democracy and politics itself as tools of the weak oppressing the strong. Ironically, these arguments are based on passages from the countercultural classic, Crowley's *Book of the Law*, or more precisely, lines like "the slaves shall serve" (II:58) or "Mercy let be off: damn them who pity. Kill and torture; spare not; be upon them" (III:18).

I will not go into extensive exegesis here, but merely point out the contradictions within the Darwinist interpretation. First of all, due to the hermetic nature of these writings every single sentence has to be read and re-read as metaphoric imagery and the overall structure of the text including the meta-text of its inception also have to be taken into account. Secondly, the notion of "Love" being "the Law" suggests a wide range of choices other than extermination and torture. Thirdly, the equation of fully aware thelemic humans to stars following their individual trajectories without conflict ("Do what thou wilt and no one shall say nay") precludes conflicting interests, but I'll leave debate about the nature of the true will to the specialists. Then, not to be underestimated, there is the eccentric character of the editor. There is no doubt that Crowley was full of spite for his unenlightened contemporaries and arrogantly condemned everyone who would not abide to the "law of the strong" – one has to wonder if this wasn't a transmuted echo of the oppressive class structure

---

10 *Zion Occupied Government;* the contemporary version of anti-Semitic Nazi-scapegoat tactics favoured by conspiracy-theorists, who are but too often involved in occultism as well, a combination proving dangerously detrimental to the mental health of hyper-compensating egos wrapped up in denial of their immanent inferiority complexes. (This, of course, is only the author's summarised observation based on multiple yet limited case examinations and is certainly not limited to occultists)

of British society he had been subjected to. Due to his strict religious upbringing, he was especially dismissive of Christians as well as Jews. He was radical in his generalisations and judgements, requesting that humanity be bred "for quality by killing off any tainted stock, as we do with other cattle? And exterminating the vermin which infect it, especially Jews and Protestant Christians?"[11]

The strongest resentments he reserved for what had defined his essence throughout the early stage of his life. Had he not been so full of twisted self-deprecation, he'd done a better job at converting his enemies instead of threatening to exterminate the vermin – such subversion also would have suited his evenly twisted humour much better. But he spat his own venom at the education he himself had had to undergo; the strict programming and conditioning of the Victorian bourgeoisie of the late 19th century, against which he rebelled all his life. Crowley's racism, as dogmatic as it might seem on first glance, was spiritually motivated, not biologically – which only makes it slightly less objectionable, but what is much worse: it provides the template for the New Right's update of cultural racism and spiritual Darwinism à la Julius Evola, whose affiliation with the Rise of Italian fascism is conveniently removed from the references made to him so frequently in Neo-folk by the same people fond of fashionably denying any interest in politics. Fools trying to fool even greater fools, but at least they're in good company: In US-style Satanism, which is also fond of playing Nazi, the intellect is discarded entirely in an attempt to short-circuit will with instinct, eliminating the exercises of ego-abolishment in favour of celebrating it; at least for as long as there is pleasure to be derived from submitting to rather than commandeering it. In short: regression equates to fun, and coming across as evil is cool. And then, as if that wasn't already enough, one picks up recent advertisement leaflets of the Golden Dawn (the Hermetic Order, not the Greek parasites who – most likely in ignorance of the Order – appropriated the name to abuse it for their political ends) showing photos of their spiritual retreat reminiscent of a bucolic suburban nightmare, complete with Ikea-style breakfast tables as furniture. Elsewhere, spiritual authorities abuse their elevated status for bland seduction attempts or to mooch off their supporters/believers – and I'm not pointing fingers solely at the Catholic Church here! For ages the easiest magick seems to have been the cheating of the unsuspecting. For completeness sake, let's not forget the silly bickering within organised occultism, itself the symptom of an isolationist drive to clinging to what's perceived as exclusive – "Us" and "Them" again, division and separation instead of ascension beyond opposites, uniting Binah and Chokmah to let the LVX superior enter through the crown of true royalty.

BEYOND THE VEIL OF SELF-SATISFACTION

With the state of (Western) organised occultism resembling rather a shabby asylum than the sublime wizard caste it imagines itself to be, desperately grasping for

---

11 Aleister Crowley & Israel Regardie (ed.): *The Law is for All*, Phoenix, Arizona 1975, 3rd edition 1986, pp. 274

elitist notions of superiority where shattering of the same would lead to actual liberation, there's little surprise that magick (but not necessarily superstition) has relocated and, similar to the frog prince in the Grimm fairy tale, turned into the ideas-become-reality-dynamics of the world wide web on a (virtually) global scale. On the personal scale a stubborn sense to "do what thou wilt" inherent to the digital natives has emerged, who lack the need to rebel against and tear down outmoded normative cultural patterns, because their predecessors already did away with those. And though as individuals we might perceive of ourselves as free from (most of) the traditional obstacles to behaviour and self-determination, their replacements are marketed to us as lifestyle choices. Offered to us by friendly and caring multinationals applying far more devious and effective magick than any occult community in existence, and harbouring destructive power in magnitudes previously restricted to governments. Taking all these signs of degeneration into account, the question arises whether or not magick itself contains an implicit factor preventing it from being used in ways not open for abuse, corruption and self-aggrandisement. However, the inherent potential of magick to attract the complex-ridden, feeble-minded and easily deceived makes it a minefield for true wisdom seekers, the path of enlightenment being littered with the carcasses of mislead philosophies, self-serving agendas and the ever-present temptation to serve vanity instead of expanding human understanding of the invisible world(s).

In fact, there is no reliable tool to measure the success of any given magickal operation except the respective magician's own perception and understanding of it, which might in itself be thwarted by his or her expectations. Suffice it to say that most of the grand magickal operations undertaken even by the most notorious of wizards have admittedly failed, so chances are that conjurers of less talent and conviction would arrive at even less impressive results. When occultists share their fondest experiences in magickal terms, phrases like "in the right place at the right time", "spontaneous and instinctual decision", "being (in) the flow of events/being in the moment" are commonly used. I've hardly ever heard convincing reports about having caused objective qualitative effects by adhering to ritual and ceremony (other than inducing mystical states of altered perception, once again proving that the actual effect of magick is first and foremost limited to the practitioners themselves). The weavings and workings of (ceremonial) magick are intricate, complicated and by their nature removed from easy analysis in a way as to prevent the possibility of actually proving its efficacy. In short, it is in all probability easier to perform a complex theatre play successfully, than performing the simplest of magickal rituals and obtaining the desired results. Anyone daring enough to posit a 100% success rate is asked to submit evidence to sustain such claims. While it may work subjectively as a tool of self-enhancement and mystical insight, eventually easing the way to a working understanding of how to constructively interact with the world to reach desired goals on a continuous and long-term basis, I fundamentally doubt the utility of magick as a broader tool to exert influence – or gain "power" – on a macro-social level. Or, to put it more bluntly: attempting to satisfy one's thirst for change in the outside world through magickal means is pointless. If it is to be effective, magick has to be applied to oneself, and the ensuing change in external reality is merely a logical consequence of that changed being interacting with it and has little if nothing to do with mystical powers or invocation of obscure deities from early history.

However, having looked at its overall inefficacy, it seems that the "will to power" cannot be satisfied by magick as it proves to be an impotent tool in socio-political matters, helpful only to project a self-image of mystery and occult prowess, inviting the fascinated to speculate. Then again, why would the kind of people interested in gaining power over others grow dissatisfied with the awe of the simple-minded who are easily persuaded to buy into myth making?

Should the Great Work still hold any utopian value at all, it will certainly not be attained by fool's worship, or fighting the wrong enemy, or fighting the right one in the wrong way. Limited views on race and reason don't help either and the possible consequences of creating a superiority complex combined with the desire to BELIEVE as caused by the Third Reich (with similar tendencies currently at work in the USA and elsewhere) should serve as a reminder to those whose spirituality and reason have not been deadened like Crowley's Christians, that the quality of magick, regardless of its outcome, is its transformative moment. Transformation enables transcendence, which is the dissolution of boundaries, which is ultimately the totality of consciousness, leaving no room for disgraceful self-limiting modes of thinking and behaviour patterns based on fear of the Other and regressive retraction into the cosiness of a *völkisch* community.

In 1925, more than two decades after the Liber AL had been "dictated" to Rose Kelly by the subconscious/archetypal raging child dubbed Aiwass, Crowley resented Christians as ever: "Catholics are dead alike to spirituality and to reason, as bad as Protestants." Almost generously though he remarked on "the" Jew that "[he] is far from hopeless outside America."[12] Such sarcastic optimism may have been the result of coming-of-age, but it could as well indicate Crowley's confessed concern with the spiritual betterment of humanity as a whole, whereas his right-wing-followers of today have constructed a bizarre, yet eclectic mixture of social-Darwinism posing as Satanism, Ariosophy and an unholy Frankenstein creature sewn together from the most unappetising limbs from the rotting corpses of Nietzsche, Crowley, Evola, with a few outright (neo) fascist writers thrown in (who just happen to be interested in pre-history), to justify their respective ideologies of essentialist, inferiorising alterity discourses of spite, scorn, and closed-mindedness. What does joining a self-declared elite convinced that everybody else is a shithead have to offer, besides collective overcompensation amounting to what is more or less a cult of self-worship akin to shared and mutually reaffirmed delusions of grandeur like those that the Nazis were so fond of infusing the masses with, that their aesthetic and propagandistic legacy continues to disrupt contemporary culture with its ripple effects of racism, both ethnic and spiritual? While the idea of an orderly, stratified society with people grouped along the lines of their intelligence, understanding, spirituality and a host of other abstract (and

---

12 ibid, p. 275

hardly ever measurable) characteristics, but preferably with oneself a member of the aristocratic caste may seem desirable, if not confirmed by your average stroll through the neighbourhood, a ride on a slow train or a trip through the next globalised pedestrian zone, beholding zoned-out shoppers engaging in materialist pleasure, the lowest form of tolerable self-indulgence, be not mistaken:

YOU ARE JUST ONE OF THEM, with a particular set of priorities, parameters and the ever-present potentiality to CONNECT WITH ALL. And mind the Golden Rule of course.

AUM.

Thelema: Aleister Crowley's Philosophy of True Will

A Preliminary Sketch

Antti P. Balk

As every self-described Thelemite undoubtedly knows, *thelêma* is the Koinê Greek word for will. The Classical Latin word for will, however, is *voluntas*, and volutarism is the school of thought that regards the will as superior to both the intellect and emotion.[1] At different points of history, the view has been applied in every academic field from metaphysics and theology to psychology and sociology. In his *magnum opus*, *The Story of Philosophy*, the celebrated, self-taught historian Will Durant defines voluntarism as the "doctrine that will is the basic factor, both in the universe and in human conduct."[2]

But what exactly is the "will"? The concept of the will itself only evolved gradually, and its proposed originators include Plato, Aristotle, the Stoics, the Epicureans, St. Augustine, and Maximus the Confessor. The term developed somewhat independently of the concept, and Plato's Academy used the word *boulêsis* to describe rational desire for the good, *thumos* to describe the desire for honour, and *epithumia* to describe the desire for pleasure. *Boulêsis* is commonly translated as "will."[3]

In the Christian era, another Greek word for willing, *thelein*, became more prominent, and the term *thelêma* is frequently used in the New Testament, along with *thelêsis* in the Septuagint version of the Old Testament. When Jesus asks for the cup to pass from him, but nevertheless for his Father's will, not his, to be done, the verb most often used is *thelein*, the noun being *thelêma*. The contemporary pagans used the verb often enough, but not the corresponding noun, with the exception of the Neoplatonist Plotinus, who has *thelêma* for the will of the One. Not until the seventh century CE did Maximus the Confessor make *thelêsis* the standard word for will.[4]

However, the most important terminological developments were in Latin, the expression *libera voluntas*, "free will," first appearing in the Epicurean Lucretius. He bases its possibility on the unpredictable swerve of atoms, but what seems to do

---

1 Not to be confused with "voluntaryism," which is the political philosophy that holds all forms of human association should be voluntary.
2 Durant 1953, 534.
3 Richard Sorabji, "The Concept of the Will from Plato to Maximus the Confessor." Pink & Stone 2004.
4 Ibid.

the work in his explanation of freedom is the swerve rather than the will.[5] Epicurus himself made a very early use of the metaphor of freedom, saying of the wise man: "He laughs down the fate which is introduced by some as mistress of all, and says instead that some things happen of necessity, some by chance, and some things are due to us. For he sees that necessity is unaccountable, and chance unstable, but what is up to us (*eph' hêmin*) has no master and it is to this last that blameworthiness and the reverse naturally belong."[6]

The Stoic Epictetus connects Aristotle's concept of *proairesis* (deliberate choice) not only with freedom, but with what is up to us (*eph' hêmin*). Aristotle himself did not, however, associate *proairesis* very closely with freedom and even dissociates it from moral responsibility. He emphasizes that voluntariness, which he links with moral responsibility, extends much more widely to the actions of animals and children, who to him are incapable of anything as rational as *proairesis*. Epictetus, on the other hand, holds that nothing is up to us except what falls under our *proairesis* and all that falls under *proairesis* is up to us. He is also the first to make clear that physical activity is never up to us, on the grounds that it could always be frustrated.[7]

St. Augustine finally makes willing ubiquitous in all action: "Yet, if we attend more subtly, even what anyone is compelled to do unwillingly (*invitus*) he does by his will, if he does it. It is because he would prefer something else that he is said to do it unwillingly (*invitus*), that is, wanting not to (*nolens*). . . .But because the effect follows his will, we cannot say control over his act was missing."[8] Augustine also expanded enormously the functions of the will. In Augustine, will performs some of the functions of directing action, it unites perception with the perceptible, memory with internal vision, and intellect with objects taken from memory. To Augustine, will is responsible for imagination. Faith, according to Augustine, is also due to will. Emotions are acts of will, and the will forms the centrepiece of Augustine's objections to lust.[9]

However, it has never been easy for the Church to admit that people have the ability to make their own free decisions. Determinism, perhaps the most significant theological doctrine of Augustine, got polished when it clashed with the opinion of Pelagius, an Irish monk who defended a heretical degree of free will.[10] In opposition to the Pelagians, who believed that man was created by God in His image and is, by nature, good, but can fall into sin through misuse of his free will (*liberum arbitrium*), Augustine argued that since the Fall of Adam, all humanity is inescapably predisposed to evil and cannot respond to the will of God without Divine Grace.[11] The Church has always held baptism to be "for the remission of sins," and the Augustinian doctrines of Original Sin and Total Depravity offered

5 Ibid.
6 *Letter to Menoeceus*, in Diogenes Laertius, *Lives of the Eminent Philosophers*, 10.133. As quoted in Sorabji.
7 Sorabji, op. cit.
8 *On the Spirit and the Letter*, 31.53. As quoted in Sorabji.
9 Sorabji, op. cit.
10 Balk 2008.
11 Josef Lössl, "Intellect with a (Divine) Purpose: Augustine on the Will." Pink & Stone, op. cit.

the first comprehensive theological explanation for the practice of baptizing infants, guilty of no actual personal sin. However, if man does not have the power to choose the good and refuse the evil, he cannot be morally accountable for his actions, which is why the Catholic Church never fully accepted Augustine's doctrines, and only out of respect for him, never publicly banned them.[12]

The centuries-long controversy between free will and predestination was finally solved by the Edwardian magus Aleister Crowley, when he posited a True Will.[13] "He who seeks the origin of evil," Crowley wrote, "seeks the source of what is not. Evil is the disordered appetite for good, the unfruitful attempt of an unskilful will."[14] Those who think they have free will reckon they can freely will this or that and just as easily will the contrary, being masters of their resolution, whereas the advocates of determinism would have us believe that the power of decision lay with God, who in his infinite wisdom has made all the decisions for all the ages. The third option, of course, is following your True Will in every situation.[15] "Then, and then only, art thou in harmony with the Movement of Things, thy will part of, and therefore equal to, the Will of God. And since the will is but the dynamic aspect of the self, and since two different selves could not possess identical wills; then, if thy will be God's will, *Thou art That*."[16]

REFERENCES:

—⁓— Balk, A.P. (2012). *Balderdash: A Treatise on Ethics*. Helsinki: Thelema Publications.

_____. (2008). *Saints & Sinners: An Account of Western Civilization*. Helsinki: Thelema Publications.

—⁓— Crowley, A. (ed.) (1909–13). *The Equinox*. Vol. I. 10 nos. London: Simpkin, Marshall, Hamilton, Kent & Co.

_____. (ed.) (1919). *The Equinox*. Vol. III. No. I. Detroit: Universal.

—⁓— Durant, W. (1953). *The Story of Philosophy: The Lives and Opinions of the World's Greatest Philosophers from Plato to John Dewey*. 2nd ed. New York: Pocket Books.

—⁓— Pink, T. & M.W.F. Stone. (eds.) (2004). *The Will and Human Action: From Antiquity to the Present Day*. London: Routledge.

---

12 Balk, op. cit.
13 Idem. 2012. Note that there is no mention of "true will" anywhere in *The Book of the Law*.
14 Éliphas Lévi. *The Key of the Mysteries*. Crowley 1909–13, X, 31.
15 Thesis-antithesis-synthesis.
16 *Liber II: The Message of the Master Therion*. Idem. 1919, 42. Emphasis in original.

THE VINDICATON OF THELEMA

Kjetil Fjell

I saw also that Horus might reconcile all religions, it being possible now to bring all countries to agree on a few fundamental principles. Science had practically driven prejudice into the dark. Faith was little more than a shibboleth which no longer influenced opinion or action. I saw my way to combine a few simple incontrovertible scientific principles into a Law which would allow the loftiest aspirations to seek satisfaction in spiritual spheres, the religious instincts to realize their sublimity through ritual, and to assist the scientific mind to see that even the most materialistic concept of the cosmos was ultimately mystical, that though mind might be merely a function of matter, yet that matter might equally well be represented as a manifestation of mind.[1]

One of the ongoing debates among modern Thelemites is whether or not Thelema is a religion, and whether or not it might better be described as a philosophy, science or political ideology. Interestingly enough this kind of internal discourse is common among religions[2] and must ultimately be viewed as a way of vindicating ones own religious beliefs in the competition against other ideas on the religious marketplace.[3]

There are two ways of measuring meaningful contributions to these four fields. One is the conventional world of peer reviewed publications and their citations among other academics, the other being the proliferation of one's ideas among groups and people. It is my argument that Crowley fails both these tests, but that he had more success in the latter than the former.

A survey of academic databases[4] that I did on the Winter Solstice 2013, reveals no citations by Crowley as a contributor to the fields of religion, philosophy, science or politics, as opposed to being an object of study. In fact even as an object of study, his contribution is recent, decidedly modern and miniscule compared to other topics. Over a hundred years after the reception of his *Book of the Law*, his legacy of thought remains untouched by academics except as an specialized study within the study of religion.

This leaves the adoption of his thoughts by the world at large. As one would

---

1 Crowley, Aleister (1979, 1989), *The Confessions of Aleister Crowley*, page 619.
2 For a discussion on the evolving discourse within religion and the field that studies it, please see Eric J. Sharpe (1994) *Comparative Religion, a history.*
3 For a thorough discussion of the mechanisms of the market of ideas as expressed within religion, please see the article by Rodney Stark (2006b), "Economics of Religion," in *The Blackwell Companion to the Study of Religion*, Ch. 3, pp. 47-67.
4 For a list of the databases consulted, please check http://en.wikipedia.org/wiki/List_of_academic_databases_and_search_engines

expect, given the slight mention of him in the research databases consulted, the religion of Thelema remains a microreligion.[5] There exists no serious political parties organized around his thoughts and his one influence on an actual active politician remains the Russian traditionalist and neo-fascist Alexandr Dugin.[6]

Given the increasing focus by Aleister Crowley on the promulgation and establishment of the Law of Thelema that had its roots in his initiation into the Grade of Magus with its curse to utter one's Word,[7] this is surprising. Crowley himself rationalised his failure and reflected that his efforts were constantly frustrated by the fact that his work for the most part attracted wooly occultists, who had no idea about how to assist him in manifesting his Word to the world at large.

It is my argument however that Crowley's problems stemmed from his own inability to contribute in any meaningful way to the three areas that he most wanted to influence, those of science, philosophy, and politics. Consequently, the people he attracted must be regarded as a result of the fact that the one field that he did make a meaningful contribution to, was the very occultism that he despised.[8]

ECCE HOMO

We do not want any more drifting 'occultists.' You want the great political leaders, great industrialists and people of that sort, the kind of persons who do not subscribe $835 in a year, but half a million dollars in a day; and every distraction or diversion of funds from the business of getting at such people is hardly better than throwing the money into the sea.[9]

Never one to underestimate the importance of his own legacy, Crowley naturally believed that it had the potential to revolutionize the fields of politics, science and philosophy. He rightly regarded his point of view to be of a radical nature and so its acceptance would not come easily.[10]

---

5 The Ordo Templi Orientis, the largest group centered around the ideas and work of Crowley in the world is an Order where the most developed countries are organized as national Grand Lodges. There are currently in 2013, three Grand Lodges in the world, where the largest of these, the Grand Lodge of USA currently has 1309 active members (source: http://oto-usa.org/static/usgl_annual_report_IVxx.pdf).

6 For a discussion of Alexandr Dugin's political activities and sympathies with among others Aleister Crowley, see *Is Aleksandr Dugin a Traditionalist? "Neo-Eurasianism" and Perennial Philosophy*, by Anton Shekhovstov and Andreas Umland in *The Russian Review* 68 (October 2009): 662–78. For a thorough presentation of Crowley's own futile ambition within the field when he was alive see *Aleister Crowley and the Temptation of Politics* by Marco Pasi (2006, 2013).

7 For a discussion of Crowley's evolving religious ambitions, please see *Varieties of Magical Experience* pp. 53–86 by Marco Pasi (2012) in *Aleister Crowley and Esotericism*. As Pasi clearly demonstrates, Crowley's presentation of Thelema in general and the Holy Guardian Angel in particular evolves to meet the challenges he has in taking control over and promulgating his Law of Thelema.

8 For more on Crowley's negative view on occultism, see his (1998) posthumously published essay "Occultism", where he reveals his problems with being associated with occultists and occultism, as well as the opening quote in the next section, a letter to W. T. Smith dated April 1st, 1943.

9 Crowley to W.T. Smith, April 1st 1943.

10 For examples of Crowley's discussion on why his ideas were not widely adopted, his contempt for the masses and vision of his program being adopted for all, see his commentary on the *Book of the Law* (1996) and the other *Holy Books of Thelema* (1998).

At times he would even regard himself as a modern Christian Rosenkreutz, whose ideas would be rediscovered through the lasting impact of his literary legacy. He was both right and wrong in this analysis. He was wrong in the sense that it was his poetry and other attempts at art that would enable his Rosetta Stone of his ideas, the first volume of the *Review of Scientific Illuminism, The Equinox*, to survive into the modern age.[11] He was however right in the sense that it was the enduring[12] interest in his books, not the conventional method of having his adherents promulgate his teachings, that would eventually allow it to survive.

For all his pretentions to impact on the real world, it is clear that Crowley could not be bothered with the slow methodical construction of an ideology that one would expect a philosopher to be engaged in. Nor did he have any time for the conventional methodological experiment and publication in peer-reviewed journals that a scientist would tirelessly do. Finally he was unable, unlike a politician, to gain the trust of the people, a group he both despised and felt that he was against.

His problem was according to him not if or even how he could make a lasting contribution to these fields, but rather how to attract the right people to put him in a position to make his mark on it. All too aware that his terrible reputation worked against him this was to happen behind the scenes. But he remained unaware that this created an even greater obstacle. If he wanted to attract people of real import and have them promulgate his Law, he needed to offer them something more than that they did not have to be associated in public with himself, a man of disrepute.

To attract people of real import he would have needed to make a disciplined argument as to what was to be gained by adopting his program. Instead he offered slogans, pamphlets and the hidden but high-risk association with himself. For him such disciplined endeavours that would lead to real contributions to these fields, were tedious distractions to his real goal in life, the prosecution of the Great Work. Within this occult sphere, however, he was perhaps the most disciplined individual and original thinker in the history of Magick.

As such it is no wonder that to the extent that he did attract people of import from these fields, it was through their interest in occultism. It is equally unsurprising that these very occultists had little interest in adopting a new religion, whose public promulgation would brand them outcasts in respectable society.[13]

His contributions to the fields of philosophy, science and politics were often written in haste, or as he would undoubtedly have preferred to refer to it, in the white heat of energized enthusiasm. As such, his contributions should be regarded as aesthetical by-products of his initiatory process, rather than real contributions to

11 Examples of this and other attempts at rationalise his lack of impact and how ultimately it is to triumph, is to be found in his autohagiography, the *Confessions of Aleister Crowley* (1979, 1989; 1985). A stronger argument could be made that Crowley's poetry and artistic output would not have survived if it had not been for the enduring interest in his occult legacy. But this was an idea Crowley did not contemplate.
12 Fuelled no doubt by his outrageous life.
13 Crowley's association with Gerald Yorke is perhaps the most illustrative of this dilemma. Crowley wanted him to get *Magick in Theory and Practice* published, and Yorke attempted in his turn to make Crowley cut out his references to Thelema. For more on their relationship, see the editorial introduction by William Breeze to *Liber ABA* (1994).

these fields. It is little wonder to anyone but Crowley himself and his most ardent supporters that he met with such abject failure to impress anyone of any worth in these fields.

Because of this and the fact that his bohemian lifestyle was designed to outrage and shock respectable citizens, including modern adherents to his Law of Thelema to this day, his life has often been regarded as a cautionary tale. His friend and former disciple Gerald J. Yorke summarized him as the first pseudo-messiah that the Hermetic Order of the Golden Dawn gave birth to.[14] Several biographies even declare that Crowley in the face of the utter ruin of his life despaired at the end at the hopelessness of his situation.[15]

Other old friends on the other hand treated him more kindly. In his biographical account of seven friends, Crowley's oldest friend, the one who had steadfastly stood by him through all those years of public ridicule and disrepute and who perhaps knew him best, Louis Marlow, remarked that Crowley did not despair in his sunset years, but he was disappointed that he had not become as rich and influential as he had hoped to become.[16]

Cognitive Dissonance

To many persons who glance at the life of A.C., and find him preeminent in many spheres, from mountaineering to magick + chess-playing, to cycling, he appears to be a poseur.[17]

Crowley himself was perplexed right until his end about why his life had not borne more influence and financial success, and consequently we find him rationalising his failure at different junctures in his life. The mainstay was that he had taken an oath, not only to endure unto the end, but give his whole life to the Great Work, and so he could not benefit from it himself. But there were other equally creative attempts at explaining why the world had not adopted his new creed.

One of them was concerned with typical religious rationalisation of one's lack of fortune and concentrated itself on the fact that Crowley had in some ways wronged the very Secret Chiefs who had put this immense task and obligation to promulgate and establish the Law of Thelema into his hands.

Interestingly enough these thoughts were at their most prominent when he was at his lowest. When he however was suffering from hypomania bordering on psychosis brought on by prolonged and excessive intake of cocaine, the world was his oyster and there were no limits to what he could accomplish, resulting in many abandoned schemes to put over the Law of Thelema.[18]

---

14 Foreword to *The Magicians of the Golden Dawn* by Ellic Howe (1972), page xix.
15 See several biographies such as John Symonds (1997) *The Beast 666*, but also more friendly biographies written by modern followers of Crowley such as Richard Kaczynski (2002, 2010) *Perdurabo, the life of Aleister Crowley.*
16 See Louis Umfreville Wilkinson (1953) *Seven Friends.*
17 Undated note in diary, probably from 1917.
18 See in particular his long discourses on the subject matter during the Cefalu years in *The Magical Record of the Beast 666* (1979), for examples of both Crowley's highs and lows and the chronic mental

When Crowley, after a long period of tribulation, felt at ease with himself and the world, he opted for an different strategy: he was not ready to put over the Law of Thelema yet, because his initiation and consequently his understanding was not yet complete. Consequently we find him writing after his initiation into the Grade of Ipsissimus, the following statement:

> *Now the Secret Chiefs had chosen him as Their representative on earth, as the vehicle of the Utterance. And because he was not yet fitted by full initiation to carry out Their designs, it was imperative that They should prevent him, even when he consented to execute Their commands, from making a premature appearance. This was not altogether easy to secure for, despite his own determination to abandon his worldly career, he had obtained eminence in two widely distinct paths of human activity; so that whatever he might choose to set forth would be certain to receive due attention from the world at large.*[19]

However, as any objective reading of his biography would conclude, no such success was forthcoming. It is my argument that it would be a more fruitful endeavour to locate naturalist causes for his resounding failure along his proposed lines of success, rather than continuing to rely on supernatural excuses and explanations to ease his (and no doubt modern day followers) cognitive dissonance.

In a sense it was the very fields that Crowley wanted to contribute to themselves, that caused problems for him. That is, it was his undisciplined use of them where he did not seek to contribute to them, but rather use them in order to further his own agenda.

THE PROBLEM OF PHILOSOPHY

Ever the pragmatic dilettante, Crowley was as pragmatic in his use of philosophy as he was of science or politics. The agenda would be clear to any skeptical and honest observer, to further his promulgation and establishment of the Law of Thelema. Consequently we see that rather than making a real and sustained effort to contribute to the world of philosophy, Crowley pragmatically used it to explain away problems with his system and approaches.

His method was as simple as it was elegant. He declared brazenly that it mattered not whether it was literally true, the important thing was that he had a method at his disposal to create change in accordance with his Will.[20]

While Crowley's pragmatic nominalism was a sensible approach[21] for a system

---

and somatic problems he suffered during his time there.

19 *The Master Therion: a biographical note*, published in *The Equinox III:10* (1985).

20 Crowley's (1994) most mature approach is exemplified in his essay *Notes towards an Astral Atlas*, where he demonstrates an pragmatic nominalism, where he refuses to acknowledge the importance of the absolute truth of the models that he presents.

21 Pragmatic nominalism has also been the approach within psychotherapy, where the focus has often been on whether or not an medical or therapeutic intervention had a positive effect on the symptoms rather than how or why it worked. That being said, there are severe problems with such an approach and modern research into psychotherapy is far more sophisticated, cf. David & Montgommery (2011)

of theurgy and thaumathurgy where one knew the answer to neither the how or the why it worked, it also provided an easy cover to retreat behind whenever someone raised a difficult answer. Thus we find Crowley, whose biography and claims to spiritually transmitted authority rested on reincarnation,[22] he would evade difficult question by claiming that it mattered not that this might not literally be true.[23]

This borderline solipsism can also be seen at work when he tries to unify his earlier claims that the Holy Guardian Angel was a distinctly individual experience with the fact that Aiwaz being his Holy Guardian Angel and a Secret Chief independent of himself, where he takes both point of views and neither.[24]

The same arguments can be seen at work when he tries to explain away incongruencies in astral work, where he declares that there is a harmony between two accounts of the same place. He continues his argument by claiming that just as if two people took the train they would focus on different things, so was it with the astral.[25]

Crowley's problem was not that he did not meet the right people, but that he did not make a sustained and serious effort at clearly formulating the basic and fundamental principles of his Law of Thelema as applied to these topics in one place. Though he made some brief attempts at building a philosophy upon his first principle, *Do what thou wilt*, it is mostly propaganda made with an eye to attract newcomers rather than engage the thoughts of true philosophers, politicians and scientists.

This problem also manifested itself in his problematic takes on science and politics. How can there be any influence when there are no first principles that allows us to rationally demonstrate the validity and reliability of his Law and from which one could build on?

THE PROBLEM OF SCIENCE

In order to get over the ethical difficulties presented by the naïve naturalism of many parts of those Scriptures, in the divine authority of which he firmly believed, Philo borrowed from the Stoics (who had been in like straits in respect of Greek mythology) that great Excalibur which they had forged with infinite pains and skill – the method of allegorical interpretation. This mighty 'two handed engine at the door' of the theologian is warranted to make a speedy end of any

---

The Scientific Status of Psychotherapies: A New Evaluative Framework for Evidence-Based Psychosocial Interventions.

22 Crowley (1979, 1989) originally fulfilled his coursework for the grade of the Adeptus Exemptus by translating Eliphas Levi's *The Key to the Mysteries*, claiming that he was an reincarnation of him. While it is true that Crowley would rectify this by publishing decades later part III of *Liber ABA, Magick in Theory and Practice*, it is equally true that he used the reincarnation claim until then. Similarly we find him identifying with Ankh-f-n-khonsu, claiming that being his reincarnation gave him spiritual authority.

23 See Crowley's (1994) attempt at rationalising his point of view on reincarnation in part III of *Liber ABA*.

24 See Marco Pasi's (2012) *Varieties of Magical Experience* for a discussion on how Crowley gradually changed his rhetoric concerning the Holy Guardian Angel to fit his agenda as a Prophet.

25 See Crowley (2010) to David Curwen on the subject in *Brother Crowley, Brother Curwen*, edited by Henrik Bogdan.

and every moral or intellectual difficulty, by showing that, taken allegorically, or, as it is otherwise said "poetically' or 'in a spiritual sense,' the plainest words mean whatever a pious interpreter desires they should mean.[26]

Crowley would often brag about his background in chemistry, particularly when he wanted to settle an argument in his favour. His was the world, or so he argued, of exact definitions and rigid experiment, not the flaky fancies of the theosophist and occultist.[27]

Crowley was a well-read and travelled man, a skilled autodidact and an pragmatic eclectic with considerable cognitive capacity for creative and deep thought. This made his system of spiritual attainment, which he at various times termed skeptical mysticism, scientific illuminism and magick, a novel branch in the annals of occultism.[28]

It is however also the history of an individual with an incredibly pragmatic take on science and so we see him advising his acolyte Charles S. Jones that it mattered little if science disagreed with the Law of Thelema when using it to promulgate its excellence. Where these two did not meet, Thelema would win, every time.

For Crowley, the very fact that he engaged in it and it was not art, was enough for it be an scientific endeavour. This explains why he brazenly would sign a petition "Scientific Essayist."[29] While he would often champion philosophical skepticism[30] a closer reading of his biography shows a man who pioneered the modern pseudo-scientific use of science in order to lend credence to his own ideas.[31]

His wrong-headed preoccupation with scientific approval is most prominent in his attempt to put over the Law of Thelema as a scientific religion.[32] Just as he would not in public[33] doubt that his legacy did in fact have an important contribution to make to the fields of science, philosophy and science, he would also never doubt that there were in actual fact an energy that made possible the work of magick and that there existed beings of immense power that wanted to communicate with mankind through prophets.

His religious hypothesis was then that there exists certain praeterhuman

---

26 From Thomas Huxley, "Evolution of Theology: an anthropological study," as quoted by Crowley (1904) in his *Sword of Song*.

27 See Crowley's authohagiography (1979, 1989) and his essay *Occultism* (1998).

28 See Egil Asprem's (2008) *Magick Naturalized: Negotiating Science and Occult Experience in Aleister Crowley's Scientific Illuminism*, for an interesting discussion in where Crowley differed from his occult compatriots. For a slightly different take, cf. Marco Pasi's (2012) *Varieties of Magical Experience*.

29 This was the occupation Crowley signed Nancy Cunard's appeal for the Scottsboro Boys in 1931.

30 See Egil Asprem's (2008) *Magic Naturalized*, but also *Liber O vel Manus Sagittae* (1994) and his authohagiography (1979, 1989), *The Confessions of Aleister Crowley*.

31 For an interesting discussion of this phenomenon and its roots in the disenchantment of the post-industrialized world, where religious authority no longer were enough, see Olav Hammer's (2003) seminal *Claiming Knowledge*.

32 See in particular *The Equinox III(1)* (1909) for his first entry in this continual effort.

33 In private he was more doubtfull however and he records in 1923 in his diary that he doubted both the active agency of the Secret Chiefs and Magick. Lucidly enough he notes that "there is something irrational & irritating that tells me otherwise."

intelligences that one may communicate with and even raise oneself to their stature.[34] The problem with Islam was not the fact that it was the result of a madman,[35] or that of a conman. Rather it was the fact that Mohammed had not left an unmodified account of his experience with the archangel Gabriel. Because the *Quran* and the story of Mohammed bore the marks of heavy editing, it was up for criticism.

The Cairo Working with its reception of the *Book of the Law*, Crowley argued, changed all of this. He had published an account of the exact circumstances of his experience in a lasting form, and the *Book of the Law* itself was photographically guaranteed to be free from editorial interference.[36]

This was what separated Thelema from superstitious religion and made it scientific, since within it was contained both external proof in the form of prophecies, as well as internal proof in the form of qabalistic riddles. The problem was of course that neither was either rigid or possible to control by others and would not, as Tobias Churton, despite agreeing with Crowley's belief that Thelema contains valid contributions to science, philosophy and politics, convince anyone but those who wanted to believe.[37]

Qabalistic proof, despite Crowley's many protestations, is not rigid and similar to mathematical proof. It is an individual and aesthetical endeavor that a true skeptic that Crowley claimed would be convinced by it, would not accept but rather claim that it reveals only that which is within the one engaging in qabalistic analysis themselves. Similarly we find his use of prophecies to be problematic in a scientific context.

Again his argument seems to stem from a wrong-headed belief that what people doubted was not that prophecy was possible to begin with, but rather that the prophet himself had somehow facilitated the prophecy to come true. Consequently he argues in *Magick Without Tears* that prophecies must be such that their nature are only divined and accepted as incontrovertibly true after they have come true, thus leaving no possibility of foul play. Needless to say, this kind of vague prophecy is exactly the opposite of what science necessitates, which are clear and unambiguous predictions which are falsifiable.[38]

The lack of principled understanding and application of scientific method and philosophy is most prominent in Crowley's last public word on the subject in *Magick Without Tears*. Here he has dropped the religious argumentation of Thelema and it is now presented as science in opposed to religion. He proudly declares that if we call it a religion, then it must only be that if it does not contradict any known scientific fact. Irony abounds when Crowley in the very next chapter criticises biology for abandoning vitalism because it does not fit with his anecdotal and religious experiences.

---

34 See the introduction to *Liber ABA* (1994) by William Breeze.

35 For if it was the work of a madman it was in fact an argument for madness, see *Liber ABA*, part I for more along this argument from Crowley (1994).

36 See Crowley's (1991) discussion concerning the importance of this in *Magick Without Tears* and alongside it an amusing exhortation against heresiarchs in Thelema.

37 See Tobias Churton (2011), *Aleister Crowley, the Biography*.

38 See Karl Popper (2002), *Conjectures and Refutations* for a discussion of the evolution and the principles of modern science.

The Problem of Politics

Despite the fact that he became increasingly preoccupied with the political aspect of the Law of Thelema after attaining to the grade of Magus, he wrote precious little concerning the actual implications. What exists is propaganda and disjointed and contradictory comments in his books, diaries, letters and several unfinished articles and one long but ultimately abandoned outline for a longer work covering all possible aspects of the application of the Law of Thelema to politics.[39]

Part of the problem is that Crowley, ever the pragmatic demagogue, shifts his rhetorics depending on who he wants to attract. I believe he was the most honest with his acolyte Norman Mudd when he notes that the system of Thelema is to mark a return to a system where there are masters and slaves. Arguing that the bulk of humanity is not worth more than his pocket lint, he pointed out that these people are not in a position to either know or do their will. So the Masters must provide for them.[40]

It seems that for Crowley what mattered was the handful of people that had the aptitude for Genius. Similarly, the question was not how one ought to secure the greatest liberty for everyone, but rather how to stop the meddlesome mediocrities interfering with the life of the spiritual giants of the world.

That Crowley landed on a system where he wanted to secure the greatest amount of freedom and leisure for the largest possible members of society, must then not be confused with sentimental feelings for the people on his part. Rather it was the system that he envisioned would make them leave geniuses at work alone.[41]

He would gladly appeal to Stalin, Hitler, the British Crown, regular workers, factory owners and even Zionists.[42] While the rhetorics varied wildly depending on the listener, offering often contradictory promises as to what would happen if they adapted the Law of Thelema, the agenda was always the same, to install Crowley as the secret prophet that would guide things behind the scenes. The principle seemed to be that with "Therion at the prow" everything would turn out alright.[43]

As he would write in his diary they would use fear to intimidate them all. The fear they wanted to prey upon was the loss of privilege which the establishment of the Law of Thelema would somehow restore or salvage. For the factory owners it was the civil unrest and possible revolution instigated by the bolsheviks, and for the workers it was certain accommodations securing a basic income, retirement and assistance in finding

---

39 What exists in more or less finished form is propaganda such as *The Scientific Solution to the Problem of Government*, and in unfinished form *Helios and the future of science*. The long outline was titled *On the problem of Labour* and contains some good attempts at serious thought along with some serious howlers (as when Crowley wants to decide upon the succession of his monarchy by a method that at best can be described as the fool winning the princess and half the Kingdom). This was however abandoned when his acolyte Frank Bennett who was intended to distribute it among the unions in Australia skewered it.
40 He makes a similar argument in *Liber Aleph* (1991) concerning the rule of the State.
41 His extensive correspondence with his acolyte Norman Mudd at the Warburg institute bears witness on these thoughts and many more concerning the political Beast 666.
42 See Marco Pasi (2006; 2013), *Aleister Crowley and the Temptation of Politics*.
43 For a similar approach by Crowley to the Tunis comment, see discussion below.

new work in order to pacify them against the bolshevik propaganda.[44]

The closest ideal to his political system would be anarcho-fascism, or as Crowley preferred to label it, *autarchy*. That is, self-governing by those who were capable and willing to discharge their duties and accept the consequences of their choices. It should come as no surprise that there were few takers except his adherents to the Law of Thelema, who in it saw the promise of a new day and bright future.

THE TUNIS COMMENT

Please note Leah Hirsig has infringed the injunction in paragraph 4 of the comment on AL and is no longer to be trusted. Any correspondence with her should be destroyed unread.[45]

For all my criticism of Crowley's failures, the reason why he did not write at length on these topics, is readily apparent. His expertise was after all within occultism, not politics, philosophy and science, so it makes a certain sense that he would leave that to more able individuals, just as he had attempted with Norman Mudd and his mathematical exposition on the *Book of the Law.*

The problem was, as already noted, that Crowley did not make a sustained and serious effort at clearly formulating the basic and fundamental principles of his Law of Thelema. The result is that there are no clear first principles derived by Crowley from the axiom or first principle of *Do what thou wilt*. The result is that the Law of Thelema as expressed by Crowley and both his contemporary as well as modern devotees to that Law, remains a religious endeavour rather than a scientific, philosophical or political one.

Crowley seems to have believed that his social program, as outlined in the rituals and the instructions of the O.T.O., would suffice to attract more serious thinkers along these lines, but one wonder how this would have ended. He did attract a serious mathematician of some note in Norman Mudd and who commented on the *Book of the Law.* Though this resulted in Crowley integrating some of Mudd's ideas into his broader commentary on the *Book of the Law,* it also resulted in the Tunis Comment, forbidding us all from engaging in such commentary in the future.

After Mudd's relentless criticism of Crowley for holding Aiwaz hostage, an attempt at schism wherein he proclaimed himself as the true leader of the movement, Crowley formulated in white heat the Tunis Comment whose principles, though often misunderstood, are surprisingly simple.

As outlined in the Comment itself along with his broader commentary on its application in *Magick Without Tears*, the Comment declares a parsimonious path away from schism and towards exegetical authority. One is warned against studying the *Book of the Law*, but may do so if it is one's will, at one's own peril.

To safeguard the movement against schism and preserving exegetical authority however we must appeal to the writings of Aleister Crowley, each of us being the

---

44 Cf. his diaries for the period of 1923-1924 for long discussions that follows these premises.
45 Memorandum by Aleister Crowley, ca. august 1928. The accompanying letter spelled out the demands he gave for rehabilitating her, which in particular centered on denouncing and incriminating Norman Mudd who similarly had infringed on the comment.

final arbiter for ourselves as to the true meaning. In doing so we must keep silent about our results, since discussion is forbidden.

Together these form the four powers of the Sphinx – to know, to will, to dare, to keep silent – as testified by its first publication in the Tunis edition of the *Book of the Law*, where Crowley ends his preface by noting exactly these four powers. They give a remarkable amount of freedom for the individual adherent to form his own point of view on the *Book of the Law*, while at the same time forbidding one from discussing the meaning of individual verses of the *Book of the Law* and thereby straying from our true paths and muddling that of others.

As he would write in *Magick in Theory and Practice*, we would be at the helm, but Therion at the prow.[46] Those that discuss its contents are to be branded centers of pestilence and shunned by the thelemic community. Crowley exercised this clause of the Comment for the first time with Norman Mudd and Leah Hirsig which denotes his clear intention with the Tunis Comment and solidifies the attack against heresiarchs in *Magick Without Tears*.

As opposed to this we would obviously be free to discuss Crowley's writings and in fact he specifically asks us to do this in *Liber CCC* and throughout his life prepared for the day when his writings, as opposed to the *Book of the Law*, would be freely discussed by experts in all fields.

A BLESSING IN DISGUISE

Ordinary discoveries proved as soon as made, are branches of one bough of the Tree of Knowledge. The Magus, the Poet, and their like perch on untouched boughs.[47]

I hold that Crowley can best be understood as an exponent of religious thought whose method was that of ecstatic revelation. If he was merely a philosopher expounding his philosophy, he was an incredibly sloppy one, a second rate Nietzsche, sprinkled a bit with Bertrand Russell. When he attempted to unite these two endeavours, science and philosophy, in politics, it becomes more problematic than just the two of them.

The Magus, just as the artist, is no manifester of a Word that may be hermeneutically interpreted. Rather it is an aesthetic by-product of his initiatic career and as such will kindle the living flame that makes gods out of all of us in mankind. He is an inspirational force rather than a theoretician and contributor to these fields. He cuts his way into the jungle and finds new sights,[48] that one day may be catalogued and understood by proper scientists. This does not detract from his

---

46 One of the demands Crowley made to Hirsig was that she sign a document that among other things read "I Leah Hirsig, Aloastrael, the Scarlet Woman, acknowledge that I have deviated from my True Path by discussing the Book of the Law."
47 Diary entry by Aleister Crowley on march 9th, 1924.
48 For a study on Crowley's novel innovation in the annals of spiritual attainment, see my forthcoming study *Attainment & Psychosis*, which covers the crossing of the abyss from a neuropsychological point of view.

value, far from it: it emphasizes his progressive uniqueness that may give a glimpse of sights hitherto unimagined.

Because Crowley's contributions to these fields were not that of careful or guarded argument and experiment, but rather the result of opportunism and illuminated insight arising from the necessities of his initiations, they should not ultimately be viewed as real contributions to these fields, but rather aesthetic by-products that may inspire others.

For all his ambition to manifest his Word on the terrestrial plane, it was his original plan of safeguarding the movement through his literary works and his ability to still shock and appall two decades after his death, that secured the Law of Thelema a second lease on life: For all intents and purposes Thelema was dying out at the end of Crowley's life and it got progressively worse after his death. Then in the 1960s the republication of his works secured a renewed interest in his legacy and today the adherents of the Law of Thelema numbers in the tens of thousands rather than the dozens as during Crowley's life.[49]

I contend that while it would be interesting to see Thelema grow up and become a real contributor to the fields of science, philosophy and politics in the same way major world religions have done so, this is not, unlike what Crowley believed, where its success will manifest. Rather it will be through the organic growth of our communities, where the Law is manifested as by-products of our lives as thelemites, that will ultimately prove our springboard into adulthood.

It will be a longer and harder road to walk, but history shows that even Christianity did not win through the acceptance of that faith by Emperor Constantine, but rather through the careful growing of its communities.[50]

Success needs to be broadly based along several endeavours. Chief of these is making Crowley's writings known, to be sure, but we need to exemplify the success that they lead to through purely aesthetic means, be this living worthwhile and responsible lives as contributing citizens to our respective communities, the raising and safeguarding of our children properly, architecture and religious art in community buildings or more progressive artistic contributions.

It is, as such, not limited to art (understood in a narrow sense), but needs to exemplify the totality of life and in the end contributions to science, philosophy and politics. But I believe that our contributions to these fields will arise in due time from our communities when they are mature enough. On that day, at long last, we are mature enough to start establishing the Law of Thelema across the globe, as opposed to merely promulgating it.

Though Crowley's organic view of Man, as having an Ego that may plan and be in charge was clearly wrong from what we know about how the brain works today,[51] the above might in fact be a true organic representation of the movement,

---

49 John Symonds (1997) has had to update the number of thelemites in his various versions of his biography on Crowley and while he writes words of fear, I think it is obvious that while distinctly impossible to rehabilitate, Crowley's aesthetics continue to inspire more and more people in the world.
50 See Rodney Stark's (2006b) seminal study on the subject, *Cities of God*.
51 Cf. Crowley's arguments concerning this in *Liber Aleph* (1991a) and compare it with the work of noted neuropsychologist Elkhenon Goldberg, *The Executive Brain*. While we may believe we are in charge,

where several different strands, working independently or together in accordance with their will, gives rise to the emergent property of the Will of the Community. A bottom-up model rather than the top-down model favored by the Beast 666.

Perhaps this is not the curse or abject failure that skeptics have supposed, but rather a blessing in disguise? One that safeguards the Law of Thelema to the greatest extent possible from dogmatism and becoming a bore.

REFERENCES

—∞— Churton, Tobias (2011). *Aleister Crowley, the biography: spiritual revolutionary, romantic explorer, occult master and spy.* London: Watkins.

—∞— Crowley, Aleister (1904). *Sword of Song.* London: Society for the Propagation of Religious Truth.

—∞— Crowley, Aleister (1919). *The Equinox III(1)* (various authors, but edited by Aleister Crowley). Detroit: Universal Books.

—∞— Crowley, Aleister (1979, 1989). *The Confessions of Aleister Crowley, an autohagiography* (edited by John Symonds & Kenneth Grant). London: Penguin.

—∞— Crowley, Aleister (1979). *The Magical Record of the Beast 666, the diaries of Aleister Crowley 1914-1920.* London: Duckworth Publishing Ltd.

—∞— Crowley, Aleister (1985). *The Equinox III(10)* (edited by William Breeze under pseudonym Hymenaus Beta). New York: Weiser.

—∞— Crowley, Aleister (1991a). *Liber Aleph, the Book of Wisdom and Folly.* New York: Weiser.

—∞— Crowley, Aleister (1991b). *Magick Without Tears* (edited by Israel Regardie). Arizona: New Falcon Publications.

—∞— Crowley, Aleister (1994, 2008). *Liber ABA* (edited by William Breeze under pseudonym Hymenaus Beta). New York: Red Wheel/Weiser.

—∞— Crowley, Aleister (1996). *The Law is for All* (edited by William Breeze under pseudonym Hymenaeus Beta and Richard Kaczynski). Arizona: New Falcon Publications.

—∞— Crowley, Aleister (1998). *The Equinox IV(1)* (edited by William Breeze). New York: Red Wheel/Weiser.

—∞— Crowley, Aleister (2010). *Brother Crowley, Brother Curwen, a Correspondence* (edited by Henrik Bogdan). York Beach: Teitan Press.

—∞— Marano, Hara Estroff (2008). *A Nation of Wimps: The High Cost of Invasive Parenting.* New York: Crown Archetype.

—∞— Goldberg, Elkhonon (2002). *The Executive Brain: Frontal Lobes and the Civilized Mind.* New York: Oxford University Press.

---

in actual fact the brain consists of several evolved modules that all engage in a tug of war that eventually determines the move forward. The ego that we believe to be in charge are mostly in charge of constructing a narrative where it misattributes the behavior of the body for volition on its part.

The Vindication of Thelema

—⚘— David, D., & Montgomery, G. H. (2011). *The Scientific Status of Psychotherapies: A New Evaluative Framework for Evidence-Based Psychosocial Interventions. Clinical Psychology: Science and Practice.* Volume 18, Issue 2, pages 89–99. Hoboken: Wiley Periodicals Inc.

—⚘— Hammer, Olav (2003). *Claiming Knowledge: Strategies of Epistemology from Theosophy to the New Age.* Leiden: Brill Academic Publisher.

—⚘— Marlow, Louis (Louis Umfreville Wilkinson), *Seven Friends.* London: The Richards Press, 1953.

—⚘— Pasi, Marco (2006). *Aleister Crowley und die Verusching der Politik.* Graz: Ares Verlag.

—⚘— Pasi, Marco (2012). *Varieties of Magical Experience* pp. 53-86 in *Aleister Crowley and Esotericism* (edited by Bogdan, H. & Starr M.). New York: Oxford University Press.

—⚘— Pasi, Marco (2013). *Aleister Crowley and the Temptation of Politics.* Durham: Acumen Publishing Ltd.

—⚘— Popper, Karl (2002). *Conjectures and Refutations: The Growth of Scientific Knowledge.* London: Routledge.

—⚘— Schaffer, David R. (2010). *Developmental Psychology: Childhood and Adolescence.* Belmont: Wadsworth.

—⚘— Sharpe, Eric J. (1994). *Comparative Religion, a history.* Bristol: Bristol Classical Press.

—⚘— Shekhovstov, A., & Umland, Andreas (2009). *Is Aleksandr Dugin a Traditionalist? "Neo-Eurasianism" and Perennial Philosophy*, in *The Russian Review* 68 (October 2009): 662–78. Hoboken: Wiley Periodical Inc.

—⚘— Spencer, Herbert (2005). *First Principles.* New York: Adamant Media Corporation.

—⚘— Stark, Rodney (2006a). "Economics of Religion," in *The Blackwell Companion to the Study of Religion*, Ch. 3, pp. 47-67.

—⚘— Stark, Rodney (2006b). *Cities of God: The Real Story of How Christianity Became an Urban Movement and Conquered Rome.* New York: Harper One.

—⚘— Symonds, John (1997). *The Beast 666.* London: Pindar Press.

—⚘— Symonds, John & Grant, Kenneth (1998). *The Magical Record of the Beast 666.* London: Gerald Duckworth & Co Ltd.

Exploring Past Lives

An Astrological Comparison between:
Aleister Crowley (12 Oct. 1875-1 Dec. 1947)
Pope Alexander VI (1 Jan. 1431-18 Aug 1503)
Edward Kelly (1 Aug.1555-1 Nov.1597)
Eliphas Levi (8 Feb.1810-31 May 1875)

Derek R. Seagrief

As the opening lines in Chapter VI, *Magick In Theory & Practice*, Crowley wrote, "There is no more important task than the exploration of one's previous incarnations. As Zoroaster says: Explore the river of the soul; whence and in what order thou hast come. One cannot do one's True Will intelligently unless one knows what it is."

Crowley called this "The Magical Memory", and wrote about its internal coherence, saying that any magical recollection is genuine if it gives the explanation of our external or internal conditions.

In the closing lines of this Chapter he concluded, "Every incarnation that we remember must increase our comprehension of ourselves as we are."

According to my occult and astrological references, there has not been any published study of Crowley's birth horoscope related to his Magical Memory, and these past-life horoscopes, where he declares his immediate past life as the French Magus, Eliphas Levi; then before that during the reign of Queen Elizabeth 1st., Dr. John Dee's magical assistant & alchemist, Edward Kelly; and prior that, the most notorious of the Renaissance Popes, Pope Alexander VI.

This article is not a detailed historical account of these different lives but an astrological exploration of the same soul's journey through the physical form of four different personalities, seeking to express one's True Will.

Can astrology deduce facts about previous incarnations from the birth chart? What do the placements of the Moon & Saturn reveal? The Nodal Axis, planets in our 12th House, or the present purpose of each incarnation as suggested by the Sun's position?

In recent years there has been a flood of astrology books giving varying methods for making such interpretations about one's previous life from one's present chart. Whilst this is a fascinating area for speculation, scientific evaluation of such teachings and their likely degree of accuracy remains an on-going study. Yet some of these methods work remarkably so for some persons and yet fall flat and meaningless for other individuals.

What most astrologers can show with considerable accuracy is the karmic journey of the soul on its evolutionary journey towards wholeness or perfection. Meeting the karma generated in past lives implies that the pattern of those past lives can be identified in the chart from the moment of birth. It is not, however, necessary to believe in reincarnation in order to ultilize an understanding of these karmic patterns.

The soul chooses a time to be born because the astrological pattern fits the experiences needed for the present stage of growth.

LIFE-TIME ASTROLOGY

One bold and original method for testing Astrological Reincarnation theories is the American astrologer A.T. Mann's "Life-Time Astrology" logarithmic time scale, which grades the entire horoscope by age. All planetary positions, personal points (Ascendant & Midheaven) and sensitive points are dated in sequence. A.T. Mann's visionary astrological theory basically matches up each sign of the zodiac with a period of human history, dating back to 50,000 years ago to AD 1950. Planets are archetypal energies, so by dating when in time these "gods" became "manifested" in your soul's history, it is possible to date the soul's lesson and the period in human history when it was experienced. These key dates are not necessarily when an incarnation was born, rather, it is the moment that the incarnation experienced its most significant life event.

CROWLEY'S LEO ASCENDANT & EGYPT

Mann points out that the Ascendant is of crucial importance since it describes the period in history that my present personality, physical appearance and environmental characteristics originate from. Crowley's birth Ascendant in early Leo registers at 2587 BC – which is the time of the first great civilizations.

The solar civilization of the Old Kingdom in ancient Egypt, and specifically the Fourth Dynasty Pharaoh Sneferu, father to Khufu (Cheops) builder of the Great Pyramid, can therefore be identified within this time frame. The Step Pyramid of Zoser was built about one hundred years earlier around 2650 BC. Old Kingdom Egypt was a stable, thousand-year pharaonic theocracy with an organized kingdom endowed with great natural resources.

The society was simultaneously materialistic and desirous of eternal life – a unique combination.

Similarly, the Indus civilization of India sprouted, fully-formed from its birth in about 2500 BC. Although both these world views were incorporated within Crowley's East-West personality, yet Old Kingdom Egypt is shown in Mann's reincarnation Time Scale to dominate his personality. Leo the Lion is associated with self-consciousness, love of self & others, creation, acting, confidence, education, speculation and game playing and the exteriorization of the self. The essence of all societies is a hierarchy of classes, elites and order of succession. We can comfortably say that the Leo personality rooted within this Egyptian Old Kingdom incarnation(s), found an appropriate vehicle in the life as Aleister Crowley of the 20th Century.

PLANETARY ASPECTS & REINCARNATION

Back in the early 1990s, film-star Shirley Maclaine transformed into new age guru and made public her interest for spirituality through various books & films. During this period she was a follower of an "Intelligence" known as Ramtha, who was channelled through a Califormian woman called J. Z. Knight. Ramtha claimed to be a wise Shaman from 35,000 BC, which aligned with Knight's birth position of Mercury in Aries. Shirley Maclaine would naturally become attracted by Ramtha (and J. Z. Knight) because she also has Mercury at 15 degrees Aries. But as time evolved she rejected Ramtha's teachings, (Jupiter the teacher) as shown through the Mercury-Jupiter opposition in her birth chart, with Jupiter in Libra symbolizing her own spiritual path in this life, which registered at 837 AD.

This whole subject of planetary aspects opens out a huge area for exploration because the suggestion is that the aspects between the planets in a birth chart describe the resultant conflict or harmony in terms of attitudes and memories relating to different lifetimes. Working with past-life wounds that influence this lifetime using A.T. Mann's method could prove to be very fruitful for therapists. This system of reincarnation theory is not, of course, the absolute truth, but more a signpost in the general direction.

ELIPHAS LEVI

By applying A.T Mann's system to Crowley's horoscope we would find that natal Mars at almost 23° degrees Capricorn would have registered in the year 1819, when Eliphas Levi was nine years of age. Mars is purposeful and located within the resourceful but traditional sign of Capricorn. The combination of planet & sign indicates high ambition to succeed in one's chosen goals, but also within established areas of historical influence, such as classical learning, history and the hierarchical structure of the Catholic Church. This was of course, the great struggle within his 65 year long life.

Son of a shoemaker, Levi was born into humble circumstances, yet gave evidence of such an unusual intelligence at an early age, that the local priest secured him education without charge. In addition to Greek and Latin, the boy genius also acquired a considerable knowledge of Hebrew, and changed his name from Alphonse Louis Constant to the pseudonym Eliphas Levi.

At what date Eliphas Levi applied himself to the study of the occult arts is not certain, but the biographical statement that in the year 1825 he entered a fateful path, which led him through suffering to knowledge, may indeed relate to his enrolment among the scholars of Saint Sulpiece Seminary – yet as this is approximately the time at which Mars registers in Crowley's horoscope, the heroic, fighting, war-like qualities of Mars would have found their way into Levi's life, individualizing him from his surroundings at this early age.

In AT Mann's system then, it would be the energies of Mars that symbolized the immediate past incarnation as Eliphas Levi. It is the heroic and pioneering qualities of Mars that Crowley inherited from this previous incarnation. This idea is further supported by the exact conjunction between Crowley's Pisces Moon at 22° degrees and Levi's Mars at 21° degrees. Mars stimulates whatever it touches and can show passion, sexuality, strong romantic attachments, as well as causing destruction – but always indicates the release of some kind of power. The Moon on the horoscope plays such an incredibly important role in all matters of psychic inheritance from the past.

Levi was a 19th Century French Magus whose influence on the Western Mystery Tradition was immense. Crowley was clearly well satisfied with his past life memory as the power-dynamo Eliphas Levi. Born into Victorian England and the hypocrisy of the times, Crowley was a prophet of a new age. During his 20th Century incarnation he acknowledged the conditioning influences by Church traditions that he too, like his predecessor Eliphas Levi, had been subjected to. And yet in this incarnation he chose not to be so restricted in his search for God & Truth was explored though all available pathways, especially the Piscean keynotes of drugs, sexuality and mystical Other Worldliness.

This English Magus, who had travelled all around the world, was responsible, almost single-handedly, for the magical revival of Paganism in the 20th Century and the establishment of a new solar consciousness, the return of the Crowned & Conquering Child Horus, which in today's terminology people call the Aquarian Age. In his earliest years, Crowley identified himself as a kind of Christian knight, doing deeds of holiness & valour which, in adult life became an identification with Ra-Hoor-Khuit, the Egyptian Sun God & God of War (the Noon Sun – or symbolically Mars exalted or in highest position in Capricorn) – in the religion of his own making.

The date of Eliphas Levi's death was about six months previous to that of Aleister Crowley's birth in 1875.

The reincarnating soul takes possession of the foetus at about this stage of development. Crowley writes that Eliphas Levi had a striking personal resemblance to Crowley's father, suggesting a certain degree of suitability from a physical genetic point of view.

Levi became a priest and teacher at a Paris Seminary, while Crowley used to accompany his father who travelled the country, preaching the true Christianity, salvation via the fundamentalist doctrine of the Plymouth Brethren.

Although he had little in common with his parents, Crowley's life is not unlike his fathers – both men belonged to a small sect of the elect, tried to convert the world to their point of view and lived amid the mysteries of religion.

In the previous life as Eliphas Levi, he was forced to leave & renounce the Church, as he pursued his occult studies, leading to a precarious existence, punctuated by a disastrous marriage to a much younger girl, who finally deserted him.

Eliphas Levi
Natal Chart
8 Feb 1810 NS, Thu
08:22 LMT -0:09:20
Paris, France
48°N52' 002°E20'
Geocentric
Tropical
Placidus
Mean Node

There are many curious similarities between the events of Levi's life and that of Aleister Crowley, such as the intention of the parents to have their son in a religious career, and their events relative to marriage. There is even the powerful attraction of Crowley to a certain quarter of Paris, which he discovered long after that Levi lived in the same neighbourhood for many years. Additionally, their publications contained similar style and content regarding magic & occult philosophy, all indications of deep seated bonding.

The birth chart of Eliphas Levi shows the mystically-inspired sign of Pisces rises with the Dark Lord of the Underworld, Pluto conjunct the Ascendant from the 12th House of the Unconscious and Mars within the 1st House of Self-identity. His profile of himself would be subjected to periodic major transformations.

He would also strive to keep much of his personality hidden, while the fiery planets in his 1st House would have pulled him towards the opposite extreme. This push-pull dilemma was characteristic of most of his incarnation.

Here is an intense personality in attunement with the hidden forces of the unconscious, and his physical presence, with the aura of the magical & mysterious would have undoubtedly proven quite overwhelming for some, while irresistible to others. Pluto is the planet of extremism and suggestive of the soul having to face the archetypal, evolutionary forces hidden deep within the darkness of the human psyche. Birthing (Ascendant) the darkness (Pluto) also represents karma connected with using, abusing and being misused by power.

For some this could prove the key to their obsession, compulsions and phobias stemming from past lives. Yet Pluto in 12th House Pisces is also connected with healing power. It could also demonstrate itself as trance mediumship or clairvoyance. The ability to work with the invisible forces of creation in a conscious way is clearly the goal of this magician.

Saturn, Lord of Fate & Karma, is conjunct Neptune, in the 9th House sign of Sagittarius, showing a mystical education coupled with enjoyment of religion and a study of universal Laws. Saturn representing tradition, reveals that he was certainly the repository for great learning, a custodian of a magical esoteric life philosophy – yet note that both Saturn & Neptune form the challenging square aspect (90° degree value) to Pluto & the Pisces Ascendant, denoting both struggle and judgment from religious authorities.

Neptune, modern planetary ruler of Pisces, was not yet discovered at the time of Levi's birth, but when in 1846 it appeared onto the modern scene, Levi was 36 years old. It was exactly during this year that he first started to publish his occult works. The 9th House where it is positioned at birth, is also the area of the horoscope connected with publications.

Jupiter is the traditional ruler of the sign Pisces and here we find the ceremonial ritualist combined with the mystical approach of religion. In Levi's chart we find, as could be expected, a prominent rising Jupiter in the 1st. House of self-identity, positioned in the pioneering Martian-ruled sign of Aries and conjunct the Moon.

The man was destined from birth to come high-profile before the public through successful education and/or through religion, as a teacher or prophet. Jupiter in this placement is a powerful testimony of a self-propagandist.

Some contradiction is shown through the 12th House Sun placement. An incarnating soul will use the social visionary strength of the Aquarian vibration to conceive new ways of being in which the needs of all humanity will be met. A Sun-sign Aquarian with Uranus (the modern planetary ruler of Aquarius) in Scorpio squaring the Sun, activating the 8th & 12th water Houses of the birth horoscope is further testimony to Levi's occult ability to bring change in society through the mediumship of new ideas. There is a radicality about these contacts, a radical departure from the normal path, which all original thinkers can claim.

But for Levi to have the Sun positioned within the 12th House, and a Pisces Ascendant suggests that he accepted an incarnation where it was necessary to experience the Christian path to Higher Faith through loss & suffering.

There are many other pathways to the experience of Faith, yet the demands of the 12th House are karmic and require major adjustment of the soul-personality to its relationship both to itself and to the world in which it lives. This necessitates a deep cleansing or purification of our past. The healing method is not so much what we must do as it is something we must become. The 12th House is deep inner work, and nothing else seems to be as important as this.

These placements also inform us that he was a soul in a previous life who had been an important prominent person, and now during this life as Eliphas Levi, would have to work more "behind-the-scenes", and have to be content with less recognition than what he deserved. This lack of recognition, or delay, can prove to be a hard lesson to learn, particularly if in the past the soul had demanded everything immediately. So clearly the finishing-up of past-life karma shown in Levi's chart is for the present life of leadership without arrogance or false humility. The soul must do the job not for the sake of reward & adulation, but for the sake of "a job well done". This was a major life theme that Crowley's inherited and his incarnation reproduced.

Inner Wheel
Alesiter Crowley
Natal Chart
12 Oct 1875 NS, Tue
23:16 GMT +0.00
Leamington Spa, UK
52°N18' 001°W31'
Geocentric
Tropical
Placidus
Mean Node

Outer Wheel
Eliphas Levi
Natal Chart
8 Feb 1810 NS, Thu
08:22 LMT -0.09:20
Paris, France
48°N52' 002°E20'
Geocentric
Tropical
Placidus
Mean Node

Levi's five planets within the 12th House and the Sun square Uranus is the 8th House also contributed to his occult ability working with spirits. There is the famous story of a visit to Bulwer-Lytton, and how Levi called up the spirit of Appollonius of Tyana in a ritual ceremony.

And it is exactly these magical rites governing the art of necromancy, spells and divination that Levi published in his book *Transcendental Magic*, first published in English in 1896.

SYNASTRY BETWEEN CROWLEY & LEVI

When comparing two horoscopes (the technique of *Synastry*), the astrologer looks for the various harmonious and challenging planetary aspects that help determine the interpretation of the dynamics within a relationship. In the above example we have Crowley's birth horoscope in the inner circle and Eliphas Levi's birth horoscope in the outer wheel.

There are many points of contact, yet not all need to be considered, and certainly the closest aspects are always of prime importance because they are the strongest.

Crowley's Libra Sun at 19° degrees makes an exact trine (120° degrees) aspect to Levi's Aquarian Sun at 19° degrees Aquarius. The Sun in Air signs for both men shows their superb mental faculties, grasp of concepts and ability to communicate the world of ideas to others. It also shows their ease of mental identification with the other's thought-forms and basic life philosophy, so if they physically met & shared the same space, they would be instant friends.

What is more significant from our reincarnation perspective is that Crowley's Saturn-Uranus opposition through the signs of Leo-Aquarius falls exactly upon Levi's Sun.

Saturn is the planet of Fate and a statement of the Past, while Uranus is the planet of Genius & Individualization, and a statement of the Future and our multi-dimensionality. If someones Saturn connects with our personal planets and especially the Sun, symbolizing our basic identity, there is always a strong attachment. The Sun is the heart-beat of the horoscope and describes the basic quality of life and the level of self-awareness passed on from one lifetime to the next. From the karmic viewpoint of psychic inheritance from one lifetime to the next, these planetary contacts are invaluable testimony.

One of the most common karmic aspects within a marriage or other love relationship is often a Saturn contact, providing a sense of security, of being comfortable as though knowing each other "for ever". For some it can be a sense of debt owed to the other. Saturn indicates where we will teach each other some major life lessons. Uranus contacts are always about acceleration, discovery and awakening us out of past patterns or the old structures of self-restriction defined through the archetype of Saturn.

Both planets represent the new kind of personal growth and consciousness that Crowley saw as the culmination of a whole series of major incarnations after relative quick succession. Indeed, one could clearly see that when transit Saturn, as the archetype of Fate & Destiny, carrying the past in its cycle around the Zodiac, had almost completed its first return to its natal position in Aquarius during March/April 1904 – thus activating his natal Saturn-Uranus opposition – this was the fated time of Crowley's contact with Aiwass and receiving *The Book of the Law* in Cairo.

And if we follow transit Saturn's movement to when it reached a conjunction to Crowley's natal Uranus at 19° degrees Leo in 1947, the opposite end of this planetary configuration, this was the time of his death at 72 years, and a period of some 43 years wherein he manifested his True Will.

Students of Kabbalah will be quick to recognize these astrological links with the 2 & 3rd Spheres on the Tree of Life, for Saturn governs the Head of the Pillar of Form and Uranus the Head of the Pillar of Force, and thus represents the magical dynamic between the Spiritual Father (Chokmah) and Spiritual Mother (Binah), with the web of life being spun between their activity and partnership.

Sphere 2: Chokmah (Wisdom) is associated with the planet Uranus & the Big Bang of Creation, initiating the descent of spirit into the lower worlds, and all governed through the Laws of Time & Karma, symbolized by Saturn and Sphere 3: Binah (Understanding).

URANUS & THE TRUE WILL

Uranus has often been identified with the archetype of the Magician and in Kabbalistic thought, the 2nd Sephiroth, which represents contact with one's Originating Spark, the True Will, or the Conductor of the Orchestra – so one of the most important planetary contacts between Crowley's horoscope and the three past life examples presented in this study would need to be the prominence of Uranus. The eccentric independent or an authentic originator of new ways of being that unifies groups of people? Ego-based rebel or revolutionary pioneer? Uranus is identical with the fire that Prometheus stole from the Gods, which made him a culture hero for humanity.

You will also see Crowley's Mercury at 13° degrees Scorpio in exact conjunction with Levi's Uranus at 14° degrees. The minds of these two men were totally identified with the Hermetic or magical world view of the inter-relationship between all things.

Another key feature astrologically speaking, in our consideration of reincarnation in Crowley's past lives, would need to be Jupiter, as the archetype of Religion and the Ritualist or one who practices Ceremonial Order. This quality reveals itself throughout all the past lives under review in our study.

Crowley's Sun at 19° degrees and Venus at 24° degrees Libra makes close opposition contact with Levi's Jupiter at 20° degrees Aries.

Esoteric teachings state that the recorded wisdom or fruit that is embedded within the soul's consciousness at the end of each incarnation is symbolized through Jupiter and this is used by the Spiritual Intelligences of the Higher Worlds to determine the direction and karmic opportunities of the next incarnation.

You will also see that Levi's Moon-Jupiter conjunction also falls upon Crowley's highest point, the 10° degree Aries Midheaven. The Moon gives a sense of belonging and Jupiter contacts always promote an expansive outlook. Another person's planet at our Midheaven angle will help us to manifest in the outer world those specific qualities.

The incarnation prior to Eliphas Levi was claimed by Crowley to be the famous Elizabethan conjurer of spirits, Edward Kelly, born some 255 years earlier.

Kelly was an ambiguous figure in English Renaissance occultism and a self-declared spirit medium who worked with Dr. John Dee in his magical investigations.

Besides his professed ability to summon spirits or angels on a crystal ball, which John Dee so valued, Kelly also claimed to possess the secret of transmuting base metals into gold.

Much of Kelly's early life is obscure, but according to Dr. John Dee's diaries we know that they first came in contact in 1582 and from this point until seven years later in 1589, Kelly became Dee's regular scryer, as they both devoted huge amounts of time & energy to these "spiritual conferences". Kelly wrote that they conducted these conferences, including "prayers for enlightenment... in the spirit of Dee's ecumenical hopes that alchemy and angelic knowledge would heal the rift of Christendom."

However, Kelly & Dr. John Dee's involvement in necromancy eventually caught the attention of the Catholic Church in Prague, and on March 27, 1587 they were required to defend themselves in a hearing.

Just before this, Kelly & Dee found patronage with the wealthy Bohemian (now Czech Republic) count Vilem Rozmberk, who shared their alchemical interests and is known to have participated in spiritual sessions with the two men. Dee's diary shows notes with Kelly's initial commitment to the alchemist goal, but somewhere along the way, that goal became clouded by Kelly's sudden desire to end their sessions. In May 1587, possibly as an act to sever the sessions, Kelly revealed to Dee that the angels had ordered for them to share everything they had – including their wives.

Nine months later on February 28 1588, Dee's wife Jane gave birth to a son, although the "cross-matching" incident remained a secret until after Dee's death.

This style of relating would have found great support from Crowley's powerful promiscuous nature, yet it has been speculated that this was a way for Kelly to end the fruitless spiritual conferences so that he could concentrate on alchemy, which under the patronage of Rozmberk, was beginning to make Kelly wealthy. Dee, anguished by the order of the angels, subsequently broke off the spiritual conferences even though he did share his wife.

Kelly left Dee in 1589. Dee returned to England while a year later Kelly was living an opulent lifestyle and Rudolf II knighted him Sir Edward Kelly on February 23, 1590. But Rudolf had Kelly arrested a year later in May 1591 and he was held in prison until his death in 1597.

On the following page is the horoscope that Dr. John Dee erected for Edward Kelly, so we can confidently accept its accuracy. At death on 1st November 1597, at the age of 42, transit Uranus & Pluto at 20-degrees Aries formed the exact conjunction to the "spine of the horoscope", the 4th House IC/10th House MC angles. Astrologers often refer to the "end of life conditions" by the 4th House angle, so the rapid separation of the root or base chakra, supporting us in the physical dimension occurred with these contacts

You will also see that Kelly was born with a dynamic Uranus-Mars-Jupiter conjunction at the "top" of his horoscope, clearly revealing his unpredictable genius, and power to impress & influence people, so at death transit Uranus had also reached its halfway cycle, what astrology terms the "Mid-Life Crisis", and his meteoric rise to fame suddenly ended when former friends became his captors. These Pluto & Uranian influences would therefore find their way into the next succeeding lives.

Born into the royal sign of Leo, Kelly naturally enjoyed the patronage of important personalities. It is quite revealing for intimate exchange of planetary energies passing from one lifetime into the next that his Leo Sun at 18° degrees on his birth chart is echoed by the next lifetime as Eliphas Levi with his Sun at almost 19° degrees in the opposite sign of Aquarius.

Saturn, planet of Fate & Karma is located at 11° degrees Aries on Kelly's birth chart – and this highly sensitive degree area is then emphasised by Levi's Moon at 14° degrees Aries and Crowley's highest point or Midheaven at 10° degrees Aries. Each man was a pioneer and came before the general public with their own unique karmic signatures. The Saturn line of energy passes down through each of these three incarnations. The diagram below shows all three horoscopes so that we can make this comparison. Crowley is the Inner Wheel, then comes Eliphas Levi in the Middle Wheel and Edward Kelley on the outside Wheel.

This astrological method of identifying sensitive degree areas between two or more horoscopes, to show karmic links is a widely accepted technique, and in interpretation, the closer the orb the more significant the contact.

Much of Kelly's early life is obscure and yet it is due to Dr. John Dee meticulous astrological notes & diaries, that we have many dates and references to their work together. He may have studied at Oxford under the name of Talbot, but whether or not he attended university, Kelly was well educated and knew Latin & Greek.

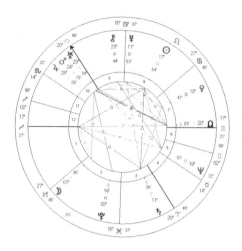

Edward Kelly
Natal Chart
1 Aug 1555 OS. Thu
16:00 LMT +0:08:52
Worcester, UK
52°N11' 002°W13'
Geocentric
Tropical
Placidus
Mean Node

He was a self-declared spirit medium who worked with John Dee in his magical investigations, showing the ability to summon spirits or angels on a crystal ball, which John Dee so valued. Kelly also claimed to possess the secret of transmuting base metals into gold. Legends began to surround Kelly shortly after his death. His flamboyant biography, and his relative notoriety among English historians, may have made him the source for the folklore image of the alchemist-charlatan.

There were major similarities in both Kelly & John Dee's horoscopes – both have a Sagittarius Ascendant, exploring new frontiers, with strong faith & belief in their goals, and both have the Sun, the present purpose of this incarnation in the 8th House, traditionally the Department of Life that deals with alchemy and transformation, death & the goods of the dead, contact with mediumship and the Ancestors. The 8th House is like a Cosmic Bank and these two men were allowed assess to what had been deposited here for centuries.

There is also the presence of a Full Moon line of energies in both men's charts. John Dee was born with the Sun at 29° degree Cancer and the Moon just entered 1° degree Aquarius, so he was born during the exact opposition, which certainly stimulated increased light, especially more light to see within the darkness. The future orientated Aquarian Moon and the interplay with the Cancerian Sun with all its focus upon the past and historical sources, shows us a Truth Seeker, wishing to make available his researches for the wider public.

Edward Kelly had the exact same Moon placement at 1° degree Aquarius, clearly showing us the powerful bond that existed between these two men, yet his Moon was on its way to the Full Moon, separated by some 16° degrees, the Sun being at 18° degrees Leo. For both men, this incarnation would be one of climax and culmination, and quite predictably, it also led to their separation.

Kelly's mediumship or contact with the invisible spheres is shown to us through the close Neptune square Sun aspect, although no knowledge about the three transpersonal planets would have existed in John Dee's time. Neptune was not

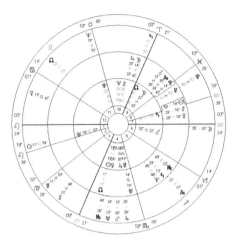

Inner Wheel
Aleister Crowley
Natal Chart
12 Oct 1875 NS, Tue
23:16 GMT +0:00
Leamington Spa, UK
52°N18' 001°W31'
Geocentric
Tropical
Placidus
Mean Node

Middle Wheel
Eliphas Levi
Natal Chart
8 Feb 1810 NS, Thu
08:22 LMT -0:09:20
Paris, France
48°N52' 002°E20'
Geocentric
Tropical
Placidus
Mean Node

Mean Node
Placidus
Geocentric
52°N11' 002°W13'
Worcester, UK
16:00 LMT +0:08:52
1 Aug 1555 OS, Thu
Natal Chart
Edward Kelly
Outer Wheel

discovered in the collective human consciousness until 1846, but naturally it already existed and exerted its influences. The Lord of the Underworld, Pluto, makes the opposition aspect to Mercury, the Communicator, positioned at 12° degrees Virgo – this contact would not have been known about either. And lastly, Uranus, the first transpersonal planet discovered in 1781, more than 200 years after Kelly's birth, occupies a most prominent position at the "top" of the chart, conjunct Kelly's Libra Midheaven and natal Mars & Jupiter.

Astrologer John Dee would have probably emphasized the Sun in 8th House Leo making the exact trine aspect (120° degrees) to the Sagittarian Ascendant as his partner's prophetic abilities.

John Dee was an intensely pious Christian, but his Christianity was deeply influenced by the Hermetic & Plato-Pythagorean doctrines that were pervasive in the Renaissance. His ultimate goal was to help bring forth a unified world religion through the healing of the breach of the Catholic and Protestant Churches and the recapture of the pure theology of the ancients. Both Dee & Kelly, with their Sagittarian Ascendants, governed by the religious principle Jupiter, were enthusiastic about this high ideal, but their journey required them to travel through Europe – and it was during these years that their differences became more apparent.

Once again you will see close planetary links between Kelly's birth chart and that of Eliphas Levi, the next incarnation. You will also see that Kelly's 18° degree Leo Sun also links with Crowley's Uranus-Saturn opposition, at 19° Leo-19° degrees Aquarius. Whereas Crowley's Sun at 19° degrees Libra & Venus nearby at 24° degrees forms the conjunction with Kelly's Midheaven at 20° Libra and Uranus at 23°, Mars at 24° degrees and Jupiter at 28° degrees. It is such contacts that the investigating astrologer looks for – and although it might not "prove" this is the same soul experiencing itself in different personalities, yet these type of references provide much stimulating food for thought. Reflect over the fact that when Kelly dies the transit Moon, as the ruler of his 7th. House cusp, symbolizing the "death

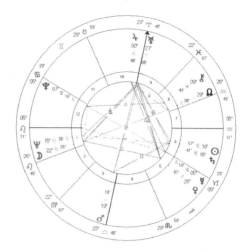

Pope Alexander V 1
Natal Chart
1 Jan 1431, Mon
18:10 LMT +0:01:28
Valencia, Spain
39°N28' 000°W22'
Geocentric
Tropical
Placidus
Mean Node

axis", was at 3° degrees Leo and the transit Sun was at 9° degrees Scorpio. Crowley was born with a 3° degree Leo Ascendant and his natal Jupiter at 7° and Mercury at 13° degrees Scorpio, would have formed the conjunction to the man's death horoscope. It is through such aspects that we can see zodiacal influences passing from one lifetime to the next.

POPE ALEXANDER VI

And our final example of Crowley's "Magical Memory" is the 212nd Bishop of Rome, Alexander VI, who was head of the Catholic Church from 11 August 1492 until his death at 72 years, on 18th August 1503, some 52 years before reincarnating as Edward Kelly.

He is considered as the most notorious of the Renaissance Popes because of his profligate life, he promoted the careers of his children, especially Cesare Borgia, and created the brother of his mistress a Cardinal. There were other public scandals, of course, yet Pope Alexander was also a well-known masterly political diplomat (Sun-Saturn conjunction in Capricorn forming the midpoint of the opposition aspect between Mars at 19° degrees Libra & Uranus-Jupiter around the Midheaven, 9th House & 10th House) He was also an enthusiastic patron of the Arts (Leo Ascendant & Moon-Neptune conjunction between 15-22° degrees Leo). And like Kelly, Pope Alexander was born with a Mercury-Pluto opposition, illustrating this Pope's enjoyment with the mysteries of the mind, taboo subjects and the occult.

Converning the birth time of Roderic Borgia, born near Valencia, Spain, who becomes Head of the Church at the age of 61, we have no reliable records, so the above horoscope has been "corrected" by me to an evening time of 18.10. It is therefore speculative, yet fulfils much of the criteria and interpretation of the man & his life's events. For one example, transit Jupiter, planet of Religion, had been in dynamic opposition aspects with his Sun-Saturn conjunction during the political process leading up to his election, and moved over his Leo Ascendant immediately

after his declaration as the new Pope.

He was born with an elevated Uranus & Jupiter, suggesting that his version of organized religion would present many surprises for his flock; whereas the more mystical approach to God is shown through the Moon-Neptune conjunction in Leo, suggesting a genuine sympathy for his spiritual career. Note the big Fire Trine linking up the Moon-Neptune conjunction in Leo to Venus (the Arts) in Sagittarius, and both forming the flowing trine aspect to Uranus in Aries at the top of the horoscope, thus suggesting that Pope Alexander was truly fiery, self-confident and inspirational.

The year he was elected to Pope in 1492 was the famous year of Columbus voyage & discovery of the New World of America. Crowley, always one for self-promotion, also took great delight in the synchronicity between Eliphas Levi's death, the birth of Aleister Crowley the same year, and the return of the Eastern mystical Teaching to the West of the Ascended Masters as presented through the creation of the Theosophical Society by Madame Blavatsky.

We can conclude that the highly sensitive degree region around 20° Leo is once again clearly emphasized; Mars is at 19° degrees Libra and this resonates exactly with Crowley's Libra Sun at 19° degrees, even the Sun-Saturn conjunction in the Pope's horoscope at 17-20° Capricorn ties in with Crowley's natal Mars at almost 23° degrees.

There is of course a wealth of astrological references when we research no less than 4-5 horoscopes, yet my main intention today is not to overwhelm my reader with abundant astrological references, but to draw your attention to specific significant planetary links between Crowley's horoscope and that of his three predecessors. It is an experiment in reincarnation research, and perhaps now after reading these "past lives", we can form even clearer picture about the man Crowley and his contribution to the Magical revival.

The last diagram is Crowley in the Inner Wheel and Pope Alexander's birth positions on the Outer Wheel. Enjoy!

THE FICTIONAL ALEISTER CROWLEY

Sandy Robertson

Dedicated to the memory of Nicholas Clayton Bishop-Culpeper

Here's an odd thought: which of these fictional characters has had the most stories written about him – Fu Manchu, James Bond... or Aleister Crowley?

Hang on, you say, Edward Alexander Crowley was *not* the product of someone else's imagination. Wrong! Real as the Great Beast may have been, as fantastic as his true adventures as mage, poet, painter, philosopher, mountaineer and libertine were, his legend hasn't daunted – indeed has encouraged – a legion of hacks, half-wits and hagiographers trying to improve on the facts in a stack of pulp fictions that outstrip in number and bizarre content the creations of Sax Rohmer and Ian Fleming.

For some years I've made notes for a projected handlist of every story that features Crowley, the Great Beast 666, that most glorious and notorious occultist of the 20th century. In the 80s, when I first began, I included a list in my *Aleister Crowley Scrapbook* (aka *The Illustrated Beast*) that comprised but a handful of titles. Today, I'm looking at about 50 to 60 instances thus far at a conservative estimate, ranging from Adrian Marcato in Ira Levin's *Rosemary's Baby* to the recent Robert Edric tome *The Monster's Lament*, starring Crowley under his own name as an old man trying a tricky soul swap with a hanged youth: sort of a Brit lit rehash of William Hjortsberg's *Falling Angel*.

In some cases when a *nom de guerre* is used, the physical description or other hints tell us beyond reasonable doubt that we are feasting on the deeds of an *ersatz* Uncle Al. Ian Fleming himself is said to have based Le Chiffre, the villainous opponent of Bond in the 1953 novel *Casino Royale*, on Crowley, though not everyone agrees. I've even heard talk that Goldfinger too is Crowley, despite the surname being harvested from architect brut Erno Goldfinger. Nevertheless, Fleming did know AC and their alleged black (magick) ops interaction in WW2 forms part of the plot of Jake Arnott's recent wide-ranging novel *The House of Rumour*, which is an elaborate phantasmagoria involving science-fiction scribes, Jack Parsons, L. Ron Hubbard and much, much more. Arnott's previous novel *The Devil's Paintbrush* also revolves around Crowley, the implement in the title not being AC's horsehair art brush but a machine gun, with our hero sympathetically counselling a disgraced (real life) Scots general in a yarn woven from a little truth and Arnott's dazzling imagination.

The difference between Fleming and Arnott is the former did not use Crowley under his own name. Many writers prefer to fashion AC *Doppelgangers*, usually black magicians whose looks, actions and even names make it impossible to avoid the conclusion that we're in Crowley-lite/like goblin territory. Some of these authors knew him personally, many did not. My late friend, the bibliophile and ultimate Crowley collector Nicholas C. Bishop-Culpeper, told me, "People say that every time I find a story with a bald satanist in it I think it's meant to be Crowley. I say of course – because usually it is!"

Somerset Maugham, a fan of *Casino Royale* so it's said, was one of the first to poach AC as model for a villain. *The Magician*, issued in 1908 and later made into a dazzling silent film by Rex Ingram, features a rotter of an occultist, Oliver Haddo, who comes across as a blend of Frankenstein and Svengali, mesmerising a young artist into marrying him before using her in hideous experiments at his country pile, Skene, the name of which is too redolent of Crowley's Loch Ness house Boleskine to be coincidence. Painter Sir Gerald Kelly apparently stated the book was partly inspired by Crowley's ill fated marriage to Kelly's alcoholic sister Rose. (I'm indebted for this tidbit to Frater Achad Osher 583's 1995 booklet, *The Character Aleister Crowley as portrayed in Novels and Short Stories* (Pangenetor Lodge), which I only recently became aware of. As he said therein, the topic of this useful tract was largely unresearched at the time of writing. It still is, I fear).

Maugham knew Crowley in Paris and in a review of the novel for *Vanity Fair* the latter got his revenge by using the Haddo name as his byline and pointing up instances of plagiarism by the author from occult texts by Eliphas Levi and others. Nevertheless, Maugham wasn't deterred from going on to also base the character Cronshaw in *Of Human Bondage* on AC. There are those who believe that Maugham sold his soul to Crowley in return for fame – believe it if you wilt.

In *The Death of the King's Canary*, a satire by Dylan Thomas and John Davenport not published till 1976, Crowley appears as Corbie – the name is Scots dialect for a crow; while the marvellously imaginative pulp magazine tales of American Manly Wade Wellman often saw his playboy occult sleuth John Thunstone battle bald-pate black magician Rowley Thorne. When asked if he wasn't worried about being sued by Crowley, the author remarked that he believed (sadly correctly) that AC's reputation was such that no jury would accept that opprobrium hinted at in print could make it sink any lower in the public mind.

Over the years authors have continued to lazily use Crowley as a convenient template for any character soaked in evil and blasphemy. Some think that the villain in M.R.James's classic tale *Casting The Runes*, Karswell, passer-on of fatal runic symbols, was based on AC but scholars like master bibliographer Timothy d'Arch Smith think it very unlikely. Another writer of early 20th century English spook fiction, H.R.Wakefield, however, liked the story so much he filched the plot *and* the character for his tale *He Cometh and He Passeth By*, featuring Oscar Clinton as yet one more 'hmm-maybe' Crowleyesque nasty. He also created another poor man's Beast in Apuleius Charlton for the story *A Black Solitude*.

I must come clean and admit that I find much of this stuff and nonsense great fun. Many sneer at the black magic novels of Dennis Wheatley (like *The Devil Rides Out*, its satanist baddy Mocata undoubtedly based on Crowley, whom Wheatley knew well enough to be gifted a personally inscribed copy of his masterwork *Magick In Theory And Practice*), yet if truth be told many practitioners of esoteric disciplines were first inspired to study these matters by such lurid tales of naked virgins and black masses in remote country piles.

Gary Val Tenuta, amiable author of the recent novel *Ash:Return of The Beast*, in which Crowley's remains are stolen, cheerfully agreed with me that yes, there's so much more to the guy than cartoon boogeyman, but said hey, if you're writing a fun horror romp and you need a black magic villain, well, he's the obvious choice! Not laudable, but truthful.

Of course, whether under his own name or obvious clone, Crowley has turned up in fiction that has dealt rather more even handedly with his legend. The late Colin Wilson's *Man Without A Shadow* (US title *The Sex Diary of Gerard Sorme*, later reissued as *The Sex Diary of a Metaphysician*) has a character who, though described as a disciple of AC, is clearly a portrait of 666 himself. Part rascal, part genius, Caradoc Cunningham is a brilliantly drawn sketch. Wilson even recreates the famous feat described by William Seabrook where the Beast fell into step behind a man, mimicking his stride then suddenly bending his knees, causing the fellow to collapse by an act of sympathetic magick. Colin wrote an unsympathetic short biography of AC, but was nevertheless interested in his outsider persona enough to provide a foreword to my Crowley *Scrapbook*. If only those two great minds had existed in the same time frame and had met, what conversations they might have had!

In the sixth book in his *Dance To The Music of Time* series, *The Kindly Ones* (1962), respected literary figure Anthony Powell used aspects of Crowley for Dr Trelawney, cult leader. He doesn't dress or look like AC but has magical lingo – no doing what thou wilt but "the vision of visions heals the blindness of sight". There's also a dubious fellow dubbed Scorpio Murtlock hovering around in there too who may also have some Crowleyesque features.

One of my all-time loosely-based-on-Crowley fictions is science-fiction author James Blish's *Black Easter or Faust Aleph-Null*, and indeed the sequel, *The Day After Judgement*. The bizarre, insane plot involves a fantastically wealthy man's whim to see what would occur were all the demons of hell loosed upon the world for a limited period with unfettered freedom to do anything they chose. To this end he buys the services of black magician Theron Ware, the go-to guy for the bad stuff. (The name sounds too like AC's alias Therion to be coincidence, though it was actually nicked from an 1896 novel, *The Damnation of Theron Ware* by Harold Frederic. Considered *risqué* in its day, it concerns the temptation and fall of a Methodist minister).

It all goes badly askew as the genies refuse to return to the bottle, so to speak. The sequel is less satisfying – I mean, how do you follow up apocalypse-by-Crowley? Still, the magickal details in *Black Easter* are fascinating old-school and Ware is so seductive one wishes there were more books about his earlier adventures.

It would be impossible for me to go into detail about all the fictional (or factional) Beasts in this short article. So far Crowley has even battled Sherlock Holmes in print at least thrice – by one of my favourite short story writers, Ron Weighell, in

The Fictional Aleister Crowley

The Case of The Fiery Messengers, in *The Case of The Philosopher's Ring* by Randall Collins, and in Guy Adams's *Sherlock Holmes and the Breath of God*. The latter is a ridiculous romp, ending in a faceoff with the Beast being exposed as a whining faker while Holmes gives a pompous pro-science/anti-spiritual speech that could have been composed by that obnoxious materialist Richard Dawkins in a bate. Maybe it was. Imagine one of Basil Rathbone's rousing anti-Nazi monologues in those great wartime Universal studios Holmes flicks – only turned to bad account. I actually find the tone more offensive than, say, something like Christopher Isherwood's daft, druggy short story *A Visit To Anselm Oakes*, or even John Symonds's *The Medusa's Head*, where Crowley meets a badder baddy in Adolf Hitler, esquire himself. As for Symonds, one always gets the feeling he resented the fact that most of his work didn't sell and that he ended by spending his life recycling the content of his biographical works *The Great Beast* and *The Magic of Aleister Crowley* under different titles again and again to a succession of less and less major publishing houses.

Some avow fellow Golden Dawn members like Dion Fortune and Algernon Blackwood vilified Crowley in their fictions. The former's Hugo Astley in *The Winged Bull* is debated as a potential AC, ditto the latter's Philip Skale in *The Human Chord* – another novel Crowley gave a bad review to.

Crowley's devoted disciple Kenneth Grant's novel *Grist To Whose Mill?*, written in the early 50s but not issued until 2012, has his mentor portrayed rather more sympathetically as Ruthven Seeley. Indeed, every time I go into a bookshop I seem to stumble across yet another factional/fictional Beastly manifestation. Some are well worth investigating, such as Richard McNeff's *Sybarite Among The Shadows*, an expansion of his short story of the same name and a vivid examination of the relationship between Crowley, his disciple Victor Neuburg and a host of others such as Neuburg's fellow poet Dylan Thomas. And yet...

Why is it when Aleister Crowley was only a few years back voted one of the 100 Great Britons of all time in a public poll by the BBC, when his image hangs in the National Portrait Gallery, when a group of enthusiasts in America (Eleusyve Productions of Seattle) are on a long term project to perform his Rites of Eleusis as innovative rock operas live and on CD and DVD, is he still seen primarily in current fiction as a horror- comic villain? Maybe I'm too pessimistic – perhaps any publicity is good publicity? But I guess that's what Crowley thought at one point – and he turned out to be wrong. Then again: James Bond and Fu Manchu... check the numbers! Read 'em and weep!

The Fenris Wolf

A RANDOM LIST OF FURTHER PSEUDO-ACS IN FICTION
(CROWLEY CHARACTER'S NAME IN BRACKETS)

—ᴟ— Warwick Deeping. *Exiles*. 1930. (Oscar Slade).

—ᴟ— Elizabeth Sharpe. *The Secrets of the Kaula Circle*. 1936. ("666"). Note: allegedly factual.

—ᴟ— R. T. M. Scott. *The Black Magician*. 1926. (Jerome Cardan).

—ᴟ— Robert Rankin. *The Witches of Chiswick*. 2003. (Hugo Rune).

—ᴟ— Ward Greene. *Ride The Nightmare* 1930 Aka *The Lives and Loves of a Modern Bluebeard*. (Bellerophon Cawdor).

—ᴟ— Frank Baker. *Talk of the Devil*. 1956 (Nathaniel Sylvester).

—ᴟ— Ethel Archer. *The Hieroglyph*. 1932 (Svaroff).

—ᴟ— Michael Delving. *The Devil Finds Work*. 1970. (Tristram Vail).

—ᴟ— Dargon (real name George MacGill). *The Nameless Order*. 1924 (Thomas Calvert).

—ᴟ— Sydney Horler. *The Evil Messenger*. 1938. (Rathin Memory).

A SELECTED LIST OF CROWLEY IN FICTION: AS HIMSELF

—ᴟ— James Harvey. *Memoirs of Aleister Crowley*. 1967.

—ᴟ— F. Gwynplaine MacIntyre. *The Woman Between The Worlds*. 1994.

—ᴟ— Nick Mamatas. *Summon, Bind, Banish*. 2007.

—ᴟ— Ron Weighell. *The Tears of God*. 2011.

—ᴟ— Mandy Slater. *Daddy's Little Girl*. 1997.

—ᴟ— Mary Hedger. *The History of Fun*. 2002.

Whence Came the Stranger: Tracking the Metapattern of Stranger in a Strange Land

Adam Rostoker

In 1961 Robert Anson Heinlein published a novel about a young Martian named Valentine Michael Smith. The book, *Stranger in a Strange Land*, burst from its modest initial reception in science fiction circles to become one of the most influential works of the 20th century. Its concepts molded the critical thinking of many important social movements and paved the way for that astonishing period of social, religious, and sexual reclamation that is misleadingly dubbed "the 60s."[1]

Arriving, as it did, at a nadir of American free thought and at a peak of media censorship, *Stranger's* publication was a minor miracle and its later mainstream success has always been considered a first class fluke. It became the first science fiction novel to penetrate public consciousness since the days of Verne and Wells and initiated an unprecedented era of respectability for science fiction that opened the door for the *Star Trek, 2001* and *Star Wars. Stranger* also marked a radical departure of form, not only for the author, but for American thought and expression in general. *Stranger* was the quintessence that transformed the nation's repressively conformist, post-war paranoia into the overtly sensual, erudite, cynical optimism that epitomized the years preceding the Reagan administration.

Entire volumes could be devoted to the influence of *Stranger* on fields as diverse (or convergent) as religion, physics, computer science, philosophy, government, anthropology, ecology and the occult. Movies, songs, and books quickly reflected its major themes. *Grok*, Heinlein's Martian neologism for deep understanding, became a household word. Every form of media, art, and science paid its respects to Heinlein's creation. The Church of All Worlds and the Covenant of The Mithril Star were two of many groups that formed around *Stranger's* principles and inspiration.[2]

As a part of its enormous cultural contribution, *Stranger* afforded a vision of the future that has proved astonishingly accurate. *Stranger* accurately predicted many of the scientific, social and political changes that mark our times from water-beds,

---

1 Most of "the 60s" as a popular movement didn't even start until around '65 and didn't really end until well after Nixon got re-elected in '72. The most active period occurred between 1968-74 and in fact, most of the '60s are still happening. Referring to "the 60s" quarantines a radical, ongoing, whole systems transition and reduces it to a mere historical fad.

2 There are at least three secret *Stranger*-inspired, nest-type organizations that survive to this day, mostly centered in communities near major universities.

faxes and teleconferencing to genetic engineering's effect on probate laws to the First Lady's private consultation with an astrologer to the rise of frightening religious fundamentalisms. Indeed, almost every major prediction of Heinlein's has been fulfilled.[3] This extraordinary grasp of the future, as well as Heinlein's humor and wisdom, make *Stranger* as fresh today as it was thirty years ago.

Yet, for all *Stranger's* phenomenal successes and successful phenomena, the novel itself presents quite a few mysteries: How does a highly respected, conservative, commercial author of primarily juvenile science fiction come to write a heretical parable concerning, among other things, sexual freedom and responsibility, anti-Christianity, anti-patriotism, and applied cultural relativism? And, how does such a parable emerge from 'sleeper' status in science fiction circles to become a major classic best-seller of 20th century literature? How do entire religions coalesce from 'a mere work of fiction' – the *Holy Bible* notwithstanding? What was the inspiration for so bold a stroke? What were you thinking, Mr. Heinlein?

The premise of this article is that Heinlein wrote *Stranger* as an allegorical recapitulation of Thelema. (The word *Thelema* is Greek for "Great Will" and refers to the body of philosophy and magickal practices codified by the late Aleister Crowley and continued by many.) This article details Heinlein's magickal interests, his relationships with the most famous of Crowley's American disciples, and his many coded references to Thelema in *Stranger* and other written works.

Moreover, we will establish that Heinlein wrote *Stranger* with the intent of initiating a Thelemic 'whole systems transition' in human thought and expression. This means that *Stranger* cannot be regarded merely as the work of a master storyteller, the product of a literary genius. Rather, *Stranger* is much better understood as a consciously wrought, carefully considered and brilliantly successful casting – a talismanic spell in itself, still dynamic, with its direct purpose being to spark human evolution along Thelemic lines. This is our hypothesis.

Establishment scientist Dr. Carl Sagan says, "Extraordinary claims require extraordinary proof," and this article presents some certifiably extraordinary information – not from science fiction and fantasy, but from real world history and real people. It's an amazing story and, as the significance of Heinlein's work begins to unfold, we'll find that *Stranger* has only just begun to inspire, shock and change us.

THE GAME IS AFOOT...

This explanation is difficult to pursue in linear form, bits of information tend to refer to one another, one story tends to bleed into another, and the required background covers a lot of history and detailed esoterica. Still, with a little luck

---

3 Heinlein's unfulfilled predictions are even more unsettling. It is revealing to track the historical paths that resulted in his missed predictions. For example, why does our era lacks robotics, greater energy efficiency, or wide-spread use of an improved technology for reading. Why do we have a (relatively) failed space program and a (relatively) failed parapsychology program? Why is there an increase of world hunger juxtaposed with historically unprecedented gluttony. Heinlein predicted enough direct hits that we might ask: What do his misses fail to account for? What mistakes have we made?

and a bit of *verdammte Quantumspringerei*, we should meet the following goals. First, we'll examine Thelema and its likeness to *Stranger*, then we'll review Heinlein's involvement with Thelema, and finally we'll dissect some of the text of *Stranger* itself, decoding a few of the more obvious clues. We'll finish with a few corollary observations that polish up our new perspective on Heinlein's motives.

One can't discuss Thelema, *per se*, without first addressing the subject of its founder, Aleister Crowley. Unfortunately, most people associate Crowley and his writings with the Satanic accusations leveled against him by the popular 'National Inquirer' media of his native Victorian England. His 'devil worshipper' reputation is reinforced by his inclusion in the pseudo-Satanic trappings of today's heavy metal music. Also, many of Crowley's most visible fans lean towards the unfortunate habit of freedom of expression – which tends to makes folks nervous and often winds up being covered today's popular 'National Inquirer' media.[4]

As recent press lynchings prove, a media rap can be more damning than a federal conviction (compare Oliver North's fortunes to that of William Kennedy Smith's accuser) and the labelling of any subject as 'occult' is sufficient to cause academicians to lose grants and the faithful to risk ex-communication. As a result, most responsible people (read: afraid 'cause they got something to lose) avoid mentioning Crowley or Thelema in public, leaving his ideas in that frightfully rich garbage pail of 20th century Establishment cast-offs. While tagging an individual or body of thought off-limits doesn't bring us closer to the truth, it certainly makes it difficult to assess Crowley's ideas on their own merit without being overwhelmed by noise about their origin. As a result, Crowley's bad boy rep has long been a millstone around Thelema's neck and even the most zealous Thelemites sometimes grumble about continuing the legacy of so vilified a man.[5]

This article is not a defense of Crowley, but it is important to understand that a philosophical exposition of Thelema intended for the general public – and *Stranger* is only one such – would have to be constructed in such a way that book burners and witch hunters couldn't associate it with Crowley. As it was, *Stranger* was actually burned by some Christians and Moslems (while being hailed by others) and Heinlein was threatened several times by the Fundies. To hide his Thelemic orientation, Heinlein counted on the intellectual dullness of his potential detractors, knowing that any God-fearing critic of un-Christian works would never stoop to reading as hated a man as Crowley and, thus, could never interpret the codes in the text. Heinlein concealed his Thelemic messages in symbols that only a fellow

---

4 Just recently in Massachusetts, a group of Thelemites who were pulled over for speeding, were hassled for being Satanists by the State Police. They were arrested, had their ritual gear confiscated, and interrogated on their religious practices. Much of the behind doors bargaining that took place over an illegal weapons charge – an athame and a finely crafted art sword – centered on the arresting officer's desire to keep the sword as a trophy. Since all charges were dropped a lawsuit is impossible, but the Thelemites lost days of time and thousands of dollars. The burning times rage unabated...

5 Near his death, Crowley published a collection of his letters in *Magick Without Tears* (republished in 1989 with Ordo Templi Orientis OTO and Falcon Press) which is widely regarded as his most accessible work. Currently OTO's longest continuously operating lodge, Thelema Lodge in Berkeley, offers a class entitled, "Magick Without Aleister" on non-Crowleyan magickal traditions in the hopes of getting something done besides living down the C-word.

Thelemite would understand. In other words, you'd have to be playing the game in order to play the game.

"THE WORD OF THE LAW IS THELEMA."[6]

Thelema begins with the observation that each life is deity and continues in lengthy, detailed commentary on the responsibilities and ramifications of godhood plus tips, hints and recipes for today's active deity. This is embodied in the three basic principles of Thelema. The first, and most famous, is: "Do what thou wilt shall be the whole of the Law."[7] While this 'Law of Thelema' is generally insufficiently translated as 'do what you like,' Crowley maintained its true meaning was that: a) Each life has a higher nature and a divine purpose. b) That each life, with differing degrees of efficiency, is currently involved in communication with the higher self for the accomplishment of their divine purpose. c) That any and every life must begin their striving by actively acknowledging and actively worshipping the divinity in themselves, in certain concepts and in every other living thing.[8] d) It is understood that the nature of one life's divinity and divine purpose may be inscrutable to another and even to him or herself.[9]

According to Crowley, the trick to the Law of Thelema is in the words "Thou" and "Wilt." The first word is formal in Old English and refers to the higher self, the deity within; and the second word refers to the divine purpose – it is a different and more potent concept than 'will'.[10]

It will become clear, especially as the intelligence herein is presented, that the Law of Thelema is the inspiration for Michael's observation "Thou art God," – notice the Thou from the Law of Thelema – "That which groks [is God]."[11]

This is a difficult concept to express in a sound bite, and although both Crowley and Heinlein did pretty well, they and both complained bitterly that language was inadequate. The brevity and odd construction of these statements contain the 'fullness' of the concept, making them something along the lines of a koan, but like the koan, there is an obvious need for depth understanding. Apprehension doesn't come without effort and deep reflection.

The Law of Thelema has another use. Crowley instructed his followers to greet

6 *The Book of the Law* (also titled *Liber Al vel Legis* and referred to as *Liber Legis*) I:39.
7 *The Book of the Law* I:40
8 We feel that this sentence, "To actively acknowledge and actively worship the divinity in oneself, in certain concepts and in every other living thing," is functional definition of *grok*.
9 *The Old and New Commentaries to Liber AL* by Aleister Crowley, edited by William E. Heidrick, see commentary on I-40.
10 Ibid, see also *The Law Is For All*, by Aleister Crowley, edited by Dr. Israel Regardie, Falcon Press, Phoenix, AZ, 1986, p. 97-98.
11 *The Original Uncut Stranger in a Strange Land*, Ace Books, 1961, 1991, p. 184. By the way, Otter Zell makes a very important point in his *Litha* 1991 *Green Egg* Editorial that the originally published, shorter version of *Stranger* is the better of the two. This author wholeheartedly agrees. Among other things, *Stranger* would not have been nearly so important had it not included Heinlein's critical definition of love. The additional apocrypha of the uncut *Stranger* are interesting and fun, but that doesn't make it a better book nor is it nearly worth the loss of the old *Stranger*.

everyone with "Do what thou wilt shall be the whole of the Law," and began all of his communications, written and oral, with these words to remind the speaker and the listener of their shared divinity.[12] Similarly, in *Stranger* the Nest even uses "Thou art God," as the first words shared among water brothers and the real world groups inspired by *Stranger* share this greeting often. Most modern Thelemites abbreviate the Law of Thelema to its Qabalic equivalent of 93, making this number something of a buzzword and greeting among the in crowd. Sadly, this abbreviation also reduces the impact of this most powerful statement.

Communicating with the divine as the center of all life and action brings us to the second major principle of Thelema: "Love is the law, love under will,"[13] which is usually said in response to "Do what thou wilt..." or in closing a speech or letter.[14]

Typically, this Law of Love is also misunderstood as mere license. Crowley interpreted to mean that any action from the higher self must be, by definition, an act of the deity and, ergo, an act of love. This is not the fearful, insecure sentimentality of modern romance, but the divine and passionate union of one part of creation with all other parts of creation.[15] As diverse as the universe itself, divine love can take many forms: according to Odin it can be death in battle, according to Vulcan it's a hard day's work raping the planet, according to Pan it's nymph and tuck, according to Hermes it's theft and seduction, *et cetera*.

Between the first two Laws, Thelema may sound like justification for the greatest possible excesses, and, well, it is. But, as Heinlein observed, these "[are laws] of nature, not an injunction, nor a permission."[16] These principles do not pretend to describe a set of inspired religious lifestyle proscriptions. Rather, they comprise demonstrable, scientifically accurate, functional observations about life and the universe. Thelema begins with the observation that each life has the freedom to create and destroy at will regardless of any later moral, ethical or aesthetic judgement. Another way of rehashing the two first principles are to quote Hassan I Sabbah who said "There is no Truth. All is permissible." Provocative? You could write a book about it.[17] This precise issue is addressed towards the end of *Stranger* when Michael has annihilated

---

12 There are many references to this in Thelemic literature. In an essay entitled *Liber DCCCXXXVII – The Law of Liberty*, Crowley writes that he always begins his speech or letters – even his greetings to his butcher – with the Law of Thelema to remind people that "[w]e are all free, all independent, all shining gloriously, each one a radiant world."

13 *Liber Legis*, I:57.

14 There are many forms of greeting exchange in fraternal groups where they serve the role of passwords, slogans, etc. A wide variety of magickal groups, military cadres, and secret societies use them for security purposes. In Thelemic groups there are many versions of the exchanges mentioned above. Some Thelemic groups greet each other with the words, "Thelema" and "Agape", the Greek words for Great Will and Great Love. And in *Bill & Ted's Excellent Adventure*, Wyld Stallyns create an utopian future based on their inspired Fool-ishness in which the greeting amongst all people is "Be excellent," and "Party on" which capture the same form, spirit and meaning.

15 This is another facet of grokking, see footnote 8. Also refer to the rest of the passage in *Liber Legis* I:57 and Crowley's notes in *Commentaries* and *Law is for All*.

16 Grumbles, p. 285.

17 Hassan was best known for the radical consciousness cult he founded back in the eleventh century at about the same time the Gnostics were getting their second wind. Known primarily for their great stash and dynamic foreign policy, later commentators called them the Assassins.

various criminals housed in prisons and in public office. Jubal asks him, "Aren't you afraid of playing God, lad?"

"Mike grinned with unashamed cheerfulness. 'I am God. Thou art God... and any jerk I remove is God, too... And when a cat stalks a sparrow both of them are God, carrying out God's thoughts."[18]

A mind-blowing responsibility comes with acknowledging the freedom to act and Heinlein points out that the law of Thelema applies to lynch mobs as well.[19] Not that this devalues these observations. Rather, it demonstrates their global application and reemphasizes the understanding that one person's Great Will may be inscrutable to another.

This dovetails nicely into the third principle of Thelema: "Every man and every woman is a star." Here is the essence of the 'all men are created equal' rap and is commonly misunderstood to mean that merely being born qualifies one for the rewards that other people may have accrued including respect, opportunity, love, security, *et cetera*. Its real meaning is that "Every man and every woman has a course, depending partly on the self, and partly on the environment which is natural and necessary for each. Anyone who is forced from his [or her] own course, either through a lack of self-understanding, or through external opposition, comes into conflict with the order of the Universe and suffers accordingly."[20]

We find this curious, worshipful tolerance a familiar theme throughout *Stranger* – a theme which balances the seeming severity of the two earlier Thelemic principles. Michael spends enormous amounts of (subjective) time and energy grokking before he acts, and thus he is in accord with himself and the universe, not counting mistakes, when he encounters a cusp. Jubal, the book's other major character, is also in constant philosophical motion, attempting to grok through the haze of his self-admitted tribal taboos. *Stranger's* whole plot may be best understood as Jubal's (and the other major characters') eventual enlightenment to this basic Thelemic principle and the defeat of their cultural filters.

Before closing the topic of Thelema, it is important to pass on a few details about how Thelema is shared and practiced. This makes it easier to frame the clues from *Stranger*. The Thelemic current seems to have roots in the writings of earlier philosophers and magicians and the movements they founded,[21] but modern Thelema stems from a brief, enigmatic text channelled by Crowley, called the *Book of the Law* or *Liber AL vel Legis* (we'll call it *Liber Legis*). It is the source from which all of Thelema is drawn.

It interesting to note that Heinlein has Michael reading "such deviant oddities as Crowley's Book of the Law" alongside other more traditional religious texts in

---

18 *Stranger*, p. 509.

19 Grumbles, p. 248.

20 *The seventh Theorem of Magick*, from *Magick in Theory and Practice*, Master Therion (Aleister Crowley), Castle Books, Seacaucus, NJ, 1991, p. xiv.

21 For example, the word Thelema may have first been used in its present form by the 16th century satirist Rabelais whose fictional Abbey of Theleme probably inspired Crowley's later Abbey of Thelema at Cefalu, Sicily. Other influences included Eliphas Levi, Dr. John Dee, and McGregor Mathers. Some Thelemites believe that Thelema is a form of esoteric Buddhism.

the first scene that presents Michael as seriously struggling with his humanity.[22] It is a very prominent, even tongue-in-cheek reference and many people, including Hymenaeus Beta, head of the world's largest Thelemic organization, recall *Stranger* as the first place they had ever heard reference to Crowley.[23]

Liber Legis is a complex, poetically striking book. It is rife with puns and references from diverse mythological, magickal, alchemical and Qabalistic sources. It is a miracle of allegory and some of its codes have been an inspiration to cryptographers since at least before WWII. Its themes are myriad and include the announcement of the New Age,[24] an age of the magickal child which follows the primeval maternal age and the current declining patriarchy. The book heralds earth changes and changes in the state of magick, offers advice and commentary on Thelema, and makes several predictions including the coming of a Thelemic magickal child who will succeed Crowley. This would seem a good idea since Crowley himself never figured out all of the kinks in *Liber Legis*, a situation which is predicted in taunting passages of the book itself,[25] nor was Crowley ever at peace with contents of the book. Only years after he received *Liber Legis*, and only when absolutely inundated by bizarre synchronicity from the text, did he begin to circulate *Liber Legis* and propagate Thelema.

He did this by printing vast quantities of *Liber Legis*, and many other remarkable texts, and selling them or (rarely) giving them away. He also founded several magickal organizations and co-opted a pre-existing magickal organization of Masonic heritage, the Ordo Templi Orientis (OTO) into his Thelemic fold. These organizations grew (and splintered and metastasized) to become large worldwide networks of both secret and public Thelemic societies. This is an epic story in itself.

These magickal orders are based on nine degrees of initiation which reflect the acquisition of magickal and mundane knowledge and illumination. There is a tenth degree, mostly administrative, which indicates the order's temporal head, and even a mysterious eleventh degree. The Order is organized (mostly) around 'lodges' where members often share living, learning and ritual space. A quick scan of Crowley's bylaws for the OTO seem to call for the creation of an extended family within the lodge and a network of lodges around the globe, united in magickal ties deemed stronger than blood and dedicated to the propagation of Thelema.[26] Does all this sound familiar? It is a very close approximation of the Nest and its influence is apparent in those real life groups inspired by *Stranger*. Coextant with the OTO is a religious body, the Gnostic Catholic Church which is organized roughly along

---

22 *Stranger*, p. 380.

23 From a conversation with Hymenaeus Beta.

24 So far as this author has found, this is the earliest mention of the term New Age in its current context.

25 These occur throughout *Liber Legis*, one example is found in Book II, verse 76, "What meaneth this, o prophet? Thou knowest not; nor shalt thou ever know. But cometh one to follow thee: he shall expound it."

26 Consult *Liber CI* by Aleister Crowley "An Open Letter to Those Who May Wish to Join the Order, Enumerating the Duties and Privileges." It precisely describes, both in scope and in detail, the ties that one finds in *Stranger* among water brothers and is only one of many similar texts. Later OTO heads greatly reduced this ideal since the OTO is a public legal entity and many of the duties are impossible under US and other law.

the lines of churches everywhere, but whose final authority rests in the head of the OTO. The GCC is known primarily for their mass which celebrates the Goddess and her union with the God. It is a deeply moving ceremony and is one of the few Thelemic rituals routinely open to the general public. It bears a very strong resemblance to the ritual witnessed by Ben Caxton in *Stranger*.[27]

So, to recap, there seems to be an astonishing similarity to the content and forms of the nest and the philosophy and practice of Thelema; yet, for the purposes of this article, such similitude is but a start. So far, we have a neat set of coincidences and a single overt mention of "Crowley's Book of the Law." Yet, for a man of Heinlein scholarship this could be dismissed as a fluke or even as two great minds thinking alike. Let's see then, if we can demonstrate that Heinlein was intimately involved with magick in general and Thelema in particular.

TIME ENOUGH FOR MAGICK

Heinlein's interests had included magick from early in his career. In 1941 he wrote the novella *Magic, Inc.*,[28] a delightfully wise and funny treatment of modern society's reaction to the 'scientific' discovery of magic. His story demonstrates a genuine scholarly inquiry into the history and practice of magic,[29] and addresses many social, economic and political ramifications of a burgeoning high-tech, magickal industry.[30] In the story, widespread industrial use of magick falls victim to a racketeering operation composed of organized crime and corrupt government officials who plot to establish a monopoly on magick and then bar its use by private citizens. (One can almost whiff the spoor of G. Gordon Liddy!) It is easy to see how the story might have arisen from Heinlein's famous opposition to gun control for the plot can be summarized: "If magick is outlawed by government, only outlaws and government will have magick."[31]

Heinlein seems to have employed magickal and Thelemic themes in many of his works, particularly the later ones. Most of his plots concerned the liberation of strong minded individuals from external control and their transmogrification into

---

27 *Stranger*, p. 423. The complete Gnostic Mass is known as *Liber XV* and is usually found as an appendix to *Magick in Theory and Practice*.

28 *Magic, Inc.*, Ace Publishing, New York, 1941. Pagan fans will be pleased to read that heroine who saves the day is a hag who rails at length that witches are many things by nature (by Nature!), but evil isn't one of them.

29 Heinlein's thaumaturgy in *Magic, Inc.* is strongly based on the elemental workings described in *Transcendental Magic*, perhaps the most widely respected occult work of the 19th century. It was written by the influential clergyman and magician Eliphas Levi with whom Crowley was greatly impressed. Later synchronicity and meditation convinced Crowley that Levi, who died shortly before the his birth, was his previous incarnation.

30 This is reminiscent of the conversations in *Stranger* (p. 486-7, 511 for example) concerning the economic vectors caused by a reliable Martian magick. Also note a recent HBO movie, *Cast A Deadly Spell*, which seems to have drawn some inspiration from Heinlein's story.

31 Grumbles, p. 62-4. Heinlein mentions *Murder, Inc.* in a 1949 letter defending his opposition to gun control – its connection to the plot of *Magic, Inc.* is obvious. Note that in our present culture, magick isn't outlawed per se, but it is repressed and its study is ridiculed. Also note that magick is pursued successfully both by government and organized crime.

their greater selves. This process of discovering and dedicating one's great destiny is inherent in "Do what thou wilt." It is a process Thelemites call apotheosis and is deemed, for many, the *raison d'être* of magick, indeed, of life itself.

Since it is clear that Heinlein was involved in magickal scholarship – and it's hard to imagine a field in which he wasn't engaged in some degree of scholarship – Heinlein's exposure to Thelema may have initially come from his vast reading. Crowley was widely (and often grudgingly) considered the greatest magickal genius of his day even by people who hated him. His Qabalistic classic *777* [32] is a standard reference among all but Orthodox Jewish sources – some of whom also note Crowley. Dion Fortune, Allan Bennett, James Joyce, Austin Osman Spare, Somerset Maugham, Sybil Leek and most other early 20th century occult superstars had much to say about Crowley, most of it contradictory, and all of their works are profoundly affected by him. Crowley's influence was not confined to magick alone: he was an avid sportsman, a fecund writer, and a 'personality' whose life affected many artists, poets, writers and scientists of his time. It is hard to imagine a man as widely read as Heinlein missing mention of "the wickedest man in the world."

Yet, until recently it was very difficult to document Heinlein's personal involvement with magick except by examining his writings. He was an intensely private man who felt his livelihood potentially threatened by the repressive moral climate of his times.[33] He seldom invited contact with the press or organized fandom and there are very few hints of his personal life available in his biographies. While some anecdotes survive that show Heinlein as some sort of Santa Claus or friendly wizard,[34] he would have been a 'maybe' on the closet magician list were it not for his relationship with three of the most famous Thelemic magicians besides Crowley: John Whiteside Parsons, Marjorie Cameron and L. Ron Hubbard who together participated in one of the most famous 20th century magickal operations, the "Babalon Working".

Hubbard, best known for his successful mid-life career transition from science fiction author to founding deity of the Church of Scientology, knew Heinlein intimately. Only several mentions of Hubbard are made in Heinlein's biographies and collected letters, but it is clear that they were close. Hubbard and Heinlein lived near each other, served as officers in the Navy, worked for the same magazines, and, from what one reads, seem to have been close personal friends.[35] Hubbard also wrote copious science fiction, and even introduced Heinlein to literary agent and

---

32 *777 and Other Qabalistic Writings of Aleister Crowley*, edited by Israel Regardie, Samuel Weiser, Inc., York Beach, ME, 1973.

33 Grumbles, p. 285 and throughout the text.

34 In the June, 1988 edition of *Locus*, author Spider Robinson describes two occasions in which Heinlein played the friendly wizard. The first Instance came years after the two had met, just once, at a science fiction event. It seems Heinlein sent Robinson a check out of the blue for the exact amount of Robinson's back rent plus $100 which arrived at the last possible moment. Robinson says that nobody – not even his agent – knew he was that broke. The second story involved the Robinson family stranded far from home on their daughter's birthday. Heinlein called – how did he know where they were or get the number? – and cheered the little girl, saying she could have a second birthday with her friends when she got home. There are many other stories like these.

35 Grumbles, p. 35.

long time friend Lurton Blassingame.[36] For that matter, Heinlein seems to have been intimate with the other messianic science fiction writers of his era, Theodore Sturgeon, Arthur C. Clarke and Frank Herbert – whose works bear closer inspection for the magickally minded.

Cameron is an influential poet, artist and actress who contributed greatly to the underground arts movement in California over the last thirty years. An advocate of Goddess worship since the '50s, her life story reads like a Tom Robbins novel. Her list of close friends and co-workers includes many key writers and film makers including Kenneth Anger, Anaïs Nin, and Louis Culling. An exhibit of her artwork was seized by LA Vice in the early '60s and became the battleground for California's first art vs. obscenity trials. (She won.) She also appeared in some of Hollywood's best and most legendary underground films. An enormously spiritual and accomplished woman who is today very reclusive – due to the demands of her "sacred grandmothering" – she was the center of the Babalon Working.

Parsons was the 'poor, little rich boy' co-founder of the California Institute of Technology and the Jet Propulsion Laboratories in Pasadena.[37] Considered one of the most brilliant rocket scientists of his day, he is credited with advancing both solid and liquid rocket fuels, enabling much of the post-war jet and rocket technology. Werner Von Braun claimed that it was Parsons, not himself, who was the true father of American rocketry. NASA owes much to this man's brilliance and energy and named a crater on the moon after him. Parsons was also a dedicated Thelemic magician involved with the OTO from late in the '30s, eventually becoming *magister templi* of the famous Los Angeles-based Agape Lodge. Crowley favored Parsons and greatly encouraged the young scientist.[38]

Parsons' true life story is every bit as compelling as Faust's. He was a remarkably handsome, noble, creative and passionate man. While inventing the technology that would eventually land us on the moon, he ran the Agape Lodge – then the world's only functioning OTO lodge – edited and published the lodge's single newsletter, the *Oriflamme,* and maintained an active participation in many of the arts and sciences. A recently published collection of his essays *Freedom is a Two-edged Sword* demonstrates his startling clarity of vision and keen understanding of magick.[39]

It should be required reading for anyone with an opposeable thumb. Parsons died the day before Midsummer in 1952 following an explosion at his home. The official explanation for the tragedy is oddly poetic and ironic – he dropped a vial of fulminate of mercury. Forty years later, conspiracy theories abound about his death, as they do for that other handsome, noble, world class hero who was dedicated to

---

36 Grumbles, p. 43. Grumbles is mostly letters between Heinlein and Blassingame.

37 There are several articles on Parsons, but the best so far, and the source cited for this article is *Jack Parsons: Sorcerous Scientist* by Douglas Chapman, in *Strange Magazine* #6, PO Box 2246, Rockville, MD 20847. The magazine is highly recommended.

38 Parsons was the first member of OTO to achieve the eigth degree by dint of time and labor, most upper degrees having been historically awarded for administrative or political expediency. There is only one other OTO member to have accomplished this and his is also a compelling story.

39 *Freedom is a Two-Edged Sword and Other Essays* by John Whiteside Parsons, edited by Cameron and Hymenaeus Beta, Ordo Templi Orientis, New York, in association with Falcon Press, Las Vegas, 1989.

the space program. How does an upper class, major league rocket scientist genius get involved with something like Crowleyism? World history is full of leading scientific minds who have found the magickal tradition both exciting and useful. Leonardo da Vinci, Dr. John Dee, Franz Kepler, Giordano Bruno, Isaac Newton, and even Copernicus all published works in what would later be dubbed "occult sciences."

Liebnitz and Boule, whose algebra is the fundament of all modern computers and communications, derived their theories from their Qabalistic work. Most of the early advances in chemistry came from alchemists, much of mathematica stems from the magickal traditions, and metaphysics was considered part of a complete education up until the end of the 19th century. It is only within the last hundred years that the Establishment has forced scientists to kick magick into the closet – and, from what one hears, magick continues to whisper through the keyhole. In fact, Parsons was introduced to Thelema and the OTO by a fellow scientist (there seem to have been several around) and later became 'sold' on Crowley and *Liber Legis* because they predicted the work of Einstein, Heidegger and quantum theory. Many leading scientists today are still very deeply moved by Crowley and Thelema.

Cameron[40] and others recall that Heinlein and Parsons were quite close friends. They may have met at the Los Angeles Science Fiction Fan club which maintained a reading room – they were certainly seen there together. It was also common for science fiction authors to tour the Pasadena-based Jet Propulsion Laboratories that Parsons co-founded. Heinlein was particularly avid in availing himself of such tours. He used to take years off to study advances in science and often wrote glowingly of NASA. So here was Parsons, the wunderkind of the rocket scientist community while Heinlein was its chief PR man and visionary. Space travel was both men's passion and livelihood. They had much in common, including their friendship with L. Ron Hubbard, who must have mentioned one to the other. Heinlein lived within driving distance of Agape Lodge which often performed the Gnostic Mass and, judging from *Stranger* and other writings, Heinlein was quite familiar with the ritual.[41]

In 1946 Hubbard and Parsons collaborated on perhaps the most famous modern magickal operation: the Babalon Working. This was an intensive, exhausting operation which allegedly opened a dimensional door for the manifestation of the goddess Babalon in human form. The Babalon Working was initiated to answer the previously mentioned prophecy of *Liber Legis*, the prophecy of Crowley's magickal heir, of which it said: "The child of thy bowels, he shall behold them".

"Expect him not from the East, not from the West; for from no expected house

---

40 From an interview with Marjorie Cameron. Heinlein was a the first person Jack Parsons ever introduced her to. She didn't care for Heinlein too much, with his ascot and pipe he was "too slick, too Hollywood. But Jack and he were quite good friends."

41 Check out Heinlein's 1952 short story, *The Year of the Jackpot* (anthologized in *The Menace from Earth*, Signet, 1959) in which protagonist Potipher Breen is a mathematician who tracks odd cycles and develops a theory of periodicity which links UFOs and flying saucers to mass human behavior and which functions at the meta level of personal will. At one point, Breen discovers a church which has reinstituted ritual nudity, "Probably [for] the first time in a thousand years, aside from some screwball cults in Los Angeles. The reverend gentleman claimed that the ceremony was identical with the 'dance of the high priestess' in the temple of Karnak."

cometh that child."[42] This prophecy continues to grip the imagination of many Thelemites and also forms the basic plotline for *Stranger*.

At the risk of getting a bit ahead of ourselves, let's take a second to compare the above quote from *Liber Legis* to the scene in *Stranger* where Madame Vesant the astrologer struggles with Michael's natal chart. She quickly becomes stumped – he comes from no expected house.[43] And since we're comparing *Stranger* quotes to Thelemic quotes, let's review Crowley's retelling of the Bacchus/Dionysus myth with an eye to the plotline of *Stranger*.

> [O]ne commemorates firstly his birth of a mortal mother who has yielded her treasure house to the Father of All, of the jealousy and rage excited by this incarnation, and of the heavenly protection afforded to the infant. Next should be commemorated the journeying westward [sunward?] upon an ass. Now comes the great scene of the drama: the gentle, exquisite youth with his following (chiefly composed of women) seems to threaten the established order of things, and that Established Order takes steps to put an end to the upstart. We find Dionysus confronting the angry King, not with defiance, but with meekness; yet with a subtle confidence, an underlying laughter. His forehead is wreathed with vine tendrils...[h]e is an effeminate figure... [who] hides horns.[44]

At this point, of course, we're well into the third part of the proof, the decoding of *Stranger*. After all, we have proven that the basic concept of Thelema is in all ways consistent with the grokking of *Stranger*. We have demonstrated that Heinlein had intimate contact, not just with Thelema and magick, but with two of the most famous Thelemic magicians in history. And, if we need more proof, there are many other little clues as well. For example, in the last letter in *Grumbles From The Grave*,[45] Heinlein uses Crowley's Thelemic motto, "Do what thou wilt shall be the whole of the Law," and Heinlein's later books use many Crowleyan, Thelemic, Qabalistic or magickal references. In fact, decoding Heinlein's work may well serve as a correspondence course in magick allegory. But before we dig further into the text of *Stranger*, let's examine the history and criteria of allegory so we have a common frame of reference for our foray.

In Search of Stranger

Throughout history, it has always been the coded or allegorical works that have truly inspired whole systems transition in contemporary thought and expression. Coincidentally, these are also the works which have endured the test of time to become classics: the fiction of Lewis Carroll[46] and Jonathan Swift, the art of

---

42 *Liber Legis*, I:55-56.
43 *Stranger*, 103-4.
44 *Magick in Theory and Practice*, p. 13.
45 Grumbles, p. 285. This was the letter to Otter mentioned in footnote 8.
46 The "Alice" series remains a classic of multiplex meaning treasured by logicians and mathematicians (for whom it is a delight), quantum physicists (for whom it was an inspiration), and qabalists (for whom

Leonardo da Vinci[47], the architecture of Gothics[48], the sculpture of Rodin[49], the drama of Shakespeare, the poetry of Blake or Swinburne – even the films of Spielberg and the songs of Don McLean or Paul Simon. These works have four characteristics in common.

First, they contain or reference obviously coded, allegorical, or metaphorical meanings which have greater dimension than the work or medium itself. Second, their finished structures represent radical departures from contemporary expressive norms. Third, their finished structures are built with a missing key – that is, the work evokes questions and provide hints to answers but stubbornly fails to provide the answers themselves, leaving the audience with the challenge to get up and seek the answers on their own or to go back to sleep.

This leads to the fourth characteristic, that the act of cognition regarding the work evokes radical evolution in thought and expression. There is a fifth thread (Discordians sigh) which is harder to establish as universally that links these coded and allegorical works to an evolving current of philosophical expression that has always interwoven mainstream culture while rarely taking its own identifiable form. This current has been labelled hermetic, alchemical, Rosicrucian, magickal, occult, Templar, *et cetera* and while dialectics occur, as well as idiosyncratic or contemporary modes, there is a clear, demonstrable line of intellectual (and ontological) heredity among these forms.

There is a large problem, however, in proving that these characteristics exist. To decode the allegory, or to have sufficient breadth to connect the lines of heredity, requires intense scholarship as well as, and this is a critically important point – experimentation with the material involved. Also, any reasonably accessible exegesis must focus on the simplest lines of connection lest the whole discussion seem to map the interpreter's process rather than the master's opus – Bohr's Copenhagen interpretation as applied to literary criticism. To avoid this problem, we'll concentrate only on major themes, referenced by a minimum of readily available works, and connected by the broadest of strokes. Perhaps a later work will illuminate the many delightful and detailed nuances.

For it is vital that the allegory itself be presented freshly; its recognition must trigger the 'Aha!' effect or its value is diminished. Indeed, we postulate that allegorical works contain a metaphorical stimulus that takes the form of a

---

it was a textbook). By the by, math, physics, and qabala are strikingly convergent in the days of Thelema – have a dinner party and invite some practitioners!

47 da Vinci's artwork represented a radical change in implied perspective and, indeed, the *raison d'être* of art itself. He caused as much outrage among established classical artists as delight in the crop of Renaissance artists he inspired. His overt sensualism, coded anti-religion, and dabbles in the "forbidden" field of natural philosophy (the precursor to experimental science) nearly got him burned alive.

48 Many authors, beginning with Fulcanelli, have detailed the strange designs of the Gothic cathedrals and their implied heretical, particularly Gnostic, meanings.

49 Rodin and his allegorical sculpture plays a great part in *Stranger*, particularly the uncut version. On pages 395-399 of *Stranger*, Jubal gives Ben a first class lesson on Rodin and allegorical sculpture. Not mentioned is that Rodin and Crowley were strong mutual admirers. In fact, Rodin was so taken by young Crowley and his poetry that he extended an invitation for a collaboration of poetry and sculpture which lasted for several projects. See *The Confessions of Aleister Crowley*, p. 338-345

stimulating metaphor. This stimulus awakens certain parts of the consciousness as effectively as any initiation – it is, in fact, the germ of initiation – and contributes to a demonstrable evolution in the efficacy and quality of creative understanding and expression: it is called enlightenment.[50] That *Stranger* is rich in this stimulus can be proven not only by the investigation that follows in this article but also in consideration of the amazing transitions that were wrought by those people who were 'turned on' to Stranger.

Let's see how *Stranger* meets the requirements for an allegorical work. First, does it contain or reference coded meanings? Yes. In fact, it is striking how many 'obvious' coded references Heinlein includes. Besides the numerous quotes and references to classical literature, Heinlein actually introduces some puzzles with text that identifies them as such. For example: there is a discussion of the true meaning of the names Abigail Zenobia, Anne and Michael's love child; and Fatima Michele, Maryam and Michael's issue[51] which is introduced as a puzzle.

Another example is the rapid changing of names: Gillian Boardman becomes Jill, Miriam becomes Maryam, and, most complex and revealing, astrologer Madame Alexandria Vesant becomes Allie Vesant and then Becky Vessey. A wonderful example of these 'obvious' puzzles is the code word 'Berquist' used in a confrontation with Captain Heinrich[52] which sets up the SS raid on Jubal's house. There are many other references, such as the Rodin sculptures mentioned above, Ben Caxton's appropriate door code of "Karthago delenda est"[53], and the neo-neo-Platonic dialogues between the angelic forms of the deceased Arch Bishops Foster and Digby.[54]

Does *Stranger's* finished structure represent a radical departure from contemporary expressive norms? Yes. Remember that any form of expression that didn't lock step with the ultra-right was taboo and, still shivering from the Commie hunts, big publishers wouldn't bite. Yet, *Stranger* spoke with what passed for brutal frankness in those days on a number of taboo subjects. Also, *Stranger* was a very long volume for those days and its length was often mentioned negatively in reviews. Finally, *Stranger* was blatantly Messianic and, at the same time, anti-Christian which offended many of the clergy.[55] Perhaps the best way to tell if *Stranger* violated norms is to scan the reviews it received. It was labelled everything from fascism to pornography, from a Utopian fantasy to a heretical nightmare. No two reviewers

---

50 Somebody ought to look for the neurotransmitters involved in "Aha!"

51 *Stranger*, p. 460-1. This is one whale of a grand puzzle, but will have to wait for later publication.

52 *Stranger*, p. 172. Let's save the readers some trouble: Despite the set-up, ours and Heinlein's, the Berquist code doesn't exist. It is just meaningful-sounding nonsense (amphigory) designed to incite Captain Heinrich (get it, Hein lein, Hein rich?) to send the posse. Then again, maybe we missed something...

53 *Stranger*, p. 85. The short version of this very complex story is that Cato, a famous Roman statesman, closed a series of passionate speeches to the Senate of Rome with the words, "Carthage is to-be-destroyed." Cato thus precipitated the Third Punic War which ended in Rome's utter destruction of the vastly under-matched Carthage. The quote's common contemporary meaning translates roughly as Kruschev's "We will bury you." or Eastwood's "Make my day!"

54 *Stranger*, p. 368-370 and throughout the text.

55 Years ago, in a conversation with a famous Catholic Archbishop, he confided that *Stranger* was the "beginning of the end" of Catholicism. It was after *Stranger* became popular that traditional churches really suffered diminishing attendance and folks started suggesting that "God is dead".

could agree on anything including whether or not *Stranger* was science fiction.[56]

In fact, Heinlein deliberately wrote *Stranger* to defy categorization and "to attack the biggest, fattest sacred cows around."[57] And, by Goddess, was he successful: "[*Stranger*] appealed to an incongruous medley of libertarians and liberals, anarchists and socialists, earnest reformers, angry rebels, and pleasure-seeking do-your-own-thingers."[58] This 'incongruous medley' continue to publish widely read articles to this day which lay passionate claim to Heinlein's inspiration while furiously dismissing those ideas which don't fit neatly into their ideologies. He is the duck-billed platypus of a dozen dirty dogmas, defiantly refusing to conform to any categorist's box.

Moreover, there's dozens of boxes that Heinlein's been kicked out of. Many are the articles which refute his claim to being an individualist, a collectivist, a socialist, a capitalist, a libertarian, a communist, a militarist, a pacificist, a sexist, a feminist, *et cetera ad nauseam* – all of which is absurd since Heinlein himself claimed none of these labels. The point is that many people from many philosophical and political camps were deeply moved by Heinlein's philosophy and intrigued by his wide and popular appeal, yet embarrassed by their inability to synthesize his ideals or track their lineage.[59] And why? They were looking in all the right [read: intellectually approved] areas. And Heinlein couldn't be found there.

Is *Stranger's* finished structure built with a missing key? Yes. The key is the Martian language, and there never was a niftier elixir vital. *Stranger's* basic idea of enlightenment is that Martian language provides such a clear framework of the universe that the human mind is opened to new vistas. The idea comes from something that Einstein said about (human) language insisting on stable coordinate systems despite physics' demonstrable evidence to the contrary. Moreover, Heinlein was a fan of Korzybski, the father of general semantics, who proved that the ability of language to entrain people reinforces a greatly flawed (linguistically derived) concept of the universe. Kipling summed it up another way with the ape chant, "We're all right because we say we are, and if we say we are it must be true."[60]

It is interesting to note that Crowley's prescription for enlightenment involved separating sensory data from its linguistic framework[61] preparatory to the real work of fathoming the universe thereby revealed. Such notables as Dr. Tim Leary, Dr.

---

56 Heinlein claimed it wasn't science fiction. He refers to it as a "Cabellesque satire on religion and sex, [and] not science fiction by any stretch of the imagination." (Grumbles, p. 262)

57 Grumbles, p. 262-3.

58 *Robert A. Heinlein: America Through Science Fiction* by H. Bruce Franklin, Oxford University Press, New York, 1968, p. 127.

59 One popular rumor spawned by the public's inability to reconcile a man who could write *Stranger* at about the same time as *Starship Troopers*, was that Heinlein's works were really written by his wife. While Virginia Heinlein seems an impressive woman in many ways, and it is clear that her input was frequent and invaluable, she wasn't Bacon to Heinlein's Shakespeare. The point of the rumor is that people were at a loss to comprehend Heinlein's vector.

60 *The Jungle Book* by Rudyard Kipling – another story of a human boy reared by aliens.

61 Part I of *Book 4* by Aleister Crowley, Samuel Weiser, York Beach, ME, 1980, is a simple, detailed description of this process. It is also uncommonly devoid of the dense, eclectically pun-laden text for which Crowley is famous, making this a good read for the beginner.

John Lilly, Dr. Israel Regardie, Dr. Wilhelm Reich, R. Buckminster Fuller, Robert Anton Wilson, and Peter Carroll – all of whom credit Crowley as being a strong influence – describe experiments designed to accomplish the intended goal of 'the Martian 101 cure.' We'll cover these in a later article.

Back to the thesis... Does grokking *Stranger* cause a level of cognition that results radical evolution in thought and expression? Yes, there are examples throughout this article. Also examine the character of the period immediately following *Stranger.* The Sexual and Consciousness Revolutions were typified by the major themes of Heinlein (and Crowley). The motto was, "Do your own thing!" The questions were: "Who is in charge of my life, my body, my soul, my world? Who says they're in charge? Who'll be my role model, now that my role model is gone?" There may have never been such a period in history when so many people were trying so hard to wake up.

Reaction to, and inspiration from, *Stranger* formed the most prominent movements and social structures of the time. Free love movements sprang up faster than the communes to hold them. Altered consciousness and ESP research moved from Defense labs into everybody's back yards. Authority freaks were strained past their limits in an effort to reestablish control over the myriad grok-flocks who realized that freedom had been a holy icon left to whither in the blind trust of patriarchs – and who now wanted it back. There is no theme present in the years before the Reagan era that wasn't promulgated in *Stranger*. Yes, this was a book that changed consciousness. It still is.

And, yes, *Stranger* does indeed have a strong link to the allegorical works it succeeded. Indeed, many of these works and the movements that arose from them are mentioned outright in the text of *Stranger*. Likewise, the keys to unlock many of *Stranger's* puzzles are found in their perusal.

But let's examine these early magickal movements a little further before we proceed with our analysis in the hopes of unearthing some critical patterns. The magickal tradition we're tracking begins back before the Egyptians, and wends its way through several identifiable groups that litter Western history. Our first stop is the Gnostics which flourished in Gaul and Iberia during the last half of the Roman Empire and later thumbed their noses at the Pope only to have their thumbs removed in the first of many Roman Catholic genocides around the first millennium.

The Gnostics were named for their emphasis on *Gnosis*, or personal illumination. They eschewed the Catholic doctrine which claimed that knowledge of the divine was accessible only through the intervention of priests. The excesses of the Gnostics seeking personal knowledge were legendary – gluttony was practiced alongside fasting, heavy drugs complimented sensory deprivation, and sexual abstinence was a kink considered equal to major league varsity group whoopee. All of these were considered part and parcel of the personal search for truth and inquirers were advised to choose many paths. (Heck, they sound like a bunch of hippies.)

Most Gnostics groups considered men in all ways equal with women – in fact it wasn't even an issue. They practiced techniques to avoid procreation, not revering the miracle of birth, but rather favoring the sacrament of sex, of 'growing closer.'

Whence Came the Stranger?

The few non-Catholic contemporary records describe these people as having been much more literate, healthier, happier, and longer-lived that the Christian- inspired ignorance, fear and squalor that surrounded them in what was correctly dubbed the Dark Ages. Their chief inspiration was a fellow named (surprise!) Valentinus, an interesting character who just missed being one of the primary influences in Christianity.[62]

His philosophy was based on personal gnosis, the inherent divinity of each man and woman, the abandonment of atonement as unnecessary, and the importance of personal freedom – all of which clearly evokes Thelema and *Stranger*. It is unclear just how Valentinus got Valentine's Day, but he did and we suspect an Illuminati conspiracy. The only other historical Valentini[63] don't fit at all and the festival's symbols are definitely both pre-Christian pagan and Gnostic.

Valentine's Day originated from the Roman Lupercalia, which was a month long fertility festival closely related to modern Mardi Gras. It was an important event – the month of February is named after the party props – and was officiated by a special class of educated priests. *Lupercalia*, which means the festival of wolf- or dog-men, has even earlier roots in the Arcadian Pan beast-man festival held at Mount Lyceum (from which we get the word and myth of lycanthropy). Part of the worship included much whoopie in the doggie style position.

The symbol of Valentinus was taken to be the heart with an arrow through it which is better understood as a doggie-style view of the yoni with a lingam through it. After all, these dudes knew what a heart looked like. This also answers why the Catholics were so all fired opposed to the doggie style position. It wasn't that they were opposed to the act – it was and is a dearly loved tradition in Rome – they were opposed any infringement on their monopoly and the best way to tell a Gnostic was by their sexual positivism. Remember that the missionary position gets its name from the Catholic church's missionaries, celibate men all, who were compelled to teach various native peoples how to fuck the One Right & True way. There were many different types and cultures of Gnostics, but what happened to them is history at its worst – they were murdered outright, every man, woman and child that the Christian butchers could find.[64]

But the movement didn't die out. Many of the Gnostics were wealthy – part of what made their genocide so attractive – and they were able to pack up and move

---

62 Valentinus was fairly influential in Rome around the first century A.D. and seemed poised for super-stardom. The famous Ptolemy, who codified the stupidest system of astronomy known to man, counted himself among Valentinus' many fans. At the peak of his career, Valentinus was offered an archbishopric in Rome in exchange for his testimony that Roman law and order took precedence over personal enlightenment. It isn't recorded what he said, all we know is that he left town and started a commune in the sticks, freeing up the position for a more viable (or at least buy-able) Christian

63 The two Catholic saints named Valentine were early Christian martyrs known for their grisly deaths and not their sermons.

64 In 1209, thirty-thousand knights and soldiers under the orders of Pope Innocent III stormed the Cathar region of Languedoc and began a massacre in which "neither age nor sex nor status [were] spared." In the city of Bezier, some fifteen thousand men, women, and children took refuge in the church only to be butchered when the commander said, "Kill them all. God will recognize his own." Some eight centuries later this callous blood-lust would become the *de facto* motto of the American forces in Viet Nam.

away to open again under a different name, just like the Nest planned to do after their Palm Springs temple was bombed.[65] As we'll see, this is one of many important common themes that link *Stranger* to the Gnostics. But where did the Gnostics go? Historians have often noted the lineage between the Gnostics, Alchemists, minstrels, Grail legends and Templars; many books have covered the subject – *Holy Blood, Holy Grail* [66] being one of the best.

It suggests that the Gnostics re-emerged as the ill-fated Knights Templar (among other groups) to reprise the familiar Gnostic and pagan theme of the Pope's hit-men whacking the competition. In the early 14th century, Pope Clement and the French King Phillipe raided the Knight's coffers on the pretext of demon worship, they also found, to their surprise, that the Templars had been a hotbed of, you guessed it, Gnostic and pagan revivalism. After the raid, the Templars scattered to prepared safe houses throughout Europe only to spring up again almost immediately as the Teutonic Knights and as the early Masonic orders and rites – some of which openly used Templar imagery.

These groups effectively combined republican and anti-Papist activities with Templar traditions and found much in common with the still practicing pagans of the British Isles. One can't meander too far into any aspect of Western history without being impressed (and often stumped) by the activities of the Gnostics, the Templars, and the Masons. These mysteries continue into the present day. A few hundred years later, a German Masonic group, inspired by the scientific and occult ferment of the 19th century, formed the Ordo Templi Orientis (Order of Oriental Templars).

It was an order held in high esteem even by the very exclusive Scottish Rite masons who were automatically conferred comparable degrees of initiation in the OTO.[67] In the early 1910s, the leader of the OTO accosted Aleister Crowley saying that he had published the great secret of the Templars in his text *The Book of Lies*. He immediately conferred the ninth degree and accordant responsibilities on Crowley, provided some magickal training, eventually made him head of the English Order and finally willed the world-wide Order to him.[68] Crowley later changed the Order to incorporate Thelema and *Liber Legis* and oversaw its pre-WWII worldwide expansion. It was with the Agape Lodge of this OTO that Parsons and Hubbard were associated.[69]

The reason for describing all of this history is that *Stranger* reprises so many of these themes. The Nest is organized around Templar lines, Michael's ideals are clearly Gnostic, and Jubal emerges in later analysis to be of deeply Templar

65 *Stranger*, p. 491-2.

66 *Holy Blood, Holy Grail* by Michael Biagent, Richard Leigh, and Henry Lincoln, Dell Publishing, New York, 1983. This is an delightfully controversial, spell-binding journey through some of the weirdest historical mysteries from the Middle Ages to modern times.

67 *History of the OTO* by William E. Heidrick, OTO, Fairfax, 1986.

68 See the Foreword to *The Book of Lies* by Aleister Crowley, Samuel Weiser, York Beach, ME, 1980. The exact details of this story are the subject of debate, e.g., the text seems to have been *Equinox I:VII* published in 1912, and not *The Book of Lies*.

69 Hubbard was never a member of the OTO. He paid no dues, received no initiations and may not have qualified for membership.

significance. But having also demonstrated that *Stranger* has its place in the body of allegorical works mentioned earlier, let's return to the text of *Stranger* itself and examine some of the puzzles and themes that have kept academics puzzling for the past three decades.

THE DOOR INTO STRANGER

In the last paragraph of the preface to the new version of *Stranger*, Virginia Heinlein departs from her brief history of *Stranger* to mention that the names of the characters have "great importance to the plot. They were carefully selected: Jubal means 'the father of all,' Michael stands for 'Who is like God?' I leave it for the reader to find out what the other names mean."[70]

That's about as subtle a challenge as a gauntlet in the face and it makes one wonder exactly why it was so important for her to mention it. Could it be that she and Robert had wanted someone to connect the dots and decode *Stranger*? Why is this so important now?

Let's go ahead and tackle the names anyway and see what we get. We'll start with Valentine Michael Smith. As Bruce Franklin writes in Robert A. Heinlein: *America through Science Fiction:*[71]

He is: Valentine, both a message of erotic love and a martyred saint; Michael, keeper of the gates of heaven, archangel who leads the heavenly hosts against the forces of evil; Smith, the American everyman. He is also a 'superman' from a culture far in advance of human culture in mysterious ways. And he is unfallen man, the New Adam who has never tasted the fruit of the Tree of Knowledge. He is likened to Dionysus, and later assumes the name of Apollo. Above all, he is the new messiah, re-enacting the crucifixion, destined to save the elect in a mortally diseased world.[72]

As we've shown, Valentine most strongly references the early Gnostic; the martyred saints fit into are another story. Michael is the archangel most closely associated with the Holy Grail, another big yoni symbol, and the elemental plane of water for which Michael has great affinity. There were several early cults to the Archangel Michael that worshipped the sword in the cup. Smith might also refer to another famous Thelemite, Wilfred T. Smith, Parsons' first magickal mentor, who headed the Agape Lodge before Parsons was appointed *magister templi* by Crowley.

Crowley disapproved of Smith who ran a fairly sex-drenched lodge and managed to sprinkle his seed widely in the Thelemic community including siring a child by Parsons' first wife. Although it is unclear why this might offend Crowley (of all people!), he nonetheless conspired to remove Smith and wrote a treatise entitled *Liber Apotheosis 132: The Hidden God*, with which he convinced Smith to retire into

70 Preface to *Stranger*.
71 *Robert A. Heinlein: America through Science Fiction*, Oxford University Press, NY, 1960.
72 Ibid, p. 128.

intense solo magickal research. This last connection may be tenuous to *Stranger*, but Smith seems to have been a remarkably charismatic man with more than a hint of religious huckster, much like the Archbishop Digby character whose Fosterite Church so influences Michael.

As we've shown, the character of Valentine Michael Smith follows Crowley's archetypal retelling of the Dionysus/Bacchus myth which later evolved into the Jesus motif. He also fulfills all but one of the prophecies of *Liber Legis* as the Thelemic messiah who follows, and is heir to, Crowley. (It is interesting to note that Parsons was once widely considered to be Crowley's heir and, as mentioned above, his Babalon Working was designed to invoke yet another heir.) There is another thought here. Ann Lynnworth, a magickal scholar and the author's co-*vivant*, suggests that Messiahs tend to take their functional forms in books: Moses, Jesus, Mohammed, Buddha all appear to the vast majority of their flock on paper. In light of her theory, it is interesting that *Stranger's* impact on society seems to follow along the lines of other Messianic faiths in their early years.[73]

The sole *Liber Legis* prophecy that Michael doesn't answer is that he fails to crack the code in *Liber Legis*.[74] What he does do is to open the New Aeon, the Age of the Magickal Child, by the revealing of the Martian language, which may be isomorphic. It is interesting to note that most of the attempts made to crack the *Liber Legis* code involve some sort of extra-terrestrial connection.[75] Although there is still much more information regarding Valentine Michael Smith, there isn't enough space in this article to cover it. Rather let's move on to examine Ben Caxton, the Winchell reporter.

Most of *Stranger's* Part 4 is devoted to Caxton's description and analysis of his experiences in the Nest and his transformation as a result. Through Caxton, the audience gets a box seat in the consciousness of a man undergoing initiation and apotheosis – not to mention a peek into the inner sanctum of the Gnostic-Templar Nest. His transformation is the very fulcrum of the novel, but who does Caxton represent? In 1910, Crowley staged the Rites of Eleusis at Caxton Hall in London.

According to Crowley, and to many of the regulars who wrote about their experiences first hand, these were initiatory experiences which caused personal evolution in the audience members. A precursor to performance art, the Rites were presented as sacred drama and received mixed, but usually bad reviews. Despite the uneven commentary, the Rites ran successfully until the outbreak of WWI in 1914.

It becomes clear that Ben Caxton, the man, represents the archetypical initiate who passes from well-accomplished manhood to something larger (godhood?)

---

73 From a conversation with Ann Lynnworth.

74 *Liber Legis*, II:76. Ann Lynnworth points out that we cannot know if Michael broke the code unless Heinlein had Michael breaking a code, which he doesn't, or unless we had already broken the code and found the answer elsewhere in *Stranger*. We haven't and the subject remains indeterminate, but doubtful.

75 Recently a Washington state Thelemic scholar, Anthra-Andromeda, published a solution to the code and claimed it heralded an extra-terrestrial Child. And Francis King, one of the most famous British Thelemites claimed Parsons' Babalon working was directly responsible for the flying saucer phenomenon that occurred shortly thereafter. For that matter, a 1907 sketch of an Enochian entity contacted by Crowley looks very similar to the beasties that Whitley Streiber writes about in Communion. Actually there are many compelling links between Crowley, the Enochian work, and UFOs.

through a series of initiations which assist in the realization of higher understandings. The process, often psychically painful, demands rigorous self-examination and the continual testing of the initiate's habitual beliefs. Caxton clearly was the subject of such an initiation. And he clearly crosses through the three Thelemically phases in his transition: a man of the earth, the lover and the hermit. This progression is described in *Liber Legis*[76] and is mirrored in most Thelemic societies.

A few more observations: Ben is Hebrew for "son of" or "heir to" and Caxton certainly winds up as an heir to Michael's fortune thereby becoming something like Jubal's grandson. Historically, there is only one Caxton of note, Britain's first commercial printer, who doesn't seem to have been so important, but the author has seen this Caxton's name on several odd monuments including the facade of Harvard's famous Widener Library so there may be more here than meets the eye.[77]

Moving along, we come to the astrologer, Madame Alexandria Vesant who clearly references the Theosophical Society and Krishnamurti movement co-founder Annie Besant. To grok the Vesant/Besant isomorph, remember that the letters B and V are qabalically equal (from the Hebrew letter Beth – the letter symbolizing magick – which is pronounced either B or V depending on the addition of a dot in its center). To emphasize this point Heinlein spoon feeds his audience a dialogue[78] in which her name is actually spelled out, which may qualify *Stranger* as the world's most blatant Book of Secrets.

Crowley – and most Thelemites to follow – had little patience for the Theosophists,[79] whom he felt were mostly misguided academics, who possessed some laudable inquisitiveness. Vesant, the *Stranger* astrologer who secretly advises the head of state through his domineering wife (Oh, Nancy, just say, Gno!), is portrayed as a well-meaning but mercenary charlatan who accidentally accesses a hidden magickal ability that is later expanded upon when she receives Michael's Martian enlightenment.[80] Next we come to the most complex character in the story, Heinlein's alter ego and the real star of the show, ladies and gentlemen – Jubal Harshaw.

Decoding Jubal is the most exciting part of the puzzle (so far anyway). It is hard to equate Jubal to any historical character, although he references many, and the only hint we have early in the game is Virginia Heinlein's note that Jubal means the "father of all."[81] The biblical Jubal isn't much help[82] although the name does translate roughly from the Hebrew into "father of all".[83] On the surface, *Stranger's* Jubal may

---

76 *Liber Legis*, I 40.

77 A final note is that Edward Bulwer-Lytton, a very popular 19th century author and politician, who wrote extensively about adventure and occult themes and whose ideas inspired many modern fictional and occult authors, wrote a popular novel entitled *The Caxtons* which may have a connection.

78 *Stranger*, p. 128.

79 *Book 4*, p14. Crowley describes Anna Kingsford, another founding Theosophist as being "handicapped by a brain that was a mass of putrid pulp." Nobody ever said he was a nice man.

80 *Stranger*, 481-2. This is one of the niftiest short explanations of astrology you'll ever read.

81 Preface, *Stranger*.

82 The biblical Jubal gets little mention. He is the son of Lamech and Adah and credited as being the inventor of instrumental music.

83 It is interesting to note that Heinlein himself is often referred to not only as the Father of Science Fic-

be paternal and he certainly seems patriarchal, but "Father of All?" Looking deeper, however, there are a few clues in the text that identify Jubal with one of the most striking aspects of the Gnostic-Templar connection. Several times in the text, a horrified Jubal is told that the only accoutrement of note in the minimalist nest is a large hologram of Jubal's head[84] which they revere as the "patron saint of the Church" and of whom Michael says he is the "one who groks all." Many of the nestlings actually worship Jubal, much to his chagrin.[85]

But wait, wasn't there another secret religion that worshipped a sacred head at its center? Indeed, one of the weirdest details to come from the raid on the Templars was that they worshipped a sacred, sometimes bearded, head which was deemed their savior and the fountain of all wisdom. Variations on the theme of a sacred head predate the Templars by thousands of years,[86] and the theme recurs often in later Templar imitators. The head was worshipped in various ways and referred to by the names Mahomet and Baphomet. Mahomet seems to derive from the Greek word for '[first] principle' or 'source' and has a history of Gnostic use. Mahomet was also contemporarily used as a word meaning simply idol, and some of the more rabid anti-Moslems of the time tried to link the word to Mohammed, accusing the Templars of collaboration with the hated Saracens.[87]

Baphomet, however, was by far the head's most common appellation and has been translated in various ways. The Moorish Spanish – the Moors were Islamic, Arabic-speaking Northern Africans who occupied Spain for several centuries and ranged far enough north to put the Black in the Black Irish – had a word *bufihimat* (pronounced *abufihamet* in the Arabic) which means "father [source] of knowledge [wisdom]".[88]

Another possible derivation is from the Greek *baphe metis*, which means "baptism of wisdom" which led some theorists to suggest the Templars were a survival of a John the Baptist cult, since John's beheading could easily have been iconized in the manner of Jesus' crucifixion. The most widely accepted translation is that of a code. Spelled backwards (backwards spelling being common in occult works), Baphomet stands for three abbreviations, *tem, oph, ab*, which enlarge to "Templi omnium hominum pacis abhas" or "the father of the temple of universal peace among men."[89]

---

tion, but also as a personal father figure for many people. In a collection of Heinlein memoria gathered shortly after his death and published as *The Man Who Sold America: Heinlein in Dementia*, edited by D.S. Black, Atlantis Press, San Francisco, 1988, many of the contributors begin be saying Heinlein was the father they never had. It seems Heinlein never had any children of his own, although the dedication of Grumbles is "For Heinlein's Children".

84 *Stranger*, p. 416. After the nest is bombed, Caxton tells Jubal that Michael salvaged only the important things through apportation including a special Martian typewriter, some clothes, some cash, and the hologram of Jubal's head.

85 *Stranger*, p. 477-8.

86 For example, several linguistic clues in *Stranger* point back to biblical mentions of Carmel whose ancient name was Rosh Kadesh, or Sacred Head.

87 *Encyclopedia of Paranormal and Supernatural*, p. 159-60.

88 *Holy Blood, Holy Grail*, p. 83.

89 *Transcendental Magic*, Eliphas Levi, p. 258.

If this sounds precocious for an abbreviation, remember that even fancier abbreviations were common before the advent of typewriters. And there's more... Baphomet survives as a major inspiration in many occult groups that follow. Different likenesses, some stemming from Templar days (and before?) are used, the most common being a (bearded) head[90] or goat's head and an allegorical portrait of an androgynous beast-man that combines aspects of goat, dog, ass and man – Eliphas Levi's rendering is perhaps the most famous example. After popping up in numerous places in Western history, Aleister Crowley adopts the name Baphomet, and the Templar seal, upon assuming the leadership of the OTO, which, the reader remembers, is allegedly the 20th century survival of the original Templars.[91]

But there's still one level deeper. Baphomet is clearly an *eidolon*[92] of the Arcadian Pan who was the major deity of the Lupercalia, the inspiration of the Greek educated Valentinus, the goat- or horned god revered by both Gnostics and pagans, and, seemingly, the inspiration of the Templars. But the Pan we're talking about isn't the simple satyr that most sanitized Christianized accounts allow, Pan of Arcadia is none other than Bacchus and Dionysus. He is called Pangenitor, the "father of all" and Panphage "the eater (grokker?) of all," and is perceived as the wild, lusty, natural, chaotic intelligence that exists beyond our linguistically enforced illusion of reality. He is symbolized by the goat man or a bearded head. Pan is a favorite of Thelemites who, like the god, deem it holy to "[u]nite passionately with every other form of consciousness, thus destroying the sense of separateness from the Whole."[93] One of Crowley's most moving poems, and dynamic invocations, is the *Hymn to Pan*. Parsons, writing after the Babalon Working, conceives of Babalon as the female eidolon of Pan. Pan and Baphomet are also the principle deities for the Chaos Magick movement, a modern offshoot of Thelema.[94]

To recap: we have a clear indication that Jubal is Baphomet and that Baphomet is translated in several interesting ways using several languages but always with the same meaning which is "source [or] father of all (wisdom)", an attribute which Michael often ascribes to Jubal.[95] But there is still one more level of meaning, and

---

90 Alchemists, for example, refer to a phase called caput mortuum or 'dead head' – Hey, Jerry Garcia! – which precedes the precipitation of the philosophers stone. And, *Zardoz* is a Qabalistically inspired allegorical film of the mid-70s (starring Sean Connery) which features a large flying head that holds a remarkable number of meanings.

91 *History of the OTO*

92 Eidolon is a technical magickal term which means an attribute that references a deity but does not encompass that deity's essence. For example, the Magus Card, Loki, fiber optic impulses, and the Trickster, are eidolons of a god called Mercury. Each of these attributes evoke hermetic energy; none of them capture his essence. A second meaning is a mask or alias that a god may choose.

93 From a widely circulated essay entitled *Duty* by Crowley. The theme of passionate union with all aspects of creation and its connection with Pan is common and appears in much the same language in a number of Thelemic works. It stems from a *Liber Legis* passage in which the goddess Nuit, who is all of creation, describes herself in quantum terms and adds: "...I am divided for love's sake for the chance of union. This is the creation of the world, that the pain of division is as nothing, and the joy of dissolution all." (*Liber Legis* I:29-30)

94 For more on Chaos Magick, read *Liber Null & Psychonaut*, by Peter J. Carroll, Samuel Weiser, 1987, 1991. Check out the Baphomet essay, p. 156-61.

95 This is an amazing example of literary punning. Jubal is the 'father of all' in four languages and a code

all the sweeter for its blatancy. Towards the end of *Stranger*, when Vesant, who calls Jubal "an old goat," asks for Jubal's birth information for a horoscope, he replies: "I was born on three successive days..."[96] This is a very odd sentence, particularly as a snappy comeback, since it involves the obsolete British term 'successive;' and Heinlein usually writes pure American. What was he up to? Compare this odd sentence from *Stranger* to the very first sentence in the introduction to *Liber Legis* which reads, "This book was dictated... on three successive days..."[97]

That's one hell of a connection. It means that Jubal equals Baphomet and that the 'source of all wisdom' equals 'the source of Thelema.' Or in other words, Jubal is the recapitulation – or even the source – of Thelema! As we pointed out however, *Liber Legis* is the source of Thelema. It is a channelled text, and its author, mentioned in the second sentence of the introduction, is an entity named Aiwass. Does he connect to all of this? In commentaries to *Liber Legis* collected in *The Law Is For All*,[98] Crowley considered Aiwass to be Baphomet. Thus Heinlein was saying that Jubal Harshaw alias Aiwass alias Baphomet alias Panphage Pangenitor, is the embodiment of Thelema, indeed the source of Thelema and the "father of all." This statement, made over the course of *Stranger* connects modern Thelema with its vast cultural legacy, its miraculous future and its 'hereditary' connection to another realm of reality. Holy Cosmic Trigger, Batman!

COROLLARY OBSERVATIONS

We're awfully close to understanding Heinlein's motives now. We've proven the link of Thelema and *Stranger*, and the link between Heinlein and Thelema. The text of *Stranger* meets the criteria for allegory and is loaded with puzzles which clearly reference magickal and Thelemic themes. But there are two remaining areas for discussion that are particularly important for this article's proof. One is Heinlein's first hand familiarity with Thelemic societies and the other is the link between *Stranger* and the Babalon Working.

Historically, Heinlein was never a member of the OTO, although he certainly may have seen the Gnostic Mass as it was open to the public. Yet his description of the people and events in the nest are oddly reminiscent of life in secret Thelemic communities. One of the first things one notices about practicing Thelemites is their radiant good health and physical charisma. In fact, there are many stories told about people becoming involved with Thelema because they had met several Thelemites and were amazed at how healthy, calm, productive and, well, 'lucky'

---

to boot! Nice footwork. Also note that punning and multi-level, hidden humor are usually indicators in this kind of research that you're on the right track.
96 *Stranger*, p. 499.
97 *Liber Legis*, Introduction 1.
98 *The Law Is For All*, Falcon Press, Phoenix, AZ, 1986, p. 79. 99 The modern OTO is not the only Thelemic society, although it is the largest single group and the source of much wonderful scholarship. It is however a public organization. There are many other secret Thelemic groups scattered all over the world, some of which have been in continuous operation for more than fifty years. Most of these observations apply to the secret societies.

these Thelemites were. Heinlein certainly makes note of the apparent increases in mental and physical health among members of the nest..

The second aspect of nest life that Heinlein mentions is the calm, synchronized, unhurried, efficient movement one finds among some Thelemites.[99] When this author first experienced the strange sense of unconscious choreography in a Thelemic lodge, the description from *Stranger* leapt to mind. It is a fascinating phenomenon and one not encountered elsewhere. It is a particularly odd observation to make about a 'cult' since, in this author's experience, most members of alternative religions are enormously, even willfully disorganized. (It is said that managing pagans is like herding cats.)

Finally, the social life in secret Thelemic communities often centers around food, work and deep play with no wasted time, exactly as portrayed in the nest. Heinlein paints an exceptionally accurate picture of an eminently healthy, vibrant people and their pleasant comings and goings, shared mealtimes, and oddly synchronized spontaneity. This precisely Thelemic picture seems improbable for him to have deduced without having been involved with a magickal community. The question is: Which one? None of the Thelemic communities or scholars this author has approached remember Heinlein as more than a terrific writer. Indeed, most are surprised by the Thelemic connection. Here is another area for research.

This recalls Heinlein's link with Parsons. As a part of the Babalon Working, Parsons 'received' a short 'book' entitled *Liber 49* or *The Book of Babalon*. Parsons claims it was the fourth chapter to *Liber Legis*, a claim which made him less than popular with Crowley and the OTO. Regardless of this claim, it is a powerful text that deals mostly with the coming of the Thelemic heir. There are two parts in particular that stand out after reading *Stranger*. The first is part of the channeled instructions to Parsons for the ritual – it advises him to clear his mind in preparation: "Consult no book but thine own mind. Thou art god. Behave at this altar as one god before another."[100]

It is interesting to note that these words were mouthed, not by Parsons, but by his Scribe, L. Ron Hubbard, who was close friends with Heinlein at about the same time the latter was working on his first shot at *Stranger*. The other Babalon Working quote which stands out, and there are many quotes which are not so overt, comes from *Liber 49* which Parsons channeled alone out in the desert – e.g., sans Hubbard:

37. For I am BABALON, and she my daughter, unique, and there shall be no other women like her. 38. In My Name shall she have all power, and all men and excellent things, and kings and captains and the secret ones at her command. 39. The first servants are chosen in secret, by my force in her – a captain, a lawyer, an agitator, a rebel – I shall provide.

Of course, throughout *Stranger*, Michael's first friends, later referred to as the "First

---

99 *Stranger*, p. 475-6.
100 *The Collected Works of Jack Parsons*, OTO, NY from the *First Ritual of the Book of Babalon*.

Called," line up in exactly that order. Captain Von Tromp of the Challenger, is the first character one meets in *Stranger*. Jubal Harshaw is an invaluable attorney to Michael as well as part time MD, and full time Baphomet. Ben Caxton is a Winchell reporter and professional fly in the ointment who mobilizes *Stranger* by using Michael as a lever with the current administration. Gillian Boardman is a nurse who literally tosses her career away to steal Michael out from under the noses of Federation Security. *Liber 49* predicts that the magickal child will have powers and guidance from beyond to assist through the early years. This seems to track with *Stranger* in the way that Michael shows an uncanny knack for attracting good people and having events roll his way and is even observed by Jubal Harshaw and others throughout the book.

All of this brings us back to one big question: Why? In Heinlein's letters he claimed that besides making money and entertaining his readers, he wanted them to think, to ask questions.[101] But that doesn't add up. Heinlein was a great writer; he could have asked all of these questions without all the codes. The answer must lie elsewhere.

So let's review: Heinlein is involved in a secret Thelemic society composed of artists, writers, scientists, and other advanced and odd minded folk. Their magick works, their lives are transformed and it is time to transmit their message to a vast number of people who desperately need to evolve. There is no interest in repeating the 'burning times' of their spiritual forebears, who rose up, were murdered, and rose again like some ontological Phoenix. And, to make matter worse, the gods had somehow selected Crowley as the channel for their newest batch of goodies only to see Crowley (and his followers) spectacularly martyred in one of the most vicious press assassinations of our century.

There was only one thing to do. We had done it many times before: Go into hiding and open up under a new name. And that is exactly what Heinlein did. He designed *Stranger* to be a magickal seed containing the spiritual and intellectual DNA of Thelema, which he placed into the fertile loam of his times, sowing a crop which includes the neo-pagan, ecosophical, sexual and consciousness movements – not to mention much of the current trend in Thelema. For any who cared to track his ideas, Heinlein encoded many additional lessons. And he included enough clues so that, some day, as a healthy, vibrant race of magickal women and men prepared to take to the stars, they'd come to know that the man who continued the sacred lineage of Valentinus, the Gnostics and the Templars, and who nursed it through the 20th century, the "man who sold the stars" was none other than, the 'father of us all', Robert Anson Heinlein.

---

101 Grumbles, p. 285.

A Preface to The Scented Garden

Emory Cranston

This text was originally commissioned as an introduction to a new and illustrated edition of Aleister Crowley's The Scented Garden *– an edition that may still be forthcoming... – Ed.*

This book is a long elaborate painstaking faked-up joke in very poor taste, parody of a typical 19th century scholarly translation from Arab or Persian literature –but containing as many scabrous references to anal sex as Crowley could think up or lift from authentic sources.

Readers who share neither AC's sexual tastes nor his peculiar sense of humor might well marvel at all the energy expended here in boisterous obscenity and deliberate blasphemy. We might forget the Victorian atmosphere of 1910 – still prudish enough to be shockable – and wonder why a brilliant occultist like Crowley would expend such effort to such an end. The bourgeoisie just isn't as *épater*-able as it used to be; the fun seems to have gone out of crude obscenities about Anglican priests and colonial sodomites.

Of course nowadays we do not burn books (unless they belong to OCCUPY WALL STREET!); this book was however indeed burnt – to AC's eternal merit. And we postmoderns seem to share with AC's contemporaries a certain squeamishness about our social values. His casual racism and phallicism will offend contemporary readers in much the same way his buggery and paganism shocked those Edwardian Customs officials. *The Scented Garden* will no doubt still seem offensive even in centuries to come. In this sense it must be deemed a success.

AC's boasts about the supposed spiritual inner meanings of the text will at first appear as more "satire". Robert Anton Wilson used to point out that Crowley was a kind of proto-Lenny Bruce. (Certainly the transcript of the court case between Crowley and Mathers for control of the London Golden Dawn Temple is one of the funniest things I've ever read.) We must not underestimate his capacity for either heavy irony or adolescent buffoonery.

But even so... Crowley was on some level a deeply serious occultist and even mystic – and it's hard to believe he'd waste so much time over a 137-page dirty joke. Is it possible he was telling the truth when he claimed that an esoteric hermeneutics would reveal some profound hidden meaning in the text?

AC knew enough Persian to read actual Persian poetry, but the main sources for *The Scented Garden* appear to be secondary: especially Sir Richard Burton's *Arabian Nights* and its infamous "terminal essay" on the "Sotadic Zone" – a text which is more

Arab than Persian. Other influences might be sought in Lane's *Modern Egyptians* and various other works by British scholars in England and India; FitzGerald's *Omar – etc.* I suspect he might've known Wilberforce-Clarke's awful translation of Hafez. Clearly he did not know of such works as Tifashi's *The Delights of Hearts*, which is as bawdy and queer as anything Crowley ever wrote, and would have delighted him. Oddly enough he does not mention the greatest of all Arab pederast poets, Abu Nuwas, although Burton's *Nights* is full of anecdotes about him and even some of his erotic poetry. Abu Nuwas is almost never mystical; there's usually nothing allegorical about his male beloveds, although he is sometimes capable of religious sentiment as well as Crowleyesque Satanism.

It also seems clear that AC had not really penetrated to the Persian Sufi school of "Witness Play" (*shahed-bazi*) – a ritual and poetic path of mystical pederasty – as exemplified by such figures as Ahmad Ghazzali, Shamsoddin Tabrizi, Awhad Kermani, or the great Jami. Crowley does mention Saadi, who devoted a chapter of his *Gulistan* ("rose garden") to Witness Play, but Crowley seems unaware that an important and widespread school of Sufism had already explored the formal possibilities of what might be called homoerotic tantra. No doubt Crowley had come across a few *ghazals* on the theme (since it would be impossible not to) but his genius intuited a great deal of the doctrine from these few shards and fragments of the whole.

The Arabo-Persian genre of obscenity (Abu Nuwas, Ahmad al-Tifashi, the *1001 Nights*, etc.) is almost never mixed with the genre of mystical pederasty. The latter is based on conventions of chaste love and gazing, longing and separation,(neo) platonic highmindedness. It is never pornographic. Of course many Sufis no doubt obeyed the Shariah and never made love to a youth or touched a bottle of wine, even during their sessions of sacred music where shaykhs like Iraqi "tore the shirts" of the young dancers and kissed them. A dervish from Damascus, who was once arrested and interrogated by that arch-bigot Ibn Taymiyya, boasted that when he kissed his lover he kissed God. "And did you go any farther than that?" "So what if we did?" answered the Sufi.

I know of no Islamic poet who ever combined the Obscene with the Mystical in the way AC has attempted in *The Scented Garden*. (Abu Nuwas has a *rubai/quatrain* very close to Omar Khayyam's famous "wilderness were Paradise enow", which could be construed as sufiistic – but *rubaiyyat* tend to "wander", and the poem in question may have been attributed to Abu Nuwas simply because it mentions "a willing boy" along with wine, bread, kebabs and the usual garden.)

Where then did Crowley get the idea of hiding esoteric teachings beneath bawdy obscenities? We need look no farther than his hero Rabelais, the original Abbé de Thélème. The Hermetic aspects of *Gargantua and Pantagruel* may be invisible to modern readers, but Rabelais's contemporaries and followers saw them clearly. Take for instance the *Fantastic Tales* of Béroalde de Verville, a 17th century Pantagruelian gallimaufry translated by the great fantasist Arthur Machen (London 1923), who was himself a member of the Golden Dawn. Oddly enough Machen himself missed the Hermetic infrastructure of the book and saw only its libertine exterior. Rabelaisan alchemy can be summed up as a proto-tantrik revaluation of excess and pleasure – precisely AC's "hidden message" in *The Scented Garden*.

Although not an expert on Crowley's magical doctrine, I suspect that *The Garden* may contain yet another Hermetic layer besides its sufiish pantheism. The long list of demons in the *Note to Poem II* – references to Cornelius Agrippa – a few throwaway lines here and there in the footnotes – may point to certain specific rites of sex magick as practiced by the O.T.O. and/or the A.A., perhaps based on legends of the Templars, their ritual sodomy and affiliations with Islamic heresy.

Contra-natural sex rites handed down from early Syro-Egyptian Gnostics such as Carpocrates or the Ophites may have been preserved or rediscovered by Occidental occultists, and reinterpreted in the light of Hindu and Buddhist Tantra, long since familiar to Western scholars. My guess is that these rites probably took on their modern form in 18th century Germany, France and England (where for example the Hellfire Club was a famous and not very serious manifestation), probably in circles devoted to Rosicrucian and Templar Masonry. Crowley's Parisian contemporary Sâr Péladan practised a heterosexual version (or so we infer from his novels) whereas homosexual variants seem to have arisen in Germany.

Western occultism of this sort is always infected to some degree with small-s satanism, if only because the Church itself has repressed all religious forms of sexuality so severely. The same holds true for some of the Sufis; Ahmad Ghazzali was a pioneer of Witness Play and also a "Defender of Iblis" (as the perfect monotheist and lover of God). This School centered in Baghdad and included also Mansur al-Hallaj the martyr as well as Ghazzali's followers. It influenced the "folk Satanism" of the Yazidis and Ahl-e Shaytan of the Iraq-Iran hinterlands and Kurdish mountains.

Indian Tantra – which almost always appears as heterosexual – also involves "demon worship", not just of Shiva and Kali (who looked like outright devils to Christians and Moslems) but also a huge cast of ghouls and afreets. Bengali Tantra (which I've studied) especially contains both exalted mysticism and plain old black magic – just like AC's cult of sex magick.

Finally *The Scented Garden* can be seen as an archetypal work of literary modernism. In that dim golden far-off haze of 1910 (just before the 20th century took its fatal turn toward total apocalyptic war) modernism was still entwined with Decadence and Symbolism, and therefore often took the form of pastiche. The fake translation was already a Romantic tradition (Ossian) as was the homage to (or serious parody of) Oriental literature (Goethe, Poe, J. Clarence Mangan, Emerson, etc.). Queerness itself (re)appeared as a form of modernism with Wilde and Proust. Even heterosexuals like Swinburne or J-K Huysmans seemed somehow "queer".

If we read Crowley's text keeping all four or five of its "levels" simultaneously in mind, *The Scented Garden*, which at first seemed like a book-length shaggy dog joke scrawled on the wall of a Gents' Lav in Piccadilly Circus, will at last begin to make some sense as the crypto-exegesis of a "spiritual pleasure", just as its author (all four or five of him) intended.

Benares, '13

THOU SHALT KEEP NOT BACK ONE DROP: ALEISTER CROWLEY AND EROTIC SUBMISSION TO THE DIVINE

Manon Hedenborg-White

Thou shalt drain out thy blood that is thy life into the golden cup of her fornication. Thou shalt mingle thy life with the universal life. Thou shalt keep not back one drop. Then shall thy brain be dumb, and thy heart beat no more, and all thy life shall go from thee; and thou shalt be cast out upon the midden, and the birds of the air shall feast upon thy flesh, and thy bones shall whiten in the sun. ... And the angels shall lay thy dust in the City of the Pyramids, and the name thereof shall be no more.
                                                                    – Liber Cheth

And it is an ecstasy in which there is no trace of pain. Its passivity (=passion) is like the giving-up of the self to the beloved.
                          – The Vision & the Voice, the Cry of the 2nd Aethyr

INTRODUCTION AND PURPOSE

The above quotes from the writings of Aleister Crowley (1875-1947) both refer to the act of mystical union with the divine. In order to attain to this mystery (according to Crowley's magical system), the adept must cross the Abyss – a void of meaningless delusion – and shatter her individuality in order to become one with all. Key to this process is the goddess Babalon, conceptualised as a sacred whore who will receive everyone into her cup provided they are willing to pay the price: that of the individual ego.

Taken together, the above excerpts may seem contradictory. The first outlines a daunting act of self-sacrifice and the utter annihilation of the adept, to the point where she is reduced to a pile of dust. The second quote, however, seems instead reassure the adept that there is nothing to fear from this process, which is actually analogous to the (generally speaking) more pleasurable act of surrendering one's self in sexual union with the beloved. The two quotes also indicate a sort of paradox in Crowley's philosophy: although his magical system and religion Thelema (the Greek word for "will") is strongly focused on developing and honing individual willpower, Crowley's poetic writings and magical practice also emphasised the ideal of self-annihilation in the infinite and union with the divine. As Crowley often likened this process to sexual union, it is perhaps unsurprising that he appears to have believed practical erotic submission to possess a particular kind of power to put the seeker in touch with divinity.

The purpose of this article is to analyse the use of erotic submission for the purposes of engaging with the divine in Crowley's sexual magic. Rather than viewing Crowley's engagement in submission simply as an antinomian strategy, a personal sexual preference, or a peculiar expression of a sadistic will to power over others, I will argue that a more nuanced understanding of Crowley's submissive magic against the backdrop of his magical system is necessary. The tension between will to power and emphasis on the cultivation of discipline and the deep-seated longing for ecstatic surrender in Crowley's magical career is mirrored in several of his writings on erotic submission that portray the process varyingly as brutally violent and blissfully exquisite, sometimes simultaneously.

DEFINITIONS AND DEMARCATIONS

In this article, I will make use of the terms "BDSM", "occultism", "sexual magic", and "submission".[1] By occultism, I mean a form of post-Enlightenment, largely de-Christianised Western esotericism that is characterised, among other things, by a strong emphasis on personal experience and a form of intuitive knowledge (gnosis).[2] By sexual magic, I mean the use of ritualised sex in occultism, for the purposes of causing change (whether for spiritual or material goals) in accordance with the will of the magician.[3]

BDSM is an acronym for Bondage-Discipline (BD), Dominance-Submission (DS), and Sadism-Masochism (SM).[4] Taylor and Ussher propose the following definition of the term, based on a discourse analytical study of how practitioners make sense of their sexual practice:

> *[BD]SM is best understood as comprising those behaviours which are characterized by a contrived, often symbolic, unequable distribution of power involving the giving and/or receiving of physical and/or psychological stimulation. It often involves acts which would generally be considered as 'painful' and/or humiliating or subjugating, but which are consensual and for the purpose of sexual arousal, and are understood by the participant to be [BD]SM.*

---

1 While I understand that the term BDSM is anachronistic when applied to early 20th century occultism, I prefer it to its predecessor "sadomasochism", as the latter is normative and connected to psychiatric and medical discourse classifying the phenomenon as pathological and practitioners as psychologically damaged.

2 Hanegraaff, 'Western Esotericism'.

3 Cf Bogdan, 'Challenging the Morals'. Hugh B. Urban defines sexual magic as 'the explicit use of orgasm ... as a means to create magical effects in the modern world'. I prefer the above stated definition as it does not have the same strict focus on orgasm. See Urban, *Magia Sexualis*.

4 It is important to understand that this term does not denote a fixed sexual identity, but is rather an umbrella term for a group of sexual practices that 'display a sufficient degree of similarity and specificity to be set apart' (Hanegraaff, 'Western Esotericism') for analytical purposes.

While this definition is useful as it highlights the complexity of the phenomenon and is grounded in practitioners' experiences, it is not ideal for an analysis of early 20th century occultism. Although Freud coined the term *sadomasochism* in 1905, thus in a sense articulating it as a distinguishable form of sexual expression,[5] the term had negative connotations and it unlikely that practitioners would have used the term as a positive form of self-identification. Therefore, I will be disregarding the part of Taylor and Ussher's definition that stipulates that practitioners themselves must understand their sexual practices as BDSM in order for it to qualify.

While sexual arousal and climax may be a side-effect of the operation, this need not be the sole or ultimate purpose of occult BDSM. Like in the case of sexual magic, it is a truism to state that an in order for a BDSM scene to qualify as 'occult', it must be conducted at least partly with some other purpose in mind than mere pleasure.[6] This article will thus be guided by an understanding of occult BDSM as comprising those behaviours which are 'characterised by a contrived, often symbolic, unequable distribution of power involving the giving and/or receiving of physical and/or psychological stimulation', often involving 'acts or modes of behaviour which would generally be considered as "painful" and/or humiliating or subjugating, but which are consensual', which are thought to be able to induce altered states of consciousness suitable for accessing superhuman intelligences or realms and/or affect change in accordance with the magician's will, and which are given meaning within an erotic discourse. It is crucial to the argument of this article that the other party to whom the submissive choses to yield need not be corporeal, and that submission can thus also entail surrender to a metaphysical force or being that is perceived as superior.

My analysis will focus primarily on one particular figure in the history of occult BDSM, in order to show how BDSM practice is used to provide access to the divine in modern occultism. Needless to say, this article does not exhaust the topic of occult BDSM. In fact, it does not even cover all uses of BDSM techniques in *fin-de-siècle* and early to mid-20th century occultism, as is surely evident from my lack of mention of, for instance, the use of the scourge and cord in Gardnerian Wicca, or Maria de Naglowska's (1883-1936) Rite of Hanging, through which a second-degree member of her magical order ascended to the third (and highest) degree. The rite consisted of a ritual hanging, during which the rope was cut just in time to save the initiate's life, followed by ritual intercourse between the (male) initiate and his priestess.[7] Furthermore, an in-depth analysis of the collection of recent writings on occult BDSM lie outside of the scope of this article,[8] and I hope that future research will delve deeper into these topics.

In Crowley's writings, as in those of de Naglowska and Gardner, BDSM practice

5 Freud, 'Three Essays'. Cf Foucault, 'History of Sexuality', on homosexuality.
6 This is also confirmed by the existent literature on both Pagan and occult BDSM. See list of references for further details.
7 Naglowska, *Hanging Mystery Initiation;* Gardner, *Book of Shadows.* It is worth noting that Hans Thomas Hakl believes it to be improbable that the Rite of Hanging was ever conducted in practice. Hakl, *Theory and Practice of Sexual Magic,* 472-473.
8 See e.g. Kaldera, *Dark Moon Rising;* Grey, *Red Goddess;* Ellwood & Lupa, *Kink Magic;* Schreck & Schreck, *Demons of the Flesh;* Dawn & Flowers, *Carnal Alchemy;* Hunter, *Rites of Pleasure.*

emerges not primarily as a way of indulging specific sexual tastes (though a penchant for such sexual practices may increase the extent to which one advocates or engages in it) or a method for coping with mental anguish or tormenting others (although it may simultaneously have filled such a function), but as a series of related techniques used both to access and enhance one's inner divine faculties as well as to enter into closer communication with externalised deities. In this sense, Crowley's practice of ritualised submission highlights some of the most fascinating paradoxes of his magical system, working alternately and sometimes simultaneously to strengthen one's own sovereignty and to put oneself at the mercy of others.

REPELLENT AND ALLURING:
TRANSGRESSIVE SEXUALITY AND THE FIN-DE-SIÈCLE

The post-Victorian years saw a strong counter-reaction against the prudish hypocrisy of the 19th century, a rejection of repressive sexual morals and a morbid fascination for the most controversial forms of sexual expression such as homosexuality and masturbation. As Michel Foucault has noted, Victorian and late-Victorian society was thus characterised by an obsession with, rather than a suppression of, sexuality. A particularly colourful expression of this phenomenon is the first literature on practical sexual magic, which emerged around this time. Like Crowley, its authors often positioned themselves in opposition to what was perceived as the repressive sexual morals of Christianity.[9]

This period also witnessed a wave of interest in deviant and uncontrollable sensuality, which was depicted as simultaneously repellent and alluring. Crowley reflected this conflicted attitude as well as anyone, and we shall come to see that this tension between fearful apprehension and wistful yearning is also mirrored in his attitudes towards submission. In a broader sense, this cultural ambivalence regarding sexuality was also reflected in the Decadent movement, of which Austrian author Leopold von Sacher-Masoch's (1836-1895) *Venus in Furs* is of particular relevance to this article. The novel tells the story of Severin, a young aristocrat who becomes infatuated with a beautiful widow by the name of Wanda von Dujanew and proceeds to become her slave. At first, Wanda agrees only reluctantly to their arrangement and Severin must convince her repeatedly that by dominating him she is fulfilling his innermost desires. However, both Severin and Wanda vacillate between feelings of excitement and repulsion at their relationship throughout the narrative. The title, *Venus in Furs,* indicates a central theme throughout the book: that of Wanda as a deified figure, a goddess who is both heavenly and satanic. Severin depicts his relationship with her as simultaneously exquisite and torturous; while he idealises and worships her, he also describes the sense of having sold his soul to the devil.[10]

Scholars have shown how the discourse on dangerous sexuality around the turn of the century time influenced Crowley's ideas.[11] Homosexuality, prostitution

---

9 Bogdan, 'Challenging the Morals'.
10 Sacher-Masoch, *Venus in Furs*. Cf Faxneld, *Satanic Feminism*.
11 Urban, *Magia Sexualis;* Nilsson, 'Scharlakansröda gudinnan'.

and non-monogamy were seen as threats to the bourgeois ideal of the married heterosexual couple.[12] Crowley's magical system both reproduced and subverted these cultural taboos through sacralisation and connection to the divine. In Crowley's mental universe, the god Pan (heralded among the Romantic poets of the 19th century as an embodiment of "merry England") is seen as a savage, same-sex lover, homosexual sex magic represents the highest degree in the O.T.O., and the stigma of promiscuity, prostitution and the *femme fatale* are cast in a new light through the image of the goddess Babalon. This transmutation of something ostensibly threatening (in this case in the eyes of bourgeois society) into something sacred and worthy of worship is emblematic of his magical system and, as we will see, is also mirrored in his attitude towards submission.

Crowley's writings and ritual work with both Pan and Babalon as well as with the Holy Guardian Angel reflect the theme of erotic submission to the divine that is hinted at in Sacher-Masoch's novel, with a similar sense of mingled fear and relief. Whether or not this work or similar literature affected his thoughts on the matter is a subject for another study, however, it is reasonable to assume that Crowley, being extremely well-read, was familiar with the book.

While the possible literary influences on Crowley's views on erotic submission exceed the scope of this article, fiction has had an unquestionable influence on the development of BDSM. In many cases, fictional accounts seem to have preceded and given birth to the real-life expressions. Examples include the terms 'masochism' and 'sadism', respectively derived from Sacher-Masoch and the Marquis de Sade, and the triskelion, derived from the ring that the protagonist of Pauline Réage's *Story of O* receives upon her initiation as a submissive into an elite society where she is taught to serve its male members sexually, which is today common symbol of the BDSM subculture. More recently, the publication of E.L. James' immensely popular *50 Shades of Grey*-trilogy has resulted in a sales boost in erotic shops as well as the creation of new lines of lingerie and sex toys. In short, it is not unreasonable to assume that the idea of the dominant as a deified tyrant and, conversely, the deity as a sexual dominant may have appeared in Crowley's mind not only as a result of the preoccupation with deviant sexuality during his lifetime, but also through the influence of a particular cultural motif.

POLARITY AND AMBIVALENCE: CROWLEY, SEX, AND MAGIC

Crowley was raised by conservative, evangelical parents, and grew up with a deep-seated hatred of the repressive sexual morals of his upbringing that bred a strong commitment to mocking and transgressing the norms of bourgeois Christianity. As demonstrated above, he entered the world of occultism at a time of intensified discourse around sexuality, particularly in its counter-normative expressions. The bourgeoning literary genre of books on sexual magic, as well as Crowley's own ideas about sexuality and its importance for spiritual transformation, both reflect and

---

12 Laskar, *Heterosexualitetens historia.*

partake in this development.[13]

Crowley began experimenting with sexual magic in his mid-30's, but did not develop any real theory of sexual magic prior to his involvement with the Ordo Templi Orientis, an initiatory fraternity founded by former Theosophist Theodor Reuss (1855-1923) in the early 20th century. Modelled on Freemasonry, the object of O.T.O. was, according to its founder, to teach the secret of sexual magic, which he believed to be the key to all masonic and hermetic systems. In 1913, Reuss allegedly approached Crowley and accused him of revealing the Order's secrets of sexual magic in his *The Book of Lies*. Crowley denied having done so, stating that he was not privy to the secrets he was claimed to have exposed. Having indicated the relevant passages in the book, Reuss conferred upon Crowley the IX°, swearing him to secrecy.[14] Crowley subsequently began exploring sexual magic in a more systematised way, and sexuality came to receive an increasingly central position in his philosophy.

In its simplest form, Crowley's sexual magic is based on the notion that orgasm creates breakages in normal consciousness that enable the magician to cause change in accordance with will. During a sex magical operation, the practitioner focuses his or her intentions on a desired goal, which is charged with ecstatic energy by means of sexual arousal and dispatched at the point of climax.[15] Crowley's sex magical theories draw largely on the teachings of P.B. Randolph and the Hermetic Brotherhood of Luxor, and are mainly based around Western esoteric, primarily alchemical, symbolism.[16] Crowley used sex magic to achieve concrete this-worldly aims, such as money, as well as for the purposes of initiation and exploring the divine.

Crowley's cosmology posits a universe constructed out of gendered, that is, male (active) and female (receptive/passive) forces constantly striving for union, a process that is often portrayed in sexual terms.[17] The notion of femininity as passive and masculinity as active is prosaically reflected in some of Crowley's magical instructions, in which he states that a woman's chief purpose in magic is to serve as a vessel and tool for the male magician.[18] While such passages have (perhaps not unreasonably) lead to him being regarded as sexist by some contemporary scholars and occultists,[19] it must be stressed that his actual magical practice did not always conform to this pattern. As I hope to demonstrate below, women sometimes took on very active roles in his rituals, and Crowley sometimes assumed a passive role in rituals aimed at exploring the divine. Furthermore, some of Crowley's principal

---

13 Foucault, 'History of Sexuality'.

14 Bogdan, 'Challenging the Morals'.

15 Crowley, 'Energized Enthusiasm', cf Bogdan, 'Challenging the Morals'.

16 Bogdan, 'Challenging the Morals'.

17 See e.g. Crowley, 'Liber XV'; Crowley, *Liber AL*. The notion of gender polarity has captivated a number of the most influential practitioners of sexual magic in Western esotericism during the 20th century. See e.g. Naglowska, 'Sacred Rite'; Evola, 'Eros and the Mysteries'; Gardner, *Book of Shadows* and *Meaning of Witchcraft*; LaVey, *The Satanic Witch*.

18 See e.g. Crowley, *Liber Aleph*, 171.

19 For scholarly critique, see Urban, 'Magia Sexualis'. For occultist critique e.g. Williams, *Woman Magician*; Lupa, 'Female Kink Magician', Schreck & Schreck, *Demons of the Flesh*.

poetic writings also idealise the notion of erotic submission to a deified lover in a sense that challenges the strictly gendered active-passive dichotomy.

Crowley's magical system contains a fundamental paradox between leading and following; between the quest for sovereignty, epitomised as the journey towards discovering and fulfilling one's True Will, and the fundamental necessity of passivity and self-annihilation for achieving enlightenment. One of the final stages in Crowley's initiatory system entails crossing the Abyss. In order to survive, the adept must destroy his or her ego and become utterly receptive to all of existence and transcending illusory dichotomies such as sacred/profane and self/not-self. If successful, the adept reaches the other side and the goddess Babalon who dwells beyond the Abyss in Binah, the third sephira on the Tree of Life. By annihilating his or her ego, becoming utterly passive and embracing all of existence (thus emulating the formula of Babalon), the magician becomes impregnated in the womb of the goddess and is reborn in the City of Pyramids. This process is described symbolically as draining one's blood into Babalon's chalice.[20] As can be seen in the first quote displayed at the beginning of this article, this is not always portrayed as a harmonious process.

Crowley also believed that Babalon had an earthly office, and viewed many of his female lovers as Scarlet Women, that is, as physical embodiments of the principle of Babalon.[21] While Crowley's writings on Babalon often tend to be poetically obscure and sometimes contradictory, his magical explorations with at least one of his most important Scarlet Women demonstrate the notion of erotic submission as a suitable attitude towards the goddess. Thus, Crowley's own magical practice was not as clear-cut in terms of polarity as some of his written work may suggest. In the following sections, I will bring attention to a number of magical operations and writings that exemplify the tension between activity and passivity.

THE EXQUISITE SACRIFICE: CROWLEY AND EROTIC SUBMISSION

In September 1906, Crowley and George Cecil Jones performed a modified and streamlined version of the Golden Dawn Neophyte ritual, stripped of unnecessary components and focused more directly on its magical formula. Presumably to this end, Crowley and Jones introduced restraining, scourging and cutting into the ritual. After some minor adaptations, the magicians once again tried the revised ritual, dubbed "Liber 671" a few weeks later, with monumental success: after six years of failed attempts, Crowley attained the knowledge and conversation of his Holy Guardian Angel.[22] Crowley also practiced a solitary version of the ritual, called "Liber Pyramidos" daily during a magical retirement in 1908, in order to connect with his Holy Guardian Angel, which I will return briefly to in the following passages.[23]

---

20 Crowley, *Book of Lies*; Crowley, *Vision and the Voice*.
21 Crowley, *Commentaries*.
22 Kaczynski, *Perdurabo*, 160. The notion of the Holy Guardian Angel is derived from the *Book of the Sacred Magic of Abra-Melin the Mage*, which details a series of rituals with the purpose of establishing contact with the magician's guardian angel, whose task it is to provide protection and spiritual guidance.
23 Crowley, 'John St John'.

"Liber Pyramidos" begins with an invocation, after which the magician proceeds to place the magical wand on the altar, use the scourge on his/her buttocks, cut a cross with the dagger on his/her chest and tightening a chain around his/her forehead. This is followed by a series of lengthy recitations and assumptions of godforms, and the ritual is finally concluded in a similar manner as it is opened, with self-scourging, cutting, and additional recitations.

The ritual combines the practice of self-mortification with violent language. The poetry recited evokes the image of a descent into utter darkness, chaos and self-loathing, an ordeal which ultimately results in ascent and deification. While it is not explicitly sexual, the ritual uses practices consistent with the above definition of BDSM to produce an altered state of consciousness that is presumably suitable to exploring the divine, and connects these practices to the theme of spiritual transformation as symbolic death and rebirth. The connection between BDSM practice and symbolic death and rebirth through the encounter with divinity would also be an important aspect of other of Crowley's magical workings involving BDSM, as I will indicate below.

When used to connect with the Holy Guardian Angel, "Pyramidos" is also given meaning within an eroticised discourse. In his diaries Crowley frequently writes about his Holy Guardian Angel in terms that are evocative of erotic submission. In the record of the abovementioned magical retirement, Crowley describes himself as a worm, slave and toad, and the Angel as his beloved, a jewel, and as a 'jealous god' who will keep Crowley 'veiled, cherished, guarded' in his harem as a 'pure and perfect spouse'.[24] This rhetoric of erotic submission to a deified lover combined with the concrete practice of self-flagellation and cutting has clear parallels with BDSM.[25] It also draws attention to one of the paradoxes of Crowley's magical system; while the purpose of the Angel is to provide protection and assistance to the magician – thus aiding him or her in the quest for spiritual transformation and sovereignty – the relationship with the Angel also demands that the magician submit, like a lover, to an at least partly separate and higher intelligence.

Crowley's essay "The Wake World" similarly portrays the relationship between the soul and the Angel as a passionate infatuation and subsequent love affair with unequal power relations and elements of self-deprecation, pain and humiliation. The essay is an allegory of initiation and advancement up the Tree of Life, and its narrative "I" is a seventeen-year-old girl in love with a Fairy Prince; her Holy Guardian Angel. Although the language used by Lola, the protagonist in the "The Wake World", is not as self-loathing as that Crowley uses in "John St. John" or "Pyramidos", Lola repeatedly emphasises her own inexperience, youth and ignorance, and describes the Fairy Prince as exceptionally beautiful and heavenly. For the purposes of spiritual transformation, Lola repeatedly proves her loyalty and obedience to the Fairy Prince, sometimes in quite painful ways. The essay combines the narrative of erotic psychological submission to a dominant, deified lover with

---

24 Crowley, 'John St John'.

25 It is worth noting that the solitary version of "Liber Pyramidos" stands out among the other magical rites discussed in this article in that the magician temporarily becomes both dominant and submissive; active and receptive; simultaneously inflicting pain and enduring it.

descriptions of actual BDSM practices similar to those used in "Pyramidos" such as self-restraint with iron chains, self-cutting and self-mortification in order to demonstrate one's love for the Angel. Lola describes being symbolically wed to her Prince:

> *First there is a tiny, tiny, tiny doorway, you must crawl through on your hands and knees; and even then I scraped ever such a lot of skin off my back; then you have to be nailed on a red board with four arms, with a great gold circle in the middle, and that hurts you dreadfully. Then they make you swear the most solemn things you ever heard of, how you would be faithful to the Fairy Prince, and live for nothing but to know him better and better. So the nails stopped hurting, because, of course, I saw that I was really being married.[26]*

Although Lola's Knowledge and Conversation of her Holy Guardian Angel ultimately furthers her own spiritual development, the relationship of the soul with the Angel as described in the essay contains strong elements of submissive worship. "The Wake World" like "Liber Pyramidos" connects the discourse of erotic submission to the divine with actual, bodily endurance of acts that could be considered painful or degrading and involve, at least temporarily, genuine surrender to divinity. In view of Crowley's ideas about the male/female, active/passive polarity it is also significant that the initiate described in "The Wake World" is female. This discursive gender-bending is further exemplified in the examples of Crowley's practice I will describe in the following sections.

IN THE COMPANY OF THE GODS: CROWLEY AND VICTOR NEUBURG

In 1909, Crowley was journeying through the Algerian desert with his lover Victor Neuburg, an initiate in Crowley's magical order A.A. who had sworn a vow of obedience to the latter. A few years earlier, Crowley had begun exploring the Enochian magical system and the so-called Aethyrs – otherworldly realms – discovered by John Dee and Edward Kelley, and had now vowed to complete the operation.[27] In simple terms, this was accomplished by Crowley reciting the relevant Call – an incantation that enabled access to the Aethyr of his desire – and then using a topaz for scrying, simultaneously describing the visions and experiences he encountered there to Neuburg, who acted as scribe.[28]

As Crowley gradually penetrated the Aethyrs, his experiences grew more intense and sublime.[29] At the fourteenth Aethyr, his progress was halted by an imposing angel who commanded him to abandon the working. Shaken, Crowley complied. Suddenly, he was inspired to perform a ritual at the summit of a nearby mountain. To this end, Neuburg and Crowley constructed a magical circle and erected an altar. What most likely happened next is an act of invocation, through which the spirit

26 Crowley, *Konx om Pax.*
27 Crowley, *Confessions*, 612.
28 Crowley, *Confessions*, 615.
29 Crowley, *Confessions*, 618

of the Greek god Pan overcame Neuburg. In Crowley's own words: 'I sacrificed myself. The fire of the all-seeing sun smote down upon the altar, consuming utterly every particle of my personality.'[30] More prosaically put, Neuburg and Crowley had anal sex, with Crowley acting as the recipient. Crowley believed that the ritual on the mountain marked the final annihilation of his personal self; a prerequisite for subsequently being able to cross the Abyss and reach Babalon.[31]

The sex magical ritual described above is interesting from several perspectives. Similar to Crowley's use of "Pyramidos" and the narrative of "The Wake World", the act both put him in touch with an externalised divinity (Pan-Neuburg), and laid the foundation for his own ascension to the divine planes through the crossing of the Abyss.[32] As is evident from his labelling of the incident as a sacrifice, Crowley did not understand this sexual act as a union of two equals. In order to be able to shatter his ego and cross the Abyss, thus becoming a shrine for the infinite divine, Crowley offered up the last vestiges of his ego and social conditioning to Pan. Like the previous examples discussed Crowley's description of the ritual also seems slightly ambivalent. While Crowley welcomes the event and its aftermath, there is no doubt that this sex magical operation was also something of a trauma for both Neuburg and Crowley. The connection of this rite to the destruction of the ego enforces the apparent correlation between erotic self-sacrifice and communing with the divine in Crowley's teachings, and epitomises the paradox of Crowley's initiation as simultaneously a struggle for greater sovereignty and a journey towards utter self-surrender.

Crowley's sexual submission to Neuburg in Algeria appears to have been his first concrete experimentation with sexuality as a means to magical advancement. If nothing else, Crowley's subsequent magical production and the emphasis on sexuality in his later writings prove that the events in Algeria marked a turning point in his life. In 1913, Crowley and Neuburg united the elements of physical BDSM practice, erotic submission and exploration of the divine in what has later been dubbed the "Paris Working", a series of twenty-four sex magical workings conducted in Paris.

Aimed at invoking Mercury and Jupiter, the individual workings were designed in accordance with Crowley's "Grimoirum Sanctissimum", which amalgamates "Liber 671" (the original, non-solitary version of "Pyramidos") with the *Goetia* and Crowley's play "The Ship". The ritual text stipulates that a priest and a maid should perform the working. However, "Grimoirum Sanctissimum" is described as containing "that which is not yet to be revealed to the X° members of the O.T.O.". This means that the ritual outlined in the text is an act of XI°, that is, homosexual magic. The position of maid thus refers to the receptive partner in homosexual

---

30 Crowley, *Confessions*, 620.

31 Crowley, 'Soul of the Desert'.

32 The understanding of Crowley's allowing himself to be penetrated as an act submission is bound to an early 20th century context (rather than based on a transhistorical assumption of penetration as inherently humiliating to the recipient). During this time, there was still a strong stigma against homosexuality, and for a person like Crowley, allowing oneself to be penetrated would in all likelihood have been understood as an act of submission.

intercourse. In Paris, Crowley generally assumed this role. The general outline of the working is this: the temple is opened according to "Liber 671", after which the maid purifies and 'kindle[s] the fire' in the priest and invokes the phallic principle. This is followed by the 'supreme sacrifice' where the priest 'enters the holiest of holies', that is, an act of sexual intercourse. The resulting sexual fluids were then collected and offered to the gods, and the ritual was finally closed with a repetition of "Liber 671".[33]

The "Paris Working" has been described as Crowley's first systematic use of sexual magic for the purposes of spiritual transformation. The ritual combines BDSM practices such as scourging, binding and cutting with homosexual sex magic, and was aimed both at the exploration of the divine and the more prosaic aim to acquire more money for Crowley. An interesting aspect of the "Paris Working" is the fact that Crowley, although he is magically superior to Neuburg and the operation seems mostly aimed at his own spiritual and material success, still chooses to assume a sexually submissive role. Like Crowley's other writings and explorations of submissive magic, this practice challenges the male/female, active/passive dichotomy he describes in other writings.

CROWLEY AND THE CUP: THE ABBEY OF THELEMA

Crowley's most radical experimentation with sexual submission in both fantasy and practice appears to have taken place at the Abbey of Thelema, the spiritual community he co-founded with his Scarlet Woman Leah Hirsig (1883-1975) at Cèfalu, Sicily in 1920 and which remained active until 1922. His diary entries from this period contain both descriptions of fantasies and acts of submission to women, who are often described in language evoking the image of Babalon. This is perhaps unsurprising, given the fact that Crowley labelled his most important female lovers his Scarlet Women. However, his attitude towards these female figures bears greater resemblance to his self-sacrificial zeal on the Algerian mountain than with the quotes from his writings that describe Babalon as inferior to the male magician and force.[34] On June 18, 1920, Crowley writes in his diary:

And I am Hers; I lift my Lance only that Blood may fill Her Cup. I die that She may live; my roots grow darkly for no fulfilment but Her flowering .... I Her slave, her fule, hidden below the Earth. ... She is ... the Infinite Space that absorbs me, dissolves me, aspires as I expire .... I drown in delight at the thought that I who have been Master of the Universe should life beneath Her feet, Her slave, Her victim, eager to be abased, passionately athirst for suffering, swooning at Her cruelty, craving Her contempt .... to bleed under Her whip's lash, to choke as Her heel treads my throat .... I want to prostitute my manhood, to abase my

---

33 Crowley, *Confessions*, 720-724; Crowley, 'Paris Working', Crowley, *Grimoirum Sanctissimum*. It is worth noting that the record of the Paris Working does not mention the use of "Liber 671" as an opening ceremony.

34 "And for this is BABALON under the power of the Magician, that she hath submitted herself unto the work; and she gardeth the Abyss." Third Aethyr, *The Vision and the Voice*, p 213.

godhead before my lady. I want my crown crushed by Her feet; I want my face fouled by Her spittle. I want my heart torn by Her boot-heel, my mind to Her skirt-hem's rustle, my soul to Her privy. … The greater I, the more hell-deep my humiliation, the viler that in Her which pushes me, the higher and the holier She![35]

The above quote reflects Crowley's sexual arousal at the thought of submission to an imposing female figure, and the manner in which he describes it: being whipped, trod upon, choked and spit upon has obvious elements of BDSM. The metaphorical language used suggests that the fantasy also had magical implications in his mind. While Crowley is likely envisioning his future relationship with his disciple Jane Wolfe (whom he yet to meet),[36] the symbolism he uses – the earth, blood filling the cup, dying and dissolving into infinite space – connects this fantasy to the image of Babalon, and the narrative of eroticised self-annihilation for the purpose of exploring the realms of the divine. It is worth restating here that this spiritual framework implies that Crowley viewed his sexual submission as more than a mere indulgence of fantasy. The quote both suggests a view of submission as a means to an end – the end, in this case, being spiritual transformation – and an appreciation of submission as an end in itself. I will return to this paradox in the final discussion.

In July the same year, Crowley engaged in a series of BDSM practices with Leah Hirsig. Among other examples, the pair conducted what Crowley refers to as a 'lesbian orgy', with Hirsig as dominant and Crowley's female alter ego Alys as submissive. It is significant that Hirsig was one of Crowley's Scarlet Women, believed by him to be an earthly manifestation of the Babalon principle, and similar to the passage above the language he uses to describe the incident connects Hirsig to the figure of the goddess and his submission to a loftier vision of spiritual self-sacrifice, annihilation and rebirth:

…[she] tore from me the last rag of manhood, violated my last veil of modesty, degraded me below the dog and the hog, revolted even my body…. From it she rose Ishtar, Love's Goddess, and drew me into Her womb; Her Babe am I…. It is for Her to nurse Her Babe…[37]

This quote, like that above, also reflects the notion of surrender to the divine and subsequent rebirth through concrete sexual submission. Despite the use of terms evoking the image of violation and castration, the connection to the goddess of love and symbolic destruction and rebirth ties into the narrative of voluntary submission that leads to both enlightenment (being reborn from the womb of Babalon) and self-destruction, simultaneous enhancement of one's inner divine faculties and being annihilated by a deity. This highlights the complexity of Crowley's attitude towards submission, which he appears to have viewed both as a sort of "skilful means" to achieve enlightenment, as well as seeing it as something genuinely desirable in itself.

---

35 Crowley, *Magical Record*, 177-178.
36 Kaczynski, *Perdurabo*.
37 Crowley, *Magical Record*.

While the two diary excerpts quoted above appear to express a sense of fascination and fear-riddled enthrallment with the idea and practice of submission, the third and final passage I will be quoting reveals a different attitude. On July 22, 1920, Hirsig decides to test Crowley for weaknesses; she punishes him for arrogance, and burns him repeatedly with a cigarette to conquer his fear of physical pain. While Crowley withstands this torment reasonably well, his resolve cracks when his Scarlet Woman commands him to consume her excrement in order to demonstrate his ability to transmute even the foulest substances into the Body of God (an ability that Crowley had previously bragged about):

> *My mouth burned; my throat choked; my belly retched; my blood fled whither who knows, and my skin sweated. She stood above me, hideous in contempt . . . . Hierophantia stood She, Her eyes uttering Light, Her mouth radiant Silence. She ate the Body of God, and with her Soul's compulsion, made me eat . . . . that which to Her teeth was moonlight, and to her tongue ambrosia; to her throat nectar, in Her Belly the One God. . . . So with my body shuddering, retching, fainting and convulsed; with my mind tempest, my heart crater, my will earthquake, I obeyed Her lash.*[38]

The above passage differs from Crowley's previous descriptions of his engagement in sexually submissive practices, in that it reflects no enjoyment whatsoever of the act. Unlike the previous diary excerpt, this passage does not connect submission to blissful annihilation of the divine. Instead, it describes what appears to be a thoroughly traumatic experience, although Crowley claims himself to be capable of appreciating the spiritual value of the exercise in theory. However, this passage is undeniably different from the previous quotes that depict submission as an act of bittersweet self-sacrifice and a spiritually valuable end in itself. Hirsig is not portrayed as the all-embracing love goddess Babalon, but as an icily radiant and terrible priestess. Crowley's compliance with her command seems to be driven primarily by the logic of spiritual transformation through transgression; submission as a way of confronting taboo in order to overcome one's fears and ultimately become stronger and more empowered for it. [39]

MASTERY AND SURRENDER

Owen writes that *fin-de-siècle* occultism with its emphasis on practical magic, represented clearly by the Golden Dawn, idealised a "masculine" type of magician, the image of which appealed to men and women alike. Ceremonial magic was epitomised by the image of the magician at the centre of the magical circle, commanding a host of otherworldly forces, whom occultists perceived as the opposite of feminised Spiritualist mediums who passively submitted and allowed themselves to be governed by forces from the "other side". Magic came to be associated with

---

38 Crowley, *Magical Record.*
39 Kaczynski, *Perdurabo.*

masculinity through its strong emphasis on willpower, which in Victorian society was associated with masculinity. Thus, modern occultism provided men with a spiritual path that did not have the feminised connotations of Spiritualism or Christianity, and an avenue for women to develop a masculine persona that was denied them in many areas of society.[40]

However, the glorification of submission in some of Crowley's writings implies that at least some branches of occultism around the turn of the century also offered men the opportunity to explore stereotypically feminine behaviours. While Crowley's magical system ascribes ontological importance to the individual will, his teachings contrast this focus on individual willpower with an idealisation of self-surrender and submission in pursuit of the numinous. Crowley's writings on uniting with the Holy Guardian Angel and the dissolution of the self in the Abyss and subsequent reincarnation through Babalon connect the notion of surrender and loss of individuality to erotic union, in a language evoking the image of sexual submission to a dominant, celestial lover. It is significant that both of these events in Crowley's own magical career were marked by acts of occult BDSM. While some of Crowley's acts of sexual submission were clearly performed with considerable trepidation, it is highly significant that several of his writings on the subject demonstrate an idea of submission as a spiritually meaningful end in itself.

In the context of BDSM, the masculine-coded image of the ceremonial magician is, perhaps, most obviously similar to the role of the dominant; controlling the microcosmic sexual scene has many parallels to the notion of imposing one's will on the macrocosmic universe through ritual. So, why did Crowley in several instances favour the receptive role in BDSM magic? Of course, this practice could be considered a mere expression of his personal sexual tastes,[41] and it is reasonable to assume that his sexual preferences played a part. However, I would argue that this does not suffice as an explanation for why Crowley chose submission during some of the defining moments of his magical career, as he could simply have chosen to indulge his fantasies of sexual submission outside of a magical context.

Scholars have also connected Crowley's exploration of transgressive sexual practices to the notion of spiritual transformation through direct engagement with that which one is frightened and repulsed by.[42] From this perspective, Crowley's experiments with erotic submission could be interpreted as mere attempts to overcome his deepest fears in order to transcend them and, ultimately, return to a dominant role. As indicated by his description of his scatological experiments with Hirsig, this rationale certainly helped push Crowley in the direction of submission in some instances. However, the other examples cited in this article indicate that Crowley appears to have perceived erotic submission not only as a repellent ordeal to be endured and ultimately conquered, but also as spiritually desirable and exquisite in itself, reflecting an idea of divinity not only as something the magician ascribes to in order to achieve power over others and the world, but also as something external that it is sometimes necessary and even desirable to give submit to and allow oneself to be governed by.

---

40 Owen, *Place of Enchantment*.
41 Cf Kelly, *Crafting the Art*, on Gerald Gardner.
42 Kaczynski, 'Taboo and Transgression'.

SUBMISSION: TRUE OR CONTRIVED?

While Crowley's fascination for submission seems genuine, it is reasonable to wonder whether his erotic submission ever involved true relinquishment of control, or whether it was simply an indulgence in the unfamiliar by a man who was secure in his power over others. In the examples cited above, Crowley chooses submission voluntarily in a clearly demarcated ritual context, and is able to return afterwards to his privileged position as a white, wealthy male. In fact, one might say that the transgressive value of his sexual submission was contingent on his otherwise dominant position in everyday life. Thus, it is reasonable to question whether role-play and power inversions simply enforce the normative order.[43]

Furthermore, Crowley was hardly passive in the rituals in which he took on a submissive or passive role. Neuburg was Crowley's magical subordinate who had taken a vow of obedience to the latter, and Owen writes that Crowley and Neuburg most likely planned the sacrifice to Pan beforehand.[44] Crowley's fantasies about Wolfe took place in the secure environment of his own mind. His experiments with Hirsig were conducted within the spiritual community he lead, and as he was the magical teacher of Hirsig and the other residents and visitors to the Abbey it would be reasonable to conclude that Crowley was really in control all along. It is clear from Crowley's magical records that he himself chose to whom he was going to submit, and that he had a higher purpose in mind when doing so. Likewise, the choice to engage in self-mortification in order to pursue his Holy Guardian Angel was hardly forced on Crowley.

However, I believe it would be overly simplistic to assume that Crowley's practice of submissive magic was but a parody of the power relations governing his everyday life. Such an assumption presupposes that ritual is mere theatrics, and that a ritual is devoid of even temporary performative effects on the psyches of the participants, as well as ignoring the spiritual centrality Crowley ascribes to submission to the Holy Guardian Angel and Babalon and the fact that he genuinely believed in his teachings on the subject.

In order to understand the psychology of submission, it is useful to apply anthropologist Roy Rappaport's (1926-1997) ideas about ritual and communication. Rappaport uses the theories of philosopher C.S. Peirce to distinguish between three forms of communication: iconic, indexical and symbolic. Iconic communication conveys information through visual likeness (such as the submersion of the tip of a lance in a chalice representing the union of archetypal male and female forces); indexical communication through correlation or indication (an erect penis indicating arousal); and finally, symbolic communication through arbitrary connections between signifier and signified (the word orgasm referring to sexual climax). Humans are, in Rappaport's view, the only creatures who have mastered symbolic communication, which enables abstract thought and the perception of time. However, symbolic communication also enables lying (where there is no

---

43 Cf Urban's discussion in *Magia Sexualis* of the relationship between taboo and transgression in Crowley's sexual magic.
44 Owen, *Place of Enchantment*.

relationship between signifier and signified). In contrast, indexical communication is more or less immune to deceitfulness, as the signifier cannot exist without the signified.

Rappaport writes that all rituals transmit indexical messages about the individual participants' positions or attitudes. These messages are not symbolic, as they cannot take place without a connection between signifier and signified. The communication of indexical messages by a ritual participant does not only convey information to observers or other participants about the former's position or attitudes, but also enforces these within the practitioner. While the power relationship between dominant and submissive is to some extent contrived, submission in a BDSM scene is an example of indexical communication, and thus cannot be entirely faked. Although a submissive may believe that her dominant will respect her limits, she is technically at his mercy and in order for the BDSM scene to be executed she must actually submit, and thus submission, contrived or not, always involves a measure of genuine loss of control. In this way, surrender to the contrived power relations of the ritual also imparts a message of actual submission and subordinance in both dominant and submissive, enhanced by the equation of the dominant with divinity. The spiritual surrender Crowley believed to be necessary for uniting with the Holy Guardian Angel or surviving the Abyss is not contrived.

Conclusion

Crowley's engagement in erotic submission is congruent with the image of the masculinised magician described by Owen in the sense that he did so to further his own spiritual development and chose the conditions under which it happened. In this respect, Crowley can be viewed as having conquered his own body and fear of powerlessness by force of will in order to manifest his inner divinity and sovereignty. However, in doing so he also willingly chose to surrender his body and soul to the control of his human-divine dominants.

The correlation between his practice of occult BDSM and the narrative of erotic submission to the divine as desirable in itself expressed in his writings indicates that these practices cannot simply be seen as an indulgence of sexual fantasies or a parody of normal relations between him and his disciples. Crowley was convinced that his self-sacrifice to Pan-Neuburg acted as a catalyst for the dissolution of his ego and consequent advancement to a higher state of being, and his description of the event suggests that it was a very powerful experience for Crowley. The language in which he describes such encounters suggests that he did not only see submission as a fear he needed to conquer and overcome. At the Abbey, Crowley's personal diary reflects an earnest commitment to the idea of himself as subservient to a deified female figure, who is described in terms reminiscent of Babalon. The notion that one must submit to one's Holy Guardian Angel in order to advance spiritually and surrender one's ego and desires in order to survive the Abyss and be reborn through Babalon indicates that Crowley viewed erotic submission itself as spiritually meaningful.

The importance of erotic submission to the divine in Crowley's magical system suggests that the idea of ceremonial magic as mostly oriented towards acquiring an increasing amount of control over one's circumstances is somewhat simplified, not least in view of the fact that Crowley is the most influential occultist of the 20th century. Moreover, it ignores the themes of worship and mysticism in many of Crowley's writings that suggest a view of divinity as something that is at least partly external to the magician and to be approached as such, not by conquering or absorbing it power but allowing oneself to be absorbed and conquered.

BIBLIOGRAPHY

—᠁— Bogdan, H., *'Challenging the Morals of Western Society: The Use of Ritualized Sex in Contemporary Occultism'*, *The Pomegranate* 8:2 (2006), 211-246.

—᠁— Chappell, Vere, *'Sexual Attitudes and Behavior Among Members of Ordo Templi Orientis'*, paper submitted to the Institute for Advanced Study of Human Sexuality, San Francisco, CA, USA, 2006.

—᠁— Crowley, A., *Commentaries on the Holy Books and Other Papers: The Equinox, Volume Four, Number One*, York Beach, ME: S. Weiser, 1996.

—᠁— Crowley, A., *'Ecclesiae Gnosticae Catholicae Canon Missae'*, *Equinox* 3:1 (1919), 247-70.

—᠁— Crowley, A., *'Energized Enthusiasm'*, *Equinox* 1:9 (1913), 19-46.

—᠁— Crowley, A., *'John St John. The Record of the Magical Retirement of G.H. Frater O.∴M.∴'*, *Equinox* 1:1 (1909).

—᠁— Crowley, A., *Konx om Pax*, Leeds: Celephais Press, 2004.

—᠁— Crowley, A., *Liber Aleph Vel CXI; The Book of Wisdom or Folly, in the Form of An Epistle of 666, the Great Wild Beast, to His Son 777, Being the Equinox Volume III No. VI*, York Beach, ME: Samuel Weiser, 1991.

—᠁— Crowley, A., *'Liber Cheth vel Vallum Abiegni sub figura CLVI'*, *Equinox* 1:6 (1911), 23-27.

—᠁— Crowley, A., *The Book of Lies*, York Beach: Samuel Weiser Inc., 1992.

—᠁— Crowley, A., *The Book of the Law, Liber AL vel Legis, With a Facsimile of the Original Manuscript as Received by Aleister and Rose Edith Crowley on April 8, 9, 10, 1904 e.v.*, York Beach, ME: Red Wheel/Weiser, 2004.

—᠁— Crowley, A., *The Confessions of Aleister Crowley: An Autohagiography*, London: Arkana, 1989.

—᠁— Crowley, A., *'The Paris Working'*, in: Crowley, A., V.B. Neuburg & M. Dest, *The Vision and the Voice with Commentary and Other Papers*, York Beach, ME: Samuel Weiser, 1998, 343-409.

—᠁— Crowley, A., *'The Soul of the Desert'*, *The Occult Review* 20:1 (1914), 18-24.

—᠁— Crowley, A., V.B. Neuburg & M. Dest, *The Vision & The Voice with Commentary and Other Papers*, York Beach: Samuel Weiser Inc., 1999.

—᠁— Crowley, A., J. Symonds & Kenneth Grant, *The Magical Record of the Beast 666*. Duckworth, 1971.

—᠁— Dawn, C. & S. Flowers, *Carnal Alchemy: A Sado-Magical Exploration of Pleasure, Pain and Self-Transformation*, Smithville, TX: Runa-Raven, 1995.

—— De Naglowska, M., *Advanced Sex Magic: The Hanging Mystery Initiation*, Rochester, VT: Inner Traditions, 2011.

—— De Naglowska, Maria, *The Sacred Rite of Magical Love: A Ceremony of Word and Flesh*, Rochester, VT: Inner Traditions, 2012.

—— Ellwood, T. & Lupa, *Kink Magic: Sex Magic Beyond Vanilla*, Stafford: Megalithica Books, 2007.

—— Evola, Julius, *Eros and the Mysteries of Love: The Metaphysics of Sex*, Rochester, VT: Inner Traditions, 1991.

—— Evola, Julius, *Revolt Against the Modern World*, Rochester, VT: Inner Traditions, 2001.

—— Foucault, M., *The History of Sexuality. Volume 1, an Introduction*, New York: Vintage, 1990.

—— Faxneld, P., *Satanic Feminism: Lucifer as the Liberator of Woman in Nineteenth Century Culture*, forthcoming PhD diss.

—— Freud, S., *Three Essays on the Theory of Sexuality*, New York: Basic Books, 1962.

—— Gardner, G., *The Meaning of Witchcraft*, London: The Antiquarian Press, 1959.

—— Gardner, G., *Witchcraft and the Book of Shadows*, Thame: I-H-O Books, 2004.

—— Grey, P., *The Red Goddess*, Scarlet Imprint, 2008.

—— Hakl, H.T., 'The Theory and Practice of Sexual Magic, Exemplified by Four Magical Groups in the Early Twentieth Century', in: Hanegraaff, W.J. & J. Kripal (eds.), *Hidden Intercourse: Eros and Sexuality in the History of Western Esotericism*, Leiden: Brill, 2008, 445-477.

—— Hanegraaff, W., 'The Study of Western Esotericism', in: Antes, P., A.W. Geertz & R.R. Warne (eds), *New Approaches to the Study of Religion*, New York: Walter de Gruyter, 2004, 490-519.

—— Hanegraaff, W.J. & J. Kripal, 'Introduction: Things We Do Not Talk About', in: Hanegraaff, W.J. & J. Kripal (eds.), *Hidden Intercourse: Eros and Sexuality in the History of Western Esotericism*, Leiden: Brill, 2008, ix-xxii.

—— Hedenborg-White, M., 'Revolutionsikon eller playboygudinna? Ett genusperspektiv på tolkningar av Babalon', *Aura* 3, 2011, 120-155.

—— Hunter, J., *Rites of Pleasure: Sexuality in Wicca and Neopaganism*, New York: Citadel Press, 2004.

—— Kaldera, Raven, *Dark Moon Rising: Pagan BDSM and the Ordeal Path*, Hubbardston, MA: Asphodel Press, 2006.

—— Kaczynski, R. 'Taboo and Transformation in the Works of Aleister Crowley', in: Hyatt, C. *Rebels and Devils: The Psychology of Liberation*, Tempe, AZ: The Original Falcon Press, 2013, sidnummer.

—— Kaczynski, R., *Perdurabo: The Life of Aleister Crowley. The Definitive Biography of the Founder of Modern Magick*, Berkeley, CA: North Atlantic Books, 2002.

—— Kelly, A., *Crafting the Art of Magic, Book 1*, St Paul, MN: Llewellyn Publications, 1991.

—— Kolmes, K., W. Stock & C. Moser, 'Investigating Bias in Psychotherapy with BDSM Clients', *Journal of Homosexuality* 50:2-3 (2006), 301-324.

—— Laskar, Pia, *Ett bidrag till heterosexualitetens historia: kön, sexualitet och njutningsnormer i sexhandböcker 1800-1920*, Stockholm: Modernista, 2005.

—᭱— LaVey, A.S., *The Satanic Witch*, Los Angeles, CA: Feral House, 2003.

—᭱— Lupa, 'The Female Kink Magician', in: Brandy Williams (ed.), *Women's Voices in Magic*, Stafford: Megalithica Books, 2009, 126-135.

—᭱— Nilsson, J., 'Den scharlakansröda gudinnan: Aleister Crowley – dekadensen och den hotfulla kvinnligheten', *Lyrikvännen* 56:4 (2009), 105-112.

—᭱— Owen, A., *The Place of Enchantment: British Occultism and the Culture of the Modern*, Chicago: University of Chicago Press, 2004.

—᭱— Pearson, Jo, 'Inappropriate Sexuality? Sex Magic, S/M and Wicca (or "Whipping Harry Potter's Arse!")', *Theology & Sexuality: The Journal of the Institute for the Study of Christianity & Sexuality* 11:2 (2005), 31-42.

—᭱— Randolph, P.B., *Eulis! The History of Love: Its Wondrous Magic, Chemistry, Laws, Modes, Moods and Rationale; Being the Third Revelation of Soul and Sex*, Toledo, OH: Randolph, 1874.

—᭱— Rappaport, Roy A., *Ritual and Religion in the Making of Humanity*, Cambridge: Cambridge University Press, 1999.

—᭱— Reuss, T. & A. Crowley, *OTO Rituals and Sex Magick*, Essex House, Thame: I-H-O Books, 1999.

—᭱— Richters, J., R.O. de Visser, C.E. Rissel, A.E. Grulich & A.M. Smith, 'Demographic and Psychosocial Features of Participants in Bondage and Discipline, "Sadomasochism" or Dominance and Submission (BDSM): Data from a National Survey', *Journal of Sexual Medicine* 5:7 (2008), 1660-1668.

—᭱— Sacher-Masoch, L.R.V, *Venus in Furs*, Waiheke Island: Floating Press, 2008.

—᭱— Schreck, N. & Z. Schreck, *Demons of the Flesh: The Complete Guide to Left Hand Path Sex Magic*, Creation Books, 2002.

—᭱— Taylor, G.W. & J.M. Ussher, 'Making Sense of S&M: A Discourse Analytic Account', *Sexualities* 4:3 (2001), 293-314.

—᭱— Urban, H.B., *Magia Sexualis. Sex, Magic and Liberation in Modern Western Esotericism*, Berkeley: University of California Press, 2006.

—᭱— Wismeijer, A.A. & A. Van Assen, 'Psychological Characteristics of BDSM Practitioners', *Journal of Sexual Medicine* 10:8 (2013), 1943-1952.

—᭱— Wright, S., 'Discrimination of SM-Identified Individuals', *Journal of Homosexuality* 50:2-3 (2006), 217-231.

What Remains for the Future?

An initial attempt at a comparison between Aleister Crowley and Rudolf Steiner

Carl Abrahamsson

The following text is a lecture originally delivered at a conference organized by Lashtal Press in Gdansk, Poland, on September 14th, 2013. – Ed.

Looking back at the 20th century, we can see that it was probably one of the most intense centuries ever. Regardless which kinds of glasses we put on to watch our own contemporary history closer, it's easy to see that the 20th century was phenomenal and revolutionary in many ways.

Aleister Crowley claimed that 1904 was an especially pivotal year, as that was the year he had authored or "received" his key text: *The Book of the Law*. By declaring the Law of Thelema and the Aeon of Horus, the child, Crowley positioned himself as prophet and interpreter through devoting his life and efforts to informing and, hopefully, enlightening others. He was pretty good at it, too. His efforts have actually brought us together here today, which is indeed a magical thing.

However, Crowley was far from alone in the participation of this aeonic shift. Several others presented similar ideas: individualism, cosmic altruism, breaking away from too rigid cultural and religious structures, an integration of alternative spiritual methods that had up until the shift been looked upon as suspect and heretical, and so on. On the whole, the Zeitgeist included a holistic spirituality, integrating thoughts, ideas and methods from other cultures, predominantly Asian. Theosophy was one main movement. That stemming from Gurdjieff and his disciples another.

Crowley's own Herculean labor of giving birth to this new Aeon has recently been well documented in several biographies, and I think most of us know his story fairly well: An initial curiosity in all things magical and esoteric, a first hand experience of philosophical systems and religious approaches through his travels, a will to inform and enlighten through his *Equinox* volumes, in which he also divulged the secrets of the previous kings of the hill, the Hermetic Order of the Golden Dawn. And then working with the Thelemic orders the AA and the OTO, as well as writing ambitiously (to say the least).

Although plagued by a great number of personal issues and problems, the impression we get of Crowley is still one of great devotion and self discipline. Whether Thelema will become the official religion of the future we have yet to see. But if we stick with the human being Crowley for now, we can see that he is currently about as established as he can be. He is out there, present in contemporary

277

consciousness, but perhaps more for his fascinating life story than for Thelema as a philosophy or religious system.

Another important interpreter and innovator of the same new age shift was the Austrian Rudolf Steiner (1861-1925). His creation of Anthroposophy has many similarities with Thelema. I'm going to try and point out some similarities, and also some differences, in order to shine the light on how it is that these two movements have both been quite successful but in very different ways and to varying degrees.

Steiner for a long time contained his own individual enlightenment, which was a result of thinking, feeling and willing but also of contacts with a spiritual master/teacher earlier on. When the time came for him to eventually bloom, during his successful career within Theosophy, he bloomed with a great appetite for sharing what he had experienced on the inner planes. He too became good at that. Theosophy was soon no longer enough for him, and he created his own system and school, Anthroposophy, just as Crowley had done after the Golden Dawn experiences and the reception of *The Book of the Law*. Initially an academic specializing in Goethe studies, Steiner gradually developed into a very creative polymath who also had the ability to enthuse people to help him out.

Crowley published his ten massive *Equinox* volumes between 1909 and 1913, under the banner of "Scientific Illuminism" and the motto "The method of science, the aim of religion". Steiner called his method "Spiritual Science", and also wrote and lectured intensely to inform the interested. In this sense, both men were very much alike. Crowley was certainly more of a rebel, but they shared an ego-transcending will to improve mankind through the integration of "non-rational" phenomena within a contemporary and very rational mind frame. Thereby bringing occult and spiritual ideas from both the outer and inner worlds into contact with modern society and its empirical standards and critical demands.

Essentially, their wisdoms are one and the same:

—~~— The human being can become enlightened and fully individual. One method of achieving this is to trust one's own intuition and be guided in inner spheres by strata of consciousness previously unacknowledged.

—~~— By going through this process, one sets standards for others and inspires them to explore themselves. Altruism by proxy.

—~~— A holistic integration of various human expressions (science, art, culture, religion etc) into this overall philosophy will also benefit and further mankind. Setting new stages and standards.

—~~— A holistic integration of teachings from different cultural spheres. The integration of yoga and meditation within a basically Western mind frame (Christianity in Steiner's case, Qabalistic mysticism in Crowley's). The idea of pragmatic synthesis.

Basically, we're seeing a teaching that empowers the individual to see the bigger picture, something that will help others too, either by concrete measures or by inspiration. Trusting one's inner experiences and non-rational, esoteric processes is of vital importance in both cases. These must, however, be tested by empirical research and validated by usefulness in spheres larger than the merely individual. Phenomena that had previously been regarded as hocus pocus or even superstitiously as the Devil's work were now being made substantial parts of entire systems of philosophy for normal people from all walks of life. Communicating with angels, elemental entities, astral intelligences etc was suddenly presented as not only matters of fact but also as recommended practices for better self-knowledge and development for modern people.

Crowley used *The Book of the Law* and Thelema as springboards for applications and implementations on different fields of human behavior and existence but seldom got further than theoretical blueprints. Steiner on the other hand networked intensely with people who had both assets and ideas of their own. For instance the collaboration with the altruistic cigarette manufacturer Emil Molt initiated the first Waldorf school at Molt's factory Waldorf-Astoria in Stuttgart in 1919. Today, there are over 1000 Waldorf schools worldwide. The construction of the first Goetheanum building in Dornach (Steiner's spiritual teaching center) was begun in 1913 but the building unfortunately burnt down in 1922. The building of the new Goetheanum, this time constructed in concrete, was finished in 1928. Work on biodynamic farming and gardening was also initiated early on, as were clinical, empirical experiments in Anthroposophic medicine. *Et cetera.*

Crowley's legacy is basically owed to a handful of individuals close to him at some point quite late in his life. I'm thinking specifically of Karl Germer, Grady McMurtry, Gerald Yorke, John Symonds and Kenneth Grant. If it weren't for the diligent archival obsession of Gerald Yorke, for instance, and his donation to the Warburg Institute at the University of London, invaluable Crowley source material would be lost forever or scattered into the digital abyss of eBay. If it weren't for these other men's exploitation of their own Crowley association, there would be no substantial Crowley presence today. The value of these few contacts, which were essentially uncontrollable for Crowley himself, has of course been enormous. The value of Crowley's own publishing efforts, ditto.

Gerald Yorke not only donated his vast collection of information and Crowleyana to the Warburg but also earlier on sent duplicates to Germer in the US and Norman Robb in Australia. Despite this enormous foresight and benevolence, things and papers disappeared along the way, as they tend to do. It seems that the most important thing to leave behind are actually good old fashioned books!

Incidentally, the first book ever that stirred Yorke's interest in things esoteric was one of Steiner's.[1]

Steiner's legacy, on the other hand, was carefully strategized by himself while still alive. The massive amount of lectures (4941 lectures are documented, but I don't know if that's even possible. He started out fairly late, around the turn of the century within the Theosophical environment, and then had approximately 25 very active years, which means some 200 lectures per year...) opened doors to new environments and a constant flow of new people in different countries. If even

---

1 Gerald Yorke interviewed by David Tibet in Gerald Yorke, *Aleister Crowley, The Golden Dawn and Buddhism.* The Teitan Press, York Beach, 2011, p. 208.

a fraction of these turned out benevolent, it was indeed a successful endeavour. The publishing of his ideas was more or less immediate through presses that were Anthroposophically supportive. The integration into society in the Germanic sphere was of course important and a very logical extension of several decades of German openmindedness in various forms of *Lebensreform* movements. The Third Reich temporarily put everything in hiatus of course, but not so much in neutral Switzerland, where the Goetheanum maintained its status as the international center of Anthroposophy – which it still is.

Steiner integrated a middle path that could but didn't necessarily involve a passionate "union of opposites" (quoting Crowley in his description of the "magick of Horus"). Yet, Steiner was aware of the transformative magic indeed. His own schematic symbol for the ideal human being was a statue he himself carved out of wood, and which is today displayed at the Goetheanum, "The representative of man – Christ between Lucifer and Ahriman". This gnostic Christ principle balances the ungrounded, spiritual loftiness of Lucifer with its ensuing pride and the gross, malkuthian materialism of Ahriman. An enlightened being who can balance these very human energies or temptations will have gained insight by the mere effort. If we allow ourselves some philosophically speculative slack within the Thelemic pantheon, the statue could perhaps equally well be called "Ra-Hoor-Khuit between Nuit and Hadit".

Steiner's progressive attitude to Christianity is without a doubt another reason why Anthroposophy has been able to grow and mature without head-on collisions with established powerful and intolerant dogmas. Crowley early on took on a persona projected on him by his fundamentalist mother: "The Great Beast". That became an image he himself nurtured throughout his life, and his antipathy towards all things Christian became one of many controversial trademarks.

However, from the perspective of religious or philosophical studies, Thelema is a decidedly neo-Gnostic system, meaning the incentive for and manifestation of enlightenment is individual. Steiner intuited and put forth exactly the same idea. But Steiner's specific psychological fundament had no need of distancing itself from the religion that had prevailed up until the 20th century, not seldom through violence and oppression. Steiner analyzed the Christian mysteries and myths thoroughly and regarded in particular the human being Jesus' Golgothan experience, when he was acting as an enlightened Christ, a gnostic master, as the single most influential happening of the past aeon. This should be regarded solely from a magical, transformative perspective though, not a dogmatic Christian one. Steiner and Anthroposophy are more in debt to Neoplatonism, pantheism, the renaissance thinkers and Goethe than to any kind of dogmatic Christian church.

Interesting to note in regard to Thelema as a cosmic mythology and its strong solar presence through Ra Hoor Khuit, is that the Christ principle in Steiner's mythology is imbued with distinctly solar force filtered through the Archangel Michael. The Golgotha experience is, in Steiner's eyes, not so much an individual self sacrifice to redeem other people's "sins" as it is a conduction of solar energy into the earth.

What Remains for the Future?

What remains if we look at their main ways of expressing themselves? Both men were voluminous writers and basically everything there is has been made available on the market. In Crowley's case recently but very ambitiously. In Steiner's case all along the decades. The availability these days not only has to do with spreading the words *per se* but also with income for the respective organisations. There is a substantial value in both men's writings, and especially now that copyright issues are more complex and floating than ever. The copyright holders are eager to maintain a presence on the market, and that the books are published in high quality editions and translations secures both revenue and interest.

Let's not forget that both men were also visual artists. Steiner was inspired by Goethe in more ways than one and ambitiously tried to convey his own inner visions in visual form. Steiner's paintings and sculptures certainly display his will to communicate a higher system of aesthetics according to Goethe's guidelines, to be used for instructional purposes. The main auditorium of the Goetheanum is an impressive, almost incredible, display of this *Gesamt* vision, in which architecture, stained glass images, mural paintings, light and acoustics work together to tell a story, teach and inspire. There are several books focusing on Steiner's visual art available today.

For Steiner, the use of art was ultimately pedagogic and magically strategic: "Beauty is not the divine in a cloak of physical reality; no, it is physical reality in a cloak that is divine. The artist does not bring the divine on to the earth by letting it flow into the world; he raises the world into the sphere of the divine. Beauty is semblance because it conjures before our senses a reality which, as such, appears as an ideal world."[2]

Crowley's paintings, drawings and the Abbey of Thelema murals at Cefalu were also creative externalizations but considerably rougher, and there seems to have been no other plan in painting them than simply to paint. Crowley's visual works exist today in private collections, and once in a while, these are exhibited (London 1998, Paris 2008, Australia 2012). There has not yet been a substantial monograph of Crowley as an artist.

Both Steiner and Crowley were extroverts, but for different reasons. Steiner was a distinct Apollonian character by Nietzsche's defintion, and Crowley very much a Dionysian one. Crowley wrote well but was inept at handling people not immediately of use to him. Steiner was not the best writer but could deliver inspiring lectures *en masse*. Crowley was lucky to have a few intelligent people around when he was about to die. And, not forgetting, Crowley's publishing efforts have indeed been talismanically successful. Steiner was more of a structured Germanic mind and basically worked himself to death to secure the immortality of Anthroposophy. His bouquet is considerably larger than Crowley's, and we are all more or less exposed to it when we eat organically produced foods, for instance, or send our kids to Waldorf schools, or use Weleda products. The pioneering research in Steiner's Spiritual Science has definitely made an impact

---

2 Rudolf Steiner, "Goethe as the Founder of a New Science of Aesthetics", in *Art – An Introductory Reader*, Sophia Books, Forest Row, 2003, p. 61.

on contemporary culture far more than Crowley's Scientific Illuminism. At least so far.

If one wanted to be a little bit mean spirited, one could present two parallel images under the umbrella of spiritual centers of the 1920s. One being a run down farm house in a Sicilian fishing village, its walls painted with obscene poetry and impressionistic demons. The other one being an architecturally advanced and radical multi million building in the Swiss countryside, designed to transmit the spirit of Goethe into the cosmos.

However, it's totally unfair to measure these concepts or systems in terms of quantity and visibility. Crowley's system, after all, is either highly personal and secretive (AA) or intra-fraternal (OTO). The Thelemic environment is more of a private sphere, in which a spiritual, magical attainment is encouraged. Whether that is of any use or interest to anyone else is not relevant unless stated so by the adept in question.

While on the subject of the OTO, I think I should mention too that Steiner met the head of the order at the time, Theodor Reuss, in 1906 in Switzerland – a meeting arranged by leading Theosophist Annie Besant. This was pre-Thelema OTO of course. These gentlemen found enough common ground to stand on that Steiner became head of an OTO lodge called Mysteria Mystica. Steiner was curious, as he had been about Theosophy, and also sought new environments in which to develop himself as a spiritual teacher. His engagement with OTO phased out quite quickly though. Reuss, Hartmann and the other early OTO protagonists had a somewhat strange reputation because it was more or less known, even back then, that OTO worked with esoteric tantric sexual rituals in the higher degrees. Perhaps this became too much for Steiner, who was more or less a celibate. Anyway, six years later Reuss knocked on Crowley's door, and the rest, as they say, is history. And another reason for why we are gathered here today.

At Christmas 1923, Steiner announced to his followers that a new and more ambitious organisation, the General Anthroposophical Society, had been set up and that from now on, the publishing of all his lectures was OK. Both these developments allowed for a much smoother, and much more public life for the philosophy itself and its many creative offshoots. He also announced a College for Spiritual Science that would teach advanced Anthroposophy at Dornach and other places. The name alone makes me think of AA as a "College of Scientific Illuminism". There was apparently something in the air that allowed for these teaching structures to manifest on similar lines, regardless of whether they were public or highly secretive.

As the old Anthroposophical Society gave way for this new and better organised one, Steiner personally issued and signed membership cards for all the old members: 12.000 of them! And the first big thing to deal with was the rebuilding of the Goetheanum, a large scale process that actually continued in terms of final decorations etc well up until the 1990s.

The word "general" is perhaps a magical clue to the success of Anthropsophy after Steiner's death and, of course, especially after the second world war. Steiner's almost Taoist approach to merge with and augment, improve, develop and never clash with or use force, allowed for an easy integration into a general mind frame of general society. Sure, some of the ideas of Atlantean civilizations, reincarnation, cosmic farming, eurythmic healing and so on may still be hard to grasp for most people, but no one can deny the common sense of eating biodynamically or at least organically grown food. Or the well documented success of the Waldorf education system, or the Camphill environments for individuals with learning disorders, etc.

Crowley's attitude was almost diametrical to this. "The key to joy is disobedience", *etc.* We can never find out if this was willed or if he was making a virtue out of necessity. I suspect that his drug addiction was the biggest real demon in his life. Not only because of the related financial and physical strains, but because of the will aspect. Although I'm sure he did want to get rid of the addiction, he simply couldn't. We can rationalize and say that just makes him all the more human, etc. Sure, but for the Great Beast himself, I believe the persona as the *agent provocateur* of a new era defined by Will, was rather unwillingly upheld, and that he would much rather have been someone considerably more welcome in the upper echelons of British society. Crowley's head-on hedonism facilitated a media image that in many ways still lingers on, and it is far from useful to Thelema as a general philosophy that has the potential to transform individual lives, with or without the technology of magic.

It is highly interesting to compare these systems that are so alike in many ways but also so very marked by their creators and their specific psychological traits. And they were both aware of it, for good and bad, and of what lay behind. In both systems, the concepts of Karma and reincarnation are present, and both men encouraged their adepts to research previous lives on the inner planes, as they had done themselves. If this wasn't done properly, one would perhaps have to make similar mistakes over again.

Steiner was unusually clear when he wrote of these principles: "Through memory, the soul preserves yesterday; through action, it prepares tomorrow."[3] And: "As a spiritual being, I must be the repetition of one whose biography can explain mine."[4] And: "I must connect to what I did yesterday if my life is to have order and continuity. Yesterday's actions have become the conditions that regulate what I do today. Through my actions yesterday, I created my destiny for today."[5]

There is in this integration of Karma an accentuation of the holistic too. Despite the fact that we are individuals, and we can only really develop on the individual level by gradual refinement, what we do also affects others, and vice-versa. These were thoughts that had been around for a long time, even in Europe. John Donne, the 17th century British poet described it well several hundred years before Theosophy: "No man is an island entire of itself; every man is a piece of the continent, a part of the main - - - Any man's death diminishes me, because I am involved in mankind. And therefore never send to know for whom the bell tolls; it tolls for thee."[6]

Perhaps Donne is a good example in this case, as he too was in between faiths, so

3 Rudolf Steiner, *The New Essential Steiner*, Edited and introduced with notes by Robert McDermott, Lindisfarne Books, Great Barrington, 2009, p. 180.
4 Ibid, p. 187.
5 Ibid, p. 192.
6 John Donne, *No man is an island*, The Folio Society, London 1997. Cover text.

to speak. Having been born a Catholic in England, Donne and his family had been exposed to intolerant harassment and even religious murder. When he eventually became a Protestant within the Church of England, he was suddenly lauded and could speak and write freely about almost anything he wished, including the need for tolerance and open-mindedness. It is in a way as if restraint brings an inherent desire for freedom. How this expresses itself has to do mainly with the Ego of the person expressing it. Donne was an intelligent opportunist who worked the system to his own benefit. That has benefited us too, as his works and ideas were allowed to remain and survive.

Crowley formulated instructions for the AA concerning knowledge of previous incarnations, as that was thought to be essential for magical development. In *Liber 913, Thisharb*, he constructed a method for the mind to work backwards in order to strengthen the individual memory to the level of transcending the present incarnation: "Memory is essential to the individual consciousness; otherwise the mind were but a blank sheet on which shadows are cast. But we see that not only does the mind retain impressions, but that it is so constituted that its tendency is to retain some more excellently than others."[7]

What remains if we look at other people's memories of these gentlemen? In Crowley's case it depends exclusively on the vantage point of the first hand writer in question. If Crowley was good to the writer, then the recollection is good. If Crowley was bad or perceived as bad to the writer, then the recollection is bad. A prime example of subjective history writing, and something which was amplified by the fact that he was so infamous as a public figure in the United Kingdom.

It is as if the impressions of the man Crowley are so predominant that more or less objective analyses of his work from his own time are non-existent. His own descriptions are literally hagiographic (as in his *Confessions*), and those of, say Fuller or Achad, could easily be seen as hagiographic by proxy. It is mainly during the most recent decades that real Crowley biographies have been written, and these have indeed been very ambitious and well researched projects.[8]

In Steiner's case, it is almost as if the person Rudolf Steiner doesn't exist. There is of course a great deal of hagiographic subjectivity in his case too, but that certainly doesn't stem from himself. He did write an autobiography at the request of his followers, but it is very low key and basically a chronological recounting of meetings and projects. And, lest we forget, he didn't have the time to finish his own biography. It only goes as far as 1907, and that was in many ways when things started to become really interesting in his life. So we are left with other people's account of his life, and mostly of the yea-saying variety.

As we can see, there are many similarities between the teachings. Crowley was predominantly interested in the technology of magic, and of refining and handling the philosophy of *The Book of the Law*. Steiner was a magnificent visionary who also worked hard at trying the resulting ideas out and making them useful for others. These gentlemen had similar goals but were very different in individual behavior and

---

7 Aleister Crowley, *Liber Thisharb*, in *Book Four*, Samuel Weiser, York Beach, 1997, p. 648.
8 For instance: Booth, Churton, Kazcynski, *et al.*

attitudes. Perhaps we can allow ourselves to regard them as two aspects of the very same phenomenon or entity, like a Horus and Set, a Lucifer and Ahriman, a Christ and a Great Beast, where each facilitates a united dynamic energy in which a human individual can have an uncensored look at him- or herself? This is undoubtedly a fascinating area of study and speculation that requires a lot more research and one that will be, I suspect, revealing and rewarding for both these cosmic philosophies of life.

LIVING IN THE SUNLIGHT

A lecture delivered on May 7, 1922

Frater Achad

In the spring of 1922 Charles Stansfeld Jones (1886-1950), Grand Master (X°) O.T.O. for North America, started a series of weekly lectures that would continue until January 1924. Although the lectures seem to have been open to the public, it appears that the audience consisted primarily of O.T.O. members or affiliates. The lectures show how the first generation of thelemites in North America would understand and interpret Thelema, but also what other magical and mystical systems that they were acquainted with. In the lecture below, for instance, Jones refers to Hindu practices such as pranayama and kundalini yoga. This first publication of "Living in the Sunshine" is based on an original typescript preserved at the O.T.O. Archives. The typescript is probably a transcription of lecture notes taken by someone in the audience. The text has been silently edited and spelling errors etc. have been corrected. I wish to express my gratitude to William Breeze for making available a copy of the typescript. – Dr. Henrik Bogdan

The subject of my talk this morning is LIVING IN THE SUNLIGHT. I do not think that we could have had a more appropriate morning for a lecture of this sort. We might, however, have a more appropriate surrounding in so far as you would all, perhaps, have been better off out of doors than in here. But the question of living in the sunlight is not one that only applies in the material sense, although, after all, that is very important.

We all realize, I think, all of us who are here this morning, how much brighter, in every way, we feel on account of the bright sunshine this morning, which has entered not only into our lungs but in our minds, and gives us a brighter and clearer outlook on the world in general. There is no doubt whatever – nobody can deny that the sunlight is one of the greatest blessings of life. Of course, as a matter of fact, without it, we should, none of us, be here at all. I want to take up the question of living in the sunlight from several aspects. First of all, we have the word "living", and the question arises as to whether or not we are all of us living, whether we are among the "quick" or what we may term "dead". I am prepared to say that there are some of us, at least, who are certainly not living 100%, in the way that they might be. They are not filled with the living forces of the universe, and by breaking thru them constantly in the way they might if they only knew the way and thought it was

286

worthwhile. El[iphas] Levi tells us that there are upon earth a number of people, so-called, whose higher self – the sun of their being, as it were – has departed from them, even in this life; and that they are little more than shells, animated by the remainder of their life forces and having a certain amount of mentality, but that they are practically dead even while they are supposed to be alive. I do not think that we have any of that type of person with us this morning, but there are others, again, who are living, but living practically in the darkness or in the shadow. You will remember last Sunday morning, I talked to you of the "Shadow Under the Table", and described this world as some of us know it, to a living in that shadow, not having realized the full light of life and, at the same time, having got accustomed to the twilight we have become more or less satisfied with it.

Now, I think there are few of us who can not increase the light within ourselves and consequently the life force within them, for life is the substance of light. We may, I think, compare this type of person to some little animal who lives under ground; or we may say, perhaps – (I do not know why) but I think perhaps people prefer to be likened to plants and flowers, rather than to animals. We might say, perhaps, they are like the young shoot in the ground who have been developing their roots to a certain extent, have been getting a firm grip upon the life of earth, but who have not yet succeeded in breaking thru the crust of earth above them and opening themselves out to the full light of the sunlight. Those who feel that their life is full of shadow should remember the comforting words of *Liber Legis*, the Book of the holy Law of the new aeon which tells us the sorrows are but shadows.[1] They pass and are done, but there is that which remains, after the sorrows and shadows have passed away, and *that* it is which we wish to concern ourselves with for it is our chance of immortality – for it does remain, and also it leads us into a life of pure joy under the law of Light, Life, Love and Liberty.

But how are we to change our condition? Probably this is more or less a question of natural growth, but once the true aspiration of growth has arisen within us, once we have become conscious of our true will, our true purpose, this growth may be greatly accelerated. We can imagine that if a flower, for instance, could become conscious instead of instinctively groping its way towards the light, if it became conscious of a desire for light, it might push forward very much more quickly and, as a matter of fact, we have heard stories which are more or less confirmed, I think, of the extremely rapid growth of plants or flowers under the influence of the will of some of the Yogis. In other words, the Yogi, or the eastern sage, knowing somewhat of the secrets of life, is able to contact the soul of the seed and to hasten its growth so that, in a few hours, we find a plant growing up and coming to maturity, which would otherwise have taken, in the course of nature, a long time. In other words, the Yogi has succeeded in, first of all, aligning himself with the will of the universe or God, and, secondly, in, to a certain extent, showing forth the powers of God by means of that will. Will is that which causes change to occur in conformity with our true will.[2] When we can succeed in learning that secret, we shall be able to grow

---

1 "Remember all ye that existence is pure joy; that all the sorrows are but as shadows; they pass & are done; but there is that which remains." *Liber AL vel Legis* II:9
2 This is a paraphrase of Crowley's most well-known definition of magic: "Magick is the Science and Art

very much more rapidly towards the sunlight than we have ever before been able to do.

Besides those who live under ground, we may say that there are those who live in the water. They are like the fishes. They see each other thru the waters, but they are unable to look above, to raise their heads above the water, especially if they are deep water fish, they may not be able to come to the surface.

They are living in a semi-transparent surrounding, and they have become quite accustomed to it. They are, as a matter of fact, what we may term children of the last aeon, children of Osiris, the Age which was governed by Pisces or fishes. There are very many who are still swimming around in the waters and who have not succeeded in imitating the bird, as far as their own life is concerned, and rising above the waters to a clear air where they may enjoy the rays of the universal sun. I suppose that this Age of Aquarius, the new aeon as we may term it, is preeminently an Age of Air. We find it heralded by the mastery of air by means of planes, and so on, and I think that we shall be able during this period to comprehend much more completely, if I may say, the bird mind. Whatever we may have been able to recognize and realize about animals, we really know very, very little from the point of view of the birds, for we have not had much opportunity to get that point of view. We shall undoubtedly gradually get it in this Age, as all these things on the physical plane are always manifestations of what is going on inside the individual and inside the race, and so on; for everything which manifests on the outer plane comes into manifestation as a result of some inner force.

I was only struck, yesterday, I think it was, by one of the very old texts in the Bible which I had previously very little understood. Sometimes, in our childhood, we learned a number of texts and so on, and we put an ordinary meaning on them, and they go on, in our mind, many years. We never trouble at all to re-examine them in the light from further and more advanced knowledge. The text I am referring to is this: "The foxes have holes, and the birds of the air have nests; but the Son of man hath not where to lay his head".[3] Now, when we were little Sunday school children, I think probably most of us had the opinion, from that text – the saying of Christ, which he answered to a man who came to him saying: "Master, I will follow thee whithersoever thou goest"[4] – we always have a [sympathetic] feeling in our heart for Christ at that time, and we think of a man as an outcast who has no place to lie down and so on. That is the kind of interpretation which is generally put upon it. Look at us – we have a nice house, and so on, and yet the Son of man hath no where to lay his head. Now, I got an idea about that, and on taking up the Bible it was afterwards much more strongly confirmed by one of the verses almost immediately following. I came to the conclusion – to give you my idea first – that the Son of man hath not where to lay his head is on account of the fact that he is constantly shining. He neither slumbers nor sleeps – in other words, because he is the true

---

of causing Change to occur in conformity with Will." Although not published until 1930 in *Magick in Theory and Practice* (Paris: Lecram Press), p. xvi, Jones had access to an early typescript of the work, now preserved in the O.T.O. Archives.
3 Matthew 8:20; Luke 9:58
4 Matthew 8:19; Luke 9:57

representative of the Sun. Now, the sun, as we know, is always shining, although many of the old religions, all of the old religions – practically every religion which is existing today, is based or has been based upon the apparent fact in nature that the sun disappeared – that he does disappear; but they had the idea that the sun died every night and was re-born or resurrected every morning; and upon that basis or solar myth was based practically all the religions for the last two thousand years. We can trace the idea, of course, in the Christian religion and many others. Now modern science has pointed out to us, more or less recently (when I say that, I mean as compared to the date on which these older religions are founded) – the fact that the sun is always shining, and it is this earth which revolves and consequently cuts off the light of the sun at times by the gross [...] and opaqueness of its own body. The sun, itself, is always shining. It does not die and is re-born. It is constantly ever-living, and that is the idea concealed beneath Christ's words. He is always shining. He is always the Son of Man.

Now, to confirm that, we will go a verse or two further – not to confirm that idea so much as to counteract the old idea that we may have had. Within three verses, we hear of the fact that Christ entered into a boat and the disciples came to him and found that he was asleep and they woke him up on account of the storm. Now, Christ would not say with his own mouth that the Son of man hath not where to lay his head, and within five or ten minutes he was asleep. Either you have got to accuse him of telling an untruth (which you would be loath to do), or to say that his words about having no where to lay his head have a decidedly different and more secret meaning; and I think, if we look at things in that way, we shall be able to interpret the saying very much better. In other words, to the man who asked him whether he could follow him all the while – he simply said, at the present time you are not capable of shining, constantly active, always reflecting and giving out light as the sun does, and that is the Son of man's particular work. But, although we may not yet be at the stage when we can become as the Sun himself, constantly shining – yet we may learn to live in the sunlight. And that, after all, is very much better than living under the earth or in the water.

Now, there is another aspect which I want to take up before I develop the subject any further; and that is – What is there living in the sunlight at the present time? This question can be taken up from more than one point of view, again. We are all living, really, on account of the sunlight. The earth upon which we live is but a spirit (?) [...] of the rays (?) of the sun. The life of the sun is in the earth, and if it were not for that life, and the one substance of which we are all made, we should not be here; we should not be able to exist at all. But this life needs to be constantly sustained; in fact, all things are in the process of becoming. They are constantly being born, constantly being preserved, and again being destroyed, in order that they may be renewed; and it is to the action of the sun, himself, the center of our solar system, that we look for the creation, preservation, and destruction of all living things as we know them.

In one of the secret rituals of a well known Order, we find the following words: "The secret of the Royal Art grows like a flower in the heart of man.

All that we can do is to aid that flower by supplying it with food, air, water and sunlight. Candidate, will the assurance of such [aid] satisfy you?"[5] That is all that any occult Order can do towards showing us the great secret of light. Realizing that within each one of us, within the heart, as it is said, the Royal Art or the secret of the Royal Art grows like a flower. It is possible to supply that flower with food which is the earth which surrounds it, the air which is necessary to it, the water which is necessary to it, and sunlight – and this can be done. Of course, they represent the four elements; the four elements which are typified in occultism by the four letters of the ineffable Name. However, there is something further needed. Jehovah – Yod – He – Vau – He must become [Yeheshua] – Yod – He – Shin – Vau – He, the Holy Spirit represented by the triple flame of the spirit must descend into these elements thus crowning man as a creature of the elements, making him into a perfect microcosm, the true fivefold star or pentagram. The Star of Unconquered Will. This Holy Spirit must arise within man, and he, himself, must seek it and find it if he would control himself and those around.

Now, to take up another aspect of what is living in the sunlight. There is something living in the sunlight which is most important to us, for it is the very life force, itself. That is what is living in the sunlight. The Hindus call it *Prana*, the life force, the one force of the universe which causes change and causes the progress of creation, preservation and destruction to continue. The one force which acts upon the one substance. In other words, the whole universe is made of a living substance of which one aspect is the life and the other the substance. Now this pranic force is everywhere around us. It is most active, perhaps, when the sun is actually shining and its rays are reaching the earth. That is why we feel our bodies to be more filled with life while the sun is shining and during the Summer months than we do in the shadow and night and cold of the winter. We have often heard the Holy Spirit designated as the Divine Breath, and the Holy Spirit comes to us as a constantly […] like a (tide)? flame. This […] is really both the light of fire and of spirit, and it is the essence and flame of the breath. It may be extracted from the air we breath if we only learn to breath rightly. This secret of the Holy Spirit is […]. It is a great mystery, but it is not so far from us as we really thought. We can let it fill our bodies with the fire and life of the Holy Spirit if we will learn to extract the Prana from the air we breath. But we have not been breathing deeply enough. The secret of Prana[yama] is control of Prana, as the Hindus call it… […] is in these two little ideas. Breathe slightly more slowly than usual and very, very deeply.

You will find all kinds of books on Yoga and breathing and so on, all kinds of exercises recommended – those of you who have studied the path, # but the secret of the whole thing is to discover a particular life breath that will just suit the individual who is practicing and this will be found by breathing slightly more slowly than normally for you, and very much deeper. It is not a question of how slow or even of how long you can make the breath or how long you can hold the breath, but

---

5 From the First Degree initiation ritual of Ordo Templi Orientis. See Francis King (ed.), *The Secret Rituals of the O.T.O.* (London: C.W. Daniel Company, 1973), p. 56.

to discover the particular breath that will tone up your being to the particular key which you manifest and comes over upon you in sympathetic vibrations with the solar forces outside. I am not going to make a lecture on breathing, this morning. I am merely pointing out, however, that there is something very much living in the sunshine and in the air we breath which is permeated by the rays of the sun.

When we have learned this secret of breath, we find another thing that we may learn from the Hindus. They tell us that coiled up at the base of the spine is a certain secret force called *Kundalini*. This is likened unto a fire. It is really the stored up Prana in our bodies, but, in a certain sense it is Karma. For the passage or canal carrying [...] passing up the central part of the spine is closed at its lower end and this Kundalini (they say mystically) three and a half coils at the lower end of the spine, beneath this closed opening, and when this can be opened, the Kundalini force takes up its rightful place which is about the navel of our bodies in a certain chakra, as it is called, a nerve plexus branching off from the spine. The solar force or the Kundalini force dwells safe within, in the solar plexus and not at the base of the spine. That is its normal home to which we must restore it. [...] and finding there are certain powers being granted to us. We find, as a matter of fact, when the force begins to [...] some of the [...] as they are called, or plexas, that we begin to see most wonderful colors. We find, in other words, that certain higher senses are developed and we are living a much fuller life than ever we had conceived before. We are like those fishes who have succeeded in raising their heads above the water, [...] – as we say – looking out in a new universe to a world which they had never previously conceived, a world of intense life. When we succeed in reaching the highest part of the spine, arouse (?) the Chakra which is called the thousand and one petaled lotus which is above the heart of the aspirant.[6]

Now, these powers are to be obtained thru the living furnished (?) of the sunlight. We are really crystallized sunlight, every one of us. Every time that we breathe, we are taking into our system some of this Prana and it is being used to keep our bodies running and at the same time, it is storing up a surplus energy which is this Kundalini force. There are certain dangers attached to these things, I must warn you. I am not giving you any details of that, for practice of that kind should be undertaken with very great care. But there are these things within us and they may be aroused by those who really aspire to the true light.

But we must truly learn to live in the sunlight. We must not be content to start on a path of this kind with any half way goal in view. We must aspire as if we are to become the sun, itself, who is the Great Spiritual Sun of the universe, which we may term God.

It is not well that we should enter upon the mystical, occult path with the intent of obtaining certain occult powers. It is only well that we should attain to our powers and complete harmony stage, which is union with God, and a conscious co-operation with our purpose in the universe. If, then, we have that end in view, which we may call the Great Work, it is safe for us to take any steps that we wish

6 This is obviously a mistake: the *sahasrara* cakra, often referred to as a thousand-petaled lotus, is located either at or slightly above the top of the head.]

that will help us towards that accomplishment, for we have in mind the very highest ends that will lead not only to our own salvation but towards the redemption of humanity. Then we will truly learn to live in the sunshine.

When we were in Vancouver, some years ago, a certain sister of the Order whom we called [Soror Hilarion][7] came to visit us with the Master Therion. She it was who first used this expression "living in the sun light" and who has most successfully shown it forth in her own life. Although I have not seen – for some [seven] years, the remembrance of her is always, as it were, a ray of sunlight. She is one of the most wonderfully bright, cheerful, soothing individuals and yet at the same time so full of passion that is arouses within one all the latent forces that I have ever known. She it was who first, to my conscious knowledge, used this expression and she had a method all her own which everyone of us may adopt. It consisted in this: she said that whatever may have been the cares and trials and troubles of the day, no matter how many people may have gone against us and appeared to be unkind to us and so on – no matter what the state of mind we have been in – there was one great secret. This world, itself, is more or less of an illusion and we create to a large extent our own illusions. As a matter of fact, when I say the world is an illusion, I will say that we are looking at it from an illusionary point of view. Now, the idea was that every morning – every night, when she laid down to sleep, she put aside the cares of the day – all little annoyances and sorrow and shadow, with a firm determination, before sleeping, to wake up with the sun and to wake up to a new day – to a clean sheet, to look at the world afresh every morning and live that day in the sun light and with the sun.

Now there we have in that simple little process a very fine idea. Practically everything we see, at one time, is sorrow and at another time is pleasure. It is a question of our view point. If we begin to learn to take the point of view of the ever-shining sun, we shall find that all around us is light and beauty, although we shall have forgotten ourselves to a certain extent, even as we should do. If we become one with the sun, we should no longer see his rays as coming and falling on us, but we should see them as we project them onto our surroundings; then wherever we throw them will be sunlight for we, ourselves, will have become the sun and the giver of light.

Now the test of [...]'s way of living is this: if we aspire to live thus, we must do all that we possibly can to refine ourselves, to cast out all that is dirty or unclean in ourselves or in our surroundings – to live royally as we are, as a representative of the sun upon earth, and not to be content that we are truly living in the sunlight or giving out the sunlight while there is any trace of darkness or distress anywhere in our surroundings

There are those who have the power of radiating light and love to all that are in their presence, so that immediately one gets into touch with such a person, one feels happy although after having left them, one may go back into the gloom of night as

---

7 Although not named in the typescript, the "sister of the Order" is clearly Soror Hilarion, i.e. Jeanne Robert Foster (1879-1970), who visited the British Columbia Lodge No. 1, Vancouver, in October 1915 together with Aleister Crowley. See Martin P. Starr, *The Unknown God: W.T. Smith and the Thelemites* (Bolingbrook: Teitan Press, 2003), pp. 37-39.]

it were. But we should become such living centers of light and love; so let it be the proof of our success whether we do still spread among any of those with whom we are in contact anything but brightness and joy and light, life, love and liberty. If we can succeed in doing that, we shall succeed in not only living in the sun light – we shall have succeeded in becoming one with the sun and look at all things from the solar point of view.

The Book of the Law, *Liber Legis*, tells us of this; it is the great charter of our Godhead, for It says that every and every woman is a star; and each star, as you know, travels in its appointed course without interference. This is what is meant by doing our true will, that we may learn our true starry or solar nature; we may learn to give out light wherever we go and we shall find ourselves avoiding all friction and trouble; we shall pass on our way fulfilling our true will or purpose like stars and constantly giving forth our light to all around us. Thus, a man seeing us will say, "who is this that makes us feel thus?" and we shall gradually be pointed to as a child of the new aeon, little children of light, the crowned children of the aeon of Horus; for this is the Age of the Crowned Child. We shall all become much more simple in our habits; we shall become perhaps a great deal more childlike in our ways, as in the past aeon we have become far too complex

But we shall give forth a source of light and pleasure that will be far, far greater and much more cheerful than all the intellectual talks that we may have been giving out before or all the little arguments, or this, that and the other, that we have been shedding forth. Everybody is shedding out some kind of an atmosphere, a genial, pleasant person, or an intellectual person, or whatever they may happen to be; but when we have succeeded in radiating the true sun within us, which is after all the true Christ Spirit, when we can say "I and my Father are One"[8] – that my Father is in Heaven and that Heaven is within me – then we shall realize what Christ meant when he talked about the Son of God, for each of us is a Son of God, and we should all have that sun giving out the strength and light and [...].

I have tried to give out some little conception of my [...] of living in the sunlight, and I hope some of you will vtry to adopt some of these simple methods. You will find your relationships with all around you taking on a more pleasant feeling, and will find joys of which I have no possible opportunity to talk to you today, arise within you; for our Lady Nuit has promised you to give, you infinite joy on earth [...] "nor do I demand aught else in sacrifice".[9] We shall attain this certainty while we still live, [...] there is (?) actually no death. There is a change, but even as the sun is constantly shining, so are we in our own true selves constantly shining. It is only when we take up a body as we have now, that the gross material of our body, as gross material of the planet, shuts us off from the sunlight of our own true being.

It is during the periods when we are out of incarnations, so to speak, that we realize more of our own true being than we do in what we call life; but life and death are but the plus and minus parts of a [...] As we change from the plus to the minus, or the minus to the plus, so in the long orbit of our lives (?) do we go on. It is all

8 *John* 10:30
9 "I give unimaginable joys on earth: certainty, not faith, while in life, upon death; peace unutterable, rest, ecstasy; nor do I demand aught in sacrifice." *Liber AL vel Legis* I:58

life, but it is a question of sleeping and waking, as it were, even as we do in this life; but once we have realized our earthly immortality, the [...] of the immortality of the universe, we shall never again enter into that darkness. [...]

The illusions of the universe may still be with us, but we shall break thru that shadow; we shall realize our [...] and we shall begin to live naturally and freely as children of God on earth and his representatives in the Kingdom.

Magick Squares and Future Beats

The Magickal Processes and Methods of William S. Burroughs and Brion Gysin

Genesis Breyer P-Orridge

This text is an excerpt from the forthcoming volume on Trapart Books (2015), "Brion Gysin: His Name Was Master", published here in honor of William Burroughs' Centennial 2014. – Ed.

Being the First Part:

Change the way to perceive and change all memory.

Our very first "memories" are hand-me-downs from other people. Various events and moments, amusing anecdotes of when we were babies and very small children. Usually stories from a period in our life that we actually cannot recall for ourselves. These are the cornerstones which we begin to add onto, building more conscious, personally recorded experiential memories. Usually, without much consideration of veracity or motive, we assume those original (whose source is usually parental) stories are true, rather than separately authored and constructed mythologies. Yet, with the best will in the world, they are edited highlights (and lowlights) from another person's perspective, interpreted by them, and even given significance and meaning by their being chosen to represent the whole of us, before our own separate SELF consciousness sets in. All the information we have at our immediate disposal as self-consciousness develops is from someone else. Everything about us is true. Everything about us is false. Everything about us is both. It is by omission that we are described exactly, creating an unfolding program not of our own choosing. We are edited bloodlines seeking an identity with only partial data and unknown motivation and expectation.

(I should point out here that Brion Gysin claimed very convincingly to recall being in his mother's womb, the traumatic drama of actually being born and the horror of arriving at the "wrong address" and all subsequent events. I personally believe(d) him. I also suspect it is a part of what made him so incredibly remarkable, important and effective as a cultural engineer and innovator, as a sorcerer of light and language, as a magickian.)

These inherited, brief memories are a little jigsaw puzzle. A picture that contains impressions of what kind of "child" we are, in the eyes of our familial others. Without malicious intent necessarily, they still tend to guide us towards an unbalanced, prejudiced perception of who we are, they can easily become at least a basic sketch of our character by our parents, a blueprint made more solid by each re-telling, less possible to challenge. Just as we tend to like to please our parents by doing what they praise, so we can also manifest and reinforce their criticisms as well. At their unintended worst, these assumptions and maps become the metaphors/enhancers/deciders/directives for a lifetime's neurotic self-image, selected recordings of who we are, who we are imagined to be, who we are instructed we are, who we are expected to become, what kind of adult we will unfold into and of course evidence of an inherited fiction from which we will be conditioned as to how we too will perceive the world and our place in and on it. Looping around and around, a self-perpetuating, self-fulfilling and prophetic sampling into which we immerse ourselves, our SELF without any great wisdom to hint we might wait and see, listen and watch, question and perhaps even re-edit in order to maximize our potential to become.

If our self-image is primarily built upon the faulty, biased, prejudiced and highly edited memory recordings of other people, with their own agenda of who we are intended to become, as defined by this perceptual process of un-natural selection. Then ways and tools that allow us to seize the means of perception become vital in our fight to construct a self, a character, an identity that is truly and independently our own. Which makes any magic that empowers us to do that both sacred and profane a matter of survival, a cause of infinite concern in terms of the evolution of both our SELF and our species. In short, a divine territory that recognizes behavior, perception, and character as malleable matter equal to all other forms of matter, distinguished (so far) only by our apparent awareness that we exist and have choices, mortality and doubt as signifiers of our individuality. If there is any right, any birth-right, it might well be the right to create one's SELF.

BEING THE SECOND PART:

In a pre-recorded universe, who made the first recordings?

In a very real sense, I do not own my early life. The first "memories" I have are actually short anecdotes describing things that happened involving me that I actually have absolutely no recollection of. Interestingly they all revolve around me doing something "naughty" which influenced others negatively (by parental standards) and for which fact I got "blamed". The mistakes of others were placed very squarely at my door. A classic "bad influence". For much of my life these shameful crises were simply accepted on trust. I have even recounted them myself, for years without doubting their veracity. Yet I have come to know how subjective, selective and personally convenient and self-serving various sources of versions of events can be, and that we consciously and unconsciously edit out all kinds of things to suit ourselves, pragmatically, or manipulatively in order to make things happen. These are the roots of a childhood theatre of behavioral depth magick. A form that sadly suffers from being born of devout ignorance, and a total lack of shamanic guidance. Magick is by one definition, if you will, the science of making things happen according to your desires in order to maximize control over one's life and immediate environment in order to create a universe that is perfecting in its kindness towards you.

This could all be innocuous, and perhaps, for many, it is. For my SELF, it has emerged as a key factor, a continuous exploration and necessity for my emotional survival as a creative being to free my SELF from imposed ways of being initiated by these uninvited guests in the recording device that is my experiential existence. My recordings are what I build my soul from. The act of independently visualized and consciously chosen creation builds that phenomenon that is what I call and perceive as "me". If I am not who I was told I was, then who am I? More importantly, can I find ways to change the original recordings and inherited construct and actually remember and become whoever it is that I am, or even better, who I dream I wish to be? Can we build our SELF? Are there methods, examples, tricks and techniques, methods and madness, analysis and delirium that empower my self?

It is very easy to fall victim to peer group pressure. Parental expectation. Emotionally crippling tales that put the blame for negative events upon your personality and behavior. We are pushed, shoved, squashed and bullied into submission and contrition. At some point in each being's life, I believe, we are presented with a critical choice, a classic, cliché, fork in our road of life. As this occurs, I would suggest that the split is between the consensus reality, consensus-perceptual "memory" pre-recordings of a more or less controlled and predictable biological time line existence and an opportunity to redefine self-perception and remix re-recordings infinitely and chaotically entirely unique and original combinations and collisions of SELF determined and SELF creating recordings assembled from, with and by freedom choice. Instead of our identity (in all possible and impossible senses of the word) being built by others we can build our own, and own it.

It was in 1967 that this critical concern overwhelmed me. Was there a system, a way to adjust, control, break-up and re-assemble behavior, personality, creativity and perception, so that novelty and surprise, the unexpected and improvisation could be applied to my identity, using my SELF as raw material, as malleable physically and mentally as any other medium? Could I change the way I perceive and change all memory? It seemed to me that there had to be a way to truly live my life as art and make my art an inseparable extension of my life. I began my search for a creativity-centered system of applied magick.

You might think that seeking out two Beatniks was a funny place to start looking for a functional, modern process of magick. But, in fact, it turned out to be exactly the right place to look, and just as I had hoped, it did change my life, and it did enable me to build, with intention and clarity, the bohemian, divinely seeking being I willed to become.

If I was constructed on the foundation of, and from, inherited memories taken on trust, on metaphors handed down with their own agenda via language and image (what one might think of as the cultural DNA of personality) then I needed to confront the omnipotence of word control. It was imperative to my survival as a sentient being to locate the most advanced alchemists, and the most radical in their field, in order to learn what I could of strategies that would force the hand of chance in favor of self-creation rather than submissive reaction.

(In Paris during the 1970's Brion Gysin pointed out to me that is was extremely significant that the first book of The Bible is known as the book of CREATION, and that he chose to point out in an early permutation "In the beginning was the WORD and the WORD was God".)

I first met William S. Burroughs in London, at Duke Street, St James in 1971 after a brief series of postal correspondence. It actually felt and seemed strange, as I had discovered his existence via Jack Kerouac as the mysterious character Bull Lee. Confirmation of his being an actual person led me to the porn district of Soho in 1965, where I snagged a copy, a first edition actually, with dust jacket by Brion Gysin, of NAKED LUNCH. It had been prosecuted for obscenity, porn shops were the only places in those days to buy W.S. Burroughs, Henry Miller, and Jean Genet and pretty much everything I was consuming as confirmation, vindication and affirmation as a 15-year-old. Six years after beginning my Beat oddesey, via books, my very first question to him, a living, breathing, beatnik legend in the flesh was…"Tell me about magic?"

BEING THE THIRD (MIND) PART:

Nothing here now but thee recordings.

William had a cut out, cardboard, life-size photo of Mick Jagger standing by his bookcase. Its significance was the rite of "Performance", not rock and roll. On the television set was a full bottle of Jack Daniels, and a remote. The first I ever saw. William was not in the least surprised by my question. "Care for a drink," he said. "Sure" I replied nervous and, for one of the only times ever in my life, in awe. "Well, … Reality is not really all it's cracked up to be, you know," he continued. He took the remote and started to flip through the channels, cutting up programmed TV. I realized he was teaching me. At the same time he began to hit stop and start on his SONY TC cassette recorder. Mixing in "random" cut-up previous recordings. But these were overlaid with our conversation. None acknowledging the other. An instant holography of information and environment. I was already being taught. What Bill explained to me then was pivotal to the unfolding of my life and art. Everything is recorded. If it is recorded, then it can be edited. If it can be edited than the order, sense, meaning and direction are as arbitrary and personal as the agenda an/or person editing. This is magick. For if we have the ability and/or choice of how things unfold, regardless of the original order, and/or intention, that they are recorded in; then we have control over the eventual unfolding. If reality consists of a series of parallel recordings that usually go unchallenged, then reality only remains stable and predictable until it is challenged. And/or the recordings are altered, or their order changed. These concepts lead us to the release of cut-ins as a magickal process.

At this point we broke open the hard liquor and each downed a large glass. Soon (it seemed) the bottle was empty.

Magick Squares and Future Beats

A Cassette Tape Recorder as a Magickal Weapon:

What I was then told changed the unfolding of my L-if-E in every possible dimension and concept of the word. He told me about how during the Chicago convention he had walked around recording the background noises of the Yippie demonstrations, the riots, the Mayor Daley repression and violence. As he walked, he would randomly hit record at intervals "cutting-in" the most recent sounds around him creating a collage that was non-linear time. What he observed happening was that as a configuration of "trouble sounds" occurred (i.e. police sirens, screams, chanting of slogans) the actual physical manifestations and/or expressions of those sounds also increased in what WE think of as the "real" physical world. His next experiment was to work with "passive" environmental audio-scapes in order to check his evidence and see if it could be replicated. As William explained it to me at that time, in what became an apocryphal action, he had decided to check more "scientifically" the theories he had been assembling with Brion Gysin regarding "reality" being a linear recording. A malleable medium or element that was subject, as such, to the intervention of edits and erasings, rub-outs and re-sculpting if you will. Not far from Duke Street (where he was then living in voluntary exile. A choice I would find my SELF compelled to make y-eras later) was a basic British/Greek café where he might sometimes relax and get the classic English breakfast of chips, baked beans, fried eggs, fried tomatoes, mushrooms and toast with a large cup of tea, or an instant coffee. Nothing special. Nowhere special. The perfect place, in fact, to encounter arrogance and snobbery, abruptness and poor manners on the part of the very people indentured to one's service. On one of those DAYS, a day when all is over-colored, over-laid, and over-bearing, William was treated with great disdain, with rudeness beyond belief. Crass, crude, rude, nasty and aggressive, insulting behavior quite beyond the acceptable pale of manners. Such was the rudeness and unpleasantness experienced by William that he swore never to eat there again. But, more than that, his disgust and anger was so intense and intentional, so unforgiving and angry in the moment that he felt quite compelled to experimental "sorcery" (his word to me, take note). What form did his curse take? Herein follows the first lesson in contemporary intuitive and functional magick.

William took his SONY TC cassette recorder and very methodically walked back and forth in front of the offending café, at breakfast-time, and other times of day, making a tape of the ongoing street noises that made the sonic background of its location. A field recording encapsulating a typical day via street sounds. Next he went back to his apartment and at various random places on the same cassette he recorded "trouble noises" over bits of the previous recordings. These were things like police car sirens and (in those days) bells; gunshots; bombs; screams and other types of mayhem from the TV news primarily. Now he went back to the café location and again walked up and down the street outside playing the cut-up cassette recording complete with "trouble noises". Apparently the tape does not need to be played very loud, in fact a volume level that blends in so that passers-by on the other side of the street, or a few feet away would not, and do not, notice the additional sounds as implanted fictions. This process was repeated several times, quite innocuously to any observer. "L'hombre invisibile" at work. Within a very short time, the café had closed down! Not only did it close down, but also the space remained empty for years, unable to be rented for love, or money.

We do well to consider, at this point, that each individual human being is inevitably the center of their own unique universe/sensory/experiential world. Only YOU are physically present every single second of your personal L-if-E and as a result, any person, or event that takes place without your physical presence is a part of somebody else's unique universe. Of course, there are times when others ARE present and then they will tend to assume they are all in ONE universe together. However, ask any cop if they get the same story from a variety of witnesses, or the same description of a suspect, and you will be told in no uncertain terms, that nobody sees, or hears, the same thing at the same time. Nor do they share equal abilities to describe or recall what they imagine their memories have recorded. In other words, even consensus reality, is just that, an amalgamation of approximate recordings from flawed bio-machines. In the background of our daily lives is almost the equivalent of a flimsy movie set unfolding created by the sum total of what people allow to filter in through their senses. This illusory material world, built ad hoc, second to second is uncommon to us all. It will only seem to exist whilst our body is passing through it. After that its continued existence is a matter of faith, and our experience of it seeming to have a certain continuity of presence. I.e., we find we can apparently GO BACK to a place that seems solid. It is quite possible that the energy or phenomenon that glues together a repeatable experience of solidity and materiality on this earth is the pressure of billions of human beings simultaneously, and in close proximity, believing in what they see and hear. Bear in mind that Astory (my preferred word for the redundant word "history") is the collected recordings of subjective previous people(s) and our species. What has survived, what was memorized or stored in some form is usually assumed to be the story of our unfolding species. Nevertheless, we are more than aware that certain events are written up with agendas included, dogmatic religions, democracies, bitter families and totalitarian regimes all collude in this process of editing. It has crossed my mind that this entire planet is a recording device itself. As archeology and anthropology and forensic science progress we are able to discover and reveal endless detail of happenings going back millions of years. Also, side by side, we have almost every period of human species Astory still continuing today. The bushmen in Africa live in a basically pre-astoric way; tribes in New Guinea in the stone age to a degree perhaps; other peoples in a barbaric middle ages; entire communities in middle America live in a fundamentalist Victorian era; and yet others, in somewhere like Silicon Valley or Tokyo, live in a technological science fiction future. This is a remarkable thought. Infinite micro-realities existing simultaneously, by their very activation creating an appearance of "reality" and infinite, social, macro-realities parallel and colliding and competing for supremacy and with it the power to edit and describe a global "reality".

At this point I feel it helpful to re-MIND the reader that this essay is necessarily, as part of an anthology, only an over-view of the complex and wide-ranging evidence consistently to be found in the creative works, in all media, of William S. Burroughs and Brion Gysin. My thereby implicit proposal is, that whilst Burroughs was, indeed, a classic literary figure of the 20th century; and Gysin was a classic 20th century renaissance artist; who together bequeathed to us through intuitive science and method, and a prophetic appreciation of meaning a pivotal approach to questions of perception and the nature and origin of literature and art. They can only be fully appreciated, and, perhaps, finally understood in terms of their central and passionate inner agendas and obsessions when re-considered and re-assessed as serious, conscious and masterful creative/cultural alchemists and practicing magickians. (N.B. A mission for which I have taken the linguistic liberty of coining the term/occupation "Cultural Engineer".)

As their works as this unexpected brotherhood unfold after their collaborations begin at "The Beat Hotel" in Paris during 1957 to 1963 and meticulously thereafter, one is immersed with them in a fascinating journey into pre-material consciousness. A place where direct and indirect communications with the nervous system occur; where nothing is fixed or permanent but everything is true and permitted; where ancient programming holds prisoner the possible truths of who and what we are, and where even words are potential enemy agents and distortion devices that assist in the suppression of our potential as beings. This wordless "interzone" was, as has been pointed out before (see "Here To Go" in the bibliography) so "inconceivable" to even such a libertarian poet as Allen Ginsberg that he felt that it "…threatened everything". It is not uncommon for people to demonstrate symptoms of fear and insecurity when the very fabric of their protective safety blanket "reality" is scattered, shattered, shredded and then further cut-up to reveal a central possibility of divinity and love within all things and perceptions of things. It can be painful to release the last connection to an inherited and linear space time "reality" assembled from filtered essence of solidifying mundanity. In a magickal universe, everything, and every THING, is malleable, changeable, interconnected at invisibly deep levels, levels so subtle and sub-atomic that consciousness and intention can affect them.

"Intention is the work of envisaging and enacting will." (Ray L. Hart in *Unfinished Man and the Imagination*. See "Even Furthur The Metaphysics of The Sigil" by Paul Cecil in the *Painful But Fabulous* bibliography)

In an often-quoted moment Gysin proposed to Burroughs "Writing is fifty years behind painting." By which he meant that painting had begun to call into question all the traditional boundaries and templates. Even reason and object were arbitrary and unnecessary markers. The only frame left was the Diggers' frame of reference. By his introduction of the cut-up in all its manifestations, Gysin the accomplished "shaman" as Burroughs so rightly designated him, gave his compadre the magickal tool(s) required for a lifetime's astonishing, and recorded as literature, revelation. Their intricate and dazzling story and their functional, demystified techniques and process continue to leak into present time in preparation for various possible futures. I believe that a re-reading of their combined body of work from a magickal perspective not only confirms what they themselves accepted about themselves, that they were powerful modern magicians. This omission does a great disservice to us all. In this post-digital age, as we each construct our own personal "reality fields" it is my conviction that a positive unfolding of our species, and an evolution that is non-destructive and anathema to polarization is absolutely central to our survival with ethical honor.

In the ever more metaphysical world of physics a parallel sequence of "discoveries" equivalent in their importance to science as the "cut-ups" system of magick is to culture, has potentially reshaped our understanding of the universe and "reality" (see *The Holographic Universe* in the bibliography). According to physicist David Bohm (simplifying and colloquialising as best as I can as a lay person) any apparent separation between matter and consciousness is an illusion, an artifact that occurs or is assembled only AFTER both consciousness and matter have unfolded INTO the "explicate" world of objects and linear/sequential time. As one might expect the OTHER realm would be the "implicate" world, which would be all those inner "worlds" (including thought) that take place outside linear time, and sensory confluence. What is coming to be accepted as a non-material field of consciousness? Bohm's researches suggested to him that "…at the subquantum level, in which the quantum potential operated, location ceased to exist. All points in space became equal to all other points in space, and it was meaningless to speak of anything being separate from anything else." Interestingly, a Cheyenne/Apache shaman told me years and years ago that there was no word for death in his clan, instead they used the word "separation" to express the concept. Similarly, the Shiva holy man Pagalananda Nath Agori Baba spent many patient hours deprogramming my western linear materiality in order for me to be better able to grasp the concept of his "path of no distinction". The Egyptian sage Hermes Trismegistus explained this absolute elsewhere idea hundreds of years ago when he was recorded as saying "The without is like the within of things and the small of things is like the large."

So now, finally, after thousands of years, we have a consensus of great significance born of this unprecedented and radical intersection between mystic, scientist, shaman and artist/creative being. Partly for lack of adequate language and partly to camouflage their subversive ideas in order to stay alive, various enlightened visionaries, often the "heretics" of their era, have employed brain-twisting metaphors to describe the Universe of objective "reality" an illusion. What scientists are trying to describe to us now is a Universe where, according to thinkers like Niels Bohr and others, subatomic particles require an observer to come into existence and without an observer's presence they do not come into existence. Even more remarkable that away from us, each observing from the center-point of our individual existence, the Universe is a measureless resonating domain of frequencies that are an open source that only gets transformed into this world as we think we recognize it after being accessed by our senses and entering our brain. There it is decoded/encoded/acoded who knows which or all and is assembled according to the dimensions of linear time and space, and, I would argue, our subjective cultural expectations. There seems to be a growing agreement at the heart of creation among those in service of the path of the divine, the scientific, and the artistic that the primary reality is one of wholeness, an indivisible unity that functions not unlike a living being, or (my favorite analogy) a coral reef. So, while we rush about, billions of us, interacting experientially with our environment and various objective events do, for all practical intents and purposes, happen to us in particular locations, on a subatomic level things are quite different. On a subatomic level, the Bohm School of science proposes that all points in space become equal to all other points in space, they are nonlocalities. So, to quote John Lennon, "Nothing is real" might have added, and it wasn't/isn't there anyway!

To sum up this section, the Universe is a unified source, an infinite, open, timeless, intricate quaquaversal frequency field in constant flux that appears to have objective form and material solidity when and because we observe it. And observe it we do. We observe it over and over, we are obsessed with recording it too (just think of all those hundreds of paparazzi documenting J Lo's every breath) and then we store it in monolithic museums, libraries, databanks. These huge repositories can act on a society's behalf to symbolize anthropological recorders and our maintenance of them, our belief in their contents in turn functions as the batteries that charge up and energize the social hologram that we have assembled as consensus reality in order to give continuity, consistency, solidity, and even significant sense of meaning with enough consistency and reliability for us to function during life as biological sentient beings. Nevertheless, it is our expectation that things will be the same, that a log will remain a log, and if enough of us keep "creating" logs as a matter of habit, eventually... yes... log jam; but it is still no more "real" despite the materiality produced by repetition. It is not a co-incidence that in more established doctrinal/dogmatic religions worldwide; in so-called "primitive" tribal and/or shamanic cultures; in the rituals of public and secret Western magickal and/or Masonic orders, or in the ecstatic rhythms and ancient beats of trance targeted music and chants that go with them repetition of key power words and phrases are as integral as is the phenomenon of call and response. Even at this deepest level of a relationship with the measureless frequency field, with the universe as a unified open source that has no locality, we are trying to solidify and maintain our sensory illusion(s). The purpose of these various "services" is to collectively reconstruct a social reality seamlessly with language, with words and names, with devotional submission to the power of its story, and thereby, ironically, to put into strict bondage through this habitual repetition the essence of life itself. Why? In order to predict and control it. Often, unwittingly, we empower the people who claim by continuity of descent by colluding in these rites. The real hidden doctrine handed down through the ages, the central agenda, is control. Why do those who control seek to maintain control? For its own sake. How do they control? By controlling the story, by editing our collective memory, conscious and unconscious. In many ways the edit is the invisible language of control and its corporate media allies. They cut and paste in order to separate us from each other by entrancing us with a pre-recorded reality that seamlessly isolates us in a world designed by those who would immerse us in service to their fundamentalist consumerism. Simultaneously divorcing us from the Universe that is creation itself in an infinite pre-sensory source.

"… writing is… not (just) an escape from reality, but an attempt to change reality, so (the) writer can escape the limits of reality." (William S. Burroughs from *Last Words*)

In his book *Last Words* Burroughs writes of the enemy and their two weaknesses being firstly that they have, "… no sense of humor" and secondly "They totally lack understanding of magic." Later he directs our attention to two other enemy weaknesses in reference to dogmatic scientific modes of enquiry by pointing out that phenomena "… that occur only once…" will automatically be invalidated by virtue of their uniqueness and that they have an "…insatiable appetite for data." Yet we have seen that everything is indivisibly unified. That there really are no hard edges, no division between mental and physical worlds, or any worlds or dimensions animate or inanimate. Instead we have been introduced to an holographic universe of infinite interconnectedness that responds to the future beat of a magickal shaman's drum. It is fundamental to understanding how to operate and interpret the challengingly effective, modern, and magickal exercises of Burroughs and Gysin, with cut-ups as their foundation and words as the disputed territory. What we have been trained from birth to believe of as a solid environment, is only a tiny fragment of what is available to our perception. At the same time, the behavioral, political and anthropological astory of our society and culture has been written and recorded by authors fulfilling an agenda of (and for) vested interests who do not have our well-being at heart, leaving most of us trapped in their current description of the universe.

"No two actual entities originate from an identical universe… The nexus (lineage) of actual entities in the universe correlate to a growth by assimilation that is termed "the actual world"". (Adapted with apology from *Process and Reality* by A.N. Whitehead.)

Back to the café. Experiments have shown we live a great deal of our lives "asleep", filtering out sensory input. Film a street as its residents are going to work in the morning. Add in a police car going past afterwards in the editing suite. Play it back to those same residents the following evening. Asked if this is a recording of the morning, almost all will say yes. They will also say they recall the police car going by. This is the phenomenon Burroughs was working with. Added to the fragility of our individual neurological recording devices is the age-old technique of suggestion. Yet, here we are faced with something perhaps even a little deeper. A conscious attack upon, and alteration of consensus reality by a formularized ritual.

"In a pre-recorded universe, who made the first recordings?" So asked Gysin and Burroughs. Further, if all we imagine to be reality is equivalent to a recording, then we become empowered to edit, re-arrange, re-contextualize and re-project by cutting-up and re-assembling my own reality and potentially, the reality of others. If this is true and effective, then a magickal act is taking place. Simplified magick has been defined as a method for changing reality in conformity with one's true will, or as a methodical demystified process that allows us to force the hands of chance in order to make things we truly desire happen based upon and within purity of intent. Crowley said that magick has "The aim of religion and the method of science." Brion Gysin talked of magick saying it was "… the Other Method, an exercise for controlling matter and knowing space, and a form of psychic hygiene." So what happened to the café? If it was only suggestion, then it would have only discouraged the people in the street whilst William was walking about playing his tape. None of them might have been customers anyway. It was NOT necessary for the café proprietors to be aware of the "curse". The premises closed and remained closed, followed by a series of brief failed businesses, long, long after William moved on to other activities.

"(The process) involves a reversal of our ordinary understanding that causes produce effects. *The cause must precede its effect* in (present) time, yet it must be presently existent in order to be active in producing its effect." (From *The Lure of God* by Lewis Ford)

According to Gysin in *Here To Go* (see bibliography) William sometimes used two cassette recorders, one in each hand and occasionally even added his own voice repeating an incantation he had written to intensify the focus of his spell. This particular incantation ended up as part of the soundtrack of *Witchcraft Through The Ages*, an obscure, and really rather kitsch Scandinavian black and white movie for which Burroughs did the voice over. A quirky anomaly resulting from the fact that beat filmmaker Antony Balch had the UK distribution rights. (see *Naked Lens* in the bibliography) Part of it went something like this:

> *Lock them out and bar the door,*
> *Lock them out for evermore.*
> *Nook and cranny, window, door,*
> *Seal them out for evermore…*

(see *Here To Go* in the bibliogrphy)

In addition to tape-recorder magick William also employed a version of the cut-up photograph as additional sorceric firepower. On that first visit, as he explained magick to me, he very generously showed me some of his journals. On one page he had stuck in two pictures. One was a black and white. Photograph of the section of the street buildings where the café was. Beneath it was a second print in black and white of the same section of street, or so it seemed at first glance. However, upon closer examination he had very neatly sliced out the café with a razor blade. Gluing the two halves of the image back together minus the offending establishment. This same principle can be applied to people one wishes to excise from one's daily L-if-E, and variations can be used according to your imagination and needs and, of course, these modern upgrades of magickal practice can be easily integrated into older traditions if one desires. For example, one could put the cut-out image into a brown paper bag with one's invocation added in pencil, black pepper, ground/broken glass, sharp blades, and vinegar and then throw it over one's shoulder into a graveyard whilst walking away without looking back.

Once one accepts a possibility that the Universe is holographic and that at the smallest subatomic levels all elements of phenomena can be affected by all others, then the probability of these operations being effective becomes far more credible. Indeed I would argue that a magickal view of the Universe is the most likely description we have proposed so far as a species. In "The Job" Burroughs discusses silence as a desirable state. What he seems to imply is that words are potentially blocks, both by their linearity in our language system and the manner in which they narrow definitions of experiential events and actions. He says, "Words… can stand in the way of what I call nonbody experience." He does not want to turn the human body into an environment that includes the universe. That would once more create limiting templates and maps of expectation that discourage new and/or radical explorations. Rationality and the fixed progression of physical biology narrow consciousness. One magickal method he proposes is then discussed.

"What I want to do is to learn to see more of what's out there, to look outside, to achieve as far as possible a complete awareness of surroundings… I'm becoming more proficient at it, partly through my work with scrapbooks and translating the connections between words and images." (From *The Third Mind* interview with Conrad Knickerbocker 1967.

One pre-requisite of most Western magickal orders is that the applicant/neophyte keep a daily magickal diary in which they note their dreams, synchronicities, apparent resolution of temporal events and desires after magickal operations. This is not so much just to document and vindicate the system being applied, as to create an ongoing awareness of the constant relationship we all actually have, moment to moment, with the other. In a universe where everything is, to quote TOPI "interconnected, inter-dimensional and integrated", or as Michael Talbot describes it, holographic, the acceleration of and practical collaboration with this interrelation of energies and their ability to assist us in affecting manifestations is more clearly revealed by methodical documentation. It seems that the more one acknowledges this confluence of mutability the more kindly its relationship to and with you. This interaction is the one symbolized by the number 23 in both Robert Anton Wilson's books, and in the mythologies flowing throughout Burroughs' fiction. It is not so much that the number 23 is a "magickal" number that does "tricks" for the person whom invokes it, it is more that the number 23 re-MINDS us of the inherent plasticity of our inherited reality and our potential to immerse our SELF in that quality to our own advantage and possible well-being. It represents a magickal vision of life rather than a linear and existential one. Significantly, Burroughs, like Kerouac and Gysin, kept dream diaries and journals. Gysin and Burroughs extending their range further by including cut-up texts, newspaper headlines, photographs, fictional routines and poems in a kaleidoscopic visualization of multi-faceted and layered "reality". Burroughs suggests a practical exercise to amplify our appreciation of, and practical familiarity with, this manifestation.

"Try this: Carefully memorize the meaning of a passage, then read it; you'll find you can actually read it without the words making any sound whatever in the mind's ear. Extraordinary experience, one that will carry over into dreams. When you start thinking in images, without words, you're well on the way." (From *The Third Mind*)

Magick Squares and Future Beats

On the 6th August 1981 I visited Burroughs in New York. He was living at 222 on the Bowery in the basement, a locale fondly nicknamed, and immortalized in various biographies as, the "Bunker". A book that Burroughs had introduced me to was "Breakthrough" by the Latvian paranormal investigator Konstantin Raudive. In his book Raudive documents hundreds of "recordings" of the voices of the spirits of the dead. His method was unusual but simple. To attach a crystal receiver to an otherwise standard reel-to-reel in the socket where a microphone would be plugged, hit record, and see what appeared on tape. What Raudive found was that within a wall of white sound and hiss, various intelligible sentences and messages that he believed were from souls in the dimensions associated with being dead, were audible. Given that we were meeting on Hiroshima Day, as Burroughs designated it, there was a feeling that perhaps quite a large number of dead souls might wish to breakthrough. We set up an old tape recorder on the kitchen table where many a dinner soirée was held over the New York years and hit record. Each of us took turns listening through headphones live to the noise and interference going down on analog tape as it slowly turned. After half an hour we played the "results" back, intently noting the slightest sonic detail. Like good, objective, laboratory researchers we made notes, both on paper and into a cassette SONY walkman I had with me. Almost in a parody of an autopsy on TV. Final report from the bunker...nothing! Oh, how we hoped for evidence, but we got just the expected hiss and short-wave "Twilight Zone" type sounds. Regardless of this, and Crowley was fastidious in reminding the initiate of this, we did not fall into the trap of "...lust for result". Sometimes only one phenomenon occurs to vindicate a theory, sometimes things seem unrepeatable. In terms of this text, what is significant is that Burroughs truly believed in the possibility of communication with the soul after physical death, long before he went public with that in his "Last Words".

As a footnote to this experiment an extra event is worthy of mentioning. During 1985 Psychic TV were recording a song about the deceased/murdered founder of the Rolling Stones, Brian Jones, called "GODSTAR". Still fascinated by the Raudive book and Burroughs' dogged exploration of its technique as a magickal tool I arbitrarily, on impulse, told Ken Thomas (my co-producer and creative engineer) to leave track 23 of the 24-track analog tape empty. After all the elements of the song were recorded in the traditional multi-track way I instructed him to re-run the master tape with every track muted except track 23. This track was to be on record, but with absolutely NO form of microphone or even a crystal receiver plugged in. Simply a tape deck running through a tape with no scientific means of recording on one track. To be honest Ken seemed to think this was both illogical and "...a bit spooky." To his credit, he went ahead and did as I asked anyway. When we played back the previously virgin, pristine and blank track 23, much to our amazement, we heard a metallic knocking at a few points! We replayed and replayed the track, it was definitely there and had certainly appeared during our "token" Raudive/Burroughs experiment; yet it seemed random, and was not a "voice". Suddenly, I had a moment of clarity and suggested Ken replay the track with the vocals of the lyric and some basic elements of the music added in the mix. The knocking sounds came very precisely under a sequence of words in the exact phrasing and position of the following, "…I wish I was with you now, I wish I could tell you somehow…" (Later I would change the lyric to, "I wish I could SAVE you somehow".) If I am truly frank, I really did take this as a sign of approval of the song and its message, that Brian Jones was murdered and received a callous treatment at the hands of the media during his last days. He became, for myself and many other fans of his iconography, a scapegoat in the essential magickal and sacred way. Sacrificed at the very least, by ignorance and greed, to the consumer and materialistic machine of linear reality. It is worth noting that at the time we were taping the song the consensus opinion, and official coroners verdict was "death by misadventure" with a lot of media hinting that he either drowned during an asthma attack, or he was so high on drugs that, despite being an athletic swimmer, he drowned right in front of his current girlfriend and guests. Our "magickal" message tended to imply there was more to the story and eventually, during the 1990's the builder Frank Thorogood confessed on his deathbed to murdering Brian Jones by holding him under water. Whatever you may choose to believe, it certainly appears that there are ways to make contact with realms considered Other via the most simple of tape recording devices.

Burroughs and Gysin both told me something that resonated with me for the rest of my life so far. They pointed out that alchemists always used the most modern equipment and mathematics, the most precise science of their day. Thus, in order to be an effective and practicing magician in contemporary times one must utilize the most practical and cutting-edge technology and theories of the era. In our case it meant cassette recorders, dreamachines and flicker, polaroid cameras, Xeroxes, e prime and, at the moment of writing this text, laptops, psychedelics, videos, dvds and the world wide web. Please note that earlier we discussed the possibility that the universe is an holographic web constructed of infinite intersections of frequencies (of truth). Basically, everything that is capable of recording and/or representing "reality" is a magickal tool just as much as it is a weapon of control.

BEING THE FOURTH PART:

Look at that picture, is it persisting?

The first question Brion Gysin asked me, in Paris in 1980 was…"Do you know your real name?" I replied, yes, (assuming it was Genesis and not my given name Neil) and then enquired as casually as I could, "Tell me about magick?"

Brion Gysin was born in Taplow, England in 1916, but, indicative of the unspecific density of his visitation on earth, and I use the word "visitation" because until his dying day, in 1986, Brion insisted that in being born human he was "delivered here by mistake". His conviction of mislocation, and with it a disruption of a different, perhaps parallel, dimensional existence, fuels his remarkably deep sense of irony and Otherness and is a central quality of his body of magickal artistic work. Gysin was a transmediator, a 20th century renaissance man, a multi-media explorer and innovator. Innately disciplined, he would continually paint and draw, extending his calligraphic journeys into what Burroughs would describe as "... painting from the viewpoint of timeless space."

During my conversations on magick with Burroughs in Duke Street, St. James, London (during the 1970's) it became more and more clear to me that Gysin was pivotal in the Astory of the magickal unfolding and the techniques of cultural alchemy, that had drawn me to his Beat *oeuvre* and from thence to make direct contact. During my conversations on magick with Gysin the cassette tape-recorder that I had with me was tolerated ONLY on the condition that certain key teachings were spoken, whilst the tape was switched off. As he presented it quite plainly to me, "... magick is passed on by the touching of hands." In other words, certain ideas and methods are handed-down master to student one on one directly in each other's physical presence. This agreement has been honored ever since, and remains so. Nevertheless, just to have confirmation from him that it was indeed true that his work was contemporary magick, not just artistic or literary experimentation was a great solace and gave me determination in my personal path.

It was Gysin who first recognized the potential of cut-ups as a means to update and upgrade writing and art, and as a contemporary application of magick. In collaboration with Ian Sommerville and Burroughs he discovered and made cheaply accessible, the Dreamachine; "The first artwork to be looked at with eyes closed". The story of and implications of which are marvelously catalogued in John Geiger's book *The Chapel Of Extreme Experience* (see below in the bibliography). In that book, for the first time, out of a kaleidoscopic cyclone, a blizzard of revolutionary scientific information and ultra-visionary creation we are exposed to an incredibly significant creative and conceptual exploration of consciousness via "flicker". In terms of possibility both Burroughs and Gysin would often quote Hassan I Sabbah, the "old man of the mountains", who from his fortress in Alamut, Iran was rumored to have controlled via assassins a huge swathe of ancient Arab civilization. His motto, "Nothing is true, Everything Is Permitted" recurs over and over, especially in Burroughs' books. It is not so far from the Thelemic precept, "Do what thou wilt shall be the whole of the Law". A theoretical connection that Burroughs appeared to acknowledge towards the end of his life.

Gysin spent 23 years living in Morocco. During that time he ran a restaurant called "1001 Nights" and would invite a group of The Master Musicians of Jajouka to play music for the guests as the entertainment. He tells the story more than once, of how that business crumbled after he found a magick spell "... an amulet of sorts, a rather elaborate one with seeds, pebbles, shards of broken mirror, seven of each, and a little package in which there was a piece of writing...which appealed to the devils of fire to take Brion away from this house." Very shortly after this discovery, he lost the restaurant and ultimately returned to Paris. On one of my first visits to Paris to meet with Gysin I was blessed with a special evening. After looking into the dreamachine for a couple of hours, Bachir Attar, then the son of the Master Musician of Jajouka, and his brother cooked me a ceremonial meal. During the feast Bachir played flute music that he told me raised the Djinn, the little people, and the spirits and bestowed great fortune upon the listener. Despite the friction of the era when the restaurant was lost, a very powerful magickal bond remained between the ancient system of magick and the most contemporary of elaborations represented by Gysin.

Calligraphic magick squares were one of the techniques most commonly applied by Gysin. He would reduce a name or an idea to a "glyph" and then write across the paper from right to left, turn the paper and do the same again, and so on, turning the paper around and around to create a multi-dimensional grid. Gysin believed this "scaffolding" allowed the Djinn, the little people to run with the intention "exercising control of matter and knowing space." The same techniques and consciously driven functional intention also permeated his paintings. In a very real sense, everything he created was an act of sorcery.

William S. Burroughs described the central difference of Gysin's painting as follows:

"All art is magical in origin... intended to produce very definite results. Art is functional; it is intended to make things happen. Take porcelain stove, disconnect it and put it in your living room, it may be a good-looking corpse, but it isn't functional anymore. Writing and painting were once in cave paintings to ensure good hunting. The painting of Brion Gysin deals directly with the magical roots of art. His paintings are designed to produce in the viewer the timeless ever-changing world of magic caught in the painter's brush. His paintings may be called space art. Time is seen spatially as a series of images or fragments images past, present, or future."

Gysin felt trapped and oppressed by materiality, but optimistically searched for techniques to short-circuit control and expectation. He accepted nothing as fixed and permanent, reducing the most intimidating formulae of language to animated permutations that become portals of behavioral liberation. If as we have seen, the Universe consists of interlaced frequencies, that pulse and resonate at various interconnected rhythms then his search was for a future beat that would liberate the body and mind from all forms of linearity. Each magick square is essentially holographic, suffused with a directed unity. Intertwined in his grids as confirmation and illustration of the magickal ideas proposed are examples of routines, exercises with words, and densely cut-up texts. What we observe is a complex, deeply serious mind, an occultural alchemist, camouflaged by passionate humor.

In Gysin's works and writings we are blessed with a perfect example of the storyteller teacher. A practiced post-technological shamanic guide to the mind, providing exercises, navigational tools and data to assist us in the essential process for magickal survival and for the exploration of this strange place in which we seem to unfold our physical existence(s). A domain we call earth, society and life but rarely call into fundamental question. Rationality and materiality have generated a depth of inertia so profound that it could destroy our potential as a species to survive or evolve. All the more reason to re-appraise and study as magickal masters the instructive works of Burroughs and Gysin as we enter the 21st Century. As science confirms their revelation of this space time neurosphere to be an holographic universe, I have no doubt that Burroughs and Gysin, re-defined as occultural alchemists and practicing magickians, are destined for an accelerating appreciation for the seminal influence of their cultural engineering experiments.

There is an exquisite mastery of perception that these discoveries unfold. Both Gysin and Burroughs use a serial seduction of detail. Meaning is shattered and scattered to become a more accurate and truthful representation of this arbitrary plane we needlessly confine by using the word-prison "reality". Consecutive events are subverted as we read, revealing the fragility and distortions that our conditioned senses filter out for simplicity of behavior and illusory reason. Nothing tends to remain as it seems, but becomes as it's seen. Contradictory experience is portrayed as equally perceived, parallel images and thoughts. Mundanity is turned strange and disturbing.

Burroughs and Gysin, as master magickians, grasp the elasticity of reality and our right to control its unfolding as we see fit and prefer. They consolidate our right to active participation in the means of perception, and their proposal of the nature of consensus being is still quite revolutionary. As we navigate the warp and weft of biological existence and infinite states of consciousness, the holographic universe that looks kindly upon us, at the magick squares of their methods and the delirious madness they supply us with, we are offered a unique perspective and afforded respite, balance and the possibility of retrieving new and valuable information for a future.

We are not talking about a matter of faith here; faith is something that has a low quotient in these experiments. Rather we are looking at prophetic predictions based upon a magickal vision of the universe and the resulting, practical applications of magickal/alchemical theories and exercises. In fact we are looking at an early, workable model of the future, in which a positive, compassionate unfolding of our latent qualities as a species is defined and described in the vainglorious hope that we "abandon all rational thought" and immerse ourselves in an ecstatic series of creative possibilities.

In a way, it is a bit like learning a martial art. We develop our media reflexes and accelerate our improvisational responses in order to maximize our individual potentialities and the interests of our chosen people or our private dream agenda. In his various essential commentaries on media divulgence Douglas Rushkoff, astutely, directs us to a re-examination of the original source of an inherited narrative of culture and life. Surprisingly, his conclusions are very similar to my assertions in relation to Burroughs and Gysin. That the very astory that began this examination, the social narrative imposed upon us as a child, that so easily programs us to maintain every possible status quo without criticism; and that compounds the notion of linearity and a serial phenomenological universe seems more clearly to be an illusion and a deliberately inert construction. A picture of "reality" that is designed by those with a vested interest in stasis to maintain our surrender to cultural impotence and all forms of addictive consumption.

The past controls through people and their surrender to a closed system, where the laws of physics remain constant, and predictability is a desirable state in an ever more rigid global world order. Yet, in fact, we are entering a digital future, an holographic universe, where at least theoretically, every sentient being on earth will be interconnected, international and interfaced entirely new navigational tools are required. The possibilities alone are endless. It is my contention that as the authorship of our own private narrative becomes increasingly autonomous, malleable and optional, that a new future, a future that is inclusive, rooted in the idea of an open source that we can affect by logical and magickal means, becomes critical to our species' survival, comprehension, and evolutionary change. A future where Burroughs and Gysin, and their modern occultural brethren, have supplied prophetic, functional skills and nonlocal points of observation which can intrinsically train us to be fittingly alert and prepared for the unpredictable aesthetic and social spasms to come.

FINAL NOTE: THE DISCIPLINE OF DO EASY:

I strongly advise any reader who has been inspired to re-consider their picture of both the "future" beats and their world picture to go online and look for the text of a short, one-page essay by William S. Burroughs titled "The Discipline of Do Easy" or "The Discipline of DE". In my own private, magickal, life a rigorous and continual application of this idea has been as central to my uncanny achievement of countless goals as the Austin Osman Spare system of sigilization.

SELECTED BIBLIOGRAPHY:

I would like to suggest that anyone whose interest has been stimulated at all by this more unorthodox point of observation and interpretation of two classic Beat figures seek out, and actually read, the books listed below, and/or re-read them with a different perspective in mind. Needless to say, there is no end in sight, even within the realms of time or mortality as to how we recreate our subjective means of perception. I really believe that listed below is a functional, inspirational and thorough library of ideas and techniques for seeing this mystery of biological and neuro-illogical L-if-E in its intended and intrinsic holographic form. As you might suspect from my text, seeking out and finding, with dogged determination and a deeply hungry appetite for soul and wisdom, for purposes of SELF determination in a world built of feedback loops of surrender and submission to consuming, to addiction to the products of an ever more banal culture that can NEVER supply satiation, aesthetic nutrition, sensual self-creation, or freedom of identity.

—⚡— MINUTES TO GO by William S. Burroughs; Gregory Corso; Sinclair Beiles and Brion Gysin 1968.
—⚡— THE PROCESS by Brion Gysin 1969.
—⚡— FUTURE RITUAL by Philip H. Farber 1995.
—⚡— BRION GYSIN LET THE MICE IN by Brion Gysin; William S. Burroughs and Ian Sommerville 1973.
—⚡— THE EXTERMINATOR by William S. Burroughs and Brion Gysin 1967.

--᠊ HERE TO GO/BRION GYSIN by Terry Wilson and Brion Gysin 1982.

--᠊ THE BEAT HOTEL by Barry Miles 2000.

--᠊ THEE PSYCHICK BIBLE by Genesis P-Orridge 1994.

--᠊ THE JOB by Daniel Odier (interviews with William S. Burroughs)

--᠊ PAINFUL BUT FABULOUS – THE LIVES AND ART OF GENESIS P-ORRIDGE by Julie A. Wilson; Douglas Rushkoff; Richard Metzger; Paul Cecil; Bengala; Carol Tessitore and Carl Abrahamsson 2003.

--᠊ CHAPEL OF EXTREME EXPERIENCE by John Geiger 2002.

--᠊ RADIUM 226.05 MAGAZINE Edited by Ulrich Hillebrand and CM von Hausswolff Spring 1986.

--᠊ BACK IN NO TIME – The BRION GYSIN READER Edited by Jason Weiss 2001.

--᠊ CYBERIA by Douglas Rushkoff 1993.

--᠊ MEDIA VIRUS by Douglas Rushkoff 1994.

--᠊ THE HOLOGRAPHIC UNIVERSE by Michael Talbot 1991.

--᠊ THE THIRD MIND by William S. Burroughs and Brion Gysin 1978.

--᠊ THE BEST OF OLYMPIA Edited by Maurice Girodias 1961.

--᠊ THE LAST MUSEUM by Brion Gysin 1986.

--᠊ WRECKERS OF CIVILIZATION by Simon Ford 1999.

--᠊ RE/SEARCH #1 – W.S. BURROUGHS/BRION GYSIN/THROBBING GRISTLE Edited by Vale 1982.

--᠊ FLICKERS-OF THE DREAMACHINE Edited by Paul Cecil 1996.

--᠊ THE SOUL'S CODE – In Search Of Character And Calling by James Hillman 1997.

--᠊ DISINFORMATION – The Interviews, Edited by Richard Metzger 2002.

--᠊ SEX AND ROCKETS – The Occult World Of Jack Parsons by John Carter 1999.

--᠊ BREAKTHROUGH – voices of the dead by Konstantin Raudive.

--᠊ THE FINAL ACADEMY – Statements Of A Kind edited by G. P-Orridge and Roger Ely with texts by Antony Balch; Felicity Mason; William S. Burroughs; Brion Gysin; John Giorno; Dave Darby; Jeff Nuttall; Ian Sommerville;Victor Bockris; Jon Savage; Eric Mottram; Barry Miles; 23 Skidoo; Cabaret Voltaire; Psychic TV; Ian Hinchcliffe; Last Few Days; Paul Burwell; Anne Bean 1982.

--᠊ THIS IS THE SALIVATION ARMY a compilation by Scott Treleaven with a foreward by Genesis P-Orridge 2003.

--᠊ THE HOLOGRAPHIC UNIVERSE by Michael Talbot 1991.

--᠊ PORTABLE DARKNESS – An Aleister Crowley Reader Edited by Scott Michaelsen with forewards by Genesis P-Orridge and Robert Anton Wilson 1989.

--᠊ THE SOUL'S CODE – In Search Of Character And Calling by James Hillman 1996.

--᠊ NAKED LENS – Beat Cinema by Jack Sergeant 1997.

--᠊ APOCALYPSE CULTURE #1 and #2 Edited by Adam Parfrey and 1987, 1990 and 2000.

--᠊ RAPID EYE #2 Edited by Simon Dwyer 1992.

--᠊ REBELS AND DEVILS –The Psychology Of Liberation, Edited by Christopher S. Hyatt with contributions by William S. Burroughs; Timothy Leary; Robert Anton Wilson; Austin Osman Spare; Lon Milo Duquette; Genesis P-Orridge; Aleister Crowley; Israel Regardie; Peter J. Carroll; Osho Rajneesh; Jack Parsons and others 1996.

–∽– GLOBAL BRAIN – The Evolution Of Mass Mind From The Big Bang To The 21st Century, by Howard Bloom 2000.

Contributors

Fredrik Söderberg is an artist based in Stockholm, and is a co-founder of Edda Publishing. He has had several major exhibitions in Sweden and abroad, and has illustrated a number of books and record covers. www.fredriksoderberg.org

Carl Abrahamsson (b. 1966) is the editor of *The Fenris Wolf* and the founder of The Institute of Comparative Magico-anthropology. He likes to write and read, take an occasional photograph and at times converse with the audio structure spirits. He is also a documentary film-maker, predominantly with the series *An Art Apart.* www.carlabrahamsson.com, www.trapart.net

Sara George (b. 1980), has studied art history at university. She likes to play with her fairy dolls house, get lost in the strange worlds of symbolist art and write fairy-tales about foxes and inner visions. www.snovitsapple.blogspot.com

Sasha Chaitow is a PhD candidate at the Centre for the Study of Myth at the University of Essex. Her PhD thesis comprises a full scale review of Joséphin Péladan's life and work, exploring his impact during the height of the French *Belle Epoque.* Sasha initially studied Fine Art at Vakalo Art School, Athens. Her interest in esoteric symbolism and the crossover between language and art led initially to an MA in English Literature (University of Indianapolis, 2004) and a second MA in Western Esotericism (EXESESO, Exeter, 2008). She has presented six solo exhibitions and her symbolic work explores a variety of esoteric themes.

Sasha has been assistant visiting professor in Religious Studies and History at the University of Indianapolis Athens since 2008, and as founding director of Phoenix Rising Academy (www.phoenixrising.org.gr), she coordinates a curriculum dedicated to bringing the academic study of Western Esotericism to a general audience.

Sasha writes for Greek national newspaper *Eleftheros Typos*, and assorted other publications in a variety of countries. She has directed two international conferences and several smaller events and colloquia, as part of Phoenix Rising Academy's activities. She has presented at many international conferences and symposia, and has contributed articles and chapters to books on Freemasonry, Intuition, Synaesthesia, Methodology in the Study of Esotericism, and Esotericism and Politics. http://peladan.org or http://sashachaitow.co.uk

Vanessa Sinclair, Psy.D. is a psychoanalyst and clinical psychologist in private practice in New York City.

Kendell Geers changed his date of birth to May 1968 and lives between Johannesburg and Brussels. He made a name for himself as an socio-political, cultural-activist, artist and animist claiming the necessity of relational ethics in a spiritual engagement through art. His performances, sculptures, videos, installations and photographs question manichean visions of the world, by calling us to a reversibility of values. His raw language explores the boundaries of art and what is permissible, provoking and arousing intense feelings of desire and danger, seduction and repulsion.

Stephen Sennitt is the editor and publisher of the well-respected and innovative occultzine NOX (published from 1986-1991). Author of many articles/essays and several books on esoteric themes, including *Monstrous Cults* and *Liber Koth*, Sennitt is currently working on a new project from which 'Sentient Absence' is extracted. E-mail: s.sennitt@ btinternet.com

Antony Hequet is a Franco-American poet & composer. His research and work are are rooted in the oral traditions of poetry. Singer and Slam Poet, he founds his performative style in the practice of Qi Gong and internal martial arts (Bagua - Dancing Cobras). Through the years he has produced and authored a number of multiform artistic creations associating music, poetry, ephemeral sculpture & installation work. These were given in spaces such as the Galleria dell'Accademia Florence Italy, Uffizi Museum Florence Italy, Château de Châteaudun France... He now is working out of the Funkhaus Berlin Nalepastraße historical sound studios. www. mund.fr http://blog.mund-production.com

Genesis Breyer P-Orridge (b 1950) is a multiversal, polymathic, pandrogenous artist-magician of legendary stature. www.genesisbreyerporridge.com

Patrick Lundborg is a writer based in Stockholm, author of the acclaimed study of psychedelic culture: *Psychedelia – Ancient Culture, Modern Lifestyle*. www.lysergia.com

Henrik Dahl is a journalist and critic specialising in psychedelic culture and art. He is the editor of The Oak Tree Review, a website featuring interviews and essays on psychedelia and the 1960s counterculture. Dahl is also a regular contributor to Psychedelic Press UK. In 2012, he was a guest editor of Swedish literature and art magazine Papi, editing an issue on intoxication. Before becoming a journalist he studied social anthropology and art history at Lund University. Dahl lives in Malmö, Sweden.

Philip H. Farber has explored the cutting edge of magick, meditation and hypnosis for nearly thirty years. He is the author of *Brain Magick: Exercises in Meta-Magick and Invocation* (Llewellyn Worldwide, 2011), *Meta-Magick: The Book of Atem: Achieving New States of Consciousness Through NLP, Neuroscience and Ritual*

(Weiser Books, 2008), *The Great Purple Hoo-Ha* (Mandrake, 2010) and *Future-ritual: Magick for the 21st Century* (Eschaton Productions, 1995). His articles on magick and popular culture have appeared in Green Egg Magazine, The Journal of Hypnotism, Hypnosis Today, Mondo 2000, High Times, Paradigm Shift, Reality Sandwich and other unique publications and web sites. He has produced several DVD packages on magical topics and teaches workshops throughout the United States, England and Europe. Phil is an instructor for Maybe Logic Academy, a Certified Hypnotist and a Licensed Trainer of Neuro-linguistic Programming, with a private practice in New York's Hudson Valley. www.meta-magick.com

Angela Edwards is a London based painter, writer and conceptual artist. She works mainly in the mediums of painting, sculpture, installation, film and extreme body performance art. Her work explores sacred sexuality, ritual, erotic primitivism, the human condition, death, transgression through extremes, the ecstatic experience, psychosexuality, western mysticism and spirituality. Her writings has been published extensively in journals, as well as in her book *Tantric Brute Grimoire*. http://angelaedwardsart.wix.com/angelaedwardsart

Vera Nikolich works her magic undercover in the tedious business world organizing and often handling paperwork; Book aficionado; Scribbler on-the-go with peculiar imagination owning an endless pile of unseen notes about everything; Diligent clerk at the Ministry of Internal; Editor of *Samekh*, a quarterly periodical of the Secret Fire Oasis, OTO.

Jason Louv runs the group futurist blog Ultraculture.org and mainlines data from the dark side at @jasonlouv

Kasper Opstrup is a writer and researcher of radical culture. For many years, he was a member of the Copenhagen based art collective 'floorless' and he holds a PhD from the London Consortium. His book, *The Way Out – invisible insurrections and radical imaginaries in the UK Underground 1961-1991*, is forthcoming on Minor Compositions in 2015.

Peter Grey is the co-founder of Scarlet Imprint (www.scarletimprint.com). The author of the acclaimed devotional work for Babalon, *The Red Goddess*. He is an exponent of the antinomian and libertarian strand of the western magical tradition. His work comes out of physical praxis. His path is one of ordeal, ecstasy, and Love.

Timothy O'Neill, b. 1951, A.B., U.C. Berkeley, Art History 1973 B.F.A., San Francisco Academy of Art College, 1979. Has been published in *Apocalypse Culture; Secret and Suppressed; Popular Alienation; Occulture, Steamshovel Press, Leonardo,* and worked as a staff writer at *Gnosis* magazine for ten years. He is a long-time member of Yogoda Satsanga and AMORC. He is currently working in San Francisco as a Performance Artist, musician, painter and writer interested in the Gnostic tradition.

The Fenris Wolf

Alexander Nym: Cultural analyst and theoretician, editor and writer, vocalist and voice actor, presenter and promoter. Primary research field is the various manifestations of (counter-)culture in film, literature and "underground" art and music in the 20th century and beyond. Regular public appearances as presenter, lecturer, panelist or performing artist. Editor of *Schillerndes Dunkel* (2010), a reference book covering the so-called "Gothic" subculture from the 70s to the present. Other publications include *Black Celebration* (2011, co-edited by Jennifer Hoffert), and contributions to *State Of Emergence* (Poison Cabinet 2011) about the NSK State phenomenon, as well as editing German editions of books about the controversial groups Laibach (Ventil 2013) and Death In June (Ploettner 2012). He holds a diplomatic passport of NSK State in Time and is co-founder and speaker of the Leipzig-based association "Collective for transnational art & culture" which is engaged in promoting exhibitions and presentations. See www.nsk-lipsk.de and www.nsk-folk-art-biennale.org

Antti P. Balk, a Finnish philosopher and historian, is best known as a translator and publisher of Thelemic literature. Author of *Saints & Sinners: An Account of Western Civilization* and *Balderdash: A Treatise on Ethics*. He lives in Tenerife, Spain.

Kjetil Fjell accepted the Law of Thelema as the letter and word of truth and the supreme rule of his life over 20 years ago and have dedicated his life to the critical study and propagation of the teachings of that book. He is an aspirant in the A∴A∴ and serves as a Sovereign Grand Inspector General and a Bishop in the O.T.O. Professionally he conducts research into cognitive neuroscience and works as a clinical neuropsychologist at a hospital. Currently he is engaged in a conceptualisation of the neuropsychological underpinnings of Will and an criticism of Crowley's reliance on psychoanalytical theories, believing that it is better to reconceptualise his system in terms of modern findings within cognitive neuroscience. He may be contacted at omphalos111@gmail.com

Derek Seagrief has written the book *The Astrology of Death: Entry & Exit – Your Birth & Death Horoscope*, published in Swedish 2012 by Ica Bokförlag (as "Dödens Astrologi: Entré och Sorti – Ditt Födelse & Dödshoroskop"). To contact the author: Email: derek@seagrief.com Website: www.seagrief.com

Sandy Robertson is the great great great grandson of Victorian astronomer James Scott. He has written on rock music, film and the occult for numerous publications including *Sounds, New Musical Express, Penthouse, Starlog, Sexadelic, Scallywag* and *Diabolique*. In partnership with Edwin Pouncey he arranged a stone for the hitherto unmarked grave of demonologist Montague Summers. His *Aleister Crowley Scrapbook* has been in print for over 25 years.

Manon Hedenborg-White is a PhD candidate in the History of Religions at Uppsala University, Sweden. Her doctoral dissertation project explores interpretations of the goddess Babalon in the 20th and 21st century from a gender perspective. She obtained her MA degree at Stockholm University. Her areas of academic interest include late-modern occultism and sexual magic, with a particular focus on issues of sexuality and the social construction of gender. She has spoken at several national and international conferences, and produced a number of articles on esotericism, gender, and paganism.

Frater Achad (Charles Stansfeld Jones, 1886-1950) was an occult writer and a favoured disciple of Aleister Crowley's. He worked with the orders A∴A∴ and Ordo Templi Orientis, predominantly in Canada. Achad wrote several books on magic and the Qabalah: *The Chalice of Ecstasy, The Egyptian Revival,* and *QBL*, to mention a few.

Made in the USA
Las Vegas, NV
04 May 2024

89532915R00187